Test Interpretation and Diversity

Test Interpretation and Diversity

Achieving Equity in Assessment

Edited by

Jonathan Sandoval

Craig L. Frisby

Kurt F. Geisinger

Janice Dowd Scheuneman

Julia Ramos Grenier

American Psychological Association

Washington, DC

First printing November 1998
Second printing July 1999

Published by
American Psychological Association
750 First Street, NE
Washington, DC 20002

Copies may be ordered from
APA Order Department
P.O. Box 92984
Washington, DC 20090-2984

In the U.K., Europe, Africa, and the Middle East, copies may be ordered from
American Psychological Association
3 Henrietta Street
Covent Garden, London
WC2E 8LU England

Typeset in New Baskerville and Futura by EPS Group Inc., Easton, MD
Printer: Data Reproductions Corp., Auburn Hills, MI
Cover Designer: Minker Design, Bethesda, MD
Technical/Production Editor: Amy J. Clarke

Library of Congress Cataloging-in-Publication Data
Test interpretation and diversity : achieving equity in assessment / edited by
    Jonathan H. Sandoval ... [et al.].—1st ed.
        p.   cm.
    Includes bibliographical references and indexes.
    ISBN 1-55798-509-X (cb : acid-free paper)
        1. Educational tests and measurements—Interpretation—Social aspects.
    2. Educational tests and measurements—Interpretation—Psychological
    aspects. 3. Educational equalization. I. Sandoval, Jonathan.
LB3060.8.T47   1998
371.26'01'3—dc21   98-26487
                                                                                      CIP

British Library Cataloguing-in-Publication Data
A CIP record is available from the British Library.

Printed in the United States of America

Contents

Contributors

Jeffrey P. Braden, Department of Educational Psychology, University of Wisconsin—Madison

Sharon Bradley-Johnson, Department of Psychology, Central Michigan State University

Barbara A. Brauer, Gallaudet University and Community Counseling and Mental Health Center, Washington, DC

Janet F. Carlson, Counseling & Psychological Services Department, Oswego State University

Lillian Comas-Díaz, Transcultural Mental Health Institute, Washington, DC

Jacqueline L. Cunningham, Allied Mental Health, Wilmington, DE

Richard P. Durán, Graduate School of Education, University of Southern California

Ruth Ekstrom, Educational Testing Services, Princeton, NJ

Craig L. Frisby, Department of Educational and Counseling Psychology, University of Missouri—Columbia

Kurt F. Geisinger, Office of the Academic Vice President, LeMoyne College

Bernadette Gray-Little, Department of Psychology, University of North Carolina at Chapel Hill

Julia Ramos Grenier, Grenier Consulting Associates, Inc., Collinsville, CT, and Graduate Institute of Professional Psychology, University of Hartford

Steven T. Hardy-Braz, Eastern North Carolina School for the Deaf, Wilson, NC

Danielle A. Kaplan, Department of Psychology, University of North Carolina at Chapel Hill

Kevin L. Moreland, Department of Psychology, Fordham University

Thomas Oakland, College of Education, University of Florida

Robert Q Pollard, Department of Psychiatry, University of Rochester Medical Center

Sarah I. Pratt, Division of Psychological and Educational Services, Fordham University

Jonathan Sandoval, Division of Education, University of California, Davis

Janice Dowd Scheuneman, Quality Assessment Services, Trenton, NJ

Stephen G. Sireci, School of Education, University of Massachusetts at Amherst

Acknowledgments

This book stands as the report of the Task Force of Test Interpretation and Diversity, formed by the American Psychological Association's (APA) Committee on Psychological Tests and Assessment. The original task force members (the editors) were joined in deliberations by Barbara Brauer and Betsy Zaborowski. Support for the project was graciously provided by the staff of the Science Directorate of APA. In particular, the editors would like to thank Dianne Brown Maranto, Dianne L. Schnieder, Adonia L. Calhoun, and Peter Pfordrescher. The majority of the credit for seeing this project through to completion, however, goes to the Science Directorate staff member, Heather Roberts Fox. She advocated for the project, attempted to herd a group of unruly cats, and never lost sight of the importance of our goals. It is her book as much as ours, although we are responsible for the errors.

Part I

Perspectives on Test Interpretation

Testing in a Changing World: An Introduction

Jonathan Sandoval

Demographic changes over the past 2 decades have increased the diversity of American society and brought transformations in many institutions. For example, one setting powerfully affected by these changes has been the public schools. Since 1985, the population of students who enter public schools without complete English proficiency has grown by about 70%. Currently, one-seventh of all U.S. school-age children speak a language other than English at home. Of these children, as many as 5.5 million, come to school without English-language skills. About 75% of these students speak Spanish, and many of the others speak Vietnamese, Hmong, Cantonese, Cambodian, or Korean (Garcia, 1995).

Moreover, distinctive settlement patterns cause the proportion of students in particular language groups to vary widely within and among communities. South Florida and New York City continue to be magnets to immigrant populations, but all urban and coastal areas are points of entry for immigrants. For example, 75% of those enrolled in California's school programs for limited-English-proficient students are Spanish speaking, but some California schools have as many as 22 different language minority groups, a situation replicated many times over in other regions across the country. Demographic projections indicate that this diversity will not diminish in the future.

What is occurring in public schools only foreshadows what will occur and has begun to occur in other settings. Increasing diversity is to be found in the workforce, the military, higher education, and hospitals. Clearly, the clientele of psychologists of all types is changing.

Psychologists have necessarily responded, albeit perhaps slowly, to the increasing numbers of clients from diverse groups. More contact with diverse individuals has led to a call for increased training and supervision of psychologists (López & Hernandez, 1986). Researchers and practitioners have joined together to form divisions within the American Psychological Association (APA) concerned with ethnic minority issues and with other diversity issues (e.g., Division 45, Society for the Psychological Study of Ethnic Minority Issues; Division 44, Society for the Psychological Study of Lesbian and Gay Issues). Groups of psychologists have formed other scientific societies and professional organizations to foster research and discussion of best practice with particular populations such as the Association of Black Psychologists and the Asian American Psychological Association. Although much attention has been focused on appropriate psychological interventions, training programs, and treatment aimed at particular groups of clients, there also has been concern about the psychological tests, assessment tools, and procedures used to make decisions that may have important consequences for individuals.

More than before, psychologists who use tests must make decisions on the basis of tests that were not developed with many of the individuals taking the test or assessments in mind. The use of tests with norms derived from primarily majority-group individuals may be increasingly inappropriate as a foundation for decision making, such as for diagnosis, for assignment to special educational programs, for employment selection, and so on. Norms are intended to reflect the general population or sometimes the group of test takers (user norms, e.g., in the Scholastic Aptitude Test), so it is natural and appropriate that norms are derived largely from majority-group test takers. The issue is how to interpret scores when comparisons with performance of the normative group are not relevant or appropriate for the purposes of the testing or when the test was validated on a group that is different from the examinee in important ways. Norms per se are not the problem. A more basic concern is that an ability or trait may be manifested differently for the groups of interest than for other groups. Stated another way, confidence in the inferences drawn from tests and assessments administered to individuals who are different in significant ways from the characteristics of the majority group may necessarily be diminished.

Although this problem in test interpretation is particularly acute for linguistic minorities, test interpretation for test takers from different socioeconomic levels, with disabling conditions, and from distinct subcultures also is fraught with difficulty. The technical standards for educational and psychological tests address the need for developers, test publishers, and test users to exercise caution when testing nonnorm group populations, but little guidance is actually provided to psychologists in applying standards or ethical principles.

In this book, the other authors and I identify the scientific and policy issues related to the interpretations of tests used with individuals for whom the tests were not developed, standardized, and validated. These issues are examined for both individual and institutional uses of tests. We provide guidelines to practicing psychologists on interpreting the test results of individuals with cultural, linguistic, or economic backgrounds that differ substantially from the majority populations and of individuals with disabilities.

Existing Guidelines for Practice

The APA and other groups have established and promulgated ethical principles and standards that govern testing practices in specific settings and with specific groups (*Standards for Educational and Psychological Testing*, 1985). Such groups include individuals with disabilities, individuals from different socioeconomic levels, individuals from different cultural backgrounds, and individuals whose primary language is not English. The joint Standards for Educational and Psychological Testing contain several standards addressing the problem of interpreting tests given to individuals who are different from the normed population.

For example, Standard 13.1 states that "for non-native English speakers or for speakers of some dialects of English, testing should be designed to minimize threats to test reliability and validity that may arise from language differences" (*Standards*, 1985, p. 74). Standard 13.3 states that "when a test is recommended for use with linguistically diverse test takers, test developers and publishers should provide the information necessary for appropriate test use and interpretation" (p. 75). In general, the standards state that one should "use appropriate caution" when interpreting test scores for individuals who are underrepresented in the normative group. Similar cautions are in order when members of a given group have not been included in the validation of an instrument.

In addition, in a different context, the revised APA Ethical Principles of Psychologists and Code of Conduct include 2.04c:

Psychologists attempt to identify situations in which particular interventions or assessment techniques or norms may not be applicable or may require adjustment in administration or interpretation because of factors such as individuals' gender, age, race ethnicity, national origin, religion, sexual orientation, disability, language, or socioeconomic status. (APA, 1992, p. 1601)

What are psychologists to do when they have identified such a situation?

The Need for More Guidance

As useful as standards and ethical principles are, they are clearly not enough to prevent destructive practices. Some cases reported to the APA's ethics committee or its Committee on Psychological Tests and Assessments, the principal cross directorate committee on testing, serve as examples of the sorts of problems psychologists encounter. In one instance, a White psychologist evaluated a Hispanic man using English-language tests via a translator and then diagnosed him as malingering because his responses were vague. This diagnosis led to the individual being denied disability benefits. In another case, a White psychologist evaluated an African American man using an objective, paper-and-pencil personality test. The profile obtained led this psychologist to diagnose a paranoid schizophrenic disorder without considering possible cultural and racial factors that may have affected the profile. This diagnosis led to the man losing his job.

Psychologists and other mental health providers believe that culture and cultural issues are important in the assessment of culturally different clients and express a need for more training focused on cultural variables (López & Hernandez, 1986; Ramirez, Wassef, Paniagua, & Linskey, 1996; Ramirez, Wassef, Paniagua, Linskey, & O'Boyle, 1994). For example, in studies by Ramirez and colleagues, clinicians did not view themselves as being successful in determining their minority clients' degree of acculturation.

High-Stakes Assessment

The position taken by me and the other editors of this book is that part of what must guide test interpretations are the consequences of the decisions based on the test. One must recognize that most tests are used to make decisions about people or to provide them with information about themselves and that they will have some effect on the test taker's life. Nevertheless, some tests will have a greater impact than others. A test that is used to determine eligibility for higher education or a job will have higher stakes than one used to determine part of the grade in a high school course or to inform a counselee of his or her interests. More recently, the laws for transferring juvenile offenders to adult court have changed in certain states. Psychological test results can make the difference between a juvenile receiving treatment or going to jail for a long time without treatment. Both the consequences and the ability to recover from incorrect decisions made are considered in evaluating the stakes. Many classroom assessments may be wrong, but there are often lots of chances to recover from error because there is much ancillary information available. Thus, the authors and I emphasize the tests and situations leading to high-stakes assessment in this work.

Other Assumptions

It is tempting, when faced with a client who does not fit the population for whom the test was developed, to abandon testing altogether. In many instances, this action will be the correct course to take. However, choosing not to test often means using alternative measures or methods that are even less satisfactory than standardized tests. The decision not to use a test also may lead to the denial of services or opportunity to those who are deserving or, alternatively, the provision of services or opportunities to those who cannot use them. One assumption in preparing this book was that there will be instances when the careful use of tests will be more fair to clients than their absolute elimination. The focal issue then becomes, How can tests be interpreted when they are used in less-than-optimal situations?

One strategy for organizing this book might have been to produce one chapter on each population of concern. As mentioned earlier in reference to California schools, such a strategy would call for 22 chapters to begin with, each on a different-language group. A book organized in this way would have dozens of chapters and probably still omit some groups. A more compelling reason why the authors and I did not wish to use conventional categories of convenience, such as racial–ethnic groups, is that this book was intended to be for psychologists and the interest was in individuals rather than groups. We appreciated that individual differences always exceed group differences and that there is a danger in stereotyping when discussing groups. Instead, we consider the effects on test performance of sociocultural and psychological variables often associated with group membership, such as bilingualism, poverty, recent immigration status, or a disabling condition. We discuss psychological variables as they affect individuals because it is they who will be interpreting tests for individuals. Although we acknowledge that much of the research has been done on gender and racial–ethnic groups, we do not stop at the usual classifications; rather, we look beyond them to considerations of effects such as acculturation and language.

Another temptation for a book on the interpretation of tests for diverse individuals would be to focus on which tests to choose to use. Other authors have identified tests that can be used with particular populations (e.g., Geisinger, 1992; Jones, 1996). As new tests become available, however, recommendations become obsolete. Obviously, one should be careful in selecting a test, and there will be many considerations that the authors and I discuss, but we do not recommend one test over another. Instead, the focus is on interpretation and the interpretation process as informed by psychological research and theory. We hope that this book will provide general principles that psychologists will be able to use repeatedly over the next few decades.

A theme that readers may encounter in this book is on critical thinking rather than a cookbook approach to test interpretation. Drawing on the notion of the scientist–practitioner, the assumption in this book is that psychologists using tests in decision making will be viewing each case as a unique problem to be solved by applying the scientific method. Part of the scientific method, such as the double-blind experiment, is designed to protect against biases in human cognition entering into the data-collection process. These biases are described in chapter 3. Ways to reason carefully during the test interpretation process, and not be influenced by irrelevant information, are discussed.

Finally, stereotyping is a difficult problem to overcome. It seems innately human to categorize the world and to form concepts about groups of individuals who have something in common. On the basis of these classifications, the authors and I develop schemes or complex concepts and constructs concerning the members of categories, schemes that include feelings, beliefs, and expectations for behavior for the members of the categories. A problem, called the "fallacy of stereotyping'' (Scriven, 1976), occurs when people act on an element of the schema as if it applied to all members of the classification.

For example, a psychologist's schema for treating individuals with attention deficit disorder may include the characteristic of impulsivity. In working with a young man whom the psychologist believes has this disorder, he or she may expect the patient to act impulsively or may notice impulsive acts more frequently regardless of whether the patient really has this characteristic. Seldom do individuals perfectly match all of the features of a prototype, although they may match several and exemplify one or two. The schemes for different diverse groups may be simple or complex depending on the clinician's experiences. Interpreting tests when a schema for the examinee has been activated requires testers to be particularly careful of stereotypes. The schemes permit testers to act efficiently and correctly much of the time, but they should not become automatically applied in every situation.

A Brief Synopsis of This Book

This book has been organized into four parts: perspectives on test interpretation, contexts for interpretation, dimensions of diversity, and looking to the future. In Part I, test interpretation is discussed from psychological and political perspectives.

In chapter 2, Geisinger reviews psychometric issues for test interpretation. In addition to reintroducing readers to classic psychometric ideas and concepts, Geisinger discusses how these principles apply to the test interpretation process for diverse individuals. Although this brief chapter is not comprehensive, Geisinger addresses specific interpretation issues and provides citations to the psychometric literature for those seeking elaboration.

In the next chapter, I review research and theory concerning how individuals make judgments. Cognitive psychologists have identified a number of heuristics judges used in making decisions and the biases inherent in these heuristics. For example, errors may be made on the basis of mental availability, when a decision maker is influenced by vivid information and information similar to recently experienced events. Because information is available in memory, new information is more likely to be connected to it. A particularly troubling bias in human cognition is related to the need to confirm expectations because psychologists are often presented with a great deal of information they must sort through in making a judgment. Expectancies based on status are at the heart of prejudice and may not be in awareness. Effective practitioners must know how these cognitive phenomena influence their day-to-day work and how to guard against making errors in judgment.

In the fourth chapter, Frisby provides a perspective by discussing the complexities inherent in concepts of "culture" and "cultural differences." He describes the implications of these concepts for practitioner problem solving in test interpretation. This chapter serves as a reaction to inadequate formulations in earlier testing interpretation literature and incorporates current research and thinking in psychology, sociology, and educational anthropology. The word *culture* is a much more complex and differentiated term than its contemporary usage suggests. There can be many distinct ethnicities and "cultures" represented within a "race" and many different "races" represented within a given "culture." The terms *culture* or *cultural differences* have different meanings depending on the context within which they are used, which may or may not have relevance for test interpretation issues. Frisby examines the assumption that cultural differences manifest themselves the same way across all individuals within test situations and helps practitioners understand the psychometric criteria for evaluating such assumptions.

Part II of this book deals with three contexts in which high-stakes decisions are made: educational, employment, and clinical. Each of these contexts has different kinds of tests, different legal constraints, and different challenges for test interpretation.

In education, issues center on (a) high school graduation, college and graduate or professional school admissions, and awards of scholarship or fellowship money using large-scale assessments and (b) placement in special educational programs using individually administered or classroom tests. In chapter 5, Scheuneman and Oakland consider the issues surrounding the use of test results in these high-stakes settings. Large-scale testing differs from most other types of testing discussed in this book in that the test score user may have little if any contact with the examinee. Hence, issues of possible test bias are particularly troublesome. Test scores must be used, however, in the face of uncertainty about the possible effects of bias on scores. Major issues in the debate about test bias are discussed that suggest why these issues are so difficult to resolve. Possible explanations for the observed differences are then reviewed, including personal characteristics of examinees that may be associated with gender or racial–ethnic group membership and properties of tests, such as test instructions, format, or time limits. Finally, the authors suggest guidelines for appropriate test use and score interpretation with diverse populations in these high-stakes educational applications.

Sireci and Geisinger's chapter on employment acquaints readers both with the general purposes of personnel testing in a personnel selection system and with the legal and social context within which personnel selection occurs. They review the concepts of adverse impact and test fairness as applied to industrial settings, especially as applied to members of various racial, ethnic, and gender groups in personnel selection settings. Next, they discuss the goal of diversifying the workforce and the impact of the Americans With Disabilities Act on employers, including recent rulings on the consideration of some types of psychological tests in employment settings, such as medical tests. After reviewing changes in the nature of the workforce, they outline the special problems in using some kinds of psychological tests (e.g., tests of physical and psychomotor ability, various work samples, or assessment center exercises) that are primarily used in personnel selection settings and that may not be equally appropriate for all members of the applicant pool. Methodological issues such as the manner in which criteria are developed, the fairness of criteria, and the technique of validity generalization also are covered. Sireci and Geisinger suggest ways that tests may be developed and used to minimize adverse impact while not sacrificing test validity. Finally, the authors consider ways of making personnel selection more fair.

In chapter 7, Gray-Little and Kaplan discuss the various uses of tests in clinical assessment that can have significant impact, positive or negative, on individuals' lives. They focus particularly on testing for psychotherapeutic and psychopharmacological intervention and for forensic decision making such as trial competence and parenting competence. The authors review the research on test validity for diverse populations, examining the tests typically used for clinical purposes. The chapter concludes with a discussion of how psychologists can conceptualize their testing practices and test interpretations in light of the information presented and practices in interpretation that can lead to more valid test interpretations.

Part III addresses various social and psychological dimensions of diversity: language, acculturation, poverty, hearing, learning, among others. Although it is impossible to consider all of the factors that must be taken into account in test interpretation, these chapters cover important aspects of client experience that must be weighed seriously in problem solving using tests.

In chapter 8, Durán and I discuss language acquisition, both in those whose native language is not English and in those who are hearing impaired. We review how language differences affect test results and how linguistic differences can be taken into account in test interpretation. We discuss the current literature on stages of bilingualism and proficiency in handling the second language. Suggestions are provided to psychologists who test individuals whose first language is not English and who interpret the results of such tests.

In chapter 9, Comas-Días and Ramos-Grenier consider the special problem of immigrants and others becoming acculturated to mainstream American customs and values. They discuss the processes of migration and immigration as well as the psychological processes that impinge on individuals who migrate or immigrate. A psychologically oriented theory of acculturation is presented, and a procedure is described that assists in the assessment of an individual's stage of acculturation. Such assessments are necessary to provide appropriate therapeutic services, educational interventions, and training programs. Comas-Días and Ramos-Grenier offer guidelines for test interpretation on the basis of information about an individual's level of acculturation.

Frisby follows this analysis by reviewing the effects of poverty and low socioeconomic status on individual development. The general purpose is to examine the correlates of poverty status that have relevance for the testing behavior of individuals and the validity of test interpretations for such users. The author pays careful attention to untangling the often-confounded effects of socioeconomic status and race or ethnicity. The concept of "poverty" is defined as being part of a continuum that has both economic and sociocultural dimensions within a given society. In addition, Frisby elucidates issues related to the concept of a "critical threshold," below which poverty status has a high likelihood of rendering test results invalid for any given individual.

Issues about individuals who are partially sighted or blind are addressed by Bradley-Johnson and Ekstrom in chapter 11. Assessment questions related to testing individuals who are blind or visually impaired have been raised for several years by many experts in the field, but, because of the Americans With Disabilities Act of 1990, psychologists face another challenge. Questions of valid use of nonstandard conditions as well as interpretation of the results of using psychometric instruments that were constructed excluding special populations present a critical challenge to psychologists concerned with the ethical and legal use of test data with individuals who are blind or visually impaired. The authors explore the major areas of concern in developing and interpreting assessment tools and methods appropriate for use with blind people. The following interpretation issues are discussed incorporating available research and perspectives of those expert in assessment with this population: (a) the use of norm-based tests with blind individuals when those tests have excluded blind people from norming populations; (b) the use of additional time for tests administered using alternative formats and the implications for correlation with predictive validity of instruments; (c) the interpretation of personality tests that may over- and underpredict pathology for individuals who are blind or visually impaired; (d) the impact of the requirement that tests be clearly linked to "essential job functions" on the ethical use of many tests of general ability for employment screening; (e) issues related to alternatives to standardized testing in many situations, including a discussion of functional assessment such as work samples with blind people using alternative techniques; (f) issues of interpreter bias when using individually administered instruments that may be adapted or only partially administered to individuals who are blind or visually impaired; and (g) general issues of misinterpretation of test results attributable to the test administrator's misconceptions about blindness and visual impairment.

Brauer, Braden, Pollard, and Hardy-Braz, in chapter 12, address the intrinsic complexities involved in providing psychological assessment services to deaf and hard-of-hearing individuals. The heterogeneity found in this diverse population requires an explanation of the terms used to describe members of various subgroups of individuals and the implications inherent in each for test-taking purposes. To provide psychologists with a better understanding of these individuals, the authors address issues such as onset, etiology, and prevalence of deafness in the United States, descriptive population demographics, family dynamics, methods of modalities of communication, educational background, and comorbidity of other disabilities. An account also has been given of the current understanding of psychological traits and characteristics of deaf and hard-of-hearing individuals that are deemed to be "cultural," the criteria used in making such determinations, and the implications for test interpretations. Examples have been provided to explicate the pitfalls often found in test interpretations that may lead to false determinations of psychopathology. The chapter concludes with an outline of possible changes to be made in psychological test giving as well as additional requirements for the practice of psychology with deaf and hard-of-hearing individuals.

The assessment of individuals with learning disabilities has come to occupy a significant portion of psychologists' time in many settings. In chapter 13, Cunningham discusses the issues surrounding the process of drawing inferences about individuals with learning disabilities on the basis of their performance on psychological and educational tests. She reviews the literature on learning disabilities and identifies ways in which underlying learning disabilities are reflected on test performance. She attempts to differentiate between primary areas of functioning that are impaired in individuals with learning disabilities (typically basic processes such as decoding) and secondary areas that may appear impaired because of the disability (an ability building on a basic process, such as reading comprehension). For some purposes, using standardized tests with individuals with learning disabilities and interpreting them in a straightforward way is appropriate, and for some purposes this practice is not appropriate. Individuals with identified learning disabilities are often tested under nonstandard conditions to accommodate the learning disability. Accommodations include increased time on tests, providing a reader, using a distraction-free location, having enlarged print, or using an amanuensis. The implications of these and other practices for test validity and interpretation are examined in detail. Cunningham also reviews myths and misconceptions about individuals with learning disabilities that may influence the test interpreter. The chapter concludes with suggested guidelines for test interpretation with individuals with learning disabilities.

In the final chapter in this section, Pratt and Moreland discuss several other dimensions of diversity not mentioned in the preceding six chapters and address issues relevant to the testing of individuals from these diverse groups. The groups discussed include those with physical and neurological impairments, those with psychological or emotional problems, and those of varying gender orientations. A few considerations that should be taken into account in interpreting tests given to members of each of these groups are discussed. A common theme here and in other chapters is that test results for individuals who do not fit the characteristics noted specifically in the norm and validation samples need to be interpreted individually, with caution, and in light of some general principles for responsible test use. The authors call for greater inclusiveness in the sampling and the development of new measures appropriate for members of these groups.

In the final section of the book, the authors look ahead, both at the need for training psychologists to respond to future demands and at the changes taking place in the technology of measurement and testing. Not only are the demographics of the country changing, but new developments in theory and practice in assessment also are occurring that may exacerbate some problems and ameliorate others.

In chapter 15, Geisinger and Carlson outline the broad steps that would need to be taken for practitioners to develop the critical thinking, decision-making, and problem-solving skills that are discussed and modeled in the previous 14 chapters. Discussed are ways in which incentives for test users may be provided to develop good test interpretation skills as well as suggestions for identifying and coping with "disincentives" for the development of quality skills (e.g., the uncritical acceptance of unwarranted conclusions derived from flawed or outdated research; the lack of adequate training materials and resources; legal and procedural constraints imposed by regulatory organizations).

In the closing chapter, I discuss the prospects for test usage for diverse groups in the future. Changes in testing technology (e.g., computer adaptive testing, computer-based interpretation, testing on demand, item response theory, and the existence of large data banks) will present new challenges and opportunities. At the same time, legal challenges and regulation of testing will continue. In addition, new dimensions of diversity may emerge as progress is made in the neurosciences. These trends and the themes of this book are integrated in the concluding chapter.

Historically, psychological assessment has proved to be an effective tool in assisting the professional practice of psychology. Although much concern has been expressed about bad practice in assessment with diverse individuals, the authors and I hope that this book will point to the promise assessment has for decision making with diverse populations. Good practice can lead to better matches between treatments, programs, or occupations and individuals in an increasingly diverse world.

References

American Psychological Association. (1992). Ethical Principles of Psychologists and Code of Conduct. *American Psychologist, 47,* 1597–1611.

Garcia, E. E. (Ed.). (1995). *Meeting the challenge of linguistic and cultural diversity in early childhood education.* New York: Teachers College Press.

Geisinger, K. F. (Ed.). (1992). *Psychological testing of Hispanics.* Washington, DC: American Psychological Association.

Jones, R. L. (Ed.). (1996). *Handbook of tests and measurements for Black populations.* Hampton, VA: Cobb & Henry.

López, S., & Hernandez, P. (1986). How culture is considered in evaluations of psychopathology. *Journal of Nervous and Mental Disease, 176,* 598–606.

Ramirez, S. Z., Wassef, A., Paniagua, F. A., & Linskey, A. O. (1996). Mental health providers' perceptions of cultural variables in evaluating ethnically diverse clients. *Professional Psychology: Research and Practice, 27,* 284–288.

Ramirez, S. Z., Wassef, A., Paniagua, F. A., Linskey, A., & O'Boyle, M. (1994). Perceptions of mental health providers concerning cultural factors in the evaluation of Hispanic children and adolescents. *Hispanic Journal of Behavioral Sciences, 16,* 28–42.

Scriven, M. (1976). *Reasoning.* New York: McGraw-Hill.

Standards for educational and psychological testing. (1995). Washington, DC: American Psychological Association.

Psychometric Issues in Test Interpretation

Kurt F. Geisinger

Jon Sandoval has set a context for the testing of members of diverse groups in U.S. society. These groups include low socioeconomic status groups, language minorities, individuals with varying degrees of one or more disabling conditions, and ethnic minority groups. Testing has been performed with remarkable effectiveness in many contexts for members of the majority group within the United States. However, disability and language differences in test takers necessitate fundamental changes in the way clinicians and other test users test individuals and interpret scores that emerge from either normal or adapted test administration procedures. Some understanding of both testing procedures and the history of testing helps clinicians and other test users understand the problems in interpreting scores from nonstandard test administrations.

Test Administration: Its Role in the History of Testing

Psychological testing has emerged from the confluence of the history of clinical or applied psychology on one hand and experimental psychology on the other. Psychological tests have been defined as samples of behavior that are objective and standardized. The term *standardization* relates specifically to the exact control of the test administration process (Geisinger, 1984). Wundt and other experimental psychologists such as Cattell (1890) influenced the zeitgeist pertaining to test administration procedures; it was urged that test administration should carefully follow experimental treatments. That is, tests should be administered in a manner that eliminates all behavioral differences (or variance) caused by the testing method other than those intended: "The logic of testing follows the paradigm of the experimental method so that the variance in the test scores is reflective of intra-individual differences rather than of differences in test administration" (Geisinger, 1994a, p. 122).

When test users call a test a "standardized test," they are actually reporting that the test administration procedures are highly uniform across all test takers. For a test to be standardized, the test developers must operationalize all aspects of the test administration process, including the testing materials, time limits, written and oral instructions, responses to questions by test takers, adaptations that are permissible in the testing process, and so forth. That test administration procedures need to be carefully followed for scores to be accurate and valid can be seen in Standard 15.1 of the *Standards for Educational and Psychological Testing* (1985). This standard states that

> in typical applications, a test administrator should follow carefully the standardized procedures for administration and scoring specified by the test publisher. Specifications regarding instructions to test takers, time limits, the form of item presentation or response, and test materials or equipment should be strictly observed. Exceptions should only be made on the basis of carefully considered professional judgment, primarily in clinical applications. (p. 83)

Clearly, the standards also caution that when test administration procedures are adapted to accommodate differences among those taking the tests, caution needs to be taken regarding the possible effects that such changes may have on the meaningfulness or validity of the scores.

The standards also urge that when testing procedures (i.e., test administrations) are adapted for the specific needs of a particular test taker, test users must study the impact of these changes in test administration with regard to their influence on scores, the validity of those test scores, the reliability of the scores, and so on. Nevertheless, such test adaptations are more likely to occur in the future and need to be studied more than they have in the past, as I explain.

The Context of Testing at the Turn of the Century

In chapter 1 of this book, Sandoval addresses some of the influences on testing as the end of the 20th century nears. In American society, this complex of factors includes a large increase in the number of immigrants in society, a tendency on the part of some immigrants such as Hispanics (Eyde, 1992) to continue speaking their native language rather than English and a general philosophical orientation on the part of society as a whole to be inclusive of all of its constituent members. With regard to this issue of inclusiveness, American society no longer wishes to relegate individuals with disabilities to institutions or to limited responsibilities. Rather, people believe that with proper accommodations, such individuals can succeed and improve society through their achievements. Similarly, people believe that those who come from other countries and whose English may not yet be fluent, or at least fluent in the academic context of test taking, should nevertheless be permitted to succeed to the best of their abilities. This freedom of opportunity has been a hallmark of American society throughout the history of the United States. The Americans With Disabilities Act of 1990 has extended particular rights to individuals with disabilities. A disability has been defined as (a) a physical or mental impairment that substantially limits one or more life activities, (b) a record of such an impairment, and (c) being regarded as having such an impairment regardless of whether the impairment substantially limits major life activities. Although the Americans With Disabilities Act was primarily oriented to employment testing, its statutes are broad and its spirit encourages others to permit those with disabilities to achieve "whatever status they seek if they meet the essential requirements of that status, regardless of their disability" (Geisinger, 1994a, p. 124). Tests must therefore be administered to individuals with disabilities using reasonable and appropriate accommodations. This permission to use appropriate accommodations, however, conflicts with the notion that those administering tests must do so uniformly for all individuals. Furthermore, in educational settings, mandates that all individuals should receive testing, regardless of their native language, have radically multiplied the numbers of languages in which tests are administered, as has been noted by Sandoval in chapter 1 of this book. In the remainder of this chapter, I describe some of the psychometric procedures that test users must follow if they are to understand better how to interpret tests that are given to members of groups who do not necessarily fit the prototype of the intended test taker.

Psychometric Issues Involved in Test Accommodation

Test users and test interpreters must become extremely careful in their reading of test manuals if they are to use tests with and to interpret test scores of members of diverse groups. Test users, for example, must read the manual to determine whether members of the groups to which they plan to administer a test have been involved in the construction of a test and have been included in norm groups as well as in the samples used for validity and reliability analysis. To the extent that the individuals from specific groups have not been included in such groups, caution must be used. Indeed, the very choice of a measure to be used should be strongly influenced by its appropriateness for the population with which it will be used. In many instances, test users must be test selectors as well. When faced with the necessity of assessing a diverse population of test takers, a responsible test user needs to raise specific questions regarding the instruments to be used. Indeed, the selection of an assessment instrument should be guided by questions about its appropriateness. To answer the question, "Is the test appropriate for the entire population of test takers?" demands resolution of several related questions. Among the questions that need to be answered are the following.

1. What Is the Composition of the Test-Taking Population?

Perhaps psychologists have not been as sophisticated as other scientists (e.g., sociologists, anthropologists) in always knowing the compositions of the samples that they study and with whom they work. Before planning a testing program, test users need to understand the composition of the group taking the examination. For example, test users need to know the extent to which English is the dominant language. They should know the number of individuals in the sample for whom English is not their dominant language. Furthermore, in the sampling of individuals whose dominant language is not English, they need to list how many speak (or write depending on the modality of the test) each of the languages other than English. Then, if one has a test-taking population that has English as the primary language and has a second language as well (e.g., Spanish), to meet the needs of the majority of remaining test takers one can possibly offer the examination in either language. In such an instance, however, one may need to decide how to make the determination of the language in which to administer the test. (Geisinger, 1994b, has described the issues involved in translating and adapting tests from one language to another.) Similarly, test users need to know what disabling conditions are present in the test-taking population and how many individuals fit each condition. To what extent do the individuals with each disabling condition vary in the extent of the disability? As with language differences, test users need to determine whether there are versions of the tests they choose to use for the different disabling conditions present in the population. They must also know the composition of the population in terms of socioeconomic status, ethnicity, gender, and other variables of interest.

2. To What Extent Can the Assessment Instrument Be Administered Without Encumbrance to All Members of the Population?

Once test users know the population to which they are administering a test, they can determine the extent to which the assessment instrument can be administered to all members of that population. If the examination is an oral one administered in English, for example, test users may need to determine how this examination is administered to those with hearing disabilities or whose dominant language is not English. If the test is a standardized one offered by a test publisher, the test manual should provide documentation on how to deal with common eventualities. Should the manual not do so, a sophisticated test user would be wise to call the test publishers for details on any adaptations in administration procedures that may be available. If the answer to the question is no, that the test cannot be administered to segments of the population, the test user or test publisher needs to determine the answer to the next question.

3. Has the Test Publisher or a Subsequent Test User or Researcher Used the Instrument in a Translated Version, Adapted Version, or an Accommodated Version, or Are There Any Recommended Alternative Testing Procedures?

As stated earlier, test publishers should include in their manual explicit information on existing test adaptations (e.g., whether there are versions of the examination available in different languages, in versions that are "culture reduced," or whether there are versions available for individuals with specific disabling conditions).

If the test user confirms that the test in question has not been used with "special populations," then the test user must consider the possibility of using other instruments that are appropriate for the diversity of the population in question, of adapting the present instrument, or of considering some alternative procedure rather than making an assessment. I use the example of a test developer or test user who wishes to assess individuals in a language different from that in which the instrument was originally constructed. Historically, test developers have translated instruments from the original or host language to a target language and then assessed the degree to which the target-language instrument matched the original version through the technique of "back translation."

In back translation, a second translator translates the target-language version of the instrument back to the original home language or host language. Individuals can then assess the degree to which the original home-language version is comparable to the twice-translated home-language version. If substantial differences occur, it is perceived that the translation to the target language is probably not acceptable. There are two problems with this procedure. First, translators who know that their work will be evaluated through the technique of back translation select words in the target language to ensure that the instrument will be back translated in a manner that makes it comparable to the original version. However, in so selecting, the translators frequently use terminology that is not optimal for the target-language version. Second, simple translations only deal with language; there is no adaptation for cultural differences that concomitantly vary among individuals from different language or cultural groups. Issues related to the translation and adaptation issues influencing interpretation of assessment instruments may be found in great detail in Geisinger (1994b). Similar issues also exist for the adaptation of instruments for those with specific types of disabilities. If a written vocabulary test is read aloud to an individual with a visual disability, the spelling and letter-by-letter cures operative in a written version of the item are not available to that test taker. In some cases, such adaptations totally change the nature of the assessment. A written test of reading comprehension is no longer a test of reading comprehension when it is provided on an audiotape and when individuals answer questions derived from their having heard the audiotape rather than their having read the text in a large type or Braille version, for example. Nevertheless, test developers and users can adapt an instrument in ways that will provide useful information if they enlist the aid of those knowledgeable about the instrument, about that which the instrument measures, and about the population to be assessed. (For example, if a test user is interested in testing individuals with visual disabilities, those who are knowledgeable about visual disabilities need to be included in the test adaptation process.) If there are accommodations in test administration procedures for members of specific populations, the test user needs to ask the next question.

4. Has the Planned Accommodation Been Assessed in Terms of the Meaningfulness of the Scores It Yields?

Questions about the meaningfulness of scores from the adapted version of the instrument or from an adapted version of a test administration relate to one of six psychometric issues: the test construction and adaptation process, the scoring of the instrument, the reliability of the scores resulting from the accommodated administration, the validity of the scores emerging from accommodated administration, the impact of the accommodated test administration on test takers, and the fairness of the scores that result from the administration. Each of these is discussed in turn.

Test Construction Processes

Several issues relate to the construction of an adapted measure. Analyses may include reviews of items on the test and test components before their placement on the examination. Such reviews can be made by groups of individuals who are members of the groups in question. Empirical methods also can be used. For example, analyses that determine whether differential item functioning can be performed to see whether adapted questions are differentially more difficult for individuals in particular groups than for the rest of the population. Similarly, components of the examination can be assessed to see whether they are not only equally difficult (in the case of cognitive-type tests) but also whether they relate to other components of the test in a similar fashion. It also is important to consider—both analytically and empirically—the issue of the amount of time that candidates will have to take a test, whether the test is adapted for use with a special population, or whether the members of that group have a condition that makes the speededness of the test problematic (e.g., a motor disability).

Scoring

Two issues are involved in the scoring of adapted or accommodated test forms for members of special groups who receive those special administrations of the test. These two issues relate to norms and equating. If a single norm group is used, and scores are interpreted on the basis of norms from the entire population, a test user must assess whether the proportion of individuals who are members of the specific group in question are members of the entire norm group. They should be represented at least to the extent to which they appear in the entire population of test takers. That is, if 5% of test takers are Spanish speaking, 5% of the norm group, minimally, should be represented in the norm sample. In some instances, specific norms based solely on the identified group (e.g., Hispanic test takers) also may be useful for purposes of test interpretation. In some instances, one may wish to interpret a given test score using both the norms from the entire sample and the norms from the special population (e.g., those with visual disabilities).

The second issue that relates to test scores is that of equating. When different forms of a test exist (as in the case of two comparable versions of a standardized college admissions measure), those two forms must be equated so that the scores emerging from both forms are interchangeable. As a regular task in the ongoing publishing of tests, test publishers equate different forms of examinations. Classical methods for equating tests forms are beyond the scope of this chapter; however, such classical methods typically involve the random selection of two groups from the general test-taking population. Each group takes one of the forms, and equivalent scores on the two forms are assigned using, for example, equipercentile equating technique. However, when one group represents the majority of test takers in the population and the other group represents a specific predefined portion of the entire population, the assumption of random assignment to group is clearly violated. Furthermore, equating procedures generally involve large sample sizes, sizes that are extremely difficult to achieve in many test-taking situations, especially when the subpopulations involved are composed of individuals with relatively rare disabilities or of individuals whose dominant language is not widely spoken within a population. Recent techniques (see Geisinger, 1994b, pp. 127–128) may permit equating with smaller samples, however. Currently, however, test users need to determine whether special accommodated test versions, whether widely used or not, have been equated to general forms of the examination. Only in such instances can one use examinations in such a way as to ensure that the scores are comparable. An informed user will determine whether test forms that have been developed for use with special populations have been equated to the original form. If they have been, interpretations are more likely to be comparable to those derived from the tests for the majority group.

Reliability

The assessment of the reliability of test scores involves a number of fundamentally related but operationally and conceptually different procedures. All forms of test reliability involve consistency, but the nature of the consistency changes depending on the type of the reliability under consideration. Included under the general concept of reliability are test–retest, alternate forms, internal consistency, and inerrater reliability, among others. These procedures indicate that a test provides consistent scores over time, across different forms of the test, within the components (typically test items) of a test, and across independent raters, respectively. Although all of these types of reliability are important for different kinds of decision making, alternate-forms reliability is especially important for interpreting scores that emerge from special test forms that have been translated or adapted from one language to another or when the test has been adapted to accommodate individuals with disabilities. It is helpful if the test developers or adapters have determined the consistency across forms, from the original form (presumably for use with the majority-group population) to the special target population for which the new form has been constructed. Indeed, the difference between reliability and validity is sometimes difficult to differentiate, and such is clearly the case in the instance of an adapted test form. Is the correlation between a new, adapted form a reliability coefficient or a validity coefficient? In this discussion, I believe that it is reliability, in that the logic of this type of assessment is in determining the consistency with which the *true score* of a test taker can be estimated across the two forms.

In instances in which the test reliability has been assessed, and the test is used either as normally administered or with an accommodated administration for a special population, it may be appropriate to assess the reliability of the examination with the special population. Indeed, the test standards (Standards 13.4, 14.6; *Standards*, 1985) encourage and suggest the estimation of test reliability when the test is administered to language minorities or when accommodations for individuals with disabilities have been made. This subgroup-specific reliability analysis may be especially appropriate when the reliability of a test has been justified on the basis of internal consistency reliability procedures (e.g., coefficient alpha). Such analyses should be repeated in the group of special test takers because the meaning and difficulty of some components of the test may change over groups, especially over some cultural, linguistic, and disability groups. Furthermore, if the time for testing has been lengthened to provide special groups more time to work on each problem on the test, the entire testing experience may involve additional fatigue and concomitant errors that affect the reliability of the assessment.

Validity

Anytime that psychologists and others use a test, they need to be concerned with the validity of that test. The term *test validity* refers to the appropriateness, meaningfulness, and usefulness of inferences that are made on the basis of the scores on the test in question (*Standards*, 1985). Psychologists have historically used several seemingly distinct methodologies to demonstrate that the measures used are valid. These methodologies have been termed *content validation, criterion-related validation,* and *construct validation.* Each of these is discussed in turn.

An assessment of the content validity of a test usually involves two components, both involving the judgment of those who are experts in the content of the test, whether it is, for example, a test of educational achievement, a job-related skill, an ability, or a personality construct. The first of these judgments involves a consideration of the adequacy of the intended test plan; the test plan is evaluated to see how well it represents the content of the characteristics being measured. The second judgment involves a review of the test materials themselves; they are in turn reviewed to see how well they operationalize the test plan: "Test plans are frequently presented using a content-by-process matrix, whereby the cognitive processes employed in the learning and application of knowledge and concepts assessed are also called for in the evaluation" (Geisinger, 1994a, p. 131). In general, when identical test forms are used with both the majority group in the population and any special populations, then content validity, if present for the majority group, also should be present for the special population. However, there are certain specific exceptions to this general rule. For a language minority group, for example, the processes involved in successfully answering test questions may to a greater or lesser extent involve English-language skills, either in addition to or instead of the intended skills. For those with disabilities, skills wholly different from those of the majority-group population may be involved.

The notion of instructional validity is related to that of content validity and is less a psychometric concept and more a legal one (see Madaus, 1983). Instructional validity is concerned with the determination of whether specific subgroups in the population whose education differs in some substantive ways from that of the majority of the population have been exposed to the instruction that is assumed and is covered on the examination. Certainly, in the case of many of the groups discussed in this book, such an assessment would appear to be appropriate.

Criterion-related validation is most commonly used when a test such as an aptitude test is used to forecast some important future behavior, which is itself measured by a criterion. This paradigm is frequently used to justify tests that are used to provide information used as part of hiring decisions and decisions for entry into selective educational programs, especially in higher education. In such instances, criteria that are estimates of one's job proficiency or one's success in education (e.g., grade point average) can be used. Tests are justified on the basis of the strength of the correlation coefficient between the test and the criterion. Standards 1.21 and 1.22 encourage the use of two types of criterion-related validation studies when certain special populations are in question. The special populations should be combined with the total population for a single study; studies also should be performed separately, so that test users can determine whether differential prediction has occurred. Differential prediction occurs when the relationship between the predictor test and the criterion is significantly different across groups. In one extreme instance, for example, a test might be valid in one sample and invalid in another. Clearly, such information is extremely important and has implications for practice. If evidence of differential prediction is found, it may suggest using the test differently for members of different groups or perhaps even not using it for members of one group. To date, however, little evidence of differential prediction has been found in the psychometric literature when one compares with majority populations either ethnic groups or groups based on disability. Such a tentative conclusion, however, should not preclude future studies of differential prediction and differential test use. Note that for many groups and in many samples, the assessment of whether differential prediction has occurred is precluded by the large number of participants required for such an analysis and by the small numbers present in the subgroups.

A determination of whether a test has construct validity incorporates many sources of evidence, including those described above regarding content validity and criterion-related validity. In addition, studies of the internal relationships of test components (such as with factor analysis) and the relationships of the test with other variables of theoretical interest are frequently considered when the construct validity of a test is assessed. The relationship between a test and other variables of interest is often considered within the framework of convergent and discriminant validity. When a test correlates with other variables that theory predicts it should, evidence of convergent validation is present. When a test does not correlate with variables that theory suggests it should not, evidence of discriminant validity is similarly present. Both of these concepts are important when test users deliberate on the validity of a special form (i.e., a translated version of a test or a test that has certain accommodations for those with disabilities). The test should correlate with other measures that assess similar characteristics, and it should not correlate with variables that imply it is measuring something other than the construct of interest.

Impact

Some in psychological testing have argued for a new term, *consequential validity*, which involves the study of both the intended and the unintended consequences that occur when testing is implemented. Insofar as testing has been seen by some as hampering the progress of minorities in American society, for example—and society does value the implicit equality of all groups in legal terms—my colleagues and I believe that the impact of tests should be studied. We do not, however, believe that evidence of the unintended consequences of testing constitutes a source of validity per se, but we nevertheless consider it unimportant. We encourage test users to consider the impact of testing in a variety of settings.

Few formal strategies exist for analyzing the impact of examinations, however. The Uniform Guidelines on Employee Selection Procedures (1978) do describe one such procedure. The guidelines mandate that many employers need to determine the passing rates of various societal groups and further advise that the passing rates of protected groups in society (e.g., African Americans, Hispanic Americans, Native Americans, Asian Americans, women) should not be below 80% that of the highest scoring group unless there is evidence that the test is highly valid for the intended purposes. For example, if White men are the highest scoring group on a given test and their passing rate is 50%, the guidelines would consider as an adverse impact on a protected group any passing rate less than 40% (80% of 50%).

Fairness

The test fairness literature is clearly beyond the scope of this chapter, but it is discussed to some extent in chapters 5 and 6 in this book. An in-depth treatment also can be found in Cole and Moss (1989). In general, the accepted definition of test fairness has emerged from the criterion-related validity methodology. A test is defined as fair if it does not lead to differential prediction. Regression lines between the predictor test and the criterion are computed for each relevant group, and their slopes, intercepts, and errors of prediction are compared. If any of these three components of the regression lines differ across groups, then the test is not thought to be fair. Definitions from the perspective of content validity and construct validity also may be found in the literature (see, e.g., Geisinger, 1992).

As noted in the Test Construction Processes section, it also is important that differential item functioning analyses be performed. When items that have been found to have unexplained differential item functioning are removed from an examination, the test is certainly more likely to be fair to all groups.

Conclusion

For the effective testing of many groups in American society, test developers and test users must adapt their testing procedures to some extent. In some instances, they can continue to use the same testing materials, but the test administration must be changed somewhat. For example, they may need to provide a large-type or Braille version of a test for individuals with visual disabilities. In the case of other groups of test takers, testing professionals must change the actual testing materials. If certain test takers do not understand written English, for example, testing professionals may need to translate the examination from English to their language. If they do translate a measure in this way, they probably also need to adapt the test for cultural differences; such a translation is really more an adaptation than it is a translation per se.

When testing professionals make changes in either testing materials or test administration, they are appreciably changing the nature of an examination. As such, many of the psychometric aspects of the test in its particular use also may become changed. Test users must assess the continued reliability and validity of the examination once it has been changed. They also raise questions about the scoring of the test, its impact on various groups in society, and whether it is fair to all groups. In this chapter I have attempted to address some of these topics. I also argue that test users must study the populations that they wish to assess to understand better the needs for testing accommodations of various types. Testing professionals also must develop ideas about the need to adapt test administration procedures and test materials so that they may be most effectively administered to all members of society.

References

Cattell, J. M. (1890). Mental tests and measurements. *Mind, 15,* 373–380.

Cole, N. S., & Moss, P. A. (1989). Bias in test use. In R. L. Linn (Ed.), *Educational measurement* (3rd ed., pp. 201–220). New York: American Council on Education/Macmillan.

Eyde, L. D. (1992). Introduction to the testing of Hispanics in industry and research. In K. F. Geisinger (Ed.), *Psychological testing of Hispanics* (pp. 167–172). Washington, DC: American Psychological Association.

Geisinger, K. F. (1984). Test standardization. In R. J. Corsini (Ed.), *Wiley encyclopedia of psychology* (Vol. 34, p. 414). New York: Wiley.

Geisinger, K. F. (1992). Fairness and selected psychometric issues in the psychological testing of Hispanics. In K. F. Geisinger (Ed.), *Psychological testing of Hispanics* (pp. 17–42). Washington, DC: American Psychological Association.

Geisinger, K. F. (1994a). Psychometric issues in testing students with disabilities. *Applied Measurement in Education, 7,* 121–140.

Geisinger, K. F. (1994b). Cross-cultural normative assessment: Translation and adaptation issues influencing the normative interpretation of assessment instruments. *Psychological Assessment, 6,* 304–312.

Madaus, G. F. (Ed.). (1983). *The courts, validity, and minimum competency.* Boston: Kluwer-Nijhoff.

Standards for educational and psychological testing. (1985). Washington, DC: American Psychological Association.

Uniform Guidelines on Employee Selection Procedures, 43 Fed. Reg. 38290 (1978).

Critical Thinking in Test Interpretation

Jonathan Sandoval

Psychologists and others use tests to help them make decisions. They rely on tests because they are fast and convenient and because they yield information not easily obtainable otherwise. Moreover, tests were developed to be more objective than individual, subjective judgment. For many purposes, as Meehl has demonstrated, the actuarial approach to diagnosis based on test results is superior to a clinical approach using nontest information (Dawes, Faust, & Meehl, 1989; Meehl, 1954). Decisions that are based on a well-developed and validated test may be superior to those based on professional intuition. According to Faust (1986),

> the advantages of tests are common knowledge, but they have rarely been considered from the standpoint of the judgment literature, particularly their function in reducing the role of judgment. It is possible that, other things being equal, the more a test reduces freedom to vary on the basis of clinical impression, the better it performs. (p. 424)

The intent here is to consider the judgment literature with respect to instances in which tests may not have been adequately validated.

It is well accepted that human decision making is influenced by strategies and heuristics that are prone to error. When actuarial approaches cannot substitute for clinical decision making, such as when test validities cannot be established for use with diverse groups, or when it is suspected that the base rates for a particular population are different from the mainstream, it then becomes important to find substitute techniques and strategies. The intent is to avoid the biases in human cognition that lead to poor decision making. One might suspect that well-trained psychologists are immune to errors of judgment or are better decision makers than other professionals. Research has not shown this to be the case. In his review, J. Wiggins (1984) asked the following:

> Are the judgmental shortcomings and biases of clinicians distinctively different from those of other professional decision makers? That is, have these *same* shortcomings been demonstrated in groups of stockbrokers, physicians, intelligence analysts, electrical engineers, etc.? (Answer: definitely yes). (p. 14)

In this chapter I review research and theory concerning how individuals make judgments (Tversky & Kahneman, 1974), with particular attention given to the kinds of decisions professional psychologists make and with reference to the special problem of making decisions about diverse clients. Herein, I use the terms *clinician* and *client* in the generic sense to denote psychological practitioners and those about whom they make judgments, respectively. The phenomena covered will include the difficulty human judges have with the representativeness of information, especially the failure to consider base-rate and sample size information. Another phenomenon is the tendency to confirm existing cognitive schemas. Decision makers make errors by detecting a correlation when none exists and not detecting a correlation when it does exist (Chapman & Chapman, 1967; Friedlander & Phillips, 1984; Kurtz & Garfield, 1978), that is, by making data fit existing ideas and by ignoring data that conflict with existing preconceptions. A third general phenomenon is the tendency to be influenced by recently activated schemas, an occurrence usually called the *availability bias* or the *anchoring bias* (Tversky & Kahneman, 1974). In encountering new information or new clients, clinicians are overinfluenced by what they have encountered in the recent past.

Decision Making and Judgment Error

Before discussing these biases and how they may be avoided, I consider correctness and errors in judgment. In decision making, a judge may make two kinds of errors in a yes or no situation (see Table 1). The judge can say yes in a situation in which the correct answer is no (a false alarm) or no in a situation in which the correct answer is yes (a miss). Of course, the judge wants to be accurate (i.e., avoid error) and say yes when yes is correct (a hit) and no when no is correct (a "don't worry"). If the effect of making either error is the same and the prob-

Table 1		
Types of Successes and Errors in Simple Judgments		
	A true situation or the outcome is "yes"	A true situation or the outcome is "no"
The decision or prediction is "yes"	A hit	A false alarm (or false positive)
The decision or prediction is "no"	A miss	A "no problem" (or true negative)

ability of a correct answer is .50, one may simply judge at random. However, the assumption is that use of tests or other information, such as a prospective student's grade point average, improves the odds of correctness above .50.

Moreover, in real life, the consequences of one sort of error are seldom equal. A false alarm may cause fewer problems than a miss, or the reverse may be the case. In industry, an error of hiring a person for a job at which he or she will fail may be worse than an error of failing to hire someone who would succeed. This is likely the case if one's client is the employer, not the job applicant. However, from the standpoint of the out-of-work job applicant, it may be worse not to be hired than to be inappropriately hired. Error consequences differ depending on one's viewpoint.

Another factor that must be taken into consideration is the base rate of the condition or status being sought. If the probability of a hit is high (i.e., if one is selecting for a job) and almost everyone would be successful in that position, then one may have lax rules for making a hiring decision. If the probability of achieving the condition or status is low, the likelihood of being correct must also be low. The probability of a hit helps determine the probability of an error. Gambrill (1990), in her excellent book on clinical decision making, pointed out that

> the predictive accuracy of a test depends on the initial risk of a condition in the person receiving the test. The probability that a client with a positive (or negative) test result for dementia actually has dementia depends on the prevalence of dementia in the population from which the client was selected—that is, on the pretest probability that a client has dementia. (p. 277)

Clinicians often ignore the fact that the base rate of a condition influences the chance of being correct. In working with clients from diverse populations, clinicians may over or underestimate how common the condition is for a particular population.

Statistical convention requires that one outcome be assigned a low probability of occurrence (.01 or .05). This is usually framed by researchers interested in differences between the treatment and control groups and deciding that there is a difference between the groups when none exists (a Type I error). The least egregious outcome, failing to find a difference when one truly does exist (a Type II error), is assigned a greater probability of error, although this error also should be minimized. The problem is that it is difficult to minimize both kinds of errors at the same time.

Malgady (1996) argued that in clinical situations, avoiding negative consequences to the minority client requires that clinicians assume the hypothesis that tests are inappropriate to use with minority clients rather than the null hypothesis that tests are appropriate (or that there is no difference in the score's meaning for minority and mainstream test takers). He thought that the consequences of decisions based on unsuitable tests are irrelevant services being delivered to minority clients. He suggested that not using tests results in fewer individuals being identified for inappropriate services, although greater numbers of clients will not receive services. Choosing the difference hypothesis is justified, he argued, because this strategy is most likely to avoid the error of acting as if minorities are the same as the majority when they are not. Malgady was addressing the general case, however; this chapter focuses on the individual. It is an open question whether clinical judgment would be better at reducing the assignment of minorities to inappropriate services. Nevertheless, the consequences of test use need to be examined from two perspectives.

Generally speaking, as decision makers, clinicians have a tendency to attend to only one cell in the 2 × 2 table shown in Table 1, the yes–yes cell, or the number of hits. Clinicians get excited when the number of hits is high. However, to get an appropriate picture of the accuracy of judgment, one needs to examine all four cells. Consider Table 2 and judge whether there is an association between the success on an interview and success in medical school for a group of 54 Latino applicants. If one looks at the yes–yes cell only, one might conclude that there is a relationship. In fact, there is no correlation between these two variables. The same proportion of high as low scores are successful. One must conclude that this interview is not useful.

Table 2

Relationship Between Fictitious Interview and Medical School Success

	Successful in medical school	Not successful in medical school
High score on the application interview	Hit ($n = 24$)	False positive ($n = 12$)
Low score on the application interview	Miss ($n = 12$)	No problem ($n = 6$)

Some Sources of Errors in Judgment

The Representativeness Bias

The problem of representativeness is deciding whether a behavior, symptom, or outcome is typical or *representative* of an underlying condition. Tversky and Kahneman (1974) defined the representative heuristic as the process "in which probabilities are evaluated by the degree to which A is representative of B, that is, by the degree to which A resembles B" (p. 1124). The psychologist must decide whether Score A is related to Disorder B, whether Score A is related to successful Treatment B, or whether Score A predicts Outcome B. In essence most of the time, the judge is inferring that if A commonly occurs with B, then A causes B. As clinicians know, however, correlation does not imply causation, but they are primed to think so. Additional factors should affect clinicians' judgments of probability, including the base rate, sample size, and regression.

Ignoring the Base Rate

One kind of representativeness error occurs when a decision maker infers cause or likelihood of cause without considering the base rate of the behavior. For example, a psychologist may note that a score pattern on a test is associated with alcoholism and occurs in 75% of the alcoholic clients with whom he or she works. However, alcoholism may be prevalent at the rate of 75% or even 80% in the psychologist's clients. As a result, the score pattern will not be useful in diagnosis.

Another error may occur when the score pattern occurs in, say,

75% of alcoholic individuals and in 60% of football spectators. In the population, there are far more football spectators than alcoholic individuals. As a result, a more accurate prediction would be that an individual with the score pattern is a football fan than that the individual is a heavy drinker.

Base rates may be higher for the behavior or for the condition in particular populations than for the general population. For example, the base rate for feelings of fatigue and weakness may be low in the general population. However, an individual with neuromuscular disease may truthfully mark an item on a personality test that indicates fatigue because the disease causes muscle weakness. Yet, such items usually contribute to a depression score on the test. Because the base rate for fatigue is much higher in individuals with neuromuscular disease, it would be easy to conclude erroneously that these individuals are likely to be depressed.

The base rates for several behaviors in a particular population may be higher or lower than in the general population. For example, there may be a lower base-rate level of impulsivity in a given childhood population leading to an underestimation of the incidence of attention deficit disorder for that group. As a result, psychologists interpreting tests for individuals from any specific group should be sensitive to the base rates of both behaviors and conditions. Although these data may not be easily available, at least the psychologist should be aware of the base-rate problem.

Insensitivity to Sample Size

Another representativeness error is a failure to take sample size into account in judging probability. Small samples yield less stable results than large sample sizes and are less representative of the true situation. Unfortunately, individuals are prone to make generalizations on the basis of limited exposure to individuals or from limited sources of information. Despite the canon that decisions should not be made on the basis of a single test score, assessors often do not collect large samples of information. This is particularly problematic for members of diverse groups because their numbers, by definition, are small and individuals from a particular group may not be seen regularly or routinely in a practice or institution. Not only will samples from diverse groups be small but they also will be selected on the basis of factors such as being able to speak English, being comfortable with the mainstream population, or availability and thus may not be representative of their group.

Regression to the Mean

Regression to the mean occurs when a person with extreme scores on a distribution at one time or in one situation earns scores closer to the mean a second time or in a different situation. Because of the way error works, clinicians should expect extreme scores to likely contain error and a repeated test to yield scores closer to the mean. Moreover, individuals are often referred to psychologists because of extreme scores or having diverged from the norm in some way.

Judges, including psychologists, often fail to expect regression to the mean in many situations in which it is bound to occur, and, when it does occur, they often invent false causal explanations. They do not expect individuals selected for high scores on the Scholastic Aptitude Test, for example, to score lower on another examination. When children of professionals do not do as well in school as their parents, the conclusion might be that the children are overindulged or that they are reacting against their parents' success; what may be operating is regression.

In a sense, clients from diverse groups by definition vary from the mean of the general population in some respect. Within their group, the individual may also vary from the mean in some way. The standard expectation should be that on reassessment or on different variables they will, because of the regression effect alone, become more similar to the mean of their subgroup. What may or may not be known to the psychologist is expected value for the specific group.

Drawing Inferences of Causation

Before clinicians can turn an observed relationship into a probability estimate, they must consider those limiting factors. Once considered, however, it may be appropriate to draw inferences of causation from correlations. In doing so, it is important to consider the following factors:

1. *The consistency of the correlation:* Does the relationship observed occur across situations, across populations, across measures, and across time? For the individual, do independent sources of information agree? Are test results in concordance from tests assessing the same construct? Do test results reflect what else is known about the client?

2. *The coherence of the correlation:* Does the relationship make sense? Does it fit an accepted or reasonable model or theory of how the world works? For the individual, does the picture make

sense? Does the test result help form a logically consistent inference about the person?

3. *The temporal relation between variables:* Does the alleged cause always precede the effect in time? For the individual, does the case history hang together? Do test results over time show a pattern? Do measures of factors related to the construct in question taken earlier in the person's development predict current performance on a measure of the construct?

4. *The elimination of competing explanations:* Has there been an active attempt to eliminate a competing hypothesis? Have other relationships been examined and discounted? Have explanations such as exposure to test content, motivation, or rapport between student and examiner been eliminated before treating the test as valid for the individual?

5. *The strength of the association:* Is the correlation strong and significant? Does the correlation explain a practical amount of variation in the effect? For the individual, is the evidence convincing? Are the test results unequivocal in spite of mitigating factors?

6. *The specificity of the association:* Does the relationship work both ways? If *A* is observed does one find *B*, and if *B* is observed does one find *A*? For the individual, does everything check both ways? If a test works to predict a criterion such as success in college, do those attaining the criterion also score highly on the test?

When these conditions hold, one may be more confident in believing that a causal relationship is operating. As a result, one may be more confident in one's judgment in linking a sign to a probable outcome.

In summary, the representative bias suggests that clinicians are not good at thinking about probabilistic information. Training in the identification of judgment errors and the use of probability theory, particularly Bayesian theory, may help (Gambrill, 1990), but the power of the representative bias is considerable (Fischoff, 1982).

Confirmatory Bias

Another well-recognized bias in human cognition is the need to confirm expectations or to verify preconceptions. Clinicians as well as other decision makers have a tendency to selectively attend to information compatible with their established practice theories. This tendency is often referred to as the "confirmatory bias."

Ironically, many clinicians use a parallel tendency in their clients when they use projective methods. The techniques are predicated on the notion that individual attitudes and cognitions about how the world operates will be displayed when the client is confronted with ambiguous stimuli. In a clinical interview, this bias in clients is called *transference.* Psychoanalytically oriented therapists are aware of the potential occurrence of countertransference and guard against their predispositions, or unconscious motives, leading them to attend to only some aspects of a case.

A cognitive interpretation for this tendency toward confirmatory biases is the resistance of schemas to change. When a conceptualization or schema is established, new information is assimilated into what is already understood; only rarely does accommodation take place with its concomitant conceptual change.

Expectancies based on status are at the heart of prejudice and may not be in awareness. As a result, when working with clients from non-mainstream groups, psychologists' schemas for this group may not be complex or may be limited compared with schemas about people similar to themselves (Park & Rothbart, 1982). Can clinicians' concepts be protected from stereotypes? Training in cross-cultural awareness is a common recommendation for psychologists dealing with clients different from themselves. One component of this training might be to emphasize the true base rates of behaviors in a particular population and stress that the behaviors may have a higher probability of accuracy in this group but that the probability is not 1.00.

Not only do judges act to confirm hypotheses, they also do not readily appreciate that things occur by chance—they want them to occur for a reason. Judges act to explain chance variation. The popularity of profile analysis on tests such as the Wechsler Adult Intelligence Scale–Revised may occur because clinicians are not comfortable with random variation in test scores. They have a need to make the data fit a schema, to find explanations for chance occurrences. Errors occur when experience and theory based on mainstream population are forced to fit diverse clients.

This tendency leads to a problem called the *illusory correlation.* Chapman and Chapman (1967) first identified this judgment error in clinical practice. An illusory correlation occurs when individuals processing information on a series of cases come to believe that correlations exist when they do not. Chapman and Chapman had clinicians review several cases in which human figure drawings were randomly paired with client symptoms in one study and Rorschach responses randomly paired with symptoms in another (Chapman & Chapman, 1969). Although there was no statistical correlation between signs and symptoms, the judges identified several that they believed to be accurate indicators. Examples of erroneous beliefs are that unusually shaped eyes in a drawing were correlated with suspiciousness and that particular Rorschach signs were correlated with homosexuality. None of their judgments had been empirically established to be accurate.

Test scores may be overinterpreted for diverse clients because clinicians will hold conceptualizations about human behavior and conceptualizations about minority clients that may be inaccurate. For example, chance variation stemming from a test taker's lack of English-speaking skills may be interpreted in a wide variety of ways depending on the background of the tester.

Clinicians interpreting tests are often advised to generate hypotheses that can be corroborated by more than one data source. Kamphaus (1993), for example, suggested that "each conclusion drawn from a psychological [test] report be supported by at least two additional data sources" (p. 160). He further suggested that interpretations should be individualized in that the tester should "search for theories and research findings to explain the child's score, in contrast to making the child's scores fit the theory of the test or some other valued theory" (p. 162). Finally, he suggested a priori interpretation in which the clinician generates hypotheses before interpretation on the basis of "previous information about the child, including reports from teachers, clinicians and parents; previous school grades; medical and developmental histories; and observations during the test session" (p. 167). The problem, of course, is that this approach feeds into the confirmatory bias, in which the test interpreter is likely to notice only that evidence from all sources are consistent with the a priori hypothesis and ignore disconfirming evidence. The problem is confounded when tests are selected and used stocastically when a second test is administered to confirm a hypothesis generated by the first. As a result, test interpreters need to look systematically at both confirmatory and disconfirmatory observations and reconcile the two carefully.

The point is, clinicians remember data that support their assumptions, may even invent supportive data, and may forget or ignore data that do not. A question to ask to mitigate the confirmatory bias is, Are clinicians looking at all of the data, or are they looking at some of them selectively? The confirmatory bias also is linked to the availability bias because ideas available to consciousness may be more likely to be corroborated.

Availability Bias

A third source of error is the availability bias. Errors based on an availability bias occur when a decision maker is influenced by vivid information and information similar to recently experienced events. Such information is more easily recalled. One explanation for this phenomenon is schema activation theory. If a schema is activated or brought to mind by vivid information, that schema will be more easily reactivated in the immediate future because of strengthened links between short- and long-term memory (Gagne, Yekovich, & Yekovich, 1993). Most people have experienced hearing a word or learning a fact for the first time and then encountering it again frequently in subsequent days.

For psychologists working predominantly with one population, a client from another population will stand out vividly. If a psychologist does not often see Pacific Islander clients, for example, a new Samoan client will bring to mind information associated with a previous Solomon Islander client. Because individuals from diverse groups may be relatively rare in the psychologist's experience, he or she may be unduly influenced when observing the same pattern in the new client that he or she saw in the old.

The availability bias is a problem, warned Achenbach, McConaughy, and Howell (1987), because

> (1) it can cause us to miss the ways in which a new case differs from other cases it superficially resembles. (2) It can cause us to match a case to an easily remembered pattern, despite greater similarity to a less available pattern. (3) It can lead us to infer correlations where none exist. (4) It can bias our estimates and predictions to reflect events most vivid to us rather than most representative of what is to be estimated or predicted. (p. 26)

A variation on the availability bias is the anchoring heuristic, the tendency to rely more heavily on information received early in the process of gathering information than on data received later. Ideas encountered first also are more available and influence subsequent perception and memory. Clinicians are known to favor hypotheses formed early in the evaluation process. Confidence in the diagnosis increases over time, even though accuracy does not (Friedlander & Phillips, 1984;

Nisbett, Zukier, & Lemley, 1981). The early ideas are simply available for confirmation. Clinicians must learn to withhold judgment until all the information is collected.

To counter the anchoring bias, assessors must be conscious about the order in which they receive information. To avoid a tendency to view clients as pathological, for example, the emphasis should be on receiving information about the positive features of the client and on similarities to the norm first, prior to a focus on differences and negative features.

A phenomenon related to the availability and confirmatory bias that manifests itself in the use of ratings is the halo effect (Murphy, Jako, & Anhalt, 1993). This is the tendency to be unduly influenced by a single positive or negative trait on the ratings of other, presumably unrelated traits. For example, the attractive appearance of an individual may lead to unearned positive ratings of competence in academic subjects. Halo effects may be triggered by race, ethnicity, gender, and other factors.

Psychologists must be on guard against information about clients that will stimulate them to attend to only some of the facts available to them. They must be wary of the unusual and of the trendy.

Cognitive Limitations in Decision Making

In addition to heuristics that lead decision makers to make errors, it also is important to acknowledge the cognitive limitations clinicians face. People have a limited capacity to process information in short-term memory. Although there are ways to organize or chunk information, people may have only seven (plus or minus two) place holders in what is termed *working memory* (Gagne et al., 1993; Miller, 1956).

This limited capacity to use information manifests itself in the inability to use additional information in decision making past an optimal amount (Golden, 1964). Psychologists given test results are only able to cope with a limited amount of information. Performance in decision making can even decline with additional information (Sines, 1959).

Judges also have a limited ability to use information that pertains to two or more dimensions (Faust, 1986). Although judges claim to be able to perform complex configural analyses, their performance on tests such as the Minnesota Multiphasic Personality Inventory can be modeled by simple linear models (N. Wiggins & Hoffman, 1968).

Another cognitive limitation is the difficulty of conceptual change in individuals. Once a conception is set or a schema is established, it is difficult to alter them. The confirmatory bias operates to maintain conceptions, as I have discussed. The robustness of incorrect conceptions has been extensively studied in the teaching of science (Sandoval, 1995).

Once a test interpreter's ideas about a test or about a population are set, it will be difficult to change them. Stereotypes and racist conceptions cannot be easily overcome. The four conditions that seem to be related to conceptual change, according to Posner, Strike, Hewson, and Gertzog (1982) are (a) dissatisfaction with existing ideas; (b) fully understanding the new, alternative idea; (c) finding the new idea to be plausible; and (d) finding the new idea to be useful in explaining a wider range of phenomena. Misconceptions may be addressed by presenting learners with anomalous data that call into question the power of existing ideas; by giving the learner accurate new theories; and by demonstrating the elegance, parsimony, and effectiveness of the idea is solving additional problems. Clinicians must use these notions as guidelines in any training program aimed at increasing cultural sensitivity in test interpretation.

Protecting Against Judgment Errors in Test Interpretation

Even-Handed Focus on Convergent and Divergent Information

The usual way of avoiding errors in judgment is to look for convergent information. Clinicians attempt to triangulate to find out where things are. The result from a test, if it agrees with other information such as interviews, biographical information, or reports of others, makes them more confident in their judgments. However, what are clinicians to do if the information is discrepant? It is well-known that different informants do not necessarily agree in rating children or adolescents, for example. These discrepancies in judgment possibly occur because judges observe the children in different settings (Achenbach et al., 1987). In addition, the results of different types of assessments such as projective tests and self-report measures may not agree (Ball, Archer, Gordon, & French, 1991) because of differences in the requirements of the methods, such as verbal fluency.

How do clinicians decide when there is a true divergence of information? Kamphaus and Frick (1996) recommended that the assessor

> try to develop explanations for the discrepancies. Can the discrep-
> ancies be explained by different demands in the various settings in
> which a child is observed? Can the discrepancies be explained by
> differences in the measurement techniques used or by certain char-
> acteristics/motivation of the informants? Can the discrepancies be
> explained by differing knowledge of the child's behavior across in-
> formants? (p. 320)

These certainly may be sources of error, but they also may be evidence
that the perceived consistencies are not real and that the hypothesis is
incorrect. Clinicians should be cognizant of discrepant information and
not try simply to explain it away.

Even if data are consistent, there still may be a problem. The internal consistency of a pattern of inputs is a major determinant of one's
confidence in predictions. An admissions officer considers all *B*s on a
transcript as a more accurate predictor of future grades than a scatter-
ing of *A*s and *C*s averaging to a *B*. However, consistent patterns are most
likely to result when a set of variables is highly redundant, correlated,
or overlapping. From statistical training, clinicians should remember
that the amount of explained variance in a regression analysis is likely
to be higher when the predictor measures are valid and independent
of one another rather than highly correlated with one another. Ironically, redundancy decreases accuracy but increases confidence in the
judgment (Tversky & Kahneman, 1974). Before clinicians are persuaded by consistent information, they must be sure that each bit of
information is independently adding useful information to their decision making.

Divergent information is equally important to convergent information about individuals. Campbell and Fisk (1959) introduced the notion of convergent validity and divergent validity for tests suggesting
that, for a test to be valid, it should correlate with some criteria and not
with others. This concept applied to test interpretation implies that in
addition to convergent information, clinicians should expect and find
divergent patterns of relationships in making inferences about their
clients. This notion is built into many diagnoses. Many conditions are
defined by a failure to establish competing causes. For example, in establishing that a child has a learning disability, federal requirements
require that other conditions be ruled out, such as the opportunity to
learn, mental retardation, and cultural factors.

In test interpretation generally, clinicians often assume that all test
takers have had an equal opportunity to learn information they are

being tested on. Perhaps this requirement is more true now, with mass communications, than it was in the past. However, clinicians must ask whether there is something obvious about the opportunity to learn or to gain skills based on the client's background that should influence their decision making. For diverse clients, factors such as poverty or language will prevent clients from full access to information and skills being tested for.

Clinicians must consider that the scientific method has been developed to help them manage bias in human judgments. Some strategies intended to reduce the chance that the experimenter will influence the results (confirmatory bias) are the random assignment of participants to treatments and the lack of knowledge on the part of the experimenters and participants about the treatment or condition (the double-blind study). The use of a comparison or control group helps clinicians to attend to the base rate (representative bias) and to distrust numbers without a sense of the distribution. The use of statistical tests also helps avoid the representative bias. The use of objective measures and operational definitions also help guard against the availability bias. Finally, the use of data recording and enumeration relieves clinicians of the need to rely on their limited memory. If they can find ways to adapt the scientific method to test interpretation, perhaps they can reduce the biases that operate in working with diverse clients.

Concluding Recommendations for Critical Thinking in Testing Individuals From Diverse Groups

Several recommendations evolve out of the foregoing discussion of bias and the need for critical thinking. Clinicians' cognitive limitations and biases are certainly going to affect them in working with clients from diverse populations.

1. *Identify preconceptions.* It is important to try to identify some of the conceptions and viewpoints clinicians have about diverse clients, both positive and negative, and recognize that they exist. Self-awareness is the first step in gaining the capacity to understand others' viewpoints. Psychologists may treasure their theories, but they also must recognize how they lead them to selective perception. Psychologists must take into account knowledge of the biases and judgment and their cognitive limitations. One aim of professional supervision is to aid in this endeavor.

2. *Develop complex schemas or conceptions of client groups.* It is important to develop a more complex schema about diverse groups clinicians may encounter in their practice. The point of cultural sensitivity training is not to create stereotypes but to build new, more complete, and accurate schemas that will help clinicians understand individuals functioning within a particular context. Clinicians must recognize that changing their conceptions about diverse groups will not be an easy or automatic task. Clear thinking skills must be complemented with knowledge about the groups to which their clients belong.

3. *Actively search for disconfirmatory evidence.* Because of the confirmatory bias, it is imperative in making judgments on the basis of tests or on other information to search constantly for disconfirming evidence and for alternative explanations for clinicians' initial hunches about clients. Clinicians must constantly attend to negative information and not simply try to explain it away (Gambrill, 1990). They must continually ask, Did the individual have the opportunity to learn the information or to express it on the test? They must not always view difficulties as being attributable to internal states of the client; instead, they must look at environmental causes as well. They can learn to shift the frames of reference they use by determining what is missing in a case or by asking questions that completely reverse their perspective, such as What if *B* caused *A* rather than the reverse?

4. *Resist a rush to judgment.* Clinicians must resist impulsivity and reserve judgment. They must wait for all the facts to present themselves and not give undue weight to vivid data, personally relevant data, or recent data. They must beware of the regression to the mean effect and not overinterpret shifts from extremely high or extremely low scores. Clinicians should aim to be reflective practitioners who continue to improve their judgment skills systematically.

5. *Seek supervision.* It is important to get feedback on decision making. In working with new kinds of clients, clinicians should consult a colleague who has experience with the population. Of course, it also is important to recognize when clinicians themselves are not competent to make a judgment about an individual or a situation; however, even if there are no options and they have to work with clients from unfamiliar backgrounds, they should seek consultation.

6. *Distrust memory.* It is useful to find ways to minimize the role of memory. Memory is a process involving construction (Bartlett, 1932) and is highly subject to the confirmatory bias. Psychologists should make recordings, take notes, and document impressions using counts, checklists, or other objective means.

Finally, when dealing with test data, clinicians must consider that the test has provided some information about performance and some norms to use as a comparison group. If the comparison does not make sense, it should not be used. However, clinicians should still realize that test data do represent some minimal performance and may represent the interplay of many forces in the client's life.

Effective practitioners must know how these cognitive phenomena influence their day-to-day work and how to guard against making errors in judgment. In some instances, the use of tests will facilitate decision making and in others they will not (Arkes, 1981). Faust (1986) observed that

> the recognition that chance is unavoidable in prediction leads to two general suggestions. First, one should not be too quick to abandon good predictors because they are fallible.... There is a tendency to believe that if only one wised up, one could be right nearly all of the time. This belief can lead clinicians to abandon state-of-the-art predictors because they do not meet their standards. One should make sure that one has a better predictor before one gives up a good one. Rejecting a proven strategy of modest validity for a personally invented judgment rule increases one's accuracy very rarely.
>
> Second, clinicians should be conservative. There are very few predictive situations in which there is justification for extreme confidence. Thus if the cost of errors is grave (e.g., potential danger), one should be cautious. At the minimum, one should find the middle point between how confident one is in one's prediction and how well people predict, or how often something occurs, under similar circumstances. (p. 428)

In working with clients from diverse backgrounds, all of psychologists' critical problem solving skills will be needed. There are no cookbooks or simple actuarial tools to fall back on. Clients deserve the clearest thinking.

References

Achenbach, T. M., McConaughy, S. H., & Howell, C. T. (1987). Child/adolescent behavioral and emotional problems: Implications of cross-informant correlations for situational specificity. *Psychological Bulletin, 101,* 213–232.

Arkes, H. R. (1981). Impediments to accurate clinical judgment and possible ways to minimize their impact. *Journal of Consulting and Clinical Psychology, 49,* 323–330.

Ball, J. D., Archer, R. P., Gordon, R. A., & French, J. (1991). Rorschach depression indices with children and adolescents: Concurrent validity findings. *Journal of Personality Assessment, 57,* 465–476.

Bartlett, F. C. (1932). *Remembering.* Cambridge, England: Cambridge University Press.

Campbell, D. T., & Fiske, D. W. (1959). Convergent and discriminant validation by the multitrait–multimethod matrix. *Psychological Bulletin, 56,* 81–105.

Chapman, L. J., & Chapman, J. P. (1967). Genesis of popular but erroneous psycho-diagnostic observations. *Journal of Abnormal Psychology, 74,* 271–280.

Chapman, L. J., & Chapman, J. P. (1969). Illusory correlation as an obstacle to the use of valid psychodiagnostic signs. *Journal of Abnormal Psychology, 74,* 271–280.

Dawes, R. M., Faust, D., & Meehl, P. E. (1989). Clinical verses actuarial judgment. *Science, 243,* 1668–1674.

Faust, D. (1986). Research on human judgment and its application to clinical practice. *Professional Psychology: Research and Practice, 17,* 420–430.

Fischoff, B. (1982). Debiasing. In D. Kahneman, P. Slovic, & A. Tversky (Eds.), *Judgment under uncertainty* (pp. 422–444). Cambridge, England: Cambridge University Press.

Friedlander, M. L., & Phillips, S. D. (1984). Preventing errors in clinical judgment. *Journal of Consulting and Clinical Psychology, 52,* 366–371.

Gagne, E. D., Yekovich, C. W., & Yekovich, F. R. (1993). *The cognitive psychology of school learning* (2nd ed.). New York: HarperCollins.

Gambrill, E. (1990). *Critical thinking in clinical practice: Improving the accuracy of judgments and decisions about clients.* San Francisco: Jossey-Bass.

Golden, M. (1964). Some effects of combining psychological tests on clinical infer-ences. *Journal of Consulting Psychology, 28,* 440–446.

Kamphaus, R. W. (1993). *Clinical assessment of children's intelligence.* Boston: Allyn & Bacon.

Kamphaus, R. W., & Frick, P. J. (1996). *Clinical assessment of child and adolescent personality and behavior.* Boston: Allyn & Bacon.

Kurtz, R. M., & Garfield, S. L. (1978). Illusory correlation: A further exploration of Chapman's paradigm. *Journal of Consulting and Clinical Psychology, 46,* 1009–1015.

Malgady, R. G. (1996). The question of cultural bias in assessment and diagnosis of ethnic minority clients: Let's reject the null hypothesis. *Professional Psychology: Research and Practice, 27,* 73–77.

Meehl, P. E. (1954). *Clinical versus statistical prediction: A theoretical analysis and a review of the evidence.* Minneapolis: University of Minnesota Press.

Miller, G. A. (1956). The magical number seven, plus or minus two: Some limits on our capacity for processing information. *Psychological Review, 63,* 81–97.

Murphy, K. R., Jako, R. A., & Anhalt, R. L. (1993). Nature and consequences of halo error: A critical analysis. *Journal of Applied Psychology, 78,* 218–225.

Nisbett, R. E., Zukier, H., & Lemley, R. E. (1981). The dilution effect: Nondiagnostic information weakens the implications of diagnostic information. *Cognitive Psy-chology, 13,* 248–277.

Park, B., & Rothbart, M. (1982). Perception of out-group homogeneity and levels of social categorization: Memory for the subordinate attributes of in-group and out-group members. *Journal of Personality and Social Psychology, 42,* 1051–1068.

Posner, G., Strike, K., Hewson, P., & Gertzog, W. (1982). Accommodations of scientific conception: Toward a theory of conceptual change. *Science Education, 66,* 211–227.

Sandoval, J. (1995). Teaching in subject matter areas: Science. *Annual Review of Psychology, 46,* 355–374.

Sines, L. K. (1959). The relative contribution of four kinds of data to accuracy in personality assessment. *Journal of Consulting Psychology, 23,* 483–492.

Tversky, A., & Kahneman, D. (1974). Judgment under uncertainty: Heuristics and biases. *Science, 185,* 1124–1131.

Wiggins, J. (1984). Clinical and statistical prediction: Where are we and where do we go from here? *Clinical Psychology Review, 1,* 3–18.

Wiggins, N., & Hoffman, P. J. (1968). Three models of clinical judgment. *Journal of Abnormal Psychology, 73,* 70–77.

Culture and Cultural Differences

Craig L. Frisby

Psychologists frequently encounter admonitions to incorporate the role of culture and cultural differences in the context of best testing and assessment practices. For example, the measurement and evaluation section in the ethical standards of the American Association for Counseling and Development encourages members to "recognize the effects of . . . cultural factors on test scores" when giving orientations or information to examinees before and after a test administration (Corey, 1988, p. 388). The American Psychological Association's Office of Ethnic Minority Affairs (1993) published guidelines for professional practice that encourage psychologists to "consider the validity of a given instrument or procedure and interpret resulting data, keeping in mind the cultural . . . characteristics of the person being assessed" (p. 46). In the recently published *Handbook of Multicultural Assessment* (Suzuki, Meller, & Ponterotto, 1996), Padilla and Medina (1996) stated the following:

> We believe that assessment is made culturally sensitive through a continuing and open-ended series of substantive and methodological insertions and adaptations designed to mesh the process of assessment and evaluation with the cultural characteristics of the group being studied. (p. 4)

Although it is clear that culture and cultural differences are important factors to consider in testing, it is far from clear what path practitioners must take to comply with these professional standards. The sources quoted above appear to advocate a combination of changed attitudes, the accumulation of more knowledge, practice at a higher skill level, or developing a greater insight into the dynamics of human behavior. It is unrealistic for practitioners to believe that any of these goals can be accomplished simply by reading a book chapter (assuming, of course, that these goals can be accomplished). Additionally, it is beyond the scope of any book chapter to integrate the massive literature base that chronicles what has been written on the topic. Nevertheless, the purpose of this chapter is to give practitioners the tools to activate critical thinking on the topic of culture and testing, with the expectation that practitioners will find some of these skills useful in drawing appropriate and defensible conclusions in the context of their experience.

Definitional Issues

The accurate definition of essential terms is the foundation for effective critical thinking. Unfortunately, there is no consensus among social and behavioral scientists about a universal definition of culture. Nevertheless, many definitions have been offered (e.g., Kroeber & Kluckhohn, 1952). For example, Herskovits (1948) viewed culture as simply that part of the environment that is constructed by humans. According to Kroeber and Kluckhohn (1952), "culture is manifested in and through personalities. Personality shapes and changes culture but is in turn shaped by culture" (p. 222). Rohner (1984) defined culture as "the totality of equivalent and complementary learned meanings maintained by a human population, or by identifiable segments of a population, and transmitted from one generation to the next" (pp. 119–120). Sue and Sue (1990) proposed that culture "consists of all those things that people have learned to do, believe, value, and enjoy in their history. It is the totality of ideals, beliefs, skills, tools, customs, and institutions into which each member of a society is born" (p. 35). Triandis and Brislin (1984) argued that culture is "often used in a vague manner and refer[s] to some combination of differences in skin color, country of origin, language, customs, socialization priorities, and some times socioeconomic class" (p. 1007).

Further complicating matters is the variability of ways in which the word culture is used semantically in everyday language. In some contexts, the word *culture* refers to the higher aesthetic accomplishments of an (arbitrarily defined) society such as its fine art, music, or literature. A "cultured" person, therefore, is someone who has accumulated a knowledge and appreciation of these aesthetic elements. In other contexts, culture is often used as a noun typically referring to a "thing" that a person may possess simply by virtue of membership in an arbitrarily defined group. For example, opponents of transracial adoptions often fear that a Black child raised from birth in a White family will be ignorant of his or her culture. In this illustration, the infant (before he or she has had any socializing experiences) is viewed as already possessing a "thing" (culture) at birth simply by virtue of group membership.

Although culture is often associated with race or ethnicity, it is frequently preceded by a modifier designed to circumscribe a group defined by any trait of the speaker's choosing. For example, it is common to hear phrases such as "youth culture," "popular culture," the "culture of poverty," "Southern culture," the "culture of the school," or "Western culture" in popular discourse. In many instances, culture (or any of its derivative forms) is used without a modifier, but in certain contexts its meaning is implicit. For example, many scholars in psychology understand implicitly that some journals operationalize "cross-cultural" psychology as comparative studies of groups living in different countries. In other contexts, the terms *cultural diversity* and *multiculturalism* are often code words that imply differences in racial, ethnic, sexual orientation, gender, or religious groups.

Attempts to bring a sense of coherence to definitions of culture, as well as its semantic manifestations, leave most individuals in a state of utter confusion—much like the proverbial blind men who attempted to understand an elephant by having access only to one of its parts. It is probably futile to attempt a consensual definition of culture in order to understand its relationship to testing issues. It seems more useful to begin by understanding origins of interest in the relationship between culture and testing from the perspective of three different (but not necessarily mutually exclusive) professional roles: (a) the theorist–researcher, (b) the practitioner–clinician, and (c) the socially conscious advocate.

The Theorist–Researcher

Scholars who are interested in the study of culture come from a variety of disciplines (e.g., political science, psychology, anthropology, sociology, education). For purposes of this discussion, scholarly work has focused on the dual goals of (a) pure theory development, which is motivated by the need to conceptualize more accurate theories and definitions of culture necessary for facilitating communication among scholars, and (b) applied research, which is motivated by the need to create new knowledge through empirical studies that investigate the relationships among culture, behavior, and cognition in specific contexts.

Why do scholars find the concept of culture useful? Most culture theorists would agree that culture is derived fundamentally from the observation that a collection of individuals can be viewed as a group because they are similar in a set of (arbitrarily identified) characteristics. Group members may or may not exist in physical proximity to one another. Nevertheless, culture theorists agree that elements of culture are shared by individuals within an arbitrarily defined group (although the form of these elements and the exact meaning of "shared" are still a matter of some debate). Brislin (1993) argued that because aspects of a group's culture are widely shared, they are taken for granted. When aspects of culture are taken for granted, there is no need for members within a culture to frequently and openly discuss aspects of their culture with each other. As a result, it may seem counterintuitive that members of a culture may have difficulty articulating these cultural aspects to those outside of the cultural group (Brislin, 1993). To those outside of a cultural group, however, culture is an inferred abstraction that is known only through the observation of similarities held by many individuals within the group.

Although scholars frequently use the concept of culture, they have struggled with a question: How does culture exist? In the history of the behavioral sciences, there have been two opposing views about the reality of culture (Rohner, 1984). There are those who hold that culture has a concrete reality of its own. Scholars who hold this viewpoint assign culture an independent existence that is wholly external to the individual. Culture exists on its own and is governed by its own laws uninfluenced by people, who are merely its carriers (e.g., White, 1949). This leads to a belief in "cultural determinism," which holds that everything that people do, feel, and think is determined by their culture. Human behavior, including perception and thought, is merely the response of the organism to cultural stimuli.

By contrast, other scholars reject the cultural determinist view and argue that culture has no concrete reality because it exists solely as an inference or abstraction in the mind of the investigator (Spiro, 1978). To these adherents, culture really exists, but it exists in the collective minds of the members of a community, much like a cognitive map that humans carry within them to guide their behavior (Rohner, 1984). The behavior of individuals in day-to-day life activities is not viewed as being guided by culture per se (a view of cultural determinists). Rather, these scholars argue that behavior "is guided by the individual's own cognitive, affective, perceptual, and motivational dispositions that may, in varying degrees, also be what the analyst ultimately comes to call culture" (Rohner, 1984, pp. 116–117). According to this view, culture is a theoretical abstraction that is not directly observable. That is, one cannot see, feel, touch, taste, or hear "culture" (i.e., knowing it directly through one's senses) because it exists only as a set of inferences or abstractions from verbal reports and other observable and measurable physical behaviors. Rohner (1984) summarized this point in the following statement: "Behavior exists in the phenomenal world; culture does not" (p. 117).

Theorists and researchers also have struggled with another question: What is the content of a culture? According to Rohner (1984), anthropologists generally agree that culture refers to a learned phenomenon. They also agree that culture refers in some generalized way to the "way of life of a people," which may or may not involve specific achievements, experiences, attitudes, beliefs, values, customs, traditions, heritage, patterns of behavior, or "life scripts." Debates among anthropologists revolve around the extent to which these specifics manifest themselves in observable behavior. Although culture can manifest itself in observable behavior, other theorists argue that the essence of culture is an unobservable inner cognitive system of shared meanings that involve symbols, ideations, and rules. Triandis (1972) referred to this phenomenon as the distinction between physical and subjective culture.

The distinction between observable and unobservable content of culture is often blurred. Observable aspects of culture include not only behavior but also permanent products that result from behavior (e.g., material artifacts such as paintings, houses, writings). At the same time, an important focus of culture theorists is the meanings associated with these artifacts. For example, to a person unfamiliar with various cultural traditions in the United States, a Confederate flag reflects little more than a piece of cloth with an interesting design on it. By contrast, one United States citizen may view this flag as an important symbol of regional pride and a glorious history, whereas another United States citizen may view this same flag as an offensive symbol of racial hatred.

Further complicating matters is the observation that nonobservable (e.g., cognitions, attitudes) and observable (behaviors, permanent products) cultural elements are linked only in a loose, probabilistic way (Rohner, 1984). Rohner illustrated this point using the analogy of a game. A game is defined by the sum of its rules. Although the rules of the game are constant, players can elect to use different strategies in playing the game, or they can use no strategies at all. Some players may even cheat or elect to discontinue the game. The point, according to Rohner, is that the objective rules of the game have an implicit reality (analogous to the aspects of culture that are not observable). Although one may make probability statements about how the players may behave as a group (which is observable), the implicit reality of the game rules cannot determine with a precise degree of accuracy how an individual player will behave.

The Practitioner–Clinician

Applied psychologists observe human behavior in somewhat controlled and structured settings. Behaviors of interest to practitioner–clinicians consist of both verbal and nonverbal behaviors of clients in the context of administering commercially available tests or assessment procedures that may or may not be standardized. Although there are many factors that influence variability in a client's behavior, culture may be an important contributor to this variation. The concept of culture helps practitioners to identify a source of variation that cannot be attributed to universal biological, maturational, or instinctual processes (universal influences) or idiosyncratic factors (patterns of behavior that are unique to an individual and not shared with anyone else). This source of variation is generally assumed to be shared with others with similar (arbitrarily identified) characteristics.

Furthermore, there is a need for practitioners to believe that all behavior is lawful, or at least that it has an explanation. The concept of culture allows practitioners to make informal judgments about the probability that a behavior will occur from individuals with given characteristics under certain conditions. Therefore, if a behavior or syndrome of behaviors occur, the practitioner will have anticipated this possibility and can partially attribute its occurrence to the role of culture or cultural differences.

In considering the role of culture, however, practitioners frequently experience a dilemma. If too much emphasis on the role of cultural differences is given in the context of evaluating a client, and the client is judged to be less disturbed (in evaluations of psychopathology) or has adequate cognitive skills (in the context of mental testing), there is a risk of inappropriately minimizing or dismissing real problems. Similarly, if important cultural difference factors are ignored, there is a risk of misinterpreting normal behavior as being pathological or less cognitively competent (López & Hernandez, 1986).

Most practitioners recognize this dilemma and are motivated by a sincere desire to adhere to best professional practices. There are numerous areas in which practitioners hope that an understanding of culture and cultural differences can assist them in developing competencies necessary for responsible and ethical test use (Eyde et al., 1993). Fundamentally, competent practitioners recognize that it makes little sense to select an instrument yielding results that are affected by cultural traits or behaviors unrelated to the specific purpose of assessment. In addition, properly trained practitioners strive to select a test normed on a standardization group containing populations with characteristics similar to relevant characteristics of the test taker. In the context of test administration, sensitive practitioners strive to create conditions that facilitate optimum performance by test takers who are culturally different from themselves. This includes the necessity of establishing rapport with examinees as well as ensuring (within the limits of acceptable test administration procedures) that every examinee follows directions so that test scores are accurate (Eyde et al., 1993).

Accurate test interpretation for culturally different test takers requires a balance between the need for clinicians and practitioners to be cautious yet thorough in test interpretation. For example, cautious practitioners understand the limitations of norms and avoid making "high-stakes" interpretations beyond these limitations. If there is a suspicion that cultural characteristics affect the validity of test scores, cautious practitioners treat any single test score as representing only one period in time that is subject to change from experience. Practitioners put this principle into practice by keeping a record of all test data for follow-up, establishing trends, and understanding how these trends apply to decision making in local situations (Eyde et al., 1993).

Thorough practitioners avoid basing important decisions on a single test score and acknowledge the need for multiple sources of convergent data to strengthen or at least provide a context for the accurate interpretation of results. After test results have been obtained, competent clinicians recognize that a thorough background history should be integrated with test results to obtain the most accurate interpretation of test data. If clinicians are unsure of the meaning of certain test information as it may relate to culture, they may consult relevant scholarship in their field or double-check their interpretations with others who are more knowledgeable about these issues (Eyde et al., 1993).

The Socially Conscious Advocate

The word *advocate* is a generic term that describes a person who supports, defends, or argues for a position or intercedes (in a political or legal sense) on behalf of a person or group. In the context of this discussion, an advocate is descriptive of scholar–practitioners who are motivated fundamentally by the desire to protect the rights, interests, and image of groups as it relates to test usage and interpretation. An analysis of the scholarly writings and research initiatives of advocates reveals the following set of implicit (and in many cases explicit) assumptions.

First, although advocates may acknowledge the complexity of the concept of culture, for all practical purposes cultural differences are equated with differences between countries of primary residence (e.g., Stewart, 1972) or differences between immigrant or native-born racial–ethnic groups living in the same country (Dana, 1993; Samuda, King, Cummins, Pascual-Leone, & Lewis, 1989).

Second, advocates argue that there are no common or universal set of tests that are appropriate for evaluating the thinking and behavior of different cultural (i.e., racial–ethnic) groups. This has led many advocates to conclude that psychological constructs such as "intelligence" and "psychopathology" are culturally relative (for specific examples and reviews of this literature, see Dana, 1993; Helms, 1992; Miller, 1995; Miller-Jones, 1989; Padilla, 1995; Schiele, 1991). Specifically, advocates argue that the social and cognitive elements of the testing situation are likely to have a different cognitive "meaning" for culturally different clients, which is a finding that has some support in cross-cultural research (e.g., Rogoff & Chavajay, 1995). Although many of these differences involved groups living in different countries, advocates generalize the "relativism of meaning" principle to any contexts in which groups living within the same country are defined as culturally (i.e., racially or ethnically) different. In the context of cognitive ability testing, advocates will subject a cognitive task to a logical analysis of the presumed social and thinking skills required for a correct answer. Next, a hypothesis is generated about how the nature of different "cultural meaning systems" held by different groups may influence test performance (e.g., Helms, 1992). Some advocates present brief anecdotes in which a culturally different client makes an incorrect response on a particular cognitive task or test item. Because all thinking processes are viewed as being culturally relative (i.e., different but not deficient), then the argument is advanced that the answer is incorrect only in the context of the "dominant" culture, but is "correct" in the context of the client's culture (for examples of this approach, see Miller-Jones, 1989; Rogoff & Chavajay, 1995).

Third, the social relationships between cultural groups is characterized as a morality play in which cultural (i.e., ethnic–racial) minorities are often viewed as being vulnerable to various degrees of misunderstanding, mistreatment, misdiagnosis, and mislabeling in the midst of a culturally dominant majority (Dana, 1993; Neill, 1995; Samuda et al., 1989). According to advocates, culturally different clients are more likely to display entering characteristics that place them at a disadvantage in the testing situation. For example, advocates often argue that culturally different individuals may be unfamiliar with the test situation or test materials, misunderstand the demands of the test situation or task, be insufficiently motivated to do their best, or generally hold cultural values that run counter to those implicit in the testing situation. As a result, the results from testing may underestimate what clients can actually do (e.g., see arguments by Larry P. plaintiffs in Elliot, 1987) or erroneously judge behaviors to be abnormal and in need of intervention when in reality they are normal in a different cultural context (e.g., Dana, 1993).

A fourth assumption of some advocates is that prima facie evidence for culturally inappropriate testing practices are reflected in significant mean differences in the average scores of culturally different groups on aptitude or achievement tests (Armour-Thomas, 1992; Meisels, Dorfman, & Steele, 1995) or different profile patterns on objective personality tests (e.g., see the review of Minnesota Multiphasic Personality Inventory–2 research by Zalewski & Greene, 1996). The overrepresentation of certain ethnic–racial groups in socially undesirable outcomes (e.g., Reschly, Kicklighter, & McKee, 1988a, 1988b) and underrepresentation in socially desirable outcomes (e.g., J. Harris & Ford, 1991) is particularly troublesome for advocates. Sometimes inappropriate testing practices are obvious, as reflected in the practice of evaluating students in a language other than their primary language (e.g., *Diana v. Califor-*

nia State Board of Education, 1970). In other situations, evidence for inappropriate testing is based on speculation (Elliot, 1987).

A fifth assumption is that these problems (as defined and framed by advocates) can be solved through some modification of a practitioner's knowledge base, test selection, test administration procedure, or test interpretation. Advocates are not monolithic in their philosophies that undergird suggested modifications. Rather, proposals for modifications vary as a function of the characteristics of the cultural group, the nature of the test, and the specific decisions that need to be made from test results.

Calls for New Knowledge

Given the criticisms of test usage with culturally different groups, it is not surprising that many advocates urge practitioners to supplement their testing practices with an in-depth knowledge of the cultural characteristics of particular groups (Helms, 1992; Janzen, Skakum, & Lightning, 1994). The material in Appendix I of the fourth edition of the *Diagnostic and Statistical Manual of Mental Disorders* is an example of varieties of culture-specific psychological disturbances not covered by the main taxonomy of disorders (American Psychiatric Association, 1994). Some advocates have argued that the basic conceptualization of the traits psychologists attempt to measure are inadequate and need to be replaced with new or expanded conceptualizations (Schiele, 1991). Other advocates have framed their criticisms in terms of an inadequate knowledge of the manner in which testing contexts differentially influence performance for culturally different children (Cole, Gay, Glick, & Sharp, 1971). Therefore, they have argued that scholars seriously consider developing theories that would identify optimal matches between culturally conditioned cognitions and their appropriate testing contexts (Grubb & Dozier, 1989; Miller-Jones, 1989). Other advocates are not fully persuaded that broad ethnic–racial group designations yield useful information about psychological functioning and have argued for the increased study of specific moderator variables that may have a more proximal influence on behavior (Betancourt & López, 1993; Dana, 1993).

Modifications in Test Selection

The type of tests proposed for use with culturally different individuals range along a continuum of maximum to minimum cultural specificity.

For example, some writers advocate the use of psychometrically sound instruments that have been specifically designed for a particular cultural group (e.g., Ritzler, 1993). Other writers retain the philosophy of maximum cultural specificity but take a radically different approach by measuring change in frequently administered tests of dominant-culture math and reading literacy skills necessary for culturally different individuals' success in American society (Shinn & Baker, 1996). At the other end of the continuum, some writers advocate the use of instruments with language minority participants that contain items that do not require verbal responses for successful completion or rely less heavily on verbal instructions for understanding (A. M. Harris, Reynolds, & Koegel, 1996).

Test Administration and Interpretation

The question of how to administer and interpret existing standardized tests with culturally different groups has varied along a continuum from conservative to radical proposals. At the conservative end of the continuum, the most ethically defensible proposal is to use only instruments that are normed and standardized on the population from which the examinee is a member. Some advocates tolerate the administration of existing instruments to culturally different individuals under less-than-optimal conditions but counsel practitioners to include disclaimers in reports that raise doubt about the accuracy of the results (A. M. Harris et al., 1996). Others have tolerated the use of existing instruments having low representation of certain cultural groups in the norms but urge practitioners to interpret scores in the context of norms derived from the examinee's specific cultural group (Tanner-Halverson, Burden, & Sabers, 1993). Some advocates have advanced the argument that culturally different children's skills are underestimated because the tester is not permitted to probe, answer questions, or encourage individuals to try an alternative answer on tests with standardized administration procedures (Miller-Jones, 1989). Elliot (1987) described an example of applying this philosophy in using the Wechsler tests with African American children (pp. 32–33). Some researchers have described procedures for cognitive testing in which the test taker is encouraged to verbalize his or her thinking processes before and after offering solutions for items, which also may involve elaborative feedback from the examiner (Carlson & Wiedl, 1992). Finally, there are advocates who have taken an extreme position and have argued that test use be discontinued with a particular cultural group for certain types of decisions (Williams, 1974).

A thorough critique of the psychometric validity and diagnostic utility of advocates' proposals for test modifications is well beyond the scope and intent of this chapter. This information can be found in psychological and educational assessment texts, anthologies of test critiques (e.g., *Mental Measurements Yearbook*; Mitchell, 1998), or relevant articles in assessment journals. Rather, points of conflict and harmony among the three approaches to the study of culture and cultural differences are identified in the remaining section. These areas of divergence and convergence are then discussed in light of their implications for testing issues. From this discussion, readers are encouraged to sharpen their critical thinking skills in evaluating the importance and limitation of the concept of culture as it relates to test interpretation.

Points Across Three Approaches to the Study of Culture and Cultural Differences

Points of Divergence

There is tension between the advocate's need to protect the rights of racial–ethnic minority groups, the practitioner–clinician's need to have reliable knowledge to guide practice, and the culture theorist's obligation to recognize the limits of knowledge and to evaluate theories in light of empirical data. This tension is most clearly seen in the different manner in which each perspective approaches the study of culture and cultural differences. Although research about culture does not depend on a consensual definition, theorists (particularly those from the anthropological sciences) are socialized to appreciate the wide range of debate about its meaning. As a result, the struggle involved in conceptualizing, reconceptualizing, or rejecting definitions of culture is seen as a normal part of the vitality of a discipline. This has led to the joke that "culture is defined by the latest anthropological monograph" (Triandis & Brislin, 1984, p. 1006). By contrast, practitioners and advocates are motivated by concrete and practical needs and do not have the luxury of changing definitions according to current and abstract anthropological theories. Because it is simpler to categorize groups by easily observable traits, the writing of practitioners and advocates implicitly equates cultural differences with geographical location and racial–ethnic differences.

Some advocates, who appear to be unable or unwilling to appreciate the complexity of culture, continue to make broad generalizations that are based on references to "White culture," "Black culture," "Asian culture," and "Hispanic culture." Many practitioners and advocates, however, are beginning to recognize the problems inherent in such generalizations. There can be many different cultures represented within a race or ethnic group as well as many races and ethnic groups represented within any given culture. For example, people with Mongoloid physical features (i.e., same broad racial group) can be found in the native-born people of America, the Pacific Islands, and numerous countries within Asia—each of which are characterized by wide ethnic, language, religious, and socioeconomic differences. Even within the broad grouping of American Hispanics, there are wide differences in an individual's country of origin (and how this influences cultural traits), length of time lived in the United States, allegiance to cultural traditions of one's homeland versus America, and proficiency with the English language. Paradoxically, "American culture" is admittedly a broad abstraction, but it nevertheless includes elements from the traditions of a wide variety of different ethnic and racial groups.

Unlike advocates, culture theorists do not confine the parameters of a culture exclusively in terms of racial and ethnic characteristics. Recall that theorists conceptualize culture in terms of characteristics shared by an arbitrarily defined group. Therefore, it follows that any individual can belong to many different cultures simultaneously (depending on how groups are arbitrarily defined). It follows that perceptions of cultural differences are somewhat arbitrary and subject to the subjective idiosyncrasies of the perceiver. An example may be helpful in illustrating this principle. Because of differences in regional mores, for example, a young college student growing up in the Northeast may be perceived as being culturally different in some respects from a cousin who grew up in the Deep South. Because region is used as a criterion for defining cultural differences in this instance, then it should follow that this same student would be considered to be culturally similar (in some respects) to an elderly neighbor who also was raised in the Northeast. However, there can be vast cultural differences between the student (coming of age in the culture of the 1990s) and the elderly neighbor (who came of age in the culture of the 1940s) that can be attributable primarily to generational differences. These differences would most likely be reflected in widely differing opinions, attitudes, and worldviews on various matters. The college student would be perceived by people from a different racial group as being culturally similar to the cousin (who lives in the Deep South) and the elderly neighbor (who came of age in the 1940s) solely on the basis of racial similarity. Similarly, some would argue that this same college student is culturally different from a close friend who belongs to a different racial group. However, when both friends take a vacation to an unfamiliar non–English-speaking foreign country, they would both most likely be perceived as coming from the same American culture in the eyes of a native-born resident of the foreign country. The point is, a person can be culturally similar to another person in the context of one set of criteria but also be culturally different from the same individual in the context of a different set of criteria. In order for the "cultural differences equals racial–ethnic differences" view to be useful for clinical assessment practice, practitioners would have to assume that (a) there is no sharing of relevant characteristics by members across different ethnic and racial groups and (b) people within each cultural group are similar to all other group members in all relevant characteristics. This, of course, is not the case. This is why writers must couch their conclusions in the form of tentative "may" statements (e.g., people from Group A may display certain testing behaviors; people from Group B may interpret the testing situation in a different manner; Examiner C may need to consider cultural factors in making Decision D).

Some cross-cultural psychologists claim that sources of bias against cultural groups can have their origins in the examiner, the tester–testee interaction, or the test itself (van de Vijver, 1994). Of these three sources, the literature on test bias reveals findings that are useful to practitioners but contradict the opinions of some advocates. In developing this discussion, clarification is needed as to what test bias is not. No test measures an underlying trait or ability perfectly because all tests are subject to random measurement error. As long as measurement error affects scores for members of different groups equally, a test cannot be said to be biased (Camilli & Shepard, 1994). Contrary to the arguments of some advocates, judgments of bias cannot be based solely on the observation of average group differences in mean scores. Although this may reflect real problems in the manner in which a test measures a construct in the lower scoring group, there also is the possibility that group differences in the underlying trait are real (and that the test is a reasonably accurate measurement of these differences).

Whenever a test (or individual test items) does not maintain its essential psychometric properties when used with different cultural groups, then test bias is said to occur. For a discussion of modern methods of detecting test bias, readers should see Camilli and Shepard (1994) and Scheuneman and Oakland (chapter 5 in this book).

Comprehensive reviews of standardized cognitive ability tests have indicated that well-developed instruments are not biased when properly used with native-born English-speaking groups such as African Americans (Eysenck, 1984; Jensen, 1980; Wigdor & Garner, 1982). In addition, studies of the accuracy of experts' "armchair" predictions of cultural bias in individual cognitive test items has not been supported by empirical evidence (Jensen, 1977; Jensen & McGurk, 1987; McGurk, 1951; Sandoval & Millie, 1980). Given these findings, it is reasonable to ask why advocates continue to criticize tests as being inappropriate for American-born English-speaking groups such as African Americans (e.g., Helms, 1992; Schiele, 1991). In a general sense, most criticisms are based on what Jensen (1984) called the "specificity doctrine":

> The essence of the specificity doctrine comprises two beliefs: (1) human mental abilities, and individual differences therein, consist of nothing other than a repertoire of specific items of knowledge and specific skills acquired through learning and experience, and (2) all psychometric tests of mental abilities measure nothing other than some selected sample of the total repertoire of knowledge and skills deemed important by the test constructor. (p. 94)

In the arguments advanced by advocates, culture can be substituted for learning and experience, and the sample of skills deemed important by the test constructor is construed as meaning bias in favor of the culture of the dominant group. However, culture theorists are much more reluctant to accept the notion that individual meaning systems or specific knowledge and behaviors can be reliably labeled as belonging to a specific cultural group. Within an arbitrarily defined population, some beliefs or behaviors may be widely shared, whereas others may be only remotely sprinkled throughout a population (Rohner, 1984). The issue of how many people have to share a set of cognitions or behaviors (before they can be labeled *culturally specific*) constitutes one of several knotty problems in culture theory (Rohner, 1984). This problematic issue spawns other problematic issues. For instance, when should one regard a cognition or behavior as no longer being part of a specific culture or as being part of a cultural system for the first time? How would a practitioner delimit one culture from another within this theoretical framework?

Recall Rohner's (1984) characterization of the culture–behavior relationship as being analogous to a game. The behavior of an individual at any given moment (such as a test situation) does not necessarily have to be congruent with "shared" cultural meanings or behaviors (a view in opposition to the doctrine of cultural determinism). In many instances, personal desires are incompatible or conflict with cultural norms. In addition, it cannot be assumed that cultural norms involve identical behaviors across all situations. When one buys food at a grocery store, the behavioral norm (independent of a person's race–ethnicity) in this instance would be to wait quietly in line to pay for food. By contrast, the behavioral norm at a football game may be to cheer loudly and boisterously for one's team. In any situation, behavior is a function of a complex interaction between characteristics of the specific situational context, what a person is capable of doing, what a person thinks he or she ought to do, what a person feels that he or she wants to do, or what a person can't help but to do. Similarly, the totality of an individual's thinking, subjective meanings, and behavior cannot easily be attributed to a single personal characteristic. For example, how would a clinician know the extent to which withdrawn behavior in the test situation is attributable to a test taker's "female-ness," her "Mexican-ness," her "youthful immaturity," or the personality trait of shyness? The bottom line is that conclusions about the frequency of shared beliefs, meanings, or behaviors and a specific group must be determined empirically and not postulated a priori. For example, Helms (1992) advanced an elaborate description of "Afrocentric" culture in speculating that the lower average achievement of African Americans on standardized cognitive ability tests may be caused by different behaviors that are underappreciated by examiners in the testing situation. However, when the items in a standardized measure of test session behavior (in the context of administration of the Wechsler Intelligence Scale for Children–Third Edition) were subjected to empirical analyses of racial bias, there were no appreciable differences in the extent to which examiners (most of whom were Anglo Whites) rated the test session behaviors of Black and White test takers (Nandakumar, Glutting, & Oakland, 1993).

Given the uncertainty of the culture–behavior link in testing, why is it important for advocates to label certain test-related behaviors as cultural (i.e., as being related to race–ethnicity)? The answer to this question can be attributed partly to the observation that linking behaviors to specific races and ethnic groups has obvious sociopolitical benefits for the groups represented by advocates. In the current political climate, charges of test bias against racial–ethnic groups (particularly in the context of aptitude or achievement testing) are taken seriously by test developers, civil rights enforcement agencies, and the court system (e.g., Elliot, 1987). According to Sowell (1993), this climate has led to the fallacy that people can judge the quality of a test taker's prior opportunities strictly from his or her test performance. This is a variation of the specificity doctrine, in which high test scores on aptitude or achievement tests are presumed to reflect greater opportunities to learn the test's content whereas low test scores are presumed to reflect limited opportunities to learn the same content (rather than objective differences in the trait measured by the test). If a higher proportion of lower scoring members belong to a protected minority group, then emotional arguments can be brought into play that include references to "restriction of opportunity," "exclusion from participation," and "prejudice favoring the privileged" (Sowell, 1993).

In principle, all that can be done in any test situation is to measure an individual's performance on a particular test at a particular time with a particular examiner. Cognitive ability tests measure what the individual can do at the time of taking the test, and it is not a measure of a person's cultural background (however one chooses to define *culture*). Similarly, there is no way to predict how a test taker "could have" performed if he or she had been exposed to some other optimal conditions in the past or future. Test scores simply assist practitioners in making conditional probability statements on the basis of the particular test. Evidence on the predictive validity of the test permits probabilistic statements about the participant's performance on an external criterion (assuming that the participant is similar in relevant characteristics to the population on whom predictive validity studies were conducted). In the context of predictive validity issues, it is possible for a test to be highly predictive of success in a job (or on a different test, course of study, training program) regardless of differences in the cultural characteristics of test takers. Although readers may wince at the thought of an examiner administering an English test to a speaker with limited English-language skills, this practice would be entirely appropriate if the purpose of the testing was to predict success for a job as copy editor for an English-language magazine (Jensen, 1980).

Points of Convergence

The previous discussion has shown that the consideration of a test's predictive validity can simplify practitioners' judgments of the relative importance of cultural differences in test interpretation. By contrast, issues related to the impact of cultural differences on test interpretation become more difficult in the context of construct validity issues. However, this is the issue about which the three perspectives can find common ground. All three perspectives allow for the possibility that a test may not be measuring the same construct (and hence have a different meaning) across widely differing cultural groups. This is most problematic in the context of comparisons between native-born acculturated American groups and poor Third World populations living in other continents (or recent refugees and immigrants to America from these countries) who are marginally assimilated to Western culture.

Scholars across a variety of disciplines seek to test the universality of important theories when evaluated in light of cross-cultural research data. For example, Rogoff and Chavajay (1995) traced research trends in the cross-cultural study of cognition from the 1960s to the early 1990s. Many of the research tasks involved Piagetian-influenced logic, classification, and memory tasks that were given to both westernized and Third World populations. Among the many principles emerging from their review are that different cultural groups vary in their level of exposure to formal schooling, familiarity with test materials, kinds of cognitive activities performed in everyday life, and understanding of the appropriate way to respond to an examiner of higher status in a test situation. In examining performance across groups on similar cognitive tasks, researchers observed that differences in performance were often related to differences in these variables (both within and across groups). Reviewers of this literature concluded that, because of this relationship, differential performance on cognitive tasks cannot be assumed to reflect differences in underlying cognitive abilities that are independent of cultural influences (Rogoff & Chavajay, 1995).

When standardized personality and cognitive tests are evaluated for construct equivalence across groups, many researchers have discovered instances in which language differences (and the cultural traits associated with them) are crucial factors that make construct equivalence difficult. To achieve construct equivalence, instruments developed and normed in American English must go through the arduous process of "back translation" (see Bracken & Barona, 1991). However, back translations are merely a starting point in the quest for construct equivalence. Cross-cultural test equivalence also must be demonstrated through appropriate factor-analytic, reliability, predictive validity, and norming studies (see reviews by Dana, 1993; Reid, 1995). If a test developer has ignored some or all of these procedures, practitioners cannot assume that a test translated into another language guarantees construct validity in culturally different groups.

In evaluating the appropriateness of test instruments, it is crucial that practitioners consider the multidimensionality of cultural differences in evaluating test publishers' descriptions of their products. For example, some test publishers will describe tests as "culture free" or appropriate for cross-cultural research. It is more accurate to characterize tests as falling along a continuum from "culture reduced" to "culture specific" or "culture loaded" (Jensen, 1980). The extreme ends of the continuum would reflect a hypothetical point that no test to date can attain. In the realm of general mental ability testing, an extremely culture-loaded test would discriminate levels of general mental ability among members of an intact family; however, all others outside of the family who took the same test would obtain scores no better than chance (Jensen, 1980). This is because the items on such a test tap mental abilities using idiosyncratic cultural content uniquely experienced only by that family. At the opposite extreme is a hypothetical culture-free test of general mental ability test that reliably discriminates both within and between all species of primates (including humans). The point is, existing tests can be characterized as being positioned along various points in the continuum between these two hypothetical end points (Jensen, 1980). Because cultural differences between groups are multidimensional, different properties of the same test can fall at different points on the culture-free to culture-specific continuum. For example, a nonverbal test may make it possible for more groups to be included in a common understanding of the task, but time limits imposed on items may violate the cultural traditions of other groups whose performance would be unfairly depressed. A test can be thought of as culture reduced (compared with other tests) when the test as a whole (and its constituent test items) maintain their psychometric properties within a more inclusive body of culturally different groups (Jensen, 1980).

Conclusion

At present, there is no consensus about a universal definition of culture. Therefore, practitioners should keep in mind that the implicit equating of cultural differences with geographical, racial, and ethnic differences, although expedient, is entirely arbitrary. Just because groups are determined to be different on one variable, it does not necessarily follow that the groups are different on all other relevant variables. In addition, judgments of the extent to which behaviors and cognitions are culturally specific (i.e., not universal in all people and not idiosyncratic to the individual) can be made with greater confidence when determined empirically. However, "empirical" should not be misconstrued as referring only to findings from data-based studies. An empirical mindset can be broadly defined to include a practitioner's extensive experience with a particular population in specific contexts. The extent to which the use of certain tests is appropriate for individuals is a function of whether important decisions depend on strong predictive validity, construct validity, or both. If a test does not demonstrate evidence of cultural bias when used with two or more groups, this is not the same as saying that there are no cultural differences that reliably discriminate between the groups. It simply means that the cultural differences in question do not significantly alter the psychometric properties of the instruments when used with individuals from these groups. Testing procedures will occasionally show strong evidence of predictive or construct validity bias that operates to the detriment of culturally different individuals. In these instances, any modification in test selection, administration, and interpretation (which themselves are less-than-perfect solutions to the problem of bias) should be defensible within the context of best professional practice, solid empirical support, and sanction from the practitioner's employers.

References

American Psychiatric Association. (1994). *Diagnostic and statistical manual of mental disorders* (4th ed.). Washington, DC: Author.

Armour-Thomas, E. (1992). Intellectual assessment of children from culturally diverse backgrounds. *School Psychology Review, 21,* 552–565.

Betancourt, H., & López, S. R. (1993). The study of culture, ethnicity, and race in American psychology. *American Psychologist, 48,* 629–637.

Bracken, B., & Barona, A. (1991). State of the art procedures for translating, validating and using psychoeducational tests in cross-cultural assessment. *School Psychology International, 12,* 119–132.

Brislin, R. (1993). *Understanding culture's influence on behavior.* Orlando, FL: Harcourt Brace.

Camilli, G., & Shepard, L. A. (1994). *Methods for identifying biased test items.* Thousand Oaks, CA: Sage.

Carlson, J. S., & Wiedl, K. H. (1992). Dynamic assessment of intelligence. In H. C. Haywood & D. Tzuriel (Eds.), *Interactive assessment* (pp. 167–186). New York: Springer-Verlag.

Cole, M., Gay, J., Glick, J., & Sharp, D. W. (1971). *The cultural context of learning and thinking.* New York: Basic Books.

Corey, G. (1988). *Issues and ethics in the helping professions* (3rd ed.). Pacific Grove, CA: Brooks/Cole.

Dana, R. H. (1993). *Multicultural assessment perspectives for professional psychology.* Needham Heights, MA: Allyn & Bacon.

Diana v. California State Board of Education, Civ. No. C-7037 RFR (N.D. Cal., 1970).

Elliot, R. (1987). *Litigating intelligence: IQ tests, special education, and social science in the courtroom.* Dover, MA: Auburn House.

Eyde, L. D., Robertson, G. J., Krug, S. E., Moreland, K. L., Robertson, A. G., Shewan, C. M., Harrison, P. L., Porch, B. E., Hammer, A. L., & Primoff, E. S. (1993). *Responsible test use: Case studies for assessing human behavior.* Washington, DC: American Psychological Association.

Eysenck, H. J. (1984). The effect of race on human abilities and mental test scores. In C. R. Reynolds & R. T. Brown (Eds.), *Perspectives on bias in mental testing* (pp. 249–292). New York: Plenum.

Grubb, H. J., Dozier, A. (1989). Too busy to learn: A "competing behaviors" explanation of cross-cultural differences in academic ascendancy based on the cultural distance hypothesis. *Journal of Black Psychology, 16,* 23–45.

Harris, A. M., Reynolds, M. A., & Koegel, H. M. (1996). Nonverbal assessment: Multicultural perspectives. In L. A. Suzuki, P. J. Meller, & J. G. Ponterotto (Eds.), *Handbook of multicultural assessment: Clinical, psychological, and educational applications* (pp. 223–252). San Francisco: Jossey-Bass.

Harris, J., & Ford, D. Y. (1991). Identifying and nurturing the promise of gifted Black American children. *Journal of Negro Education, 60,* 3–18.

Helms, J. E. (1992). Why is there no study of cultural equivalence in standardized cognitive ability testing? *American Psychologist, 47,* 1083–1101.

Herskovits, M. J. (1948). *Man and his works: The science of cultural anthropology.* New York: Knopf.

Janzen, H. L., Skakum, S., & Lightning, W. (1994). Professional services in a Cree native community. *Canadian Journal of School Psychology, 10,* 88–102.

Jensen, A. R. (1977). An examination of cultural bias in the Wonderlic Personnel Test. *Intelligence, 1,* 51–64.

Jensen, A. R. (1980). *Bias in mental testing.* New York: Free Press.

Jensen, A. R. (1984). Test validity: *g* versus the specificity doctrine. *Journal of Social and Biological Structures, 7,* 93–118.

Jensen, A. R., & McGurk, F. C. J. (1987). Black–White bias in "cultural" and "noncultural" test items. *Personality and Individual Differences, 8,* 295–301.

Kroeber, A. L., & Kluckhohn, C. (1952). *Culture: A critical review of concepts and definitions.* New York: Vintage Books.

López, S., & Hernandez, P. (1986). How culture is considered in evaluations of psychopathology. *Journal of Nervous and Mental Disease, 176,* 598–606.

McGurk, F. C. J. (1951). *Comparison of the performance of Negro and White high school seniors on cultural and noncultural psychological test questions.* Washington, DC: Catholic University Press.

Meisels, S. J., Dorfman, A., & Steele, D. (1995). Equity and excellence in group-administered and performance-based assessments. In M. T. Nettles & A. L. Nettles (Eds.), *Equity and excellence in educational testing and assessment* (pp. 243–261). Boston: Kluwer Academic.

Miller, L. S. (1995). *An American imperative: Accelerating minority educational advancement.* New Haven, CT: Yale University Press.

Miller-Jones, D. (1989). Culture and testing. *American Psychologist, 44,* 360–366.

Mitchell, J. V. (Ed.). (1998). *Mental measurements yearbook* (13th ed.). Lincoln: University of Nebraska–Lincoln, Buros Institute of Mental Measurements.

Nandakumar, R., Glutting, J. J., & Oakland, T. (1993). Mantel-Haenszel methodology for detecting item bias: An introduction and example using the guide to the assessment of test session behavior. *Journal of Psychoeducational Assessment, 11,* 108–119.

Neill, M. (1995). Some prerequisites for the establishment of equitable, inclusive multicultural assessment systems. In M. T. Nettles & A. L. Nettles (Eds.), *Equity and excellence in educational testing and assessment* (pp. 115–149). Boston: Kluwer Academic.

Office of Ethnic Minority Affairs. (1993). Guidelines for providers of psychological services to ethnic, linguistic, and culturally diverse populations. *American Psychologist, 48,* 45–48.

Padilla, A. M. (Ed.). (1995). *Hispanic psychology: Critical issues in theory and research.* Thousand Oaks, CA: Sage.

Padilla, A. M., & Medina, A. (1996). Cross-cultural sensitivity in assessment: Using tests in culturally appropriate ways. In L. A. Suzuki, P. J. Meller, & J. G. Ponterotto (Eds.), *Handbook of multicultural assessment: Clinical, psychological, and educational applications* (pp. 3–28). San Francisco: Jossey-Bass.

Reid, R. (1995). Assessment of ADHD with culturally different groups: The use of behavioral rating scales. *School Psychology Review, 24,* 537–560.

Reschly, D. J., Kicklighter, R., & McKee, P. (1988a). Recent placement litigation. Part I: Regular education grouping: Comparison of Marshall (1984, 1985) and Hobson (1967, 1969). *School Psychology Review, 17,* 9–21.

Reschly, D. J., Kicklighter, R., & McKee, P. (1988b). Recent placement litigation. Part II: Minority EMR overrepresentation: Comparison of Larry P. (1979, 1984, 1986) with Marshall (1984, 1985) and S-1 (1986). *School Psychology Review, 17,* 22–38.

Ritzler, B. (1993). TEMAS (Tell Me A Story). *Journal of Psychoeducational Assessment, 11,* 381–389.

Rogoff, B., & Chavajay, P. (1995). What's become of research on the cultural basis of cognitive development? *American Psychologist, 50,* 859–877.

Rohner, R. P. (1984). Toward a conception of culture for cross-cultural psychology. *Journal of Cross-Cultural Psychology, 15,* 111–138.

Samuda, R. J., King, S. L., Cummins, J., Pascual-Leone, J., & Lewis, J. (1989). *Assessment and placement of minority students.* Toronto, Ontario, Canada: Hogrefe.

Sandoval, J., & Millie, M. P. W. (1980). Accuracy of judgments of WISC-R item difficulty for minority groups. *Journal of Consulting and Clinical Psychology, 48,* 249–253.

Schiele, J. H. (1991). An epistemological perspective on intelligence assessment among African-American children. *Journal of Black Psychology, 17,* 23–26.

Shinn, M., & Baker, S. (1996). The use of curriculum-based measurement with diverse learners. In L. A. Suzuki, P. J. Mueller, & J. G. Ponterotto (Eds.), *Handbook of multicultural assessment: Clinical, psychological, and educational applications* (pp. 179–222). San Francisco: Jossey-Bass.

Sowell, T. (1993). *Inside American education: The decline, the deception, the dogmas.* New York: Free Press.

Spiro, M. F. (1978). Culture and human nature. In G. D. Spindler (Ed.), *The making of psychological anthropology* (pp. 331–360). Berkeley: University of California Press.

Stewart, E. C. (1972). *American cultural patterns: A cross-cultural perspective.* LaGrange Park, IL: Intercultural Network.

Sue, D. W., & Sue, D. (1990). *Counseling the culturally different.* New York: Wiley.

Suzuki, L. A., Meller, P. J., & Ponterotto, J. G. (Eds.). (1996). *Handbook of multicultural assessment: Clinical, psychological, and educational applications.* San Francisco: Jossey-Bass.

Tanner-Halverson, P., Burden, T., & Sabers, D. (1993). WISC-III normative data for Tohono O'odham Native-American children. In B. A. Bracken & R. S. McCallum (Eds.), *Wechsler Intelligence for Children: Third edition. Journal of Psychoeducational Assessment. Advances in psychoeducational assessment* (pp. 125–133). Brandon, VT: Clinical Psychology.

Triandis, H. C. (1972). *The analysis of subjective culture.* New York: Wiley.

Triandis, H. C., & Brislin, R. W. (1984). Cross-cultural psychology. *American Psychologist, 39,* 1006–1016.

Van de Vijver, F. J. R. (1994). Bias: Where psychology and methodology meet. In A. M. Bouvy, F. J. R. van de Vijver, P. Boski, & P. Schmitz (Eds.), *Journeys into cross-cultural psychology* (pp. 111–126). Amsterdam: Swets & Zeitlinger.

White, L. (1949). Ethnological theory. In R. W. Sellars, V. J. McGill, & M. Farber (Eds.), *Philosophy for the future.* New York: Macmillan.

Wigdor, A. K., & Garner, W. R. (Eds.). (1982). *Ability testing: Uses, consequences and controversies.* Washington, DC: National Academy Press.

Williams, R. L. (1974, May). Scientific racism and IQ: The silent mugging of the Black community. *Psychology Today,* pp. 32–41.

Zalewski, C., & Greene, R. L. (1996). Multicultural usage of the MMPI-2. In L. A. Suzuki, P. J. Meller, & J. G. Ponterotto (Eds.), *Handbook of multicultural assessment: Clinical, psychological, and educational applications* (pp. 77–114). San Francisco: Jossey-Bass.

Part II

Contexts for Interpretation

High-Stakes Testing in Education

Janice Dowd Scheuneman and Thomas Oakland

Nowhere is testing more commonly used than in education. From kindergarten through graduate and professional schools, tests are a part of every student's life. Tests may be measures of knowledge, academic skills (e.g., reading, writing, or language proficiency), general intelligence or intellectual abilities (e.g., verbal reasoning or analytical ability), special aptitudes (e.g., music or art), or vocational interests. Tests may be administered either to groups or to individuals by teachers, counselors, school psychologists, or administrators. They may be administered in school settings or in special testing centers as part of large-scale admissions testing. More recently, tests also have been administered by computers in universities or commercial testing centers.

Most common among the tests encountered by individuals are those developed by teachers to use in support of their own instruction. These tests are strongly associated with the classroom setting with all students having an opportunity to learn the material covered by the examination. The term *educational testing*, however, more typically refers to group-administered standardized tests of subject area knowledge or academic skills, abilities, or aptitudes. Although such tests are less well matched to what is taught in the schools, and hence may be less useful to teachers than their own tests, the availability of scores on the same or comparable tests across many classrooms makes them useful to school and district personnel for a number of possible purposes, such as school-level evaluation or community accountability. When scores on standardized tests are returned to teachers, they are able to evaluate the results relative to their knowledge of the abilities and other attributes that their students display in the classroom, helping to mitigate the possible adverse effects that might follow from inappropriately low scores.

In other instances, important consequences for individuals may follow from the use of educational testing results, instances that may be viewed as "high-stakes" testing situations. During the elementary school years, group or individually administered test scores are typically used when students are being considered for placement into special programs. At higher levels, high school graduation may be contingent on passing state-developed standardized tests. Decisions concerning admissions to programs for gifted students, to private secondary schools, to college and university undergraduate programs, and to graduate and professional schools may depend in part on scores on standardized multiple-choice tests. Awards of scholarship or fellowship funding also are likely to involve test scores at some point in the decision process.

High-stakes decisions based on test scores also may be made by people to whom the student is not well-known. In placement decisions, test results that poorly reflect a student's ability may result in inappropriate placement if other information about the student is inadequate. In admission decisions, with its reliance on scores from large-scale administrations of examinations such as the SAT and the ACT, applicants are not likely to be known personally to the admissions officer. As the use of test scores becomes increasingly removed from personal knowledge of the examinee, instances of mismeasurement are more likely to go undetected.

For students outside the population mainstream due to their racial–ethnic background, socioeconomic status (SES), or disability, the use of test results in high-stakes situations does not always appear equitable. For example, African American, Hispanic American, and Native American youths seem more likely to be placed in special education classes and less likely to be placed in classes for gifted and talented students. The average of scores obtained by students from these groups, including those whose first language is not English, are generally lower than the average of scores obtained by the White English-speaking majority on tests used for high-stakes decisions. Such patterns of test results have led to charges that tests are biased against members of these groups.

Although the focus of this book is to move away from the commonly used demographic groups based on gender or racial–ethnic group, the "protected groups" under the equal opportunity regulations, almost all research discussed in this chapter is based on these groups. Much of the controversy surrounding the issues of test use for high-stakes decisions comes from the political and social implications of the data for these groups. Hence, the discussion in this chapter centers around racial–ethnic and gender groups, despite the considerable heterogeneity within each. In this chapter we first consider issues surrounding high-stakes testing in education. In the following sections we address the possibility of bias in many widely used achievement and aptitude tests. Possible sources of performance differences between groups defined by race–ethnicity or gender are then reviewed. Finally, we suggest guidelines for appropriate test use, first for individually administered tests for educational placement and then for large-scale admissions tests used for other high-stakes applications.

High-Stakes Testing

At one time, White men with favorable economic standing and good family connections were unapologetically favored for desirable outcomes such as college admissions. The introduction of standardized testing into selection procedures was expected to afford opportunity to those who were not similarly advantaged. Scores from tests such as the SAT or ACT were thought to provide a level playing field for applicants who submitted grades and references from institutions other than the well-known preparatory schools. Standardized tests have been and remain a force for democratic access to higher education and to the advantages that accrue from that education. Despite the charges of test bias and gate keeping, many women and minority-group members achieve high test scores that help them gain access to classes for gifted students, to colleges and universities, and to graduate and professional schools. Nevertheless, problems with the use of tests remain. Some of the concerns about the use of tests with female and minority examinees are considered in the following sections.

Educational Placement

The rate of referrals for special educational services is generally higher for minority-group children than for White children. Overall, students from minority groups often perform more poorly, on average, on educational tests and are represented in greater numbers among families of lower SES, who also tend to perform more poorly on tests. Some citizens, parents, and educators believe, therefore, that special education placements are politically motivated, designed perhaps to reestablish segregated schools or to permit a lower quality of education for minority students. They believe that tests provide unfair representation of these students' abilities. For example, they argue that students classified as mentally retarded are not dysfunctional outside of school. The issue of biased testing has been the predominant concern in court cases involving inappropriate educational placement. Although instances of test misuse have occurred that feed these negative perceptions, appropriate appraisal of individual students should ensure proper placement of all students.

High School Graduation

At present, many states in the United States require students to pass a standardized examination or series of examinations to receive a high school diploma. These tests are intended to guarantee that a certain minimum standard of competency is met by every graduate. Typically, such a test is developed specifically for the state in which it is used and its content matched to that state's required curriculum or specified standards so that every student should have had an opportunity to learn the material tested on the examination. Ideally, all youths should meet such standards after spending 12 or more years in an educational system. Not all students do pass, however, and African American and Hispanic American youths are more likely to be among those who fail to meet these standards (Geisinger, 1992; Johnson, 1989).

Language minority students who are not fully proficient in English are particularly at risk for failing high school graduation examinations. Although some states waive the test requirement for these students or, more rarely, permit them to test in their own language, these students are often required to meet the same standard as other students. Meeting this standard is an especially difficult task for students who first encountered English-language instruction at the high school level (Geisinger, 1992; O'Malley & Pierce, 1994).

Admissions Testing

Despite the widespread fear of parents and students who view the SAT and ACT as barriers to higher education and the attention received by these tests in both the research literature and the popular press, few if any colleges and universities use test scores as the only criterion for admissions. Even at the most selective schools, where test scores can be more important than at schools with fewer applicants, many other sources of information about a candidate are used in the admissions decision. The relationships of high school grade point average (GPA) and of test scores to college GPA are both significant, each typically predicting about 25–30% of the variance in first-year GPA. If both measures are used together, test scores add only about 5% to high school grades even for White students (Linn, 1990). Many other factors play a part in a student's success in attaining a college education, including student motivation and persistence and the fit between the student's personal qualities and the environment in the college attended. Admissions officers at most colleges and universities are trained professionals who are well aware of the need for various types of information on applicants for use in their decision making.

At the graduate or professional school level, however, admissions decisions are typically made by people with subject matter expertise who may have little training in testing and test use. Decisions to provide financial support also may be made at the same time and by the same individuals as the admissions decision. Misuse of test scores is more likely to occur when important decisions are made by untrained individuals. The most common errors would be placing undue weight on test scores relative to other application materials and overinterpreting small score differences between individuals. To the extent that female and minority examinees, on average, earn lower scores on admissions tests, both of these errors may result in undervaluing the qualifications of applicants from these groups.

Scholarship Decisions

Although most of the attention on the use of large-scale testing has focused on admissions, the use of scores in granting scholarships is perhaps more problematic. A minimum test score is sometimes used to form a pool of applicants for whom more information will be obtained before the award decision is made. This practice has been criticized by women's groups in particular, who point out that tiny mean score differences can create large differences in the proportion of girls or women in the eligible pools.

The National Collegiate Athletic Association has set a minimum score for the SAT and ACT that must be met by student athletes to participate in intercollegiate sports, effectively limiting athletic scholarships and often admission to those with scores above that minimum. Although the apparent intent of these regulations is to ensure that student athletes are capable of college work, little evidence has been garnered to demonstrate that it does so. The relationship of test scores to college grades typically found with students in more academically oriented programs may not hold up well for student athletes (Petrie, 1993). Furthermore, most measurement professionals consider the use of a test score alone to make important decisions a misuse of tests.

Bias in Educational Testing

Bias in the context of testing has become an emotionally laden term connoting prejudice, unfairness, or intentional discrimination. Bias, however, also is a neutral statistical term used to describe a statistic that systematically over- or underestimates the true value of an unknown parameter (such as the population mean). Following this definition, a biased test would be one that systematically over- or underestimates the unknown "true" mean score of examinees from a particular group.

In measurement theory, if a test could be administered several times to the same individual, such that no advantage would be gained from repeating the same material and that fatigue never became a factor, the mean of the scores obtained from these administrations would be equal to the individual's true score on that test. When tested once, an individual's score is assumed to be the sum of his or her true score plus or minus some amount of measurement error. Hence, a single observed score is always in an unknown relationship with the individual's true score (although it will generally be close to it), so that any statistical bias associated with that observed score would be indeterminant. For a large group of individuals, however, the mean of the observed score for the group will equal the mean of the individual true scores plus the mean of the error terms. For an unbiased test, the mean of the error terms is assumed to be zero. (The standard deviation of the error terms is called the "standard error of measurement.") This indicates that the mean of the observed scores equals the mean of the true scores of the individuals in the group. If the test score is biased for a group of examinees, however, the mean of observed scores will be systematically (nonrandomly) higher or lower than the mean of the true scores for that group.

In practice, bias in testing is discussed relative to mean observed score differences between groups defined by characteristics such as race, ethnicity, first language, or gender. The underlying issue is whether the observed group differences between test scores means accurately reflect group differences in true scores. Suppose, for example, that two groups with different means are being compared and that the test score is biased so that the observed score mean underestimates the true ability of the group with the lower mean observed score. The difference between the observed score means of two groups will then be larger than the differences between their true score means. Unfortunately, "true score" is a theoretical concept; true scores are always unknown and cannot be studied directly. Hence, the research in test bias has been based on a number of statistical models that operationalize bias in terms of its expected effects. This evidence tends to fall into categories defined by the model or procedure used, most often regression and factor-analytic procedures.

Research Evidence Using Regression Procedures

In admissions testing, bias has been evaluated most often in the context of criterion-related validity. The most common procedure uses GPA to measure an examinee's academic performance. In the typical analysis, the aptitude test scores of different groups would be used to predict their GPA for the first year of college (Cleary, 1968). The reasoning is that if the test is biased against a group, the grades predicted for that group would be lower than the grades actually earned.

Results of many studies using the Cleary (1968) method have shown that admissions test scores predict grades equally well for different racial–ethnic groups and that, when differences are found, the actual first-year GPA for the group with lower mean admissions test scores tends to be lower rather than higher than predicted (N. S. Cole & Moss, 1989; Jensen, 1980; Linn, 1990; Pennock-Roman, 1990). Studies contrasting men and women, however, have occasionally shown the expected pattern of a small degree of underprediction for women (Gemache & Novick, 1985; Kessel & Linn, 1996; Linn, 1990). More recently, the Cleary procedure has been improved by taking into account group differences in course selection patterns and differential grading practices in various academic areas. Observed differences in prediction between groups then tend to be reduced or to disappear (Elliot & Strenta, 1988; McCornack & McLeod, 1988; Pennock-Roman, 1990; Young, 1991).

Despite its popular acceptance as a procedure for detecting test bias, this method also has limitations. First, the use of first-year GPA as an achievement measure and ultimately as a measure of success in college is questionable (Flaugher, 1978; Wild & Dwyer, 1980). Second, because of statistical properties of regression analysis, different definitions based on regression can lead to mutually contradictory results. To illustrate, suppose that a second definition of an unbiased test is one on which people who earn the same grades in college have the same admissions test scores. If a test is unbiased using this second definition, of necessity that same test will be biased by the Cleary procedure, and, similarly, a test that is unbiased by the Cleary procedure must be biased by the second definition (Darlington, 1971; Thorndike, 1971). Third, when simulated data are used, the Cleary procedure simply fails to detect real differences unless these differences are large and may show overprediction for a group when test scores actually have a small degree of bias against them (Linn, 1984; Shepard, 1987).

Another concern about using test scores in the admissions decision is the effect on errors of prediction and whether the use of tests leads to fair admissions decisions. For example, a retrospective study of different admissions criteria examined the effects of different admissions procedures had they been used to admit the students currently enrolled at a large state college (Goldman & Widawski, 1976). The addition of SAT scores to high school GPA would have improved prediction slightly for more minority students, with the result that fewer students who would later fail would have been accepted (false-positive errors) but at the cost of accepting fewer students who would later pass (false-negative errors). Also using retrospective procedures, Keller, Crouse, and Trusheim (1994) found that addition of SAT to high school GPA improved the prediction of college grades but that it would have resulted in the admission of fewer female and Black students if no other information was used in the admissions decision.

Research Evidence Using Factor Analysis

Factor-analytic studies address whether tests measure the same constructs or underlying abilities for members of different groups (Reynolds, 1982). The tests most often studied using this method have been individually administered intelligence tests such as the Wechsler Intelligence Scale for Children–Revised (WISC-R). As with the regression studies, the results generally indicate that the factors measured by the test were largely the same for different groups (e.g., Jensen & Reynolds, 1982; Kaufman, 1975).

Nevertheless, minor differences in factor structure have been found, suggesting that the constructs measured are highly similar but not identical. For example, several researchers examining WISC-R performance for different groups showed that a third factor was supported clearly only for White children (Gutkin & Reynolds, 1981; Johnston & Bolen, 1984; Reschly, 1978; Sandoval, 1982). A study of a college placement examination finds three factors: Verbal, Reasoning, and Spatial. The Verbal factor was more highly correlated with the other factors for the Black examinees, suggesting that they experienced a higher verbal load for items measuring the other skills (Hennessy & Merrifield, 1976).

Are Tests Biased?

Overall, the evidence is substantial that tests are unbiased and valid for use with both sexes and with minority populations, a conclusion that is widely accepted among those familiar with the research literature. However, enough problems exist with the evidence to support the concerns held by many researchers and practitioners about the equivalence of test scores for different groups. The evidence is generally consistent with the view that test scores are lower for some group members than would be expected if their true scores were known, even though the scores correlate with the same criterion measures as for the majority of students. Although articles continue to appear on different procedures or applications, the debate about test bias has largely faded among measurement professionals, with neither side of the argument fully convinced by the other. The issue of whether tests are biased, at least to some degree, is now and probably will remain unresolved.

This uncertainty leaves the test user in a quandary. Test scores will undoubtedly remain an important component of high-stakes decision making in education for the foreseeable future. The challenge will be to interpret scores appropriately for all examinees. Meeting this challenge will require mindful awareness of the factors that may cause scores to be lower than they should be for some individuals.

Sources of Group Performance Differences

In the United States, the cultures of the diverse racial–ethnic groups have substantial similarities as well as differences. Culture also is likely to vary within racial–ethnic groups according to factors such as geographic regions and SES levels. Moreover, individuals who consider themselves to be members of a particular racial–ethnic group differ considerably in the degree to which they identify with its culture (see chapter 4 in this book). Cultural differences do not seem to apply when contrasting men and women or boys and girls, who are typically raised together in the same families. Nevertheless, men and women and boys and girls as well as individuals from different racial–ethnic groups may have characteristic ways of responding to situations that may affect their test performance differently.

One avenue through which culture exerts its influence on test performance is through the types of tasks and activities that are typically performed and valued within that culture. For children raised in a minority culture, the cumulative effect of these experiences may be to emphasize competencies and cognitive abilities that are somewhat different from those required by tests. This implies that minority children may be able to display the appropriate skills but with less facility and probably with more errors than children whose culture has emphasized the development of competencies more similar to those measured by the test (Miller-Jones, 1989). In general, observed performance differences suggest that the greater the similarity of an individual's socioeconomic and cultural background to that of the majority population, the better the test performance will be (Helms, 1992; Scheuneman, 1987a).

The adequacy of instructions for a test also may be affected by the familiarity of tasks. For many students, simple instructions may be adequate because they are able to form mental analogies with similar tasks they have performed in the past. A study of intercity children used interviews to determine how well the directions for several individually administered tests were understood. Most children had little idea of what was required of them from the standard instructions. The exception was the directions for the Columbia Mental Maturity Scale, which uses a classification task similar to ones often demonstrated on *Sesame Street* (Scarr, 1981).

Effects of Language Background

For most English-language tests, a lack of English fluency may significantly affect test performance (see chapter 8 in this book). For example, among foreign applicants to U.S. colleges, scores on the Test of English as a Foreign Language, commonly known as TOEFL, tend to be associated with their SAT Verbal scores. Performance on tests requiring the use of language may be affected even for bilingual examinees who are competent in English. Mean performance on reading and vocabulary measures by Asian American examinees is often markedly lower than their mean performance on the mathematical sections of the same tests. Studies of differential item functioning, which evaluate the relative difficulty of individual test items for two groups, have shown that Hispanic examinees on the SAT find English homonyms and homographs particularly difficult. They may perform better than White examinees, however, when terms are Spanish cognates, particularly if a term is used more commonly in Spanish than it is in English (Schmitt, 1988; Schmitt & Dorans, 1991).

Effects of Personal Characteristics

The interests and motivations of different groups in a testing situation also may affect test performance. For example, two groups may not be equal in their ability to persist at a task that has little interest or perceived value for them. Moreover, interest is likely to be associated with incidental learning, which may take place outside the classroom. Students may thus simply know more about an area that holds interest for them (Banks, McQuater, & Hubbard, 1978).

Studies investigating the relative difficulty of test items for different groups have shown that examinees from a minority group perform better on materials, such as reading passages, that are about them or others with whom they easily identify or that appear to be of greater interest or relevance to them (Carlton & Harris, 1989; Scheuneman, 1987b; Schmitt & Dorans, 1991). Women and minority examinees often do less well on reading passages with science content, a finding that has generally been attributed to lack of interest and hence prior learning (Lawrence, Curley, & McHale, 1988; Scheuneman & Gerritz, 1990).

Effects of Other Personal Characteristics

Researchers also have considered whether minority or female examinees differ from White male examinees in characteristics such as test anxiety, test wiseness, locus of control, risk taking, or other attributes thought to affect test performance. Results of such studies have been mixed, and no clear patterns have emerged. Studies of these personal characteristics using multivariate designs have suggested that the lack of clear findings may be attributable to interactions of these characteristics with each other or with combinations of race–ethnicity, gender, and SES (Scheuneman, 1987a). For example, interactions between race and sex have been found on measures of test anxiety (Payne, Smith, & Payne, 1983; Reynolds, Plake, & Harding, 1983).

Examinee's test-taking skills and behaviors on individually administered tests also have been examined (Glutting & Oakland, 1993; Watson, 1951). Three qualities that characterize test behavior—attentiveness, nonavoidance of task, and cooperative mood—have been shown to be significantly related to student performance on individually administered measures of intelligence and achievement. Correlations average .27 between these qualities and scores on the third edition of the WISC (WISC-III). Students who exhibited more problems with these behaviors generally obtain lower scores on the WISC-III and Wechsler Individual Achievement Test. No significant differences in these behaviors were found between students who differed by gender, social class, and ethnicity (Oakland & Glutting, 1998).

Effects of Testing Method

The majority of standardized tests used in high-stakes educational testing use multiple-choice formats. Studies comparing performance differences between male and female examinees suggest that women do less well on multiple-choice questions than they do on essays or other constructed-response measures. These differences have been found across national boundaries (Bell & Hay, 1987; Bolger & Kellaghan, 1990; Murphy, 1982) and within ethnic groups in the United States (Mazzeo, Schmitt, & Bleistein, 1993).

The College Board Advanced Placement Examinations, which permit high school students to obtain credit for college-level courses, provide useful data to evaluate possible differences attributable to the effects of testing methods because the tests include both multiple-choice and constructed-response sections. Studies of the American History, European History, English Language and Composition, Biology, and Chemistry examinations all showed patterns in which female examinees performed less well on the multiple-choice sections of the tests than would have been expected from their performance on the constructed-response sections. In addition, the correlations with course grades in the corresponding subject areas were similar for the constructed-response section scores and the multiple-choice scores, despite the lower reliability of the constructed response. This suggests that the constructed-response sections, which show smaller group differences, are at least as valid as the multiple-choice sections (Breland, Danos, Kahn, Kubota, & Sudlow, 1991; Bridgeman & Lewis, 1994; Mazzeo et al., 1993).

Effects of Multiple-Choice Formats

In general, multiple-choice tests have the virtues of high reliability, ease of administration and scoring, and broad coverage of the domain being tested. Their disadvantage is that performance may be affected by factors such as the examinee's propensity to guess, time management, and test-taking strategies that may be unrelated to the construct being measured by the examination.

Guessing

On multiple-choice tests, unless a correction for guessing is used, an examinee should respond to all items because even a random guess may sometimes produce a correct answer. Even on tests with guessing corrections, guessing can be an effective strategy if the examinee can eliminate some of the incorrect options. Hence, those who guess when they do not know the answer are likely to score higher than students of comparable ability who do not. Studies of the number of omitted items on examinations without guessing corrections suggest that women and minority examinees, particularly Black examinees, may omit responses at a higher rate than do White male examinees (Ben-Shakhar & Sinai, 1991; Gafni & Melamed, 1994; Grandy, 1987; Zhu & Thompson, 1995).

Test Speededness

Time limits are usually set to standardize the testing process and for administrative convenience rather than to impose an element of speed into the tested construct. Although unintended, time limits may result in different degrees of speededness depending on individual differences in the rate of working as well as in test-taking strategies such as skipping items that need more work and returning to them later. Test speededness is thought to affect the scores of examinees with learning disabilities as well as members of minority groups. Speededness may result, for example, in failure to finish a test, inadequate time to go back to omitted items, or just a pressure to respond quickly that can work against the examinee's optimal performance. The speededness of a test is often measured in terms of the percentage of examinees finishing a test, but this measure does not reflect the other effects of time pressure. The inadequacy of measures of speededness makes meaningful comparison of its effects in different groups problematic (Rindler, 1979).

A study in which a test was administered under both standard and extended time limits showed that performance generally improved slightly with more time but that the score improvement was similar for examinees from different groups (Wild, Durso, & Rubin, 1982). In another study, White examinees who completed the test had higher scores than those who did not, a typical pattern that suggests that speed is positively correlated with the ability being tested. Black examinees who completed the test had lower scores than those who did not, however, suggesting that speed and ability are negatively correlated (Evans, 1980). The percentage of each group completing the examination was similar, but speededness had a different meaning for the two groups. In some differential item functioning studies, which control for examinee ability, items near the end of the tests show larger performance differences than items appearing earlier (Ironson & Subkoviak, 1979; Schmitt & Bleistein, 1987; Sinnott, 1980).

Time is a less salient concept in many Hispanic cultures than in the dominant White culture, and consequently Hispanic examinees may take longer to respond to testing tasks. In a study using computer administration that recorded the response time to individual items, Hispanic students took longer to respond to multiple-choice items than did White students of similar abilities. The time differences were similar on both verbal and nonverbal material. Hispanic students said they did not translate the items into Spanish before responding, suggesting that language was not the only reason for the slower response rate. The speed of cognitive processing is slower in a second language than in the first, however, and effects of stress and fatigue are much greater when performing in a second language than in the first language. Fatigue, particularly in longer tests, may be one source of performance differences for language minority examinees (Llabre, 1991).

Use of Individualized Testing for Placement

Within the school setting, high-stakes decisions most often concern placement of children into programs for special education services or gifted students. Although group-administered tests may be used to screen for students at risk or with exceptional abilities, such placements are usually made following an evaluation that includes individually administered tests. Unlike group tests, individual tests require a professional with graduate training to administer, score, and interpret results. Such testing is thus more costly than group testing, but it yields more information about the child.

When individual testing is used, school and medical records as well as information provided by the child's family enable those conducting the examination to determine the relevance of the measures and, when needed, to tailor the selection of appraisal methods in light of the student's history and current conditions. In addition, information for the appraisal comes from a variety of professionals in the school, including administrators, counselors, school psychologists, speech and language specialists, and teachers. Interpretation of scores is made with input from these professionals and the child's parents.

The process of conducting an individual assessment also must consider issues such as the ways in which assessment information may be used. The value and importance of assessment are established by the nature of the outcomes from the assessment. For example, assessments conducted to determine eligibility for special education placement may be judged to be effective if the assessment results in an accurate diagnosis together with sound and effective educational programs, minimizes the use of pejorative and harmful labels, and is conducted efficiently.

Conventional test use, even with individualized measurement, may be problematic if the student was raised outside the United States, particularly in a Third World nation; received no prior schooling or was educated in an atypical setting; is not fluent in English; or does not display suitable test-taking skills. These students are less likely to have been exposed to content commonly assessed by measures of cognitive abilities, to be familiar with methods commonly used in standardized testing, and to exhibit trust and faith in the examiner. In conducting an appraisal with such children, the examiner needs to pay considerable attention to ensure that these and related student qualities do not jeopardize the validity of the measurement.

Federal Legislation Governing Individual Assessment

Guidelines for test use and procedures to follow in evaluating children with special education needs are addressed by Public Law 94-142, the

Education for All Handicapped Children's Act. Two revisions, Public Law 99-457, resulting in the Individuals With Disabilities Education Act (IDEA), and Public Law 105-17 (IDEA Amendments of 1997), reaffirmed its original and principal provisions. These laws legislate that students with special education needs are entitled to a free public education in one or more settings that provide services needed to support the student's continuous educational development. Although school systems are not responsible for overcoming the disability, they are responsible for providing an educational program calculated to help promote the student's academic development. Furthermore, the program should be provided within a setting that least restricts the student's interactions with others who do not have special education needs.

These laws specifically address issues pertaining to the selection and use of tests when making decisions about whether a special education placement is suitable for a given student. Tests must assess specific areas of need, be validated for the specific purposes for which they are used, and be administered by individuals with suitable training in their use. The qualities being assessed should not be inadvertently attenuated by the nature of the student's physical or sensory deficits.

Although these three laws clearly have had the most striking impact on assessment for special education, other federally initiated legal action instrumental in prohibiting discrimination also has affected assessment practices. Two prominent pieces of legislation (and their expansion through judicial and administrative interpretation) are Section 504 of the Rehabilitation Act of 1973 and the Americans With Disabilities Act. For example, Section 504 states that students are eligible for services if they have or had a physical or mental impairment that substantially limits a major life activity (i.e., caring for oneself, performing manual tasks, walking, seeing, hearing, speaking, breathing, learning, working), have a record of such an impairment, or are regarded by others as having a handicapping condition. This definition considerably broadens the definition of handicapping conditions beyond that found in IDEA and makes many more students eligible for assessment services. The need for assessment and intervention services by adult college students with learning disabilities also has been addressed in part through the Americans With Disabilities Act. (See Oakland & Laosa, 1977, and Sandoval & Irvin, 1990, for further discussion of the legal issues.)

Guidelines for Appropriate Individual Testing

The process of testing for individual assessment involves a complex mixture of conditions that characterize an examinee, the examiner, the testing environment, the test, and the ways tests are interpreted and test data used. Each of these factors is particularly important when using tests to evaluate students for whom the test may not have been designed. (Standard references on the appropriate testing of individuals include Kaufman, 1990, 1994; Reynolds & Kamphaus, 1990; Salvia & Ysseldyke, 1988; and Sattler, 1988.)

Examinee Conditions

The use of educational and psychological tests assumes that examinees are physically able to perform the tasks requested of them. Their medical status (e.g., chronic ill health, allergies, and other medical conditions) must not interfere with their performance. Needs associated with nutrition, sleep, elimination, and other basic biological conditions must be met. Examinees' vision, hearing, motor skills, and other sensory processes must be sufficiently developed to enable an accurate assessment of skills and abilities. Test use also assumes that examinees' abilities to attend, concentrate, and sustain motivation are age appropriate and adequate (Bracken, 1991; Sattler, 1988).

Attention to examinees' test-taking attitudes, skills, and behaviors also is important. Test interpretation assumes that examinees have suitable attitudes. They should feel that they are able to do what is required by the test and have a positive attitude toward the testing process and the examiner. In addition, attitudes should differ as a function of the types of tests being used. For example, on cognitive measures, examinees' attitudes should support their doing their best work by displaying their highest and best qualities and abilities. On measures such as personality, temperament, and self-concept, examinees' attitudes should support their displaying qualities that are typical for them, not their best. Examiners must ensure these attitudinal qualities are present.

Examinees' language abilities can strongly affect their test performance. Language typically involves receptive (i.e., the ability to receive and interpret by listening and reading) and expressive (i.e., the ability to express by speaking and writing) abilities and skills. Although some tests have been constructed to minimize the impact of deficiencies in one or more of these language functions, others rely heavily on receptive and expressive language skills as a prerequisite to test performance. Examiners must remain alert to possible skill deficiencies in these areas.

Examiner Characteristics

Examiner characteristics also may influence test performance. Examiners are expected to display various qualities that help create a suitable test-taking environment. Personally, they are expected to be confident, warm, and cordial. Professionally, they are expected to be well-prepared and to set limits consistent with the standards that govern the administration of the test (Sattler, 1988).

Both female and male examiners demonstrate these qualities; however, on occasion, female examiners may elicit somewhat higher test scores than male examiners. Examiners who differ by race also demonstrate these personal and professional qualities. Children's test performance generally is not affected by the examiner's race (Sattler, 1988). However, in some situations, examiners and examinees should be matched by race, particularly when the examinee expresses a strong positive attitude toward (or strong negative attitudes against) those of a particular race or ethnic group (Terrell, Terrell, & Taylor, 1981).

Testing Environments

The environments within which tests are given can influence test performance. Test environments should be physically comfortable (e.g., suitable furniture, a temperature that is neither too cold nor hot) and free of auditory and visual distractions. Examinees who are shy or uncomfortable in this new environment require extra time to become acclimated.

Test Content

Tests typically consist of a series of items that require examinees to indicate their knowledge, behaviors, or preferences. For example, students may be asked in what direction one would travel to go from Boston to New York, if they tie their shoes with no help from others, or whether they would prefer to play soccer or ride a bicycle. Test content should be reviewed to evaluate whether the items are sufficient in number and representative of the domain being assessed and whether the individuals being assessed have familiarity with the test content and task requirements that is comparable to that of the students on whom the test was standardized.

Decisions about the degree of familiarity with the test material often are difficult. Decisions tend to be subjective and rest on knowledge of the examinee's background and experiences. Decisions should not be made on the basis of an examinee's nationality, race, gender, social class, or other demographic qualities. The more similar an examinee's background and experiences are to those that characterize the standardization sample, the greater confidence clinicians have that the test is suitable.

Use of Test Data

The value of testing lies in its impact on the ways the information is used. Individual appraisals are intended to bring together information to describe and explain important qualities, minimize further difficulties, and promote growth and development. Educators are not expected to ensure that every student is performing at an average level. They are expected to enable students to display continuous educational progress consistent with their aptitude. Test data that can be used to accurately classify students as well as to establish pathways for their continued education progress generally will meet professional and legal standards governing test use with children and youths.

Use of Large-Scale Testing Results

A user of test results from large-scale administrations of multiple-choice tests also is responsible for the mindful interpretation of scores. First, the examinee should be prepared to take the test. Second, test scores should be interpreted within the context of other information about the student, including high school or undergraduate records and references. Factors affecting test scores, such as those discussed in earlier sections of this chapter, should be kept in mind. Third, the purpose of the testing and the intended consequences of the use of the test scores should be examined.

Training the Test Taker

The effectiveness of special training or coaching on admissions test performance has been controversial. Coaching generally is likely to result in limited gains, but differences among training programs and students create important exceptions. Effective and stable improvement is more likely to result from longer term courses that foster the learning of academic knowledge or skills than from short courses that provide tricks to promote score gain. Students who initially earn low scores and those whose test scores are inconsistent with their academic records are most likely to benefit from training in test-taking skills. Relatively little has been done to evaluate coaching specifically for minorities, although the results suggest that appropriately designed training sessions can be effective in raising test scores (Bond, 1989). One study indicates that training resulted in small score gains for Black students and increased the numbers of items they completed during the time period, suggesting that improved scores may have been attributable to better pacing, familiarity with instructions and item formats, reduced anxiety, and increased confidence (B. P. Cole, 1987).

The College Board has developed a test preparation package aimed specifically at sophomore Hispanic students for the Preliminary SAT/National Merit Scholar Qualifying Test, an examination often used as an indicator of later performance on the SAT as well as one component of the selection process for National Merit scholars. This package consists of materials for 23 lessons addressing topics such as test format and directions, test anxiety, and appropriate guessing strategies as well as supplementary mathematics lessons. Practice tests also are included (Gaire, 1991). An evaluation of the materials shows that students were more likely to take the tests after completing the program and had more positive attitudes toward college and college preparatory courses. When students were asked if the course material was new to them, the majority reported previous familiarity only with using answer sheets. A substantial minority, however, reported that at least some of this information was new, suggesting that test familiarity should not be taken for granted even in high school populations (Pennock-Roman, Powers, & Perez, 1991).

Guidelines for the Appropriate Use of Large-Scale Testing Results

Test scores from large-scale administrations can be used appropriately for admission or scholarship decisions if test scores are interpreted in light of the other information that is typically a part of an application package.

Context for Test Scores
When evaluating an application for admission or scholarship funding, the available information should form a coherent picture of the applicant. If the test score is inconsistently low in light of this picture, relatively little weight should be assigned to it. A test score higher than expected may indicate late maturation or improving motivation. Other records should be consulted to evaluate the plausibility of such a hypothesis and the likelihood that correspondingly improved work will follow.

Disaggregated Normative Information
The normative information provided with large-scale admissions testing does not typically refer to a nationally representative sample. The norms

summarize the performance of examinees who have taken the examination over some time period, usually including only first-time test takers. This summary information includes the minority students taking the examination, ensuring that they are represented in the norms in the same proportion as in the examinee group. Students are not generally included in the normative data if they took the examination under nonstandard administrative conditions such as might be provided for students with disabilities.

When making decisions about minority students, the overall normal group, even though it includes minority examinees, may not be the most suitable reference group. Statistical reports are often obtainable from test publishers that provide data separately by racial–ethnic group and gender. These data enable a comparison of an examinee's performance with others in his or her own racial–ethnic group that can be used in conjunction with the other available information. Such information may not be representative of that group, however, and care should be taken to ensure that the reports are based on a large enough sample to make a comparison with that group meaningful.

Local Validation of Test Scores

Ideally, admissions test scores are validated for admission to a particular college or university. If this is done, validation of scores should occur before the implementation of an admissions policy so that a criterion measure such as grades can be collected for all entering students. The effects of the policy, had it been implemented, can then be evaluated. Attention also should be directed to the criterion measures used in the evaluation. First-year GPA is a convenient measure but may not reflect the desired outcome of the educational program. Consideration should be given to alternative measures such as retention beyond the first year or successful completion of a degree program. (See Wild & Dwyer, 1980, for a discussion of the selection of criteria for evaluation of admissions procedures.)

Performance Assessment

Many critics of multiple-choice testing have argued that fairer test use will result from performance assessments, including student-constructed responses, essays, projects or experiments, portfolios, or other samples of student work. Some evidence suggests that essays or examination formats that require the student to produce the response to a test question result in higher scores for female examinees than they obtain on multiple-choice tests covering comparable material, as was discussed earlier in this chapter. Clear evidence of the relative advantage or disadvantage of different item formats for performance of racial–ethnic groups has yet to emerge.

Performance assessments, although offering many advantages for supporting instruction and learning, have several possible drawbacks for large-scale, high-stakes testing. First, these tests are less reliable, sometimes much less reliable, than multiple-choice tests, an undesirable feature for a high-stakes examination. Part of this unreliability comes from the subjective scoring procedures these examinations require, but it also results from a lack of generalizability across tasks from the same content domain. That is, studies of many different performance instruments show that performance on one task is nearly unrelated to performance on another task ostensibly measuring the same general knowledge or skill area (Linn, Baker, & Dunbar, 1991). Many tasks may therefore be needed to yield a reliable score, possibly resulting in several hours of testing because performance assessment tasks are more time-consuming than those with multiple-choice formats.

Another concern for high-stakes testing is that essays, portfolios, or other samples of student work that may be required for decision making may or may not have been created entirely as the result of the student's own effort. Some examinations provide standardized conditions for writing essays during the testing session to ensure that the result is the student's work. Others have argued that the editing and revision processes that normally take place following an initial draft are an important part of writing that cannot be included within the typical standardized testing time limits.

Other issues concerning the use of performance assessments for high-stakes purposes include the security of test content when few items are used, a possible lack of validity due to unrepresentative content of a small number of tasks, and comparability of different test forms administered to different individuals (Mehrens, 1992). Many of these concerns about performance assessment will need to be resolved before these measures can be evaluated as a high-stakes assessment alternative that may provide better measurement for minority or female examinees.

Retention Policy

If the goal of the admissions decision is to select students who will successfully complete the college program, factors other than examinee characteristics may need to be taken into account. Policy research has indicated that colleges and universities who have been successful in retaining and graduating minority students are those that offer a variety of supportive services to these students and others who are different from the majority of the student body. The nature of the interpersonal environment appears to be nearly as important as the student's capabilities in ensuring a successful college experience.

Conclusion

Some of the concerns expressed about the use of large-scale and individualized testing with minority and female examinees are legitimate. Charges of test bias may or may not be justified, but the percentage of observed differences between groups that may be attributable to bias is probably small at worst, and standardized measures of cognitive skills and abilities appear to be essentially valid for test takers with adequate English-language skills. Properly administered individual measures enable examiners to be alert to conditions that might contribute to bias and to alleviate some of their efforts.

The issues of bias are complex, and no practical solutions have been forthcoming for changing tests to avoid any inherent biasing factors. Important changes in the nature of the tests occurring anytime soon is unlikely. In this chapter we have reviewed some of the sources of performance differences between groups and have discussed the issues of test use for placement, admissions, and other high-stakes educational decisions. The challenge is to make positive use of the power of these examinations in light of some uncertainty about the meaning of the scores for some examinees.

References

Banks, W. C., McQuater, G. V., & Hubbard, J. L. (1978). Toward a reconceptualization of the social-cognitive bases of achievement orientations in Blacks. *Review of Educational Research, 48*, 381–197.

Bell, R. C., & Hay, J. A. (1987). Differences and biases in English language examination formats. *British Journal of Educational Psychology, 57*, 212–220.

Ben-Shakhar, G., & Sinai, Y. (1991). Gender differences in multiple-choice tests: The role of differential guessing tendencies. *Journal of Educational Measurement, 28*, 23–35.

Bolger, N., & Kellaghan, T. (1990). Method of measurement and gender differences in scholastic achievement. *Journal of Educational Measurement, 27*, 165–174.

Bond, L. (1989). The effects of special preparation on measures of scholastic ability.

In R. L. Linn (Ed.), *Educational measurement* (3rd ed., pp. 429–444). New York: Macmillan.

Bracken, B. A. (1991). The clinical observation of preschool assessment behavior. In B. A. Bracken (Ed.), *The psychoeducational assessment of preschool children* (2nd ed., pp. 40–52). Boston: Allyn & Bacon.

Breland, H. M., Danos, D. O., Kahn, H. D., Kubota, M. Y., & Sudlow, M. W. (1991). *A study of gender and performance on Advanced Placement History Examinations* (Report 91-4). New York: College Entrance Examination Board.

Bridgeman, B., & Lewis, C. (1994). The relationship of essay and multiple-choice scores with grades in college courses. *Journal of Educational Measurement, 31,* 37–50.

Carlton, S. T., & Harris, A. M. (1989, March). *Characteristics of differential item performance on the Scholastic Aptitude Test: Selected ethnic group comparisons.* Paper presented at the meeting of the National Council on Measurement in Education, San Francisco, CA.

Cleary, T. A. (1968). Test bias: Prediction of grades of Negro and White students in integrated colleges. *Journal of Educational Measurement, 5,* 115–124.

Cole, B. P. (1987). College admissions and coaching. *Negro Educational Review, 38,* 125–135.

Cole, N. S., & Moss, P. A. (1989). Bias in test use. In R. L. Linn (Ed.), *Educational measurement* (3rd ed., pp. 201–219). New York: Macmillan.

Darlington, R. B. (1971). Another look at "cultural fairness." *Journal of Educational Measurement, 8,* 71–82.

Elliot, R., & Strenta, A. C. (1988). Effects of improving the reliability of the GPA on prediction generally and on comparative predictions for gender and race particularly. *Journal of Educational Measurement, 25,* 333–347.

Evans, F. R. (1980). *A study of the relationships among speed and power, aptitude test scores, and ethnic identity* (RR-80-22). Princeton, NJ: Educational Testing Service.

Flaugher, R. L. (1978). The many definitions of test bias. *American Psychologist, 33,* 671–679.

Gafni, N., & Melamed, E. (1994). Differential tendencies to guess as a function of gender and lingual–cultural reference group. *Studies in Educational Evaluation, 20,* 309–319.

Gaire, L. (1991). The development of TestSkills: A test familiarization kit on the PSAT/NMSQT for Hispanic students. In G. D. Keller, J. R. Deneen, & R. J. Magallan (Eds.), *Assessment and access: Hispanics in higher education* (pp. 235–242). Albany: State University of New York Press.

Geisinger, K. F. (1992, August). Testing limited English proficient students for minimum competency and high school graduation. In *Focus on evaluation and measurement* (Vol. 2). Washington, DC: U.S. Department of Education, Office of Bilingual Education and Minority Language Affairs.

Gemache, L. M., & Novick, M. R. (1985). Choice of variables and gender differentiated prediction with selected academic programs. *Journal of Educational Measurement, 22,* 53–70.

Glutting, J., & Oakland, T. (1993). *GATSB: Guide to the assessment of test session behavior.* San Antonio, TX: The Psychological Corporation.

Goldman, R. D., & Widawski, M. H. (1976). An analysis of types of errors in the selection of minority college students. *Journal of Educational Measurement, 13,* 185–200.

Grandy, J. (1987). *Characteristics of examinees who leave questions unanswered on the GRE General Test under rights-only scoring* (GRE Research Report No. 83-16P). Princeton, NJ: Educational Testing Service.

Gutkin, T. B., & Reynolds, C. R. (1981). Factorial similarity of the WISC-R for White and Black children from the standardization sample. *Journal of Educational Psychology, 73*, 227–231.

Helms, J. E. (1992). Why is there no study of cultural equivalence in standardized cognitive ability testing? *American Psychologist, 47*, 1083–1101.

Hennessy, J. J., & Merrifield, P. R. (1976). A comparison of the factor structures of mental abilities in four ethnic groups. *Journal of Educational Psychology, 68*, 754–759.

Ironson, G. H., & Subkoviak, M. J. (1979). A comparison of several methods of assessing item bias. *Journal of Educational Measurement, 16*, 209–225.

Jensen, A. R. (1980). *Bias in mental testing.* New York: Free Press.

Jensen, A. R., & Reynolds, C. R. (1982). Race, social class, and ability patterns on the WISC-R. *Personality and Individual Differences, 3*, 423–438.

Johnson, S. T. (1989). Test fairness and bias: Measuring academic achievement among Black youth. In W. D. Smith & E. W. Chunn (Eds.), *Black education: A quest for equity and excellence* (pp. 76–92). New Brunswick, NJ: Transaction.

Johnston, W. T., & Bolen, R. M. (1984). A comparison of the factor structures of the WISC-R for Blacks and Whites. *Psychology in the Schools, 21*, 42–44.

Kaufman, A. S. (1975). Factor analysis of the WISC-R at eleven age levels between 6½ and 16½ years. *Journal of Consulting and Clinical Psychology, 43*, 135–147.

Kaufman, A. S. (1990). *Assessing adolescent and adult intelligence.* Needham, MA: Allyn & Bacon.

Kaufman, A. S. (1994). *Intelligence testing with the WISC-III.* New York: Wiley.

Keller, D., Crouse, J., & Trusheim, D. (1994). The effects of college grade adjustments on the predictive validity and utility of SAT scores. *Research in Higher Education, 35*, 195–208.

Kessel, C., & Linn, M. C. (1996). Grades or scores: Predicting future college mathematics performance. *Educational Measurement: Issues and Practice, 15*(4), 10–14.

Lawrence, I. M., Curley, W. E., & McHale, F. J. (1988, April). *Differential item functioning of SAT Verbal Reading subscore items for male and female examinees.* Paper presented at the meeting of the American Educational Research Association, New Orleans, LA.

Linn, R. L. (1984). Selection bias: Multiple meanings. *Journal of Educational Measurement, 21*, 33–47.

Linn, R. L. (1990). Admissions testing: Recommended uses, validity, differential prediction, and coaching. *Applied Measurement in Education, 3*, 297–318.

Linn, R. L., Baker, E. L., & Dunbar, S. B. (1991). Complex performance-based assessments: Expectations and validation criteria. *Educational Research, 20*(8), 15–21.

Llabre, M. M. (1991). Time as a factor in the cognitive ability test performance of Latino college students. In G. D. Keller, J. R. Deneen, & R. J. Magallan (Eds.), *Assessment and access: Hispanics in higher education* (pp. 95–104). Albany: State University of New York Press.

Mazzeo, J., Schmitt, A. P., & Bleistein, C. A. (1993). *Sex-related differences on constructed response and multiple-choice sections of Advanced Placement Examinations* (Report No. 92-7). New York: College Entrance Examination Board.

McCornack, R. L., & McLeod, M. M. (1988). Gender bias in the prediction of college course performance. *Journal of Educational Measurement, 25*, 321–331.

Mehrens, W. A. (1992). Using performance assessment for accountability purposes. *Educational Measurement: Issues and Practice, 11*(1), 3–9, 20.

Miller-Jones, D. (1989). Culture and testing. *American Psychologist, 44*, 360–366.

Murphy, R. J. L. (1982). Sex differences in objective test performance. *British Journal of Educational Psychology, 52*, 213–219.

Oakland, T., & Glutting, J. (1998). Assessment of test behaviors with the WISC-III. In A. Prifitera & D. Saklofske (Eds.), *WISC-III: A scientist–practitioner perspective* (pp. 289–310). San Diego, CA: Academic Press.

Oakland, T., & Laosa, L. (1977). Professional, legislative, and judicial influences on psychological and educational assessment practices in the schools. In T. Oakland (Ed.), *Psychological and educational assessment of minority children* (pp. 21–51). Larchmont, NY: Brunner/Mazel.

O'Malley, J. M., & Pierce, L. V. (1994). State assessment policies, practices, and language minority students. *Educational Assessment, 2*, 213–255.

Payne, B. D., Smith, J. E., & Payne, D. A. (1983). Grade, sex, and race differences in test anxiety. *Psychological Reports, 53*, 291–294.

Pennock-Roman, M. (1990). *Test validity and language background: A study of Hispanic-American students at six universities.* New York: College Entrance Examination Board.

Pennock-Roman, M., Powers, D. E., & Perez, M. (1991). A preliminary evaluation of TestSkills: A kit to prepare Hispanic students for the PSAT/NMSQT. In G. D. Keller, J. R. Deneen, & R. J. Magallan (Eds.), *Assessment and access: Hispanics in higher education* (pp. 243–264). Albany: State University of New York Press.

Petrie, T. A. (1993). Racial differences in the prediction of college football players' academic performance. *Journal of College Student Development, 34*, 418–421.

Reschly, D. J. (1978). WISC-R factor structures among Anglos, Blacks, Chicanos, and Native American Papagos. *Journal of Clinical and Consulting Psychology, 3*, 417–422.

Reynolds, C. R. (1982). Method for detecting construct and predictive bias. In R. A. Berk (Ed.), *Handbook of methods for detecting test bias* (pp. 199–227). Baltimore: Johns Hopkins University Press.

Reynolds, C. R., & Kamphaus, R. (Eds.). (1990). *Handbook of psychological and educational assessment of children.* New York: Guilford Press.

Reynold, C. R., Plake, B. S., & Harding, R. E. (1983). Item bias in the assessment of children's anxiety: Race and sex interaction on items of the revised Children's Manifest Anxiety Scale. *Journal of Psychoeducational Assessment, 1*, 17–24.

Rindler, S. E. (1979). Pitfalls in assessing test speededness. *Journal of Educational Measurement, 16*, 261–270.

Salvia, J., & Ysseldyke, J. (1988). *Assessment in special and remedial education.* Boston: Houghton Mifflin.

Sandoval, J. (1982). The WISC-R factorial validity for minority groups and Spearman's hypothesis. *Journal of School Psychology, 20*, 198–204.

Sandoval, J., & Irvin, M. G. (1990). Legal and ethical issues in the assessment of children. In C. R. Reynolds & R. W. Kamphaus (Eds.), *Handbook of psychological and educational assessment of children* (pp. 86–104). New York: Guilford Press.

Sattler, J. (1988). *Assessment of children* (3rd ed.). San Diego, CA: Author.

Scarr, S. (1981). *Race, social class, and individual differences in IQ.* Hillsdale, NJ: Erlbaum.

Scheuneman, J. D. (1987a). An argument opposing Jensen on test bias: The psychological aspects. In S. Modgil & C. Modgil (Eds.), *Arthur Jensen: Consensus and controversy* (pp. 155–170). London: Falmer Press.

Scheuneman, J. D. (1987b). An experimental, exploratory study of causes of bias in test items. *Journal of Educational Measurement, 24*, 97–118.

Scheuneman, J. D., & Gerritz, K. (1990). Using differential item functioning procedures to explore sources of difficulty and group performance characteristics. *Journal of Educational Measurement, 27*, 109–131.

Schmitt, A. P. (1988). Language and cultural characteristics that explain differential item functioning for Hispanic examinees on the Scholastic Aptitude Test. *Journal of Educational Measurement, 25,* 1–13.

Schmitt, A. P., & Bleistein, C. A. (1987). *Factors affecting differential item functioning for Black examinees on Scholastic Aptitude Test analogy items* (RR-87-23). Princeton, NJ: Educational Testing Service.

Schmitt, A., & Dorans, N. J. (1991). Factors related to differential item functioning on the Scholastic Aptitude Test. In G. D. Keller, J. R. Deneen, & R. J. Magallan (Eds.), *Assessment and access: Hispanics in higher education* (pp. 105–132). State University of New York Press.

Shepard, L. A. (1987). The case for bias in tests of achievement and scholastic aptitude. In S. Modgil & C. Modgil (Eds.), *Arthur Jensen: Consensus and controversy* (pp. 177–190). London: Falmer Press.

Sinnott, L. T. (1980). *Differences in item performance across groups* (RR-80-19). Princeton, NJ: Educational Testing Service.

Terrell, F., Terrell, S. L., & Taylor, J. (1981). Effects of race of examiner and cultural mistrust on the WAIS performance of Black students. *Journal of Consulting and Clinical Psychology, 49,* 750–751.

Thorndike, R. L. (1971). Concepts of culture fairness. *Journal of Educational Measurement, 8,* 63–70.

Watson, R. (1951). Test behavior observation guide. In R. Watson (Ed.), *The clinical method in psychology* (pp. 148–159). New York: Harper.

Wild, C. L., & Dwyer, C. A. (1980). Sex bias in selection. In L. J. T. van der Kamp, W. F. Langerak, & D. N. M. de Gruijter (Eds.), *Psychometrics for educational debates* (pp. 153–168). New York: Wiley.

Wild, C. L., Durso, R., & Rubin, D. B. (1982). Effect of increase test-taking time on test scores by ethnic group, years out of school, and sex. *Journal of Educational Measurement, 19,* 19–28.

Young, J. W. (1991). Gender bias in predicting college academic performance: A new approach using item response theory. *Journal of Educational Measurement, 28,* 37–47.

Zhu, D., & Thompson, T. D. (1995, April). *Gender and ethnic differences in tendencies to omit responses on multiple-choice tests using number-right scoring.* Paper presented at the meeting of the American Educational Research Association, San Francisco, CA.

Equity Issues in Employment Testing

Stephen G. Sireci and Kurt F. Geisinger

Employment tests are frequently used in the employment arena to screen many job applicants for a limited number of jobs and to promote employees within an organization, especially in civil service settings. The decisions made on the basis of scores derived on employment tests often mean the difference between work and unemployment or between upward mobility and stagnation.

Given such serious consequences, it is no surprise that equity issues surrounding employment tests have received considerable attention in the psychometric literature, in the courtroom, and on Capitol Hill. Laws, guidelines, and other promulgations for fair and appropriate employment testing practices have generated intense controversy and heated debate. In almost every instance, antagonists on both sides of the debate support their position on the basis of fairness and equity, and sometimes fairness is placed in apparent contrast to productivity. The purpose of this chapter is to summarize these equity issues, critique empirical methodology and research in this area, and provide suggestions for promoting fairness in employment testing.

Employment Tests and Workforce Diversity

One of the greatest strengths of the U.S. workforce is its diversity. A diverse workforce promotes innovation, creativity, and problem solving within the workplace, qualities that are critical in a competitive global economy. Testing a diverse workforce presents formidable challenges for those using employment tests. Acknowledging workforce diversity requires ensuring that employment tests are fair to all employees and job applicants. Thus, the challenge for those who use employment tests is to demonstrate that the testing process is not biased against common (identifiable) subgroups of the examinee population.

Subgroups of examinees (i.e., potential employees) can be categorized in many ways. Examples include people of different racial, ethnic, or religious groups; people with disabilities; bilingual and English-as-a-second-language (ESL) individuals; males; females; people of different age groups; and those adopting "alternative" lifestyles such as gays and lesbians. Many of these groups have made their concerns known to testing professionals by filing court cases against users of employment tests, claiming that the tests were biased against them (some of these cases are reviewed later). It is important for test users to forestall such claims by proactively considering unintended interactions between the testing process and various subgroups composing the examinee population as well as the potential intended benefits of using assessment instruments. Examination of unintended effects of testing is a critical component of evaluating the validity of an employment test (or battery of tests).

Purposes and Criticisms of Employment Tests

There are several purposes of employment tests. The most common purpose is to select the "best" employees to fill a limited number of jobs. However, employment tests also are used to promote individuals within an organization or classify employees according to different jobs (Zeidner & Johnson, 1994). In all cases, employment tests are used to achieve economic gains for organizations. The information provided by employment tests facilitates decision making and allows employers to maximize workforce productivity (Brogden, 1949; Cronbach & Gleser, 1957; Roe & Greuter, 1991; Rudner, 1992; Schmidt, 1988). In many employment settings, such as the government, the military, and other large corporations, the ratio of the number of job applicants to available positions may make other forms of selection (e.g., assessment centers) either not feasible or lacking utility. In addition to the economic gains, employment tests also are used to provide equitable criteria for selection and classification decisions.

Criticisms against the fairness of employment tests stem from the fact that these tests are often seen as preventing people from securing valuable jobs. Some critics assert that employment tests are not valid for all groups of job applicants. Even when no evidence of test bias is found, employment tests have been challenged as being unfair against certain groups. Many of these challenges originated with concerns raised during the Civil Rights movement of the 1950s and 1960s. Others, such as concerns of sex discrimination, language bias, and promoting obstacles for individuals with disabilities, were raised more recently. Before discussing the methodology used to deal with these important concerns, we present a brief review of the political and legal history of challenges to employment testing.

Issues in Testing Racial–Ethnic Minorities

Title VII of the Civil Rights Act of 1964 directly influenced employment testing by prohibiting discrimination in personnel selection on the basis of race, color, religion, sex, or national origin. Passage of this act accelerated research on score differences among subgroups of examinees and the effect of such differences on the selection ratio of these groups. Litigation related to Title VII led to the theory of adverse impact, which maintained that tests that rejected minority applicants at a higher rate than nonminority applicants were discriminatory, unless the tests could be shown to be job related.

The influence of the Title VII legislation was evident in the U.S. Supreme Court case *Griggs v. Duke Power Co.* (1971). Discrimination against African Americans was charged against Duke Power because of hiring requirements that included a high school diploma and above-average scores on two professionally developed selection tests (the Wonderlic Personnel Test and the Bennett Mechanical Comprehension Test). These requirements produced an adverse impact against African American applicants, and, because insufficient evidence of the job relatedness was produced by the employer, the Supreme Court ruled against Duke. In a subsequent case, *Albemarle Paper Co. v. Moody* (1975), the Supreme Court emphasized the criticality of evidence of job relatedness and applauded employment tests for providing an opportunity to evaluate applicants objectively on a standardized basis (Bolick, 1988).

Federal conceptions of adverse impact and standards of job relatedness were clarified in the Equal Employment Opportunities Commission (EEOC), U.S. Civil Service Commission (CSC), U.S. Department of Labor (DOL), and U.S. Department of Justice's (DOJ), 1978 Uniform Guidelines on Employee Selection Procedures. Rules were developed that permitted members of protected groups to litigate when their population subgroups were not hired or promoted at the rate comparable to that of the majority group. Such a situation was termed *adverse impact*. In terms of adverse impact, the guidelines promulgated the "four-fifths rule," which stated that a passing rate for a group that is less than four fifths of the passing rate for the highest scoring group constitutes adverse impact. For example, under this guideline, if 50% of the highest scoring group (typically the majority group) passed the test, then adverse impact would be present if the passing rate for any protected group was less than 40% (i.e., four fifths of 50%). To continue to use an employment measure in spite of its adverse impact, employers were primarily required to demonstrate that it is job related in any of three ways. The guidelines described acceptable forms of evidence to support job relatedness: content, criterion-related, and construct validity. Conditions needed to demonstrate job relatedness using any of these approaches are articulated in the guidelines.

Legislation on adverse impact in employment testing generated criticisms of reverse discrimination against nonminority job applicants. Critics of the four-fifths rule argued that minority applicants obtain preferential treatment at the expense of nonminorities. Although in *United Steelworkers v. Weber* (1979) and *Fullilove v. Klutznick* (1980), the U.S. Supreme Court ruled that minority preference for the purpose of reducing adverse impact is acceptable, in *Watson v. Fort Worth Bank and Trust* (1988) the court indicated clearly that strict adherence to the guidelines was not endorsed. Rather, the *Watson* ruling asserted that the burden of proof for adverse impact and lack of job relatedness rests on the plaintiff. The plaintiff's burden of proof was reemphasized by the court in *Wards Cove Packaging Co. Inc. v. Antonio* (1989).

Within-Groups Norming and the Civil Rights Act of 1991

Interpretation of the EEOC guidelines and the U.S. Supreme Court rulings led to several practices in employment testing designed to reduce adverse impact. These practices included norming employment tests separately for different minority and nonminority groups (within-groups norming), giving minority-group applicants "bonus points" (or using different passing or "cut" scores for minority and nonminority groups), and banding procedures. Use of these methods generated controversy between proponents for reducing adverse impact and proponents for reducing reverse discrimination. Because banding procedures are more technically complex than the other procedures, we describe them later. Within-groups norming, bonus points, and multiple cut scores are described in the present to preface the political context leading to changes mandated by the Civil Rights Act of 1991.

The use of both bonus points and multiple cut scores on employment tests is self-explanatory. The former method adds a certain number of points to the test scores of applicants belonging to particular minority groups; the latter method uses different "passing scores" on the selection test for different groups. Like within-groups norming, the purpose of these methods is to reduce score differences between minority and nonminority groups that result from the "top-down" method of selection, which involves selecting applicants according to the rank order of their test score (i.e., the highest scoring applicant is selected first, the second highest applicant is selected second, etc.). The top-down method maximizes selection utility with respect to the criterion performance measures against which employment tests are validated (Cascio, Outtz, Zedeck, & Goldstein, 1991; Schmidt, 1988, 1994; Society for Industrial and Organizational Psychology [SIOP], 1987), and using the top-down method in combination with within-groups norming represents an attempt to maximize selection utility and workforce diversity.

Within-groups norming involves computing percentile rank scores from raw test scores separately for nonminority and minority groups. Separate sets of percentile ranks are computed for relevant subgroups of the applicant pool such as Whites, African Americans, Hispanics, American Indians, and so on. This process results in identical percentile rank scores that may correspond to different raw scores across groups. For example, suppose within-groups norms are used for men and women on a hypothetical computer literacy test, and the highest scoring woman earns a score of 88, whereas the highest scoring man earns a score of 79. The within-groups percentile rank scores for these two applicants would be the same (i.e., 99), and so they would be considered equally qualified even though their raw scores differed by 9 points. When the various groups differ widely in their test score distributions (e.g., mean test scores), the adjustment can have a major impact. If the distributions of various groups, on the other hand, overlap greatly the adjustment may be trivial.

The purpose of within-groups norming is to produce selection ratios for minority and nonminority groups that are congruous to the proportion of these groups in the applicant pool. For example, if an applicant pool comprised 300 White applicants (75%) and 100 African American applicants (25%), and 40 job openings were available (a 10% selection ratio), 30 White (75%) and 10 African American (25%) applicants would be selected using within-groups norms (i.e., the top 10% in each group).[1] Thus, the approach approximates a so-called "quota system," in which the proportion of each group present in the selection population parallels their proportion in the final sample.

Although within-groups norming is successful for removing adverse impact against minorities, it has been severely criticized because of the large differences in raw scores that can result for applicants in different groups with identical percentile rank scores (Casio et al., 1991; Gottfredson, 1994; Zedeck, Outtz, Cascio, & Goldstein, 1995). Using within-groups norming, it is not uncommon to select minority-group applicants over nonminority applicants when the raw scores for the minority applicant are more than 1 SD lower than a large proportion of nonselected nonminority applicants. Furthermore, there is evidence that within-groups norming can create a negative impact against nonminorities (McKinney & Collins, 1991). Critics of within-groups norming argue that the prices paid for eliminating adverse impact on the protected group is reverse discrimination, which is tantamount to bias against nonminority applicants and a reduction in the utility of the test to select the best employees.

The controversy surrounding within-groups norming was highly publicized when the United States Employment Service (USES) implemented within-groups norming on the General Aptitude Test Battery (GATB). This test has been used by the USES to screen applicants for a wide variety of jobs and is currently the largest employment screening test in the United States (Sackett & Wilk, 1994). Separate norms were produced on the GATB for African Americans, Hispanics, and others. Because of the high-stakes consequences of this test, the practice of within-groups norming generated criticisms of reverse discrimination. Most prominent among the critics was the Department of Justice, which charged that the practice was unconstitutional. In 1986, a blue ribbon panel committee was convened by the National Academy of Sciences

---

[1] Obviously, this is a contrived example. Note that within-groups norms may be calculated on a national norm group rather than on a particular pool of job applicants, and so the exact proportion of minority group representation in the applicant pool may not be represented in the group of applicants selected.

(NAS) to study the problem of race-based scoring of the GATB. The book-length report of the committee (Hartigan & Wigdor, 1989) supported the practice of within-groups norming on the GATB but was extremely controversial.

The committee report (Hartigan & Wigdor, 1989) acknowledged the criticisms of reverse discrimination stemming from within-groups norming. However, they upheld this practice with respect to the GATB because top-down selection resulted in screening out a disproportionate number of minorities. Because the GATB is primarily an early screening device in a multiple-hurdle selection system, the committee concluded that the adverse impact resulting from top-down scoring was inappropriate.

The criticisms of within-groups norming extended to the popular press and Congress shortly after release of the NAS report. Charges of reverse discrimination heightened, and the Supreme Court reversed earlier decisions regarding challenges to affirmative action (*Martin v. Wilks*, 1989). Ultimately, legislative debate surrounding the Civil Rights Act of 1991 led to a ban on score adjustment on the basis of "race, color, religion, sex, or national origin" (Civil Rights Act of 1991, 1998, Section 106). This ban on score adjustment grew directly from criticisms against the USES GATB system (Sackett & Wilk, 1994) and the NAS report. As described by Gottfredson (1994),

> already struggling to deny that their 1991 civil rights bill was a quota bill, its embarrassed sponsors acceded to pressure to ban score adjustments. . . . The NAS committee's seemingly compelling rationale for race norming quickly receded into oblivion as public outrage escalated over the bald racial preferences the practice actually seemed to entail. (p. 958)

Although within-groups norming was prohibited by the act, it was unclear whether other forms of score adjustment, such as banding procedures (described later), were justified. The debate over score adjustments on employment tests for minority groups stems from differences between testing professionals who believe that tests are valid when no evidence of bias is present (and evidence for predictive validity is found) and those testing professionals who believe employment tests provide only limited information with respect to predicting future work performance. The former view is exemplified by Gottfredson (1994), who concluded that

> the disparate impact of [cognitive ability employment tests] is not due to their imperfections but to substantial racial differences in

the job-related skills, abilities, and knowledge they reveal. . . . Their use cannot be abandoned without considerable sacrifice in work-force productivity. (p. 955)

The later view is exemplified by the NAS committee report on the use of the GATB:

The modest validities of the GATB cause selection errors that weigh more heavily on minority workers than on majority workers. This outcome is at odds with the nation's express commitment to equal employment opportunity for minority workers. In the committee's judgment, the disproportionate impact of selection error provides scientific grounds for the adjustment of minority scores so that able minority workers have approximately the same chances of referral as able majority workers. (Hartigan & Wigdor, 1989, p. 7)

Note that cognitive abilities tests used in personnel selection were at the center of this debate because such tests exhibited larger differences in performance among minority and nonminority groups and were considered by some to provide only limited predictive information about future job performance (Sackett & Wilk, 1994).

Legal and Psychometric Issues in Testing Individuals With Disabilities

In addition to legislation on employment testing and minorities, recent laws also have influenced practices concerning testing people with disabilities. In fact, Scarpati (1991) concluded that "lawsuits have clearly been the single source through which testing the handicapped has changed in concept and in practice" (p. 253). A landmark case affecting the testing of individuals with disabilities was *Hobson v. Hanson* (1967), in which the use of psychological tests was questioned for the purpose of diagnosing mental retardation in low-income, special education, and minority students. A federal court ruled that psychological tests produce misleading scores for these individuals, and its decision disallowed a diagnosis of mental retardation on the basis of the administration of only one test by one individual.

Section 504 of the Rehabilitation Act (1973) and the Americans With Disabilities Act (ADA; 1990) prohibit discrimination against people with disabilities in a variety of contexts. Although these laws did not contain language specific to employment testing, they do prohibit discrimination against job applicants solely on the basis of their disability. Thus, under ADA legislation, if a disability precludes an applicant from taking the standard administration of an employment test, but not from performing well on the job (perhaps with the aid of an accommodation to perform the job), then some form of testing accommodation is warranted (Geisinger, 1994b). According to Klimoski and Palmer (1994), the ADA may be understood as follows:

> The ADA does not guarantee equal outcomes, establish quotas, or require preferences favoring individuals without disabilities. Rather, the ADA is intended to ensure access to equal employment opportunities based on merit. The ADA is designed to "level the playing field" by removing the barriers that prevent qualified individuals with disabilities from having access to the same employment opportunities that are available to qualified individuals without disabilities. (p. 45)

The critical issue in testing job applicants with disabilities is determining whether accommodations to standardized testing conditions should be granted. Accommodating employment tests for these individuals requires test developers to remove barriers related to the testing situation that are construct irrelevant, but impede the performance of individuals with disabilities on the test. A second critical issue is ensuring the validity of test scores for all examinees. As Phillips (1994) described, measurement specialists must "balance the social goal of integrating the disabled against the measurement goal of accurate test score interpretation" (p. 93).

Guidance with respect to whether an accommodated test administration is required under the law can be found in Eyde, Nester, Heaton, and Nelson (1994) or Nester (1994). Types of accommodations granted in employment testing vary widely according to the particular disability presented. Such accommodations include altering test instruments, modifying instructions or time limits, or modifying the medium through which examinees provide their responses to test questions. Prevailing accommodations for sensory and motor disabilities include an audio cassette version, a reader, or Braille or large-print versions of a test for visual impairments; use of a scribe or computer to assist recording of answers for motor or verbal disabilities; and sign language interpreters or video cassette recorders for students with hearing impairments. A variety of accommodations also are granted for applicants with learning disabilities, such as attention deficit disorder, dysgraphia, dyslexia, and dyscalculia.[2] These accommodations include providing fre-

---

[2] Another critical issue in the testing of applicants with learning disabilities is documentation of the disability. Unlike physical disabilities, which are typically conspicuous, learning disabilities are subtle. To qualify for an accommodated test administration, applicants with learning disabilities are typically required to produce documentation of the disability, certified by a licensed professional (see Scarpati, 1991, and chapter 13 in this book).

quent breaks, oral presentation of instructions or test questions, use of a calculator or computer, extension of standardized time limits, and taking the test in a private room rather than in a group setting. Many of these accommodations also are granted to individuals with psychiatric and metabolic disabilities. A full discussion of the types of accommodations that can be provided can be found in Eyde et al. (1994) and Nester (1994).

In addition to modifying the medium of test presentation of the testing environment, changes in the content of a test also are used to accommodate individuals with disabilities (see Geisinger, 1994b; Nester, 1994). Nester (1994) categorized changes in test content as being "change in individual test questions, change in the question type, and change or deletion of a knowledge, skill or ability . . . that is being measured" (p. 31). A common example is reducing the number of test questions containing graphics or other visual cues that present problems for applicants with visual impairments. Another example is the elimination of questions that presume access to spoken English that may disadvantage deaf students (e.g., idioms related to sound such as "a roaring ocean"). With respect to testing examinees with hearing impairments, Mounty (1990) illustrated that allowing deaf examinees the opportunity to provide their answers to essay and listening subtest questions in sign language significantly improved their test scores.

The equivalence of scores from accommodated and standardized test administration conditions is a fundamental aspect of test fairness. Changes in the content of the test, or in the standardized administration procedures, can change the construct measured (*Standards for Educational and Psychological Testing*, 1985; Geisinger, 1994a; Phillips, 1994; Willingham et al., 1988). For example, removing or replacing test questions containing graphs or other visual information may alter the cognitive skill being measured from "decoding information" to "reading comprehension." Similarly, reading test questions aloud to dyslexic people may change the construct measured from "reading comprehension" to "oral comprehension." Eliminating or extending time limits also will affect the construct measured for speeded tests. For example, if the ability to file documents in a timely manner is a critical aspect of the job domain, eliminating or extending testing time limits is likely to reduce the predictive validity of the assessment. Elimination of the "speededness" (or timing) factor in this case may change the construct measured from "filing efficiency" to "alphabetizing."

The *Standards for Educational and Psychological Testing* (1985) and

Geisinger (1994b), among others, have pointed to the lack of research in the area of evaluating construct equivalence across standardized and adapted versions of tests. As noted by Geisinger (1994b), "the time has come for test authors and publishers to engage in more developmental research on modified test administrations" (p. 125). Notable exceptions to the paucity of research in this area is the work performed by Willingham et al. (1988) based on people with disabilities who took the Scholastic Aptitude Test (SAT) or the Graduate Record Examination (GRE). Rock, Bennett, and Kaplan (1987) and Rock, Bennett, and Jirele (1988) compared the factor structures of these tests across standard and nonstandard administrations (including Braille, audio cassette, and extended time modifications) and concluded that the factor structures from modified administrations could be interpreted similarly to those resulting from standardized administrations. Braun, Ragosta, and Kaplan (1988) investigated the predictive validity of these tests across "standard" and "disabled" groups of students. Although overlap in the predictive validity for these two groups was found with respect to first-year college grades, both under- and overprediction of grades were discovered for certain groups of students with disabilities. The overwhelming consensus from these studies is that more research in this area is needed. Except for the research on the SAT and GRE that has been mentioned, little research of consequence has been performed.

Unfortunately, research on the score comparability of standardized and accommodated tests has not emerged in the arena of employment testing. The primary reasons for this lack of research are the traditionally small number of applicants with disabilities who are tested with employment tests and the large variety of types of accommodations reported even for individuals within the same disability group. Nevertheless, the passage of the ADA has sharply increased the number of requests for special testing accommodations (Phillips, 1994).

Gender Discrimination Issues

Another set of challenges to the fairness of employment tests involves discrimination of these tests against women. Although some challenges pertain to tests of cognitive skills (e.g., Doolittle & Cleary, 1987; Linn, 1982), for the most part, challenges of bias against women are raised against physical abilities (PA) tests. PA testing is becoming increasingly popular in personnel selection and is commonly used as part of the selection battery for firefighters and police officers (Arvey, Nutting, &

Landon, 1992; Fleishman, 1988; J. Hogan, 1994). Commensurate with the increase in use of PA tests is increased litigation against use of these tests for personnel selection (Arvey et al., 1992; J. Hogan & Quigley, 1986). The reasons for these litigations are similar to those raised by minority groups in challenging cognitive ability tests: PA tests produce large score differences between male and female candidates that facilitate adverse impact against women.

Litigation against PA employment tests has focused on whether these tests measured critical aspects of the job domain and, if so, whether the aspects identified were overemphasized in the selection process (Arvey et al., 1992). Denning (1984) and J. Hogan (1991) identified three factors underlying PA employment tests: muscular strength; coordination, flexibility, and balance; and cardiovascular fitness (the skinfold test). As a group, men overwhelmingly outperform women on measures of muscular strength, but women fare better on aerobic tasks and measures of balance (Arvey et al., 1992; cf Sackett & Wilk, 1994). Because the differences between men and women across these three factors may counterbalance one another (e.g., women's flexibility compensates for muscular strength), a critical component of fairness in PA testing is to demonstrate that the measures of PA used are job related. For measures of physical strength to be heavily weighted in the selection process, it must be demonstrated that they are essential for success on the job.

Testing Linguistically Diverse Individuals

Criticisms of the fairness of employment tests sometimes also extend to testing linguistic minorities, many of whom also are members of racial and ethnic groups. Most employment tests are administered in English, which may present a barrier to bilingual, ESL, or non–English-speaking job applicants for demonstrating their job-related knowledge, skills, and abilities. These criticisms are most viable when employment tests are administered in English and English is not demonstrated to be an essential component of the job domain. As stated in the *Standards* (1985): "In employment testing, licensing, and certification testing, the English language proficiency level of the test should not exceed that appropriate to the relevant occupation or profession" (p. 75).

Donlon (1992) provided an extensive review of litigation on the testing of Hispanics in both educational and employment settings. His review illustrates that court cases involving testing linguistic minorities are complex. For example, in *Rivera v. City of Wichita Falls* (1982), a Texas court ruled that the Basic Occupational Language Test for Police Officers was not discriminatory against Hispanics because its reading selections were representative of standard training materials used in Texas police academies and it demonstrated predictive validity. However, in *Chance v. Board of Examiners* (1971), a New York court ruled that an oral test used as part of a selection battery for principals and other school administrators was biased against Hispanics because the board did not demonstrate that the level of English proficiency measured was commensurate with that needed for success on the job. Thus, content validity appears to be a critical feature in defending the use of employment tests with linguistic minorities.

Issues in testing linguistic minorities have traditionally been underresearched (Olmedo, 1981). However, there has been a recent increase in research in this area. Some of this research points to problems inherent in testing linguistic minorities and questions the validity of cross-lingual assessment (Camara, 1992; Prieto, 1992; Valdés & Figueroa, 1994). Other research provides suggestions for increasing the sensitivity of the assessment process to linguistic minorities (Geisinger, 1992a), increasing score comparability across different language versions of tests (Angoff & Cook, 1988; Ellis, 1989; Hambleton, 1993; Martin & Berberoglu, 1991; Sireci, 1997), and methods for evaluating the validity of different language tests (Geisinger, 1994a; Hambleton, 1994). A significant contribution in this area are the Guidelines for Adapting Educational and Psychological Tests, developed by the International Test Commission (summarized by Hambleton, 1994). These guidelines review problems inherent in translating tests and provide suggestions for maximizing construct equivalence across languages.

In the area of employment testing, little research has been done on testing linguistic minorities. A notable exception is the study by Ramos (1981), who found that providing Hispanic job applicants test batteries with instructions in Spanish led to gains in their test scores. The results of that study suggested that giving job applicants the choice of taking employment tests with English-language instructions, or instructions in another language, may reduce adverse impact against linguistic minorities. Other research in the area of testing linguistic minorities is the inclusion of linguistically diverse ethnic groups in predictive validity studies such as those described earlier. These studies have not shown test bias against linguistic minorities using cognitive abilities tests (Wigdor & Garner, 1982). Similarly, Ramos (1992) found that assessment center devices were as predictive of managerial success for Hispanics as for non-minority-group members and found no evidence of bias against Hispanics using assessment center techniques. Nevertheless, large score differences between linguistic minority groups and English-language groups persevere on cognitive and assessment center test batteries. Valdés and Figueroa (1994) qualified these findings by asserting that "predictive validity is not consistently found when language proficiency is controlled for" (pp. 102–103). Using data presented by Jensen (1974), Valdéz and Figueroa illustrated that only after including a nonverbal measure of cognitive ability (i.e., Raven Progressive Matrices Test) in the predictive validity model was the bias of the verbal measure of ability (i.e., the Peabody Picture Vocabulary Test) evident. Given these findings, and a lack of a substantial knowledge base supporting the validity of testing bilinguals, Valdéz and Figueroa (1994) called for suspending the testing of linguistic minorities until the validity of such practices is defendable.

The abandonment of employment testing practices would undermine equity in personnel selection (Ramos, 1992). However, there are steps that can be taken to ameliorate threats to the validity of test scores gleaned from testing linguistic minorities (Camara, 1992; Geisinger, 1992a, 1994a; Hambleton, 1993, 1994). These steps include acknowledging linguistic diversity in the test construction process (including dialectic diversity within languages), evaluating score validity across language groups, and evaluating the validity of translated measures.

Geisinger (1996) put forth a model in which individual Hispanics, as members of one demographically important linguistic minority group, should be evaluated with respect to their language competence before their actual assessment. If their written or spoken English is critical to job success, then they may be assessed with the traditional (English-language) measure. (Fairness analyses should be performed, as discussed in the following section.) If English-language ability is not critical to job success and the most valid measure is sought, personnel specialists may consider testing some Hispanics in Spanish; this model may require translating or adapting a measure from English to Spanish. (See Geisinger, 1994a, or Hambleton, 1994, for steps to be taken to translate or adapt a measure.) Finally, a third model would involve the formal assessment of language skills as part of the employment process, especially when they have been found to be either useful or critical in job success on the basis of a carefully performed job analysis.

Evaluating Test Fairness

In the preceding sections we reviewed legal, political, and social issues pertaining to the use of employment tests on various subgroups of examinees. Included were brief summaries of the results of investigations of test fairness. However, we did not provide a description of the theory and methodology used to evaluate test fairness. Therefore, in this section we provide a brief description and critique of judgmental and empirical methods for evaluating test fairness.

The fundamental requirement for the validity of inferences derived from test scores is a comprehensive system of evidence supporting use of the test for the purpose for which it is used. Types of validity evidence are typically categorized into different aspects such as content related, criterion related, and construct related (*Standards*, 1985). In employment testing, content-related and predictive validity (a form of criterion-related evidence) are most often adduced to support the validity of inferences derived from test scores. Validity theorists describe content and predictive validity as components of construct validity, which is considered to be the general, unifying concept (Cronbach, 1988; Geisinger, 1992b; Guion, 1977, 1995; Messick, 1989, 1995a, 1995b; Shepard, 1993). However, in practice, the terms *content validity* and *predictive validity* are endorsed by employment test specialists because they accurately describe distinct forms of validity evidence and are consistent with the types of evidence required to support test use in the Uniform Guidelines on Employee Selection Procedures (EEOC, CSC, DOL, & DOJ, 1978).

Predictive validity evidence was described previously in considering bias against minority groups, women, and individuals with disabilities (i.e., consideration of differential predictive validity). This form of validity evidence describes the extent to which test scores predict future behavior. In employment testing, these future behaviors, called *job-related criteria*, include a variety of measures of job performance such as supervisory ratings, sales figures or other measures of employee output, work sample tests, attendance and other personnel records, or promotion rates (cf. Campbell, 1994). Evidence of predictive validity suggests that meaningful information about expected job performance can be derived from test scores.

Content-related validity is the extent to which the test represents the content domain it purports to measure. In the context of employment testing, content-related evidence of validity maintains that the test adequately represents the essential features of the job. Thus, to demonstrate content validity, items and tasks composing an employment test must be relevant to job performance and provide a representative sampling of job-related behaviors. Content validity is a goal of the test construction process. It emanates from an operational definition of the job domain, usually accomplished via job analyses (i.e., comprehensive analyses of the knowledge, skills, and tasks considered requisite for success on the job; see Colton, Kane, Kingsbury, & Estes, 1991). Content validity is evaluated throughout the test construction process by panels of subject matter experts who review test specifications, items, and final test forms. These subject matter experts evaluate the relevance, representativeness, and coverage of the test content relative to the job domain.

Content validity is the fundamental element of fairness in employment testing because it constrains the knowledge, skills, and abilities measured by tests to those necessary for success on the job. By striving to maximize content validity, test developers minimize the probability of measuring factors that are not job related and contribute bias into the measurement process. More comprehensive descriptions of the theory and practice of content validity are provided by Crocker, Miller, and Franks (1989), Guion (1977), Hambleton (1984), Sireci (in press), Sireci and Geisinger (1995), and Smith and Greenberg (1993).

Because construct validity refers to the meaning and consequences associated with inferences derived from test scores, it is the most general and complete conceptualization of test validity, comprising content, predictive, and any other evidence contributing to score meaning (Messick, 1989, 1995a, 1995b). When general ability tests are used in employment testing, rather than tests designed to measure specific job domains, it is presumed that these general ability constructs are critically related to job performance. In these situations, test users generally use a construct validity framework for evaluating the appropriateness of tests in particular settings. In particular, the concept of validity generalization (Schmidt, 1988; Schmidt & Hunter, 1977) invokes a construct validity perspective.

Guidelines and standards relevant to the theory and practice of evaluating the validity of employment test scores are provided by the *Standards for Educational and Psychological Testing* (1985), the Principles for the Validation and Use of Personnel Selection Procedures (SIOP, 1987), and the Code of Fair Testing Practices (Joint Committee on Testing Practices, 1988). Because fairness is subsumed under the concept of validity, research and practice in the area of test validity ultimately define fair testing practices. Specific forms of evidence used to evaluate the fairness of employment tests include judgmental and statistical methods for evaluating test bias.

Judgmental Methods for Evaluating Test Fairness

Judgmental methods for evaluating test bias are used during the test construction process. For example, the *Standards for Educational and Psychological Testing* (1985) recommend that

> when selecting the type and content of items for tests and inventories, test developers should consider the content and type in relation to cultural backgrounds and prior experiences of the variety of ethnic, cultural, age, and gender groups represented in the intended population of test takers. (p. 26)

To meet this requirement, test developers often use "sensitivity reviewers" to determine whether tests contain material that is offensive (e.g., racist or sexist material), controversial (e.g., concerning matters that are emotionally or politically volatile), or material that may provide an unfair advantage or disadvantage to certain groups of examinees (Ramsey, 1993; Sireci & Mullane, 1994). The goals of sensitivity review can be classified into three general categories: (a) identification of offensive or controversial material, (b) identification of unfair material, and (c) regard for population diversity. In striving to accomplish these goals, sensitivity reviewers consider language usage, ethnocentrism, minority-group representation, and minority-group portrayal within the assessment context.

Empirical Investigation of Test Bias

Although critical for ensuring test fairness and the appearance of the same, screening tests using judgmental review, even when carefully, systematically, and representatively performed, does not necessarily signify a lack of bias (Angoff, 1993; Sireci & Mullane, 1994). Rather, empirical methods also are necessary. Statistical methods for evaluating test bias have centered on evaluating bias in the test as a whole, generally within a criterion-related validity perspective, and evaluating bias at the item or task level. Test bias analyses have predominantly used the regression model to determine whether differential predictive validity is observed between minority and nonminority groups. Investigations of bias at the item–task level are termed analyses of differential item functioning (DIF). These analyses evaluate bias by matching examinees in minority and nonminority groups on the attribute measured and then determining whether matched examinees differ significantly in terms of their expected item–task performance. Test bias and DIF procedures are briefly described. For a comprehensive explanation of these procedures, see Cleary (1968), Cole and Moss (1989), Cronbach (1976), Jensen (1980), and Schmidt (1988) for analyses of test bias and Holland and Thayer (1988), Holland and Wainer (1993), and Millsap and Everson (1993) for DIF analyses.

Evaluating Test Bias Using Regression Models

Regression models have been widely applied to investigations of differential predictive validity (e.g., see chapter 5 in this book). The overwhelming majority of results have not produced evidence of test bias (Hunter & Schmidt, 1991; Schmidt, 1988, 1991). When differences in prediction have been found, they were typically in the direction of overpredicting for the minority group. In critiquing studies that detected test bias, Schmidt (1988) and Hunter and Schmidt (1991) concluded that these findings were attributable to statistical artifacts such as reduced statistical power (associated with smaller minority-group sample sizes), restriction of range, or unreliability of test or criterion measures. Schmidt (1988) asserted that the regression model is the most appropriate model for evaluating employment test bias and concluded that no evidence of bias against minority groups had been detected using this procedure. This position was underscored in the SIOP's (1987) principles:

> There is little evidence to suggest that there is differential prediction for the sexes, and the literature indicates that differential prediction on the basis of cognitive tests is not supported for the major ethnic groups (Schmidt, Pearlman, & Hunter, 1980; Hunter, Schmidt, & Rauschenberger, 1977). There is no compelling research literature or theory to suggest that cognitive tests should be used differently for different groups. (p. 18)

The SIOP position has been sharply criticized as being too broad. Linn (1994), for example, acknowledged the findings of previous research in this area but described several artifacts that could account for these findings:

> The most common finding of overprediction for African Americans or Hispanics . . . is consistent with a conclusion that predictive bias is either nonexistent or actually in favor of the minority group. There are, however, artifacts that could produce the overprediction.

In particular, less than perfect reliability of the predictor, specification error (e.g., the exclusion of an important predictor from the equation), and differential selectivity for the two groups being compared can yield an artifactual overprediction for the group with lower scores on the test. (p. 365)

Furthermore, Linn (1994) pointed to the research of Houston and Novick (1987), who found test bias against African Americans using the regression model, and Dunbar and Novick (1988) and Linn (1982), who found bias against women, also using regression models. Linn (1994) and other critics of the position of Schmidt (1988) and the SIOP principles (e.g., Camara & Brown, 1995; Messick, 1989, 1995a) condone the use of the regression model for evaluating test bias. However, they cautioned against overgeneralizing the conclusions of such analyses and instead suggested consideration of threats to the internal validity of the model (Rubin, 1988). These critics asserted that, although the regression model is useful, defining test validity strictly in terms of predictive equations is inadequate. Messick (1989, 1995a), for example, has long argued that an evidential basis of validity is insufficient support for test use. Rather, the intended and unintended consequences of test use and interpretation must be considered. As described by Camara and Brown (1995),

in personnel selection, the utility of the criterion-related model must be re-examined, especially considering potential contamination by irrelevant modifiers of test performance. . . . Personnel assessment may lead to . . . negative consequences when its use results in a less diverse workforce, a reluctance to seek employment or complete the necessary steps in the screening process by particular individuals or groups, or when rigid or inappropriate cut scores hamper the selection of the best employees. (pp. 6–7)

Thus, evaluating the fairness of employment tests is not reducible to the predictive validity model. In theory, the social and psychometric aspects of employment testing can be separated (Gottfredson, 1994; Schmidt, 1988); however, in the use and evaluation of employment tests, they are inseparable.

Evaluating DIF

The predictive validity model is a valuable tool for contributing information about the fairness of scores obtained from administrations of cognitive tests to diverse groups of individuals. The area of DIF involves statistical evaluation of the items composing employment tests. These evaluations are useful in the development of employment tests for screening out potentially biased items or for removing items that exhibit bias.

Although there are a variety of methods for evaluating DIF (Holland & Wainer, 1993; Rogers & Swaminathan, 1993), the Mantel–Haenszel (MH) procedure (Dorans & Holland, 1993; Holland & Thayer 1988) is the most popular in practice and provides a good conceptual foundation for understanding other methods. The MH statistic is an extension of the chi-square test of independence between variables (Mantel & Haenszel, 1959). The MH test extends the traditional two-way chi-square test to the three-way situation. In terms of evaluating DIF, the MH procedure takes the form of a 3-D ($2 \times 2 \times M$) contingency table: two groups × two levels of item response (correct or incorrect) × M score levels of the matching variable. The null hypothesis evaluated using the MH procedure is that the odds of answering the item correctly at any given level of the matching variable (i.e., M) is the same in both (minority and nonminority) groups. If one group exhibits a higher probability (i.e., better odds) of answering the item correctly than the other group, the item is considered to be functioning differentially with respect to the groups. In more traditional terminology, the item is considered to be biased against the group illustrating the lower probability of success on the item. The MH procedure is appropriate only for evaluating items that are scored right or wrong, such as multiple-choice items. For items scored in a polytomous fashion, DIF detection procedures based on logistic regression (Swaminathan & Rogers, 1990) appear the most promising.

Matching examinees across groups is the key feature for determining DIF. Because of the lack of valid external criteria, the total score on the test is most often used as the matching variable. MH procedures typically use raw test scores as the matching variable. Procedures based on item response theory match examinees according to their estimated position on the underlying latent variable. Although these matching procedures go a long way toward distinguishing between item bias and group differences, if the test as a whole is biased, matching on the total test score or theta will obfuscate the detection of bias.

Emerging issues in evaluating DIF are evaluating groups of items simultaneously (so-called "testlet-DIF"; Wainer, Sireci, & Thissen, 1991) or evaluating bias at the level of total test scores (Shealy & Stout, 1993). These studies can lead to the detection of DIF aggregation (i.e., bias against a particular group that is not observable at the item level but is detected when a group of items are analyzed simultaneously) or DIF cancellation (i.e., items exhibit DIF at the item level, but when investigated at the test or testlet level, the counterbalancing effects of other items "cancel" the DIF effect). These areas offer promise for contributing to evaluations of the fairness of employment tests. Unfortunately, applications of these procedures to employment testing have lagged far behind those in educational testing.

Banding Methods for Promoting Workforce Diversity

Even after no evidence of test bias is found, adverse impact from employment tests may result. This situation can lead to criticisms that the selection process did not consider the goal of workforce diversity. These issues were discussed previously relative to within-groups norming. In this section we describe a newer method of score adjustment called *banding*, which aims to balance the social goal of reducing adverse impact and the measurement goal of maximizing selection utility.

Banding methods for personnel selection (Cascio et al., 1991; Zedeck et al., 1995) operate from the premise that observed test scores contain measurement error and that applicants with different observed test scores may actually have similar "true" scores. Given this premise, estimates of measurement error are used to create test score "bands" within which applicants are considered to be equal. Using this approach, more minority applicants are considered "equivalent" to nonminority applicants, compared with the top-down method. Additionally, banding methods typically result in smaller test score differences between minority and nonminority applicants selected for employment, than would result from using within-groups norming.

The construction of test score bands is generally a function of the measurement precision of the test, as gauged by the standard error of measurement. The standard error of measurement is an index of the average amount of error contained in a given test score. It historically has been proposed as a means for creating an interval around an examinee's observed test score to estimate his or her true score given measurement error (Anastasi, 1988; Harvill, 1991; Nunnally, 1978). The standard error of measurement is calculated by multiplying the standard deviation of the test scores by the square root of 1 minus the estimated reliability of the test scores ($SEM = s_x \sqrt{1 - r_{xx}}$. The standard error of measurement is multiplied by $\sqrt{2}$ to compute the standard error of difference, which is used to create the width of a test score band. The standard error of difference is an index of statistically significant difference (reliable difference in the Cascio et al., 1991, terminology) between test scores. The standard error of difference was first proposed by Gulliksen (1950) for determining reasonable limits for the difference between the true scores of two individuals.

The creation of test score bands depends on the amount of difference considered statistically significant to those making the selection decisions (analogous to selection of a Type I error level). For example, if it is decided that errors in identifying statistically significant test scores will be tolerated no more than 5% of the time, the bandwidth is created by multiplying 1.96 (the z score corresponding to an alpha level of .05) by the standard error of difference. If errors attributable to chance in distinguishing statistically significant test scores can be tolerated 10% of the time, then the bandwidth is created by multiplying 1.64 and the standard error of difference, and so on. A test score band is created by subtracting the bandwidth from the highest observed score on the test.

The banding process is best understood by example. Suppose the scores for an employment test have an estimated reliability of .90 and a standard deviation of 10. The standard error of measurement for these scores would be 3.16, and the standard error of difference would be 4.47. Assuming a risk level (an alpha level of .05), the bandwidth for this test would be 8.76 (1.96 × 4.47) test score points. Suppose further that the highest score on the test was 98 (on a scale ranging from 0 to 100). Given these hypothetical data, the test score band would range from 89.24 to 98. The highest score defines the top of the band, and the bottom of the band is defined by subtracting the bandwidth from the highest score. In this scenario, all scores between 90 and 98 (assuming only integer scores) would be considered equivalent (similar to classroom scores between 90 and 100 given a grade of A; Murphy & Myors, 1995; Zedeck et al., 1995). Adverse impact is reduced if, using the banding procedure, lower scoring minorities within the band are selected who would not have been selected in a strict top-down procedure. Sometimes, individuals are randomly selected within bands. In some circumstances, individuals could be selected from within a score band on the basis of other factors.

Theoretically, there are four different methods for selecting applicants using test score bands. These four methods differ with respect to whether the banding method is "fixed" or "sliding" and whether selection of applicants within the band is random or "diversity based" (Cascio et al., 1991). The random selection method selects candidates at random within a band, whereas the diversity-based method selects proportions of candidates within a band in proportion to the representation of minority and nonminority applicants in the total pool. (The selection of minority and nonminority candidates within a band is generally performed in top-down fashion.) Random selection of applicants within a band has not been suggested for practical use because it may not typically yield reduction in adverse impact (Cascio et al., 1991); thus, only fixed and sliding bands are used for diversity-based selection.

In fixed banding, the test score band for selecting applicants is held constant until selection decisions exhaust all applicants within a band. If additional selections are necessary, a new band is created by subtracting the bandwidth from the next available highest score. In the sliding band method, after the highest scoring candidate is selected, a new band is created using the next available highest score as the top of the band (i.e., the top of the band slides down to the new highest score).

Cascio et al. (1991) provided a comprehensive comparison of the four banding, top-down, and within-groups norming procedures. These comparisons were based on results from a firefighter selection test administered to 3,377 applicants in a large urban city. Their overall finding was that the diversity-based sliding band method was most effective for achieving workforce diversity and led to score differences between selected minority and nonminority applicants that were far lower than those obtained using within-groups norming. Their results also indicated that fixed and sliding banding procedures varied substantially depending on the chosen Type I error level, banding method, and selection ratio. These findings suggest that users of banding methods consider different options in creating bandwidths and in using fixed or sliding bands. Methods that result in smaller differences in test scores between the lowest scoring minority applicant selected and the lowest scoring nonminority applicant selected, and that achieve gains in reducing adverse impact, are preferable.

Although the use of banding methods purports to have advantages over top-down and within-groups norming methods, they have been sharply criticized on both statistical and logical grounds (Schmidt, 1991; Schmidt & Hunter, 1995). These criticisms correctly point out that the logic of banding methods are contrary to their implementation; specifically, it is contradictory to consider applicants within a band equivalent and then to use a top-down method within a band. The logic of considering applicants within a band equivalent, while the lowest scorer within the band is considered significantly different from the highest scorer outside the band, also has been criticized. A third criticism involves the absence of statistical theory for using statistical tests on individual scores (or, more specifically, on individual true scores).

Schmidt (1991), Schmidt and Hunter (1995), and Gottfredson (1994) argued strongly against the use of banding methods because of the reduction of the optimal utility of the selection model and because of concerns about reverse discrimination. These arguments have not undermined acceptance of banding procedures. The primary reason for the popularity of banding procedures is that they appear to reduce adverse impact in a manner that minimizes discrepancies between the performance of selected minority and nonminority applicants. For example, in the analyses reported by Cascio et al. (1991), for a selection ratio (the percentage of applicants hired) of 2.5% and using an alpha level of .13, complete representation of the proportion of minority groups in the applicant pool was achieved in the selected group of examinees, all of whom scored at or above the 92nd percentile in the total population of applicants. Obviously, the ability to achieve workforce diversity while simultaneously selecting only the top 8% of the applicant pool is an attractive choice for employers. The popularity of banding methods is evident by their endorsement in the literature (Murphy & Myors, 1995; Sackett & Wilk, 1994; Scientific Affairs Committee, 1994). However, the utility of banding is undermined when it results in substantial score differences between selected minority and nonminority applicants (Gottfredson, 1994).

The debate between Cascio and colleagues on one hand and Schmidt and colleagues on the other includes questions about the representativeness of the data presented by Cascio et al. (1991; see Schmidt, 1991; Zedeck et al., 1995; Schmidt & Hunter, 1995). Although Zedeck et al. presented new data illustrating the representativeness of the original data used to support the banding methodology, unfortunately, they did not apply banding methods to the newer data sets, and so the utility of banding procedures needs continued research.

Although we acknowledge the attractive features of banding, there are some other limitations of this methodology that are worth noting. Foremost is the question of a true ceiling effect on a selection test. If the highest scorer achieves a perfect score, the test score may not accurately gauge the examinee's predicted performance. The logic of drawing a confidence interval around a perfect score does not apply, and so a perfect score would be inappropriate for forming the top of a score band. A related issue was touched on by Cascio et al. (1991), who indicated that errors of measurement are not identical across the entire score distribution. Future research in banding procedures needs to explore the use of conditional standard errors of measurement, that is, the errors of measurement at specific score intervals. Straightforward procedures for estimating conditional standard errors of measurement are available within a classical testing paradigm (Kolen, Hanson, & Brennan, 1992; Livingston, 1982; Lord, 1957), and if item response theory models are used in the development of employment tests, the conditional standard error of measurement at any particular score is easily obtainable (Hambleton, Swaminathan, & Rogers, 1991).

Another concern regarding banding methods is the type of reliability coefficient used. As is well known (e.g., Anastasi, 1988), an internal consistency coefficient is not appropriate for calculating the reliability (or standard error of measurement) of a test comprising highly heterogeneous content areas or measuring diverse skills or that is concerned with the stability of scores over time.

Ancillary Issues

Tacit Knowledge as a Predictor of Job Performance

Tests of general cognitive ability (e.g., the GATB) are among the most prominent employment measures used across different job settings. As illustrated earlier, these methods also are controversial because they exhibit large score differences between minority and nonminority groups. A criticism against relying heavily on tests measuring general cognitive abilities for predicting job performance is that these tests largely depend on verbal ability, which may not be critical for job success (McClelland, 1973). It has been suggested that employment test batteries include measures of practical intelligence or tacit knowledge as well as measures of general cognitive ability (Sternberg, 1994; Sternberg, Wagner, Williams, & Horvath, 1995). The term *tacit knowledge* refers to knowledge that is goal oriented, acquired with little or no help from others, and necessary for adapting to one's own environment. Recent research, summarized by Sternberg et al. (1995), illustrates that measures of tacit knowledge improve the prediction of job performance above and beyond that provided by measures of general cognitive ability.

Measuring tacit knowledge in employment testing emphasizes that the context within which a person functions (i.e., the job environment) must be considered when evaluating potential performance. Tests of general cognitive ability are criticized as being inadequate for measuring "person–context interaction" (Sternberg, 1994). Sternberg et al. (1995) pointed out that even the highest estimates of the predictive validity of general cognitive abilities tests account for only about 25% of the variance of job performance measures.

Although extensive research has evaluated comparing measures of tacit knowledge with measures of general cognitive ability, little research has been done to determine whether tacit knowledge tests reduce adverse impact. Eddy (1988) and Sternberg et al. (1995) provided preliminary evidence that minorities and nonminorities do not differ significantly on measures of tacit knowledge. However, this research is in its infancy, and no data have been presented on the performance of individuals with disabilities on these tests.

Personality Testing

In addition to measures of cognitive ability, personality tests also have been championed as valid predictors of job performance (Barrick & Mount, 1991; Cascio, 1995; Goldberg, 1994; Tett, Jackson, & Rothstein, 1991). Research in this area has focused on the predictive validity of the "Big Five" dimensions of personality (i.e., extraversion, agreeableness, conscientiousness, emotional stability, and openness to experience) and their related traits. In particular, the variables of conscientiousness (Barrick & Mount, 1991) and diligence (Dunnette, 1983; Fleishman, Quaintance, & Broedling, 1984) have been cited as being especially valid predictors of job performance. As summarized by Goldberg (1994), cognitive ability is not the only feature critical for success on the job: "There is widespread agreement that noncognitive factors are heavily implicated in many, if not most, aspects of job-related activities. Intellectually able individuals falter on the job when their personality traits are not congruent with task requirements" (p. 257).

Although claims have been made that personality variables used in personnel selection do not produce adverse impact for minorities and other groups (Goldberg, 1994; R. Hogan, 1991), continued research in this area suggests that these findings are equivocal. For example, some personality attributes, such as conformity, are more prevalent in some cultures. Camara (1992) and Ramos (1992) noted that Hispanics tend to score higher on need for approval and conventionality measures, which may impede predictions of their job performance. A related concern is that people having strong religious beliefs may appear "pathological" on some personality screening measures (Lilienfeld, Allinger, & Mitchell, 1995).

A particular area of controversy in the use of personality measures in employment testing is integrity (honesty) testing. Integrity tests attempt to measure counterproductivity or dishonesty and have been shown to be valid predictors of job performance in some cases (Ones, Viswesvaran, & Schmidt, 1995; Sackett, Burris, & Callahan, 1989). However, these tests have been criticized for several reasons, including the potential for applying inappropriate labels to prospective employees (i.e., "dishonest"), high false-positive rates (i.e., honest people being categorized as dishonest), susceptibility to "fakability," and a lack of adequate definition of the integrity construct (Camara & Schneider, 1994, 1995). To our knowledge, the bias of these tests against minorities and other groups has not yet been investigated. However, Lilienfeld et al. (1995) pointed out that these tests may be unfair to individuals with a criminal past who no longer engage in criminal activities (especially if they are truthful about their past behaviors).

Biodata

The use of biodata in employment testing has a long history (e.g., Goldsmith, 1922; Owens, 1976). These data are descriptions of an individuals' life history, such as accomplishments or involvement in activities such as sports or civics. The logic underlying the use of biodata in personnel selection is that a person's experiences influence his or her future behavior; thus, the experiences are predictive of such behavior (Mael, 1994). The effect of biodata on adverse impact has not been extensively studied; however, Camara (1992) suggested that these data have the potential to reduce adverse impact with respect to some minority groups, and Reilly and Chao (1982) found biodata to be almost as valid as cognitive tests for predicting job performance. On the other hand, Mael pointed out that biodata may discriminate against victims of difficult life situations such as those with disabilities. Biodata also may discriminate against younger people. Scoring biodata for the purposes of prediction raises additional problems. Mumford and Stokes (1992) suggested that the differential scoring of biodata for men and women may be required for predictive validity to hold, but Sackett and Wilk

(1994) noted that this practice would violate the Civil Rights Act of 1991.

Suggestions for Promoting Equity in Employment Testing

In this chapter we introduced a myriad of equity issues in employment testing. Although a comprehensive discussion of these issues is beyond the scope of this chapter, our review of the research provides several suggestions for promoting equity in employment testing.

First, there is much that users and developers of employment tests can do to build fairness into a personnel selection system. When tests for specific jobs are used, a comprehensive job analysis is warranted to ensure that the critical features of the job are represented in the test specifications and extraneous content is not included. Content validity analyses using subject matter experts, and sensitivity reviews using trained sensitivity reviewers, should be used to make sure that the test content represents the test specifications and is appropriate for all examinees. When commercially available tests are selected, it must be ensured that these tests are relevant to the knowledge, skills, and abilities considered to be essential for job performance.

Second, employment test developers should incorporate procedures for evaluating DIF at the item tryout stage. By eliminating items or test components that exhibit bias against certain groups, the probability of observing bias in final test scores will be reduced.

Third, users of employment tests should consider the wide variety of measures that are available for predicting performance and should use multiple measures whenever possible. In addition to tests of general cognitive ability, job-related tests of cognitive skills, PA tests, personality tests, vocational inventories, and biodata have been shown to be valid predictors of performance for certain jobs. The ideal combination of multiple measures for particular jobs should increase selection utility and minimize adverse impact. Relying solely on general cognitive ability tests that are predominantly verbal is generally not recommended unless verbal skills are demonstrated to be a critical job requirement.

Fourth, if criterion-related validation is used, good criteria must be used. Although supervisor ratings may well be valid as well as expedient, they also are subject to various biases. Indeed, it is possible that even the use of objective criteria may adversely affect members of some groups and should be carefully studied for fairness.

Fifth, evaluation of the validity of the selection system should be continuous. This ongoing evaluation should include consideration of the consequences of the selection system, especially in relation to adverse impact.

Sixth, if adverse impact is observed, methods for adjusting test scores should be considered. Banding methods should be investigated. Within-groups norming methods are not currently recommended. The investigation of banding methods should evaluate different banding options, such as the choice of the alpha level used to define the bandwidth and the use of conditional versus average standard errors of measurement. Those options that minimize score differences between selected employees and different groups, whereas simultaneously reducing adverse impact between these groups, are preferable.

Seventh, any selection system should incorporate accommodations for testing linguistic minorities. Such accommodations are currently mandated for people with disabilities. Aspects of the testing process that are not construct relevant but impede performance on the examination for these groups must be eliminated. Accommodations that are not likely to alter the construct measured should be provided. In some cases, alternative selection systems, such as individualized testing, should be provided.

Finally, the utility of a selection system can be greatly improved by factors outside the testing context. In particular, the recruitment of competitive minorities, women, and individuals with disabilities into the applicant pool will increase workforce diversity and organizational productivity (Rudner, 1992).

References

Albemarle Paper Co. v. Moody, 422 U.S. 405 (1975).

Americans With Disabilities Act of 1990, 42 U.S.C. § 12101 et seq (1990).

Anastasi, A. (1988). *Psychological testing* (6th ed.). New York: Macmillan.

Angoff, W. H. (1993). Perspectives on differential item functioning methodology. In P. W. Holland & H. Wainer (Eds.), *Differential item functioning* (pp. 3–23). Hillsdale, NJ: Erlbaum.

Angoff, W. H., & Cook, L. L. (1988). *Equating the scores of the Prueba de Aptitud Academica and the Scholastic Aptitude Test* (Rep. No. 88-2). New York: College Entrance Examination Board.

Arvey, R. D., Nutting, S. M., & Landon, T. E. (1992). Validation strategies for physical ability testing in police and fire settings. *Public Personnel Management, 21,* 301–312.

Barrick, M. R., & Mount, M. K. (1991). The big five personality dimensions and job performance: A meta-analysis. *Personnel Psychology, 44,* 1–26.

Bolick, C. (1988). Legal and policy aspects of testing. *Journal of Vocational Behavior, 33*, 320–330.

Braun, H., Ragosta, M., & Kaplan, B. A. (1988). Predictive validity. In W. W. Willingham, M. Ragosta, R. E. Bennett, H. Braun, D. A. Rock, & D. E. Powers (Eds.), *Testing handicapped people* (pp. 109–132). Needham Heights, MA: Allyn & Bacon.

Brogden, H. E. (1949). When testing pays off. *Personnel Psychology, 2*, 171–183.

Camara, W. J. (1992). Fairness and fair use in employment testing: A matter of perspective. In K. F. Geisinger (Ed.), *Psychological testing of Hispanics* (pp. 215–231). Washington, DC: American Psychological Association.

Camara, W. J., & Brown, D. C. (1995). Educational and employment testing: Changing concepts in measurement and policy. *Educational Measurement: Issues and Practice, 14*, 5–11.

Camara, W. J., & Schneider, D. L. (1994). Integrity tests: Facts and unresolved issues. *American Psychologist, 49*, 112–119.

Camara, W. J., & Schneider, D. L. (1995). Questions of construct breadth and openness of research in integrity testing. *American Psychologist, 50*, 459–460.

Campbell, J. P. (1994). Alternative models of job performance and their implications for selection and classification. In M. G. Rumsey, C. B. Walker, & J. H. Harris (Eds.), *Personnel selection and classification* (pp. 35–51), Hillsdale, NJ: Erlbaum.

Cascio, W. F. (1995). Wither industrial and organizational psychology in a changing world of work? *American Psychologist, 50*, 928–939.

Cascio, W. F., Outtz, J., Zedeck, S., & Goldstein, I. L. (1991). Statistical implications of six methods of test score use in personnel selection. *Human Performance, 4*, 233–264.

Chance v. Board of Examiners, 330 F. Supp. 203 (S.D. N.Y. 1991), *aff'd*, 458 F.2d 1167 (2nd cir. 1971).

Civil Rights Act of 1991, 42 U.S.C.S. § 200e-2(a)(1) (1998).

Cleary, T. A. (1968). Test bias: Prediction of grades of Negro and White students in integrated colleges. *Journal of Educational Measurement, 5*, 115–124.

Cole, N. S., & Moss, P. A. (1989). Bias in test use. In R. Linn (Ed.), *Educational measurement* (3rd ed., pp. 201–219). Washington, DC: American Council on Education.

Colton, D. A., Kane, M. T., Kingsbury, C., & Estes, C. A. (1991). A strategy for examining the validity of job analysis data. *Journal of Educational Measurement, 28*, 283–294.

Crocker, L. M., Miller, D., & Franks, E. A. (1989). Quantitative methods for assessing the fit between test and curriculum. *Applied Measurement in Education, 2*, 179–194.

Cronbach, L. J. (1976). Equity in selection: Where psychometrics and philosophy meet. *Journal of Educational Measurement, 13*, 31–41.

Cronbach, L. J. (1988). Five perspectives on the validity argument. In H. Wainer & H. I. Braun (Eds.), *Test validity* (pp. 3–17). Hillsdale, NJ: Erlbaum.

Cronbach, L. J., & Gleser, G. (1957). *Psychological tests and personnel decisions.* Urbana: University of Illinois Press.

Denning, D. L. (1984, August). *Applying the Hogan model of physical performance of occupational tasks.* Paper presented at the 92nd Annual Convention of the American Psychological Association, Toronto, Ontario, Canada.

Donlon, T. F. (1992). Legal issues in the educational testing of Hispanics. In K. F. Geisinger (Ed.), *Psychological testing of Hispanics* (pp. 55–78), Washington, DC: American Psychological Association.

Doolittle, A. E., & Cleary, T. A. (1987). Gender-based differential item performance in mathematics achievement items. *Journal of Educational Measurement, 24*, 157–166.

Dorans, N. J., & Holland, P. W. (1993). DIF detection and description: Mantel-Haenszel and standardization. In P. W. Holland & H. Wainer (Eds.), *Differential item functioning* (pp. 35–66). Hillsdale, NJ: Erlbaum.

Dunbar, S. B., & Novick, M. R. (1988). On predicting success in training for men and women: Examples from Marine Corps clerical specialties. *Journal of Applied Psychology, 73*, 545–550.

Dunnette, M. D. (1983). Aptitudes, abilities, and skills. In M. D. Dunnette (Ed.), *Handbook of industrial and organizational psychology* (pp. 473–520). New York: Wiley.

Eddy, A. S. (1988). *The relationship between the Tacit Knowledge Inventory for Managers and the Armed Services Vocational Aptitude Battery.* Unpublished master's thesis, St. Mary's University, San Antonio, TX.

Ellis, B. B. (1989). Differential item functioning: Implications for test translations. *Journal of Applied Psychology, 74*, 912–920.

Equal Employment Opportunities Commission, U.S. Civil Service Commission, U.S. Department of Labor, and U.S. Department of Justice. (1978). Uniform guidelines on employee selection procedures. *Federal Register, 43*, 38290–38309.

Eyde, L. D., Nester, M. A., Heaton, S. M., & Nelson, A. V. (1994). *Guide for administering written employment examinations to persons with disabilities* (Publication No. PRDC-94-11). Washington, D.C.: U.S. Office of Personnel Management, Personnel Research and Development Center.

Fleishman, E. A. (1988). Some new frontiers in personnel selection research. *Personnel Psychology, 41*, 679–697.

Fleishman, E., Quaintance, M., & Broedling, L. A. (1984). *Taxonomies of human performance: The description of human tasks.* New York: Academic Press.

Fullilove v. Klutznick, 448 U.S. S. Ct. (1980).

Geisinger, K. F. (1992a). Fairness and selected psychometric issues in the psychological testing of Hispanics. In K. F. Geisinger (Ed.), *Psychological testing of Hispanics* (pp. 17–42). Washington, DC: American Psychological Association.

Geisinger, K. F. (1992b). The metamorphosis in test validity. *Educational Psychologist, 27*, 197–222.

Geisinger, K. F. (1994a). Cross-cultural normative assessment: Translation and adaptation issues influencing the normative interpretation of assessment instruments. *Psychological Assessment, 6*, 304–312.

Geisinger, K. F. (1994b). Psychometric issues in testing students with disabilities. *Applied Measurement in Education, 7*, 121–140.

Geisinger, K. F. (1996, September). *The testing of Hispanics in civil service settings.* Paper presented at the Personnel Testing Council of Metropolitan Washington, Washington, DC.

Goldberg, L. R. (1994). Basic research on personality structure: Implications of the emerging consensus for applications to selection and classification. In M. G. Rumsey, C. B. Walker, & J. H. Harris (Eds.), *Personnel selection and classification* (pp. 247–259), Hillsdale, NJ: Erlbaum.

Goldsmith, D. B. (1922). The use of the Personal History Blank as a salesmanship test. *Journal of Applied Psychology, 6*, 149–155.

Gottfredson, L. S. (1994). The science and politics of race norming. *American Psychologist, 49*, 955–963.

Griggs v. Duke Power Co., 401 U.S. 424 (1971).

Guion, R. M. (1977). Content validity: The source of my discontent. *Applied Psychological Measurement, 1,* 1–10.

Guion, R. M. (1995). Commentary on values and standards in performance assessment. *Educational Measurement: Issues and Practice, 14,* 25–27.

Gulliksen, H. (1950). *Theory of mental tests.* New York: Wiley.

Hambleton, R. K. (1984). Validating the test score. In R. A. Berk (Ed.), *A guide to criterion-referenced test construction* (pp. 199–230). Baltimore: Johns Hopkins University Press.

Hambleton, R. K. (1993). Translating achievement tests for use in cross-national studies. *European Journal of Psychological Assessment, 9,* 57–68.

Hambleton, R. K. (1994). Guidelines for adapting educational and psychological tests: A progress report. *European Journal of Psychological Assessment, 10,* 229–244.

Hambleton, R. K., Swaminathan, H., & Rogers, H. J. (1991). *Fundamentals of item response theory.* Newbury Park, CA: Sage.

Hartigan, J. A., & Wigdor, A. K. (Eds.). (1989). *Fairness in employment testing: Validity generalization, minority issues, and the General Aptitude Test Battery.* Washington, DC: National Academy Press.

Harvill, L. M. (1991). Standard error of measurement. *Educational Measurement: Issues and Practice, 10,* 33–41.

Hobson v. Hanson, F. Supp. 401 (D.D.C., 1967).

Hogan, J. (1991). Structure of physical performance in occupational tasks. *Journal of Applied Psychology, 76,* 495–507.

Hogan, J. (1994). Theoretical and applied developments in models of individual differences: Physical abilities. In M. G. Rumsey, C. B. Walker, & J. H. Harris (Eds.), *Personnel selection and classification* (pp. 233–259), Hillsdale, NJ: Erlbaum.

Hogan, J., & Quigley, A. M. (1986). Physical standards for employment and the courts. *American Psychologist, 41,* 1193–1217.

Hogan, R. (1991). Personality and personality measurement. In M. D. Dunnette & L. M. Hough (Eds.), *Handbook of industrial and organizational psychology* (2nd ed., pp. 873–919). Palo Alto, CA: Consulting Psychologists Press.

Holland, P. W., & Thayer, D. T. (1988). Differential item functioning and the Mantel-Haenszel procedure. In H. Wainer & H. I. Braun (Eds.), *Test validity* (pp. 129–145). Hillsdale, NJ: Erlbaum.

Holland, P. W., & Wainer, H. (Eds.). (1993). *Differential item functioning.* Hillsdale, NJ: Erlbaum.

Houston, W. M., & Novick, M. R. (1987). Race-based differential prediction in Air Force technical training programs. *Journal of Educational Measurement, 24,* 309–320.

Hunter, J. E., & Schmidt, F. L. (1991). Meta-analysis. In R. K. Hambleton & J. N. Zall (Eds.), *Advances in educational and psychological testing* (pp. 157–183). Norwell, MA: Kluwer Academic.

Hunter, J. E., Schmidt, F. L., & Rauschenberger, J. M. (1977). Fairness of psychological tests: Implications of four definitions for selection utility and minority hiring. *Journal of Applied Psychology, 62,* 245–260.

Jensen, A. R. (1974). How biased are culture-loaded tests? *Genetic Psychology Monographs, 90,* 185–244.

Jensen, A. R. (1980). *Bias in mental testing.* New York: Free Press.

Joint Committee on Testing Practices. (1988). *Code of fair testing practices in education.* Washington, DC: American Psychological Association.

Klimoski, R., & Palmer, S. N. (1994). The ADA and the hiring process in organizations. In S. M. Bruyere & J. O'Keeffe (Eds.), *Implications of the Americans With*

Disabilities Act for psychology (pp. 37–84). Washington, DC: American Psychological Association.

Kolen, M. J., Hanson, B. A., & Brennan, R. L. (1992). Conditional standard errors of measurement for scale scores. *Journal of Educational Measurement, 29,* 285–307.

Lilienfeld, S. O., Allinger, G., & Mitchell, K. (1995). Why integrity testing remains controversial. *American Psychologist, 50,* 457–458.

Linn, R. L. (1982). Ability testing: Individual differences, prediction and differential prediction. In A. K. Wigdor & W. R. Garner (Eds.), *Ability testing: Uses, consequences, and controversies: II* (pp. 335–388). Washington, DC: National Academy Press.

Linn, R. L. (1994). Fair test use: Research and policy. In M. G. Rumsey, C. B. Walker, & J. H. Harris (Eds.), *Personnel selection and classification* (pp. 363–375), Hillsdale, NJ: Erlbaum.

Livingston, S. A. (1982). Estimation of the conditional standard error of measurement for stratified tests. *Journal of Educational Measurement, 19,* 135–138.

Lord, F. M. (1957). Do tests of the same length have the same standard error of measurement? *Educational and Psychological Measurement, 17,* 510–521.

Mael, F. A. (1994). If past behavior really predicts future, so should biodata's. In M. G. Rumsey, C. B. Walker, & J. H. Harris (Eds.), *Personnel selection and classification* (pp. 273–291). Hillsdale, NJ: Erlbaum.

Mantel, N., & Haenszel, W. (1959). Statistical aspects of the analysis of data from retrospective studies of disease. *Journal of the National Cancer Institute, 22,* 719–748.

Martin v. Wilks, 490. U.S. S. Ct. 755 (1989).

Martin, M. R., & Berberoglu, G. (1991). Initial efforts in construct validation for the Turkish Marlowe-Crowne Social Desirability Scale. In B. Thompson (Ed.), *Advances in educational research: Substantive findings, methodological developments* (pp. 25–36). Greenwich, CT: JAI Press.

McClelland, D. C. (1973). Testing for competence rather than for intelligence. *American Psychologist, 28,* 1–14.

McKinney, W. R., & Collins, J. R. (1991). The impact on utility, race, and gender using three standard methods of scoring selection examinations. *Public Personnel Management, 20,* 145–169.

Messick, S. (1989). Validity. In R. Linn (Ed.), *Educational measurement* (3rd ed., pp. 13–103). Washington, DC: American Council on Education.

Messick, S. (1995a). Standards of validity and the validity of standards in performance assessment. *Educational Measurement: Issues and Practice, 14,* 5–8.

Messick, S. (1995b). Validation of inferences from persons' responses and performances as scientific inquiry into score meaning. *American Psychologist, 50,* 741–749.

Millsap, R. E., & Everson, H. T. (1993). Methodology review: Statistical approaches for assessing measurement bias. *Applied Psychological Measurement, 17,* 297–334.

Mounty, J. L. (1990). Testing deaf individuals: Equity in test conditions and test format in D. Ellis (Ed.), *In tune with the future: Selected proceedings of the 1990 AHSSPPE Conference* (pp. 13–18). Columbus, OH: Association on Handicapped Student Service Programs in Postsecondary Education.

Mumford, M. D., & Stokes, G. S. (1992). Developmental determinants of individual action: Theory and practice in the application of background data. In M. D. Dunnette & L. M. Hough (Eds.), *Handbook of industrial and organizational psychology* (2nd ed., pp. 61–138). Palo Alto, CA: Consulting Psychologists Press.

Murphy, K. R., & Myors, B. (1995). Evaluating the logical critique of banding. *Human Performance, 8,* 191–201.

Nester, M. A. (1994). Psychometric testing and reasonable accommodation for persons with disabilities. In S. M. Bruyere & J. O'Keeffe (Eds.), *Implications of the Americans With Disabilities Act for Psychology* (pp. 25–36). Washington, DC: American Psychological Association.

Nunnally, J. C. (1978). *Psychometric theory.* New York: McGraw-Hill.

Olmedo, E. L. (1981). Testing linguistic minorities. *American Psychologist, 36,* 1078–1085.

Ones, D. S., Viswesvaran, C., & Schmidt, F. L. (1995). Integrity tests: Overlooked facts, resolved issues, and remaining questions. *American Psychologist, 50,* 456–457.

Owens, W. A. (1976). Background data. In M. D. Dunnette (Ed.), *Handbook of industrial and organizational psychology* (pp. 609–644). Chicago: Rand McNally.

Phillips, S. E. (1994). High-stakes testing accommodations: Validity versus disabled rights. *Applied Measurement in Education, 7,* 93–120.

Prieto, A. J. (1992). A method for translation of instruments to other languages. *Adult Education Quarterly, 43,* 1–14.

Ramos, R. A. (1981). Employment battery performance of Hispanic as a function of English or Spanish test instructions. *Journal of Applied Psychology, 66,* 291–295.

Ramos, R. A. (1992). Testing and assessment of Hispanics for occupational and management positions: A developmental needs analysis. In K. F. Geisinger (Ed.), *Psychological testing of Hispanics* (pp. 173–193), Washington, DC: American Psychological Association.

Ramsey, P. A. (1993). Sensitivity review: The ETS experience as a case study. In P. W. Holland & H. Wainer (Eds.), *Differential item functioning* (pp. 367–388). Hillsdale, NJ: Erlbaum.

Reilly, R. R., & Chao, G. T. (1982). Validity and fairness of some alternative employee selection procedures. *Personnel Psychology, 35,* 11–62.

Rivera v. City of Wichita Falls, 665 F.2d 531 (1982).

Rock, D. A., Bennett, R. E., & Jirele, T. (1988). Factor structure of the Graduate Record Examination's General Test in handicapped and nonhandicapped groups. *Journal of Applied Psychology, 73,* 382–392.

Rock, D. A., Bennett, R. E., & Kaplan, B. A. (1987). Internal construct validity of a college admissions test across handicapped and nonhandicapped groups. *Educational and Psychological Measurement, 47,* 193–205.

Roe, R. A., & Greuter, M. A. M. (1991). Developments in personnel selection methodology. In R. K. Hambleton & J. N. Zall (Eds.), *Advances in educational and psychological testing* (pp. 187–226). Norwell, MA: Kluwer Academic.

Rogers, H. J., & Swaminathan, H. (1993). A comparison of the logistic regression and Mantel-Haenszel procedures for detecting differential item functioning. *Applied Psychological Measurement, 17,* 105–116.

Rubin, D. B. (1988). Discussion. In H. Wainer & H. I. Braun (Eds.), *Test validity* (pp. 241–256). Hillsdale, NJ: Erlbaum.

Rudner, L. M. (1992). Pre-employment testing and employee productivity. *Public Personnel Management, 21,* 133–150.

Sackett, P. R., Burris, L. R., & Callahan, C. (1989). Integrity testing for personnel selection: An update. *Personnel Psychology, 37,* 491–529.

Sackett, P. R., & Wilk, S. L. (1994). Within-group norming and other forms of score adjustment in preemployment testing. *Amerian Psychologist, 49,* 929–954.

Scarpati, S. (1991). Current perspectives in the assessment of the handicapped. In

R. K. Hambleton & J. N. Zall (Eds.), *Advances in educational and psychological testing* (pp. 251–276). Norwell, MA: Kluwer Academic.

Schmidt, F. L. (1988). The problem of group differences in ability test scores in employment selection. *Journal of Vocational Behavior, 33,* 272–292.

Schmidt, F. L. (1991). Why all banding procedures are logically flawed. *Human Performance, 4,* 265–277.

Schmidt, F. L. (1994). The future of personnel selection in the U.S. Army. In M. G. Rumsey, C. B. Walker, & J. H. Harris (Eds.), *Personnel selection and classification* (pp. 333–350). Hillsdale, NJ: Erlbaum.

Schmidt, F. L., & Hunter, J. E. (1977). Development of a general solution to the problem of validity generalization. *Journal of Applied Psychology, 62,* 529–540.

Schmidt, F. L., & Hunter, J. E. (1995). The fatal internal contradiction in banding: Its statistical rationale is logically inconsistent with its operational procedures. *Human Performance, 8,* 203–214.

Schmidt, F. L., Pearlman, K., & Hunter, J. E. (1980). The validity and fairness of employment and educational tests for Hispanic Americans: A review and analysis. *Personnel Psychology, 33,* 705–724.

Scientific Affairs Committee. (1994). An evaluation of banding methods in personnel selection. *The Industrial-Organizational Psychologist, 32,* 80–86.

Section 504 of the Rehabilitation Act of 1973, 29 U.S.C. § 701 *et seq* (1973).

Shealy, R. T., & Stout, W. F. (1993). An item response theory model for test bias and differential test functioning. In P. W. Holland & H. Wainer (Eds.), *Differential item functioning* (pp. 197–239). Hillsdale, NJ: Erlbaum.

Shepard, L. A. (1993). Evaluating test validity. *Review of Research in Education, 19,* 405–450.

Sireci, S. G. (in press). *The construct of content validity. Social Indications Research.*

Sireci, S. G. (1997). Problems and issues in linking assessments across languages. *Educational Measurement: Issues and Practice, 16,* 12–19, 29.

Sireci, S. G., & Geisinger, K. F. (1995). Using subject matter experts to assess content representation: A MDS analysis. *Applied Psychological Measurement, 19,* 241–255.

Sireci, S. G., & Mullane, L. A. (1994). Evaluating test fairness in licensure testing: The sensitivity review process. *CLEAR Exam Review, 5*(2), 22–28.

Smith, I. L., & Greenberg, S. (1993). Content validity procedures. *CLEAR Exam Review, 4*(2), 19–22.

Society for Industrial and Organizational Psychology. (1987). *Principles for the validation and use of personnel selection procedures* (3rd ed.). College Park, MD: Author.

Standards for educational and psychological testing. (1985). Washington, DC: American Psychological Association.

Sternberg, R. J. (1994). The PRSVL model of person-context interaction in the study of human potential. In M. G. Rumsey, C. B. Walker, & J. H. Harris (Eds.), *Personnel selection and classification* (pp. 317–332). Hillsdale, NJ: Erlbaum.

Sternberg, R. J., Wagner, R. K., Williams, W. M., & Horvath, J. A. (1995). Testing common sense. *American Psychologist, 50,* 912–927.

Swaminathan, H., & Rogers, H. J. (1990). Detecting differential item functioning using logistic regression procedures. *Journal of Educational Measurement, 27,* 361–370.

Tett, R. P., Jackson, D. R., & Rothstein, M. (1991). Personality measures as predictors of job performance: A meta-analytic review. *Personnel Psychology, 44,* 703–742.

United Steelworkers v. Weber, 433 U.S. 193 (1979).

Valdés, G., & Figueroa, R. A. (1994). *Bilingualism and testing: A special case of bias.* Norwood, NJ: Ablex.

Wainer, H., Sireci, S. G., & Thissen, D. (1991). Differential testlet functioning: Definitions and detection. *Journal of Educational Measurement, 28,* 197–219.

Wards Cove Packaging Co. Inc. v. Antonio (1989). 43 FEP Cases 130.

Watson v. Fort Worth Bank and Trust, 56 U.S.L.W. 4922 (1988).

Wigdor, A., & Garner, W. R. (Eds.). (1982). *Ability testing: Uses, consequences, and controversies.* Washington, DC: National Academy Press.

Willingham, W. W., Ragosta, M., Bennett, R. E., Braun, H., Rock, D. A., & Powers, D. E. (Eds.). (1988). *Testing handicapped people.* Needham Heights, MA: Allyn & Bacon.

Zedeck, S., Outtz, J., Cascio, W. F., & Goldstein, I. L. (1995). Why do "testing experts" have such limited vision? *Human Performance, 8,* 179–190.

Zeidner, J., & Johnson, C. D. (1994). Is personnel classification a concept whose time has passed? In M. G. Rumsey, C. B. Walker, & J. H. Harris (Eds.), *Personnel selection and classification* (pp. 377–410). Hillsdale, NJ: Erlbaum.

Interpretation of Psychological Tests in Clinical and Forensic Evaluations

Bernadette Gray-Little and Danielle A. Kaplan

Psychologists and the public have debated the appropriate use of psychological tests with diverse populations since the first wide-scale application of mental tests in the early part of this century (Block & Dworkin, 1976; Cronbach, 1975). Today, the large number of psychological tests, their many uses, and the increasing diversity of the population make current discussions more complex. At issue is the development of tests that reliably indicate individual differences in the trait being measured and that provide equally valid, or unbiased, information on individuals from different groups. The mere observance of a mean difference in the test performance of two groups is not sufficient to establish bias because the differences may be veridical. Instead, the term *bias* generally refers to the differential validity of a test for various groups. Establishing test validity for a single group is challenging; establishing differential validity is doubly complicated by the need to identify an acceptable criterion.

Because psychological tests are used to make decisions that may have a critical impact on the people being tested, there is no acceptable alternative to trying to ensure that tests are appropriate for the diverse populations served by clinicians. In clinical settings, misdiagnoses— whether based on interview or psychological testing—can have serious health consequences. First, a misdiagnosed patient is denied the most appropriate treatment. Second, many psychotropic medications have serious side effects, and misdiagnosis exposes patients to needless risks (Pavkov, Lewis, & Lyons, 1989). When testing is conducted for forensic assessment, equally important decisions affecting legal responsibility and personal freedom are at stake. In this chapter we consider the appropriate interpretation of psychological tests with diverse groups in two important contexts: clinical evaluation and forensic evaluation. The clinical use of psychological tests is illustrated by discussions of psychiatric and neurological assessment; the forensic use of tests is represented by evaluations for competency to stand trial and for parenting competency.

Clinical Evaluation: Psychiatric Diagnosis

Diagnosis and Diversity

In clinical settings, psychological tests are used to assist in diagnosis and treatment planning. Diagnosis involves determining the nature, and the source when possible, of distress and abnormal behavior as well as classifying the person in terms of diagnostic nomenclature, typically the *Diagnostic and Statistical Manual of Mental Disorders* (*DSM*). Thus, the use of psychological tests for clinical diagnosis is intimately linked with psychiatric diagnosis. A review of the literature on the psychiatric diagnosis of ethnic minorities supports three interrelated conclusions that have important implications for psychological testing. First, there is a relationship between ethnicity and diagnosis such that race and ethnicity are sometimes predictive of diagnosis, independent of symptoms. Second, diagnosticians are subject to bias in their clinical judgments. Third, there are variations in the expression of distress and psychopathology among racial and ethnic groups in the United States; these variations may affect the interpretation of psychological tests and the accuracy of diagnostic judgments.

Association of Diagnosis to Race and Ethnicity
Numerous studies conducted over the past three decades support the conclusion that diagnosis is related to race or ethnicity (Adebimpe, 1979; Fabrega, Mezzich, & Ulrich, 1988; Flaskerud & Hu, 1992; Pavkov et al., 1989; Simon, Fleiss, Gurland, Stiller, & Sharpe, 1973; Strawkowski et al., 1995). One common finding is that affective disorders and personality disorders are diagnosed less frequently in Blacks than Whites, and affective disorders are possibly diagnosed more frequently among Asian Americans (Aldwin & Greenberger, 1987; Kuo, 1984). Another is that Blacks are diagnosed with schizophrenia three or more times more

often than Whites in various clinical settings (Lawson, 1986; Strawkowski et al., 1995). On the surface, the finding of more frequent diagnosis of schizophrenia in Blacks (or of depression in Whites) begs the question of whether there is bias in diagnosis or merely racial differences in the occurrence of the disorder. However, epidemiological surveys based on standardized psychiatric interviews do not support the level of difference found in clinical studies (Lawson, 1986; Strawkowski et al., 1995), nor does the difference appear to be explainable in terms of the level of symptomatology (Craig, Goodman, & Hauglaund, 1982; Flaskerud & Hu, 1992; Simon et al., 1973; Strawkowski et al., 1995).

In a study that controlled for the level of individual psychopathology with the Schedule for Affective Disorders and Schizophrenia (SADS) and the Global Assessment Scale (GAS), Pavkov et al. (1989) found that race (being Black) was a significant predictor of diagnosis, although it was entered last into a regression analysis that included not only SADS and GAF but also age, sex, and level of help seeking. The socioeconomic status (SES) of Black and White patients in this study was comparable. Similar results were reported by Mukherjee, Shukla, Woodle, Rosen, and Olarte (1983), who found that ethnicity was a significant predictor of misdiagnosis with schizophrenia for both Hispanic and Black patients. Comparable errors can be found in the use of psychological tests. For example, Pritchard and Rosenblatt (1980) described research demonstrating that clinicians were less accurate in classifying the Minnesota Multiphasic Personality Inventory (MMPI) profiles of Black patients than of White patients. Attempts to explain the association between race and ethnicity and diagnosis have invoked diagnostician bias and group variation in the expression of distress.

Bias in Diagnostic Judgments

Numerous factors may affect the accuracy of professional diagnostic judgments. In this section we are concerned with the influence of patients' sociocultural characteristics on diagnostic accuracy. Some literature on this topic suggests that members of minority groups are given more severe diagnoses than Whites with the same or comparable symptoms. For example, Loring and Powell (1988) found that Black patients received more severe diagnoses than White patients from both Black and White psychiatrists, although the effect was more pronounced for White psychiatrists. Other studies in this area show that members of minority groups may be given either more severe or less severe diagnoses than Whites. Strickland, Jenkins, Myers, and Adams (1988) found

that, although as a group of Black and White clinical psychology graduate students did not rate Black and White clients as being different in
their overall level of psychopathology (normal, neurotic, or psychotic),
there was a Therapist × Patient Race interaction. White therapists un-
derrated the level of psychopathology of Black patients and Black therapists overrated psychopathology in White patients. In addition, the
Black patient was rated as being less verbally skilled by White therapists
and less appropriate for treatment by Black therapists, although all patients were presented by videotape and worked from a verbatim transcript.

Allen's (1992) survey revealed that 174 White mental health counselors assigned less severe diagnoses to patients described in vignettes
as Native American (or no information was given) than to a patient
described as White. A similar trend was found in Martin's (1993) study,
in which experienced doctoral-level psychologists considered aggressive
and delinquent behavior less indicative of psychopathology among
Black than White adolescents. The underpathologizing of the minority
client in Allen's (1992) and Martin's (1993) research may be attributable to social desirability, resulting in a counterstereotypic response. It
also is possible that diagnosticians considered deviant behavior to be
more normative among minority groups and therefore viewed the "apparently deviant" behavior as normal.

The results of these studies strongly suggest that diagnostic judgments may be influenced by a patient's race or ethnicity over and above
the level of symptomatology. Patterns of both over- and underpathologizing of minority clients may reflect a transition in which mental
health professionals struggle to conceptualize the impact that race or
ethnicity may have on the understanding of symptoms but do not have
the benefit of theory or a coherent factual base to guide this process
(Betancourt & López, 1993).

Base-rate errors. Errors in diagnosing minority clients may be partially attributable to the faulty use of base rates (Finn & Camphuis,
1995) or to the social distance between the diagnostician and patient
(Gray-Little, 1995; López, 1989). Although there are distinct advantages
to the use of base rates in making diagnostic decisions and interpreting
test data, their use is subject to both logical and empirical error (Finn
& Camphuis, 1995). Logical errors occur when a correlational or causal
link is made between two events with high co-occurring base rates. For
example, one of the four clinics examined by Pavkov et al. (1989) had
both a high percentage of Black patients and a high rate of diagnosed

schizophrenia. Assuming a causal link between the two occurrences would lead diagnosticians to expect a high rate of schizophrenia among Black patients who attended this clinic and perhaps to assign that diagnosis when it was not warranted by a strict interpretation of the symptoms. Empirical errors occur from using erroneous base rates. When base rates are founded on misdiagnosis, such as overdiagnosis of schizophrenia in Hispanic or underdiagnosis in Asian American patients at a given clinical site, the institutional base rates will be inaccurate and their use will lead to further error.

Social distance. Social distance between the diagnostician and the patient also may lead to diagnostic error (Rosenfield, 1984). There is evidence that people form more complex schema about those who are similar and that they have less complex structures for memories regarding out-group members (Park & Rothbart, 1982). In a clinical setting, this may result in a more limited range of diagnoses being considered for out-group members. When recalling information about a member of an out-group, it also is possible that clinicians rely on stereotypical or counterstereotypical information more often because of poor information storage and retrieval. Note that simply being a member of the same racial or ethnic group as the patient does not eliminate the potential effects of social distance (Loring & Powell, 1988; Strickland et al., 1988) because social distance can be caused by other status characteristics as well. Moreover, the process of education and successful socialization into a profession may involve the internalization of standards and biases current in the profession.

Variations in the Expression of Distress

Research from anthropology and psychiatry provides ample evidence of cultural and social variations in the expression of distress (Fabrega et al., 1988; Jones & Gray, 1986; Kleinman, 1986; Westermeyer, 1987). Such variations render accurate diagnosis more difficult whether psychological tests or interviews are used for assessment. Variations in the expression of disorder have been studied primarily in relation to affective disorders and schizophrenia. The manifestations of major depression in some ethnic groups compromise the boundary between affective disorders and somatization. In particular, Asian American and Hispanic patients have been found to report more somatic symptoms when depressed than White Americans (Fabrega, Rubel, & Wallace, 1967; Maduro, 1983; Marsella, Kenzie, & Gordon, 1973; S. Sue & Morishima, 1982). These are not isolated findings; Kleinman (1986) observed that "the research literature indicates that depression and most other mental illnesses, especially in non-Western societies and among rural, ethnic, and lower-class groups in the West, are associated preponderantly with physical complaints" (p. 52).

The clarity of the distinction between affective disorder and thought disorder also may vary for different racial and ethnic groups; both African Americans and Hispanics with bipolar disorder have been observed to report hallucinations more often than Whites with the same diagnosis (Lawson, 1986). Several years ago Liss, Welner, Robins, and Richardson (1973) performed a chart review of 256 patients to examine the fit between symptoms and diagnosis. They found a better fit for White than for Black patients and that among Black patients, there was a greater frequency of delusion and hallucinations regardless of whether patients were diagnosed as schizophrenic. Some variations in the expression of distress may be unrelated to the criteria typically used in diagnosis, but others mean that psychiatric formulations of disorders are not an equally good fit for all groups.

The Role of Psychological Testing

Many psychological tests have the advantage over the traditional clinical interview of providing a standard stimulus and set of norms for interpretation (Anastasi & Urbina, 1997); thus, it is possible that some of the problems associated with diagnostician bias can be reduced. Psychological tests, however, also rely on compilations of signs and symptoms and reports of behavior; hence, their use does not obviate problems associated with variations in the expression of symptoms of distress or the fit between symptoms and diagnostic categories. Thus, in the interpretation of psychological tests, the culturally sensitive examiner will need to be attuned to these issues, which may threaten the accuracy of diagnosis.

Surveys of current practices in training and clinical settings show that aside from intelligence tests, the Rorschach Inkblot Test, the Thematic Apperception Test (TAT), and the MMPI are the tests most commonly taught in training programs and most frequently used in clinical settings (Lubin, Larsen, Matarazzo, & Seever, 1985; Piotrowski, Sherry, & Keller, 1985; Ritzler & Alter, 1986). The use of these tests with racial and ethnic minority groups is discussed next. We also consider the Millon Clinical Multiaxial Inventory (MCMI), which has an increasingly important role in the assessment of personality disorders (Piotrowski & Keller, 1989).

Projective Tests: The Rorschach

Projective tests offer opportunities and pitfalls in the assessment of racial and ethnic minorities. It is not unusual for advocates of projective techniques to take the stance that the ambiguity of projective test stimuli precludes cultural bias; for example, it is sometimes argued that everyone who takes the test is in comparably unfamiliar territory. This point of view was enunciated clearly by Holtzman (1980), who argued that (a) projective techniques provide an adequate sample of behavior on which to judge personality and psychopathology; (b) the determinants of the responses are basic and similar for all groups; and (c) the responses therefore provide equally adequate assessment of all groups. There are numerous challenges to Holtzman's first assumption, *the projective hypothesis,* which undergirds the entire process of projective assessment. Our primary concern, however, is with the second and third assumptions.

The conviction that the determinants of Rorschach responses are universal and that the test provides equivalent assessment of all groups seems to be honored in the inattention to the issues of race and ethnicity in major works on the Rorschach (e.g., Aronow, Reznikoff, & Moreland, 1994; Exner, 1986). Anastasi and Urbina (1997) and Blatt (1990) noted two traditions in Rorschach scoring and interpretation. The first is the tradition of Hermann Rorschach and others who viewed the Rorschach as an assessment of perception to interpret primarily in terms of its structural or quantitative characteristics. This tradition is seen in the work of Beck and Klopfer and others who developed empirically based scoring systems that emphasize the reliability and validity of Rorschach scores. The most elaborate scoring and interpretative approach within this tradition, however, is Exner's comprehensive system, which merges and augments elements of earlier systems (Exner, 1986). In support of the cross-cultural utility of the Rorschach, it has been argued that normal groups of different nationalities are more similar than depressed and nondepressed individuals within a given culture (Ritzler, 1996); however, there has been little work on comparisons of racial and ethnic subgroups within the United States. Given that Exner's comprehensive system is the system taught in training programs, the absence of attention to these issues is an important weakness.

A diametrically different approach to the Rorschach technique is found in those who emphasize the content and idiographic elements of Rorschach interpretation (Aronow et al., 1994; Phillips, 1992; Phillips & Smith, 1953). Advocates of this approach prefer to view the Rorschach as an ambiguous situation that allows the examiner to observe how the individual constructs meaning rather than as a test (Blatt, 1990). Proponents of this approach often view reliance on formal or structural features of the Rorschach protocol as evidence of lack of sophistication. For example, Aronow et al. (1994) emphasized the importance of individualizing interpretation as well as the interpersonal nature of all clinical work. They also noted that variables such as education and occupation (i.e., SES) are important in interpreting the Rorschach. Nonetheless, their work included no reference to the use of the test with racial or ethnic minorities and, aside from age norms, no formal attention was given to social status. These omissions are troublesome in light of the finding that some features of the Rorschach protocol, such as the number of responses and the type of projection, may be influenced by the patient's educational level, characteristics of the examiner, and the quality of rapport (Abel, 1973; Pedersen, 1987).

Most of the studies directly addressing the use of the Rorschach with racial and ethnic groups in this country were conducted prior to the 1970s and provide limited guidance for present-day use. Krall (1983), Scott (1981), and Howes and DeBlassie (1989) are among the few to address this topic since 1980. Those authors generally supported the use of the Rorschach with the groups they studied; however, Ritzler (1996) cautioned that level of acculturation and use of the client's preferred language may influence Rorschach responses, and Kaplan and Saccuzzo (1993, 1997) also indicated that race variables influence test results.

The promise of the Rorschach is that its flexibility makes it usable with people from all groups. The shortcoming is that there are currently no norms or interpretative guidelines for use with minorities, although race and ethnicity may influence numerous aspects of the Rorschach protocol. Our review suggests that social distance between the examiner and patient may affect rapport and ultimately the production of Rorschach responses in a way that may limit interpretability. For that reason, competent use of the Rorschach with minority individuals will ultimately depend on the examiner's sophistication with the Rorschach, on his or her ability to establish a rapport that fosters patients' responding, and on personal skill in interpreting Rorschach responses in a culturally sensitive manner.

There are still profound questions about the psychometric adequacy of the Rorschach. Although progress has been made in establishing standardized administration and scoring procedures (Exner, 1986), fundamental problems still exist in establishing norms, reliability, and validity for the Rorschach. (See Kaplan & Saccuzzo, 1997, for a discussion of the continuing struggle to establish psychometric adequacy for projective techniques.) If an examiner cannot be satisfied that the Rorschach has something reliable and meaningful to say about individual clients, then issues of its sensitivity to group variations will be irrelevant.

Apperceptive Tests

There is apparently a "second blooming" of interest in apperceptive tests that parallels a revitalization of interest in the Rorschach (Bellak, 1993). The TAT is the best known apperceptive test for adults and has been used extensively for research and clinical purposes. There are various scoring schemes, such as those by Holt, Tompkins, and Eron, available for use with the TAT (Bellak, 1993). Some scoring schemes emphasize content analysis, whereas others are largely geared to analyzing the structural features of the TAT protocol, but there is no widely accepted scoring system that is comparable to Exner's (1986) comprehensive system for the Rorschach (Bellak, 1993). For that reason, in clinical practice, the TAT is almost always used idiographically.

The TAT stimuli are less ambiguous than those of the Rorschach, and their depiction of human figures in culturally saturated scenes makes universality highly questionable. The fact that group membership and sociocultural factors may be reflected in the stories was recognized in interpretive guidelines developed more than 40 years ago. Comparisons of ethnic and racial differences on the standard TAT have produced mixed findings. Megargee (1966) considered the response patterns of Blacks and Whites to be similar when education and IQ were controlled. However, D. Johnson and Sikes (1965) found group difference in responses to themes of achievement, frustration, family unity, and parental acceptance in a comparison of Mexican American, Black, and White patients with similar education and diagnoses. Chin (1983) also noted that in her experience, TAT themes related to shame and authority figures seemed both qualitatively different and more frequent among Chinese Americans; whether these themes reflect psychopathology or normal cultural variations will have to be weighed by the examiner.

The adaptation of the TAT for racial and ethnic minorities has a long history (see reviews by Bellak, 1993; Dana, 1993; Henry, 1987; Snowden & Todman, 1982). Protocols from members of ethnic and racial minorities were often characterized by low response rates, which was attributed to the failure of minority group members to identify with TAT characters. Therefore, the TAT has been adapted for use with specific groups to facilitate identification and, thereby, to increase the response production. Thompson (1949) and Bailey and Green (1977) adapted the TAT for use with Blacks; these adaptations involved modification of the facial features, hair, and clothing styles. Dana (1993) described adaptation of the TAT stimuli and interpretative guidelines for several Native American groups, such as the Lakota, the Navaho, Hopi, and Zuni (Dana, 1993). For the most part, these adaptations have resulted in modest response increases in Black and Native American populations, but low responding remains a concern. The cause of the low responsiveness in these groups is not fully understood. Inadequacy of the stimuli, patients' lack of acceptance of the testing situation, education levels, and problems in rapport may all contribute.

Williams and Johnson (1981) developed an essentially new apperceptive test, Themes Concerning Blacks, which depicts Black characters in new settings. Although the Themes Concerning Blacks offers the advantage of a scoring system, it has not been widely adopted for use in clinical settings and its equivalence with the standard TAT has not been evaluated. Constantino, Malagady, and Rogler (1988) developed Tell-Me-a-Story (TEMAS) for use with Hispanic populations, primarily children and adolescents. TEMAS, which differs from the TAT in using chromatic color and in the ethnicity of the characters, has undergone extensive development. It features matching sets of cards for different racial–ethnic groups and a scoring system for use with Hispanics, Blacks, and Whites. Ritzler (1996) observed that its concentration on minority-group experience in New York City may limit the TEMAS primarily to use with an urban population. The availability of interpretative guidelines and norms for different groups, however, offers some features that the original TAT does not, and TEMAS is likely to enjoy increased popularity. (See Dana, 1993, and Lang, 1992, for a review of TEMAS.)

A variety of other projective techniques, including forms of sentence completion tests, word association, drawing tests, and early memory procedures, are used in clinical settings. However, the use of these approaches is often idiosyncratic to the tester, and the approaches have not been studied for the assessment of personality and psychopathology in diverse groups.

Objective Tests

The Minnesota Multiphasic Personality Inventory. In clinical practice, the MMPI is used primarily to assist in personality assessment and psychiatric diagnosis. The MMPI is well suited, by design, for diagnostic use. It is composed of a set of 10 clinical scales corresponding to major diagnostic categories and three validity scales to aid in the detection of response patterns that might invalidate test interpretation. These 13 scales are referred to as the basic scales (see Exhibit 7.1). Our focus is on the basic scales; however, a large number of specialized scales have been derived from the same item set to measure many features of personality. In constructing the MMPI, the distinction between abnormal and normal responses on the clinical scales was determined by contrasting the responses of criterion groups (patients with the target diagnosis) with a control group (composed of White Minnesotans). The advantage of the criterion group strategy is that it requires few assumptions about the meaning of the test items. However, the applicability of such tests to diverse groups hinges on their essential similarity to original criterion and control groups. A restandardization effort, the MMPI-2, was undertaken in the early 1980s to address what was seen as a major flaw of the original MMPI, an unrepresentative and outdated control group.

A comprehensive analysis of the appropriateness of the MMPI for various groups might include the following: (a) demonstrating a comparable factorial structure for various groups, which would indicate that the test is measuring the same thing in the groups; (b) consideration of similarity in scale elevations; and (c) establishing that scale scores or other indexes have similar predictive validity in clinical settings. In re-

---

Exhibit 7.1

Minnesota Multiphasic Personality Inventory

Validity Scales

L Lie scale, a rationally designed measure of social desirable responding.
F Infrequency scale, endorsement of unusual items that others endorse infrequently.
K Defensiveness, an empirically defined scale, measuring favorable self-portrayal.

Clinical Scales

1. Hypochondriasis
2. Depression
3. Hysteria
4. Psychopathy
5. Masculinity-Femininity

6. Paranoia
7. Psychasthenia
8. Schizophrenia
9. Hypomania
0. Social Introversion

ality, there have been few studies examining the similarity in factorial structure for various racial and ethnic groups. Bernstein, Teng, Grannemann, and Garbin (1987) used a principal-components analysis with a large sample of Black, Hispanic, Native American, and White respondents and reported an invariant structure across all four groups; however, Beck et al. (1989) found different factor structures for Black and White inpatients.

By far the most common type of research has examined the average scale scores obtained by Whites compared with various other groups; research on predictive validity is less common. Because research findings vary across racial and ethnic groups, we discuss the use of MMPI separately for Blacks, Asian Americans, Hispanic Americans, and Native Americans. With regard to each group, "experts" differ about the appropriateness of the standard interpretation of the MMPI.

Blacks. In a series of studies beginning in 1962, Gynther and associates (Gynther, 1972; Gynther & Green, 1980; McDonald & Gynther, 1963) reported significant racial differences on the MMPI validity and clinical scales. In particular, Gynther warned that the frequent elevation of Scales 8 and 9 among Blacks may result in the overdiagnosis of serious pathology, a warning that seems to echo findings from the literature on psychiatric diagnoses. Gynther's (1972) review of MMPI research led him to suggest that differential norms for Blacks should be considered.

Pritchard and Rosenblatt (1980), after a consideration of the same literature, argued that there was insufficient evidence to justify different norms for use with Blacks. In support of this position, they cited studies showing that racial differences are reduced or eliminated when moderator variables such as education, SES, and profile validity were controlled. Their analysis of six studies, which presumably examined predictive validity, led them to argue that predictive validity was similar for Blacks and Whites. A similar conclusion was reached by Greene (1987) and Dahlstrom, Lachar, and Dahlstrom (1986), who expressed concern that use of special norms lowered, rather than improved, the accuracy in predicting psychiatric diagnosis. (The use of different norms or race-sensitive scales in interpreting the MMPI often resulted in dramatic reductions in the level of psychopathology diagnosed in Blacks; Costello, 1977; Dahlstrom et al., 1986.)

More recently, Gynther (1989) presented a summary of six previous reviews of Black–White comparisons on the MMPI and repeated the warning that in interpreting MMPI profiles for Blacks, elevations on

Scales *F*, 8, and 9 should be played down as a way to enhance accuracy and avoid overpathologizing Black test takers. This recommendation reflects the following rationale: In comparisons of Scales 8 and 9 in normal and psychiatric samples, the average scores of Blacks exceeded those of Whites by an effect size of at least .5 (5 or more *T*-score points) in more than 25% of the comparisons; White averages on these same scales exceeded those of Blacks only 2% of the time; in the majority of the comparisons, there were no effect sizes that were as large as 5 *T*-score points (from data presented in Greene, 1987). Differences smaller than 5 *T*-score points are described as not clinically significant; however, when diagnostic decisions are based on cutoff scores, as they often are in individual cases, small score discrepancies will make a difference in a percentage of the cases. Thus, a consideration of what 4, 5, or 10 scale points might mean in individual clinical applications is important. Gynther's caution also is warranted in light of Pritchard and Rosenblatt's (1980) finding of poorer accuracy in classifying profiles from Black patients.

Research findings based on the MMPI-2 seem to parallel those with the MMPI. For example, Goldman, Cooke, and Dahlstrom (1995) compared the responses of Black and White normal college men and women on the MMPI and MMPI-2. The means for all four groups were lower on the MMPI-2 than on the MMPI, with the greatest reduction occurring for Black men. Black men and women received significantly higher scores than Whites on Scales 6, 8, and 9, although only the difference for Scale 8 for men exceeded 5 *T*-score points. This study did not include data on the behavioral correlates of the differences. Grillo's (1991) results with a university sample of normal students was similar; he found that more Blacks than Whites were identified as having elevated code types and that race alone or in interaction with other moderator variables was a significant source of variance for all the validity scales and half of the clinical scales. Shondrick, Ben-Porath, and Stafford (1992) found a higher Scale 9 for Black men (7 *T*-score points) in a group undergoing forensic assessment. Timbrook and Graham (1994) examined racial mean difference and predictive validity for the MMPI-2 in an adult sample. Among men, the means for Blacks were significantly higher on Scale 8 and for women on Scales 4, 5, and 9. None of the differences exceeded 5 *T*-score points, however, and the accuracy of relevant MMPI scales in predicting partner ratings (for characteristics such as depression, anxiety, and social discomfort) was similar for the two groups. McNulty, Graham, Ben-Porath, and Stein (1997)

found similar correlations between MMPI-2 scores and conceptually related therapist ratings for Black and White mental health center clients,
which they interpreted as evidence of a comparable validity for the two
groups.

In summary, the MMPI and MMPI-2 seem to be appropriate instruments for use with Blacks. The behavioral implications of their
higher elevations on Scales *F*, 8, and 9 have not been established un-
equivocally for either normal or clinical populations. For that reason,
higher elevations on these scales should be interpreted conservatively.
In addition, great caution should be exercised in the interpretation of
profiles with questionable validity.

Asian Americans. There are relatively few comparative MMPI studies involving Asian Americans. In a study of a normal sample, Marsella,
Sanborn, Kameoka, Shizuru, and Brennan (1975) found that Chinese
American women and Japanese American men had higher elevations
on Scale 2 than their White counterparts. S. Sue and Sue (1974) examined scale elevations among Asian American and non-Asian college
students at a psychological services center and found more elevated
scales for Asian American men on Scales *L* and *F* and on all clinical
scales except 3, 5, and 9. Among women, Asian Americans had higher
scores on Scales *L*, *F*, and 0. Regardless of gender, Asian American students had higher distress on items measuring somatic and family problems. The latter finding is consistent with the psychiatric literature,
which has suggested reports of more somatic symptoms for Asians and
Asian Americans (S. Sue & Morishima, 1982). Cogburn, Zalewski, Farrell, and Mendoza (1993) found that although Asian American college
students received lower scores on Scale *K* than Whites, they scored
higher on the other validity scales and on more than half of the clinical
scales. Tsushima and Onorato (1982) reported that, among a group of
medical patients, White men had higher Scale 4 elevations than a
matched diagnostic sample of Japanese American men; no differences
were found for women. More recently, Keefe, Sue, Enomoto, Durvasula,
and Chao (1994) examined the MMPI-2 performance of Asian American and White college students. Asian Americans were divided into two
levels of acculturation on the basis of their scores on the Suinn–Lew
Self-Identity Acculturation Scale. On scales showing differences in elevation, the direction was that scores of Whites were lowest followed by
the more acculturated, and then by the less acculturated Asian Americans.

In summary, there is inadequate research with Asian Americans to draw definitive conclusions about the appropriateness of the MMPI or MMPI-2. To date, little research has been conducted with clinical samples, and we found no studies assessing the behavioral correlates of the elevations found in these samples. Greene (1987) observed that heightened somatic concerns represent a consistent finding in the MMPI protocols of Asian Americans, a pattern that is consistent with psychiatric and anthropological literature. Research by Keefe et al. (1994) also indicates that the level of acculturation is an important consideration in the use of the MMPI with Asian Americans.

Hispanic Americans. Campos (1989) performed a meta-analytic review of 16 studies that compared Whites and Hispanics on the MMPI. The only consistent finding was that Hispanics scored higher on the L scale, by approximately 4 T-score points. Campos also concluded that the MMPI had comparable validity in predicting job performance for police officers. Comparisons of specific diagnostic groups such as male sex offenders (Velasquez, Callahan, & Carillo, 1989) and schizophrenic patients (Velasquez & Callahan, 1990a) have at times yielded similar results. However, in a study of psychiatric patients that controlled for diagnostic category, Velasquez, Callahan, and Young (1993) found higher scores on Scales L, F, 4, and 8 for Hispanic schizophrenia patients; among depressed patients, Whites were higher on Scale 5 and Hispanics were higher on Scale 6; there were no differences between Hispanic and White patients with antisocial personality disorder. Velasquez and Callahan (1990b) also found that alcoholic Hispanics scored significantly lower on Scales 4, 5, and 0 than alcoholic Whites—a finding that is parallel to research comparing alcoholic Blacks and Whites. Weisman, Anglin, and Fisher's (1989) comparison of Chicano and White narcotic addicts also showed that Whites had higher scores on Scale F and all clinical scales except Scale 2.

Whitworth and McBlaine (1993) compared Hispanic and White college students on the MMPI-2. White students scored higher on Scales K, 3, and 4, and Hispanic students scored higher on Scale L. However, none of the differences were as high as 5 T-score points. Whitworth's (1988) earlier research indicated that Mexican Americans who took the MMPI in English received a higher score than Whites only on Scale L, whereas those tested in Spanish received higher scores than the other two groups on Scales L and F and most of the clinical scales. Karle and Velasquez (1996) reported, however, that the English and Spanish versions (Garcia-Peltoniemi & Azun, 1993) of the MMPI-2 yielded equivalent results when both were administered to a group of bilingual, bicultural college students. Their results suggest that acculturation, not language preference per se, is the important factor in interpreting the MMPI in comparisons of normal individuals.

Greene (1987) concluded that there seemed to be fewer Hispanic–White than Black–White differences on the MMPI. There is still little research with Hispanic psychiatric populations, however, and, with one or two exceptions, no research comparing the predictive validity of the MMPI for Hispanic and White populations. Velasquez et al. (1993) argued that it is too soon to conclude that the MMPI can be used without reservation with Hispanics. Our review suggests that the examiner should be alert to the possibility of high L scale scores with Hispanic patients. The L scale is typically associated with the desire to make a socially desirable presentation. We discuss this issue further in the section on forensic assessment.

Native Americans. Few studies assess the comparability of the MMPI for Native American clinical populations (Dana, 1993). Pollack and Shore (1980) examined several different diagnostic groups of patients from Pacific Northwest tribes and noted that the most impressive finding was the similarity of profiles across the diagnostic groups. For example, the authors noted that "nonpsychotic, depressed Indian patients could not be distinguished from schizophrenic patients on any clinical scale, and there were no significant differences between antisocial-alcoholic patients and those with situational reactions" (Pollack & Shore, 1980, p. 947). Butcher, Braswell, and Raney (1983) found that the MMPI profiles of the Native Americans included in their study of psychiatric patients were less deviant than those of both Black and White patients. Graham (1993), however, reported a pattern of higher scores on the validity and clinical scales (greater than 5 T-score points) among the small group of Native Americans included in the MMPI-2 normative sample.

The pattern of MMPI results for Native Americans is so inconsistent that no general conclusion can be drawn from it. It is worth remembering, however, that Native Americans represent many linguistic and cultural traditions, and it will be important to know whether inconsistent findings are attributable to this diversity or to other unexplored factors, such as residence or nonresidence in reservation communities, which may be related to acculturation.

Studies of the behavioral and diagnostic correlates of MMPI scale scores are sorely needed to enhance interpretation for all the groups discussed. Given the problems that we have discussed regarding clinical diagnoses, future studies of predictive validity should use standardized diagnostic interviews as the criterion. If not, psychologists are faced with a circular argument that has no apparent solution.

Millon Clinical Multiaxial Inventory. The MCMI is an objective inventory that was designed to assess personality disorders and major symptomatic disorders described in the *DSM.* The original scale was published in 1983 and a revision, the MCMI-II, was published in 1987 (Millon, 1987). The items and scales that constitute the MCMI were originally developed on a rational basis to tap dimensions of Millon's personality theory and were eventually refined through internal consistency analysis and the use of criterion groups (Choca, Shanley, & Van Denburg, 1992; Kaplan & Saccuzzo; 1993). MCMI raw scores are converted into base-rate scores, which indicate the probability that the characteristic or disorder is present rather than indicating the level of a characteristic. In practical use, a base rate of 75 is interpreted as a definite indication that the characteristic being measured is present, whereas a base-rate score of 85 is interpreted as evidence that the characteristic is pervasive in the individual.

Numerous scales can be interpreted from the MCMI. The standard scales consist of 8 scales of personality style, 5 scales indicating severe personality disorder, and 9 scales that measure symptom disorders such as anxiety, mania, drug abuse, and psychotic thinking (Choca et al., 1992). The MCMI also provides a validity index. The match between *DSM* personality disorders and those measured by the MCMI is controversial (Widiger & Sanderson, 1987). Some investigators have found a good correspondence between the MCMI and structured clinical interviews (Torgersen & Alnaes, 1990), but others have reported a high rate of false-positive results compared with clinical diagnosis (Wetzler & Dubro, 1990).

The adequacy of the MCMI for ethnic and racial groups was confronted early in its development with the publication of conversion tables for Black, Hispanic, and White test takers (Choca et al., 1992). These norms have met with mixed success in studies of item-level responding, mean scale scores, similarity of factor structure, and predictive validity. Our search revealed several studies featuring Black–White comparisons, one study involving Native Canadians, and no recent research with the MCMI on Asian or Hispanic groups in the United States.

In general, research comparing scale scores indicates that higher scores are obtained by Blacks than Whites even when race-appropriate norms are used. Choca, Shanley, Peterson, and Van Denburg (1990) compared Black and White inpatients using race-appropriate norms. When patients were matched for diagnosis, more than 25% of the items showed different endorsement patterns by race; Blacks received higher scores on 8 of 20 scale comparisons, whereas Whites were higher only on the scale assessing dysthymia. Hamberger and Hastings (1992) found significant race differences on several scales in a group of psychiatric inpatients.

Research addressing the factorial structure of the MCMI with different racial groups has generally been supportive of a similar factor structure. For example, despite finding mean racial differences, Choca et al. (1990) found that separate principal-components factor analyses revealed identical factor structures. Weekes, Morison, Millson, and Fettig (1995) contrasted the MCMI performance of White, Native, and Metis (mixed) Canadian incarcerated criminals. Principal-components analyses for the White group and the two other groups combined resulted in similar four-factor solutions.

Research on predictive validity has been mixed. Choca et al. (1990) found that the positive predictive power (true-positive results) of the MCMI was higher for Whites on scales measuring anxiety disorders and affective disorders, but lower on scales for substance abuse and psychosis. There were no racial differences in the prediction of personality disorders. Calsyn, Saxon, and Daisy (1991) found that although fewer than half of the cases of drug abuse could be predicted by the Drug Abuse scale of the MCMI, the prediction was slightly better for Blacks than for Whites. Greenblatt and Davis (1992) demonstrated equal power in predicting anger and psychosis in groups of Black and White psychiatric inpatients. When Davis, Greenblatt, and Pochyly (1990) compared the effects of race, education, and diagnosis on several MCMI scales (scored with race-appropriate norms), however, their results indicated that the diagnostically relevant MCMI scales were not helpful in distinguishing between schizophrenic and nonschizophrenic patients but that race made a significant difference in four of the six scales compared. As evidence of predictive validity with Native Canadians, Weekes et al. (1995) noted that higher MCMI scores for alcohol abuse obtained by the Native and Metis groups in their study were confirmed by independent clinical assessment.

In general, research on the MCMI indicates that scale elevations are different for Black and White patients and that predictive validity is not equivalent for the two groups. If future research continues to confirm a similar factor structure for Blacks and other minority groups, adjustments can be made in the norms that are used with each group. At present, however, the norms available for Blacks do not seem to have accomplished their intended outcome. Little is known about the effectiveness of the specific norms in interpreting MCMI results for Hispanic individuals.

Clinical Evaluation: Neuropsychological Assessment

Discrepancies in performance between majority- and minority-group members on neuropsychological instruments have been well documented. For example, in a study in which an urban sample of Black and White geriatric patients was tested with the Boston Naming Test, more than 20% of the variance in test scores was directly attributable to ethnicity and SES (Lichtenberg, Ross, & Christensen, 1994). Similar variance has been found in the performance of Hispanic and non-Hispanic patients with Alzheimer's disease on Trail Making tests A and B and the Fuld Object Memory Test, with English-speaking patients scoring higher on both (Taussig et al., as cited in Cervantes & Acosta, 1992). Ethnic and racial differences on neuropsychological assessment instruments have been attributed to factors of language, education, and SES (all issues to which the culturally sensitive assessor should be alert when selecting and interpreting an appropriate test battery).

It is sound testing practice to use tests in combination to elicit diverse samples of behavior (Anastasi & Urbina, 1997). Cervantes and Acosta (1992) also suggested using multiple measures of the same construct to compensate for bias in a particular instrument. The value of this strategy was illustrated in Bernard's (1989) study of the performance of Black, White, and Hispanic young men from poor educational backgrounds on the Halstead–Reitan Neuropsychological Test Battery. No racial or ethnic differences in the rates of impairment were found when the entire test battery was administered and an overall impairment index calculated. However, significant differences in mean individual subtest scores were found across race and ethnicity for three subtests: Category, Rhythm, and Finger Tapping. Of these, differences in mean scores on Finger Tapping resulted in a disproportionate percentage of both Black and White participants being classified as impaired. Thus, although the Halstead–Reitan as a whole appears to produce scores that are relatively bias free, care must be taken in the administration and interpretation of individual subtests with diverse populations. Furthermore, administration of multiple tests may increase the chance that test results that indicate impairment are not an artifact of the client's dissimilarity to a specific normative group.

To reduce the bias that may result from linguistic difficulties, some researchers have developed translated forms of standard neuropsychological assessment instruments. There are now foreign-language versions of the Wechsler Adult Intelligence Scale–Revised (WAIS-R) and the Mini-Mental Status Examination (MMSE), which may help clinicians gain a clearer picture of the capabilities and deficits of clients whose dominant language is not English. However, Chavez and Gonzales-Singh (1980) cautioned that the simple translation of an instrument from English to the native language of the individual being assessed may be insufficient to eliminate bias. Work by Escobar et al. (1986) in which Hispanics were tested with the MMSE illustrates this point nicely. The researchers found higher rates of cognitive impairment among Spanish-speaking participants than among English-speaking participants, even when the native Spanish speakers were assessed using a widely used Spanish version of the MMSE (Karno et al. as cited in Escobar et al., 1986). An item analysis of the translated MMSE revealed that 5 of the 30 items, primarily those related to orientation, attention and calculation, and language vocalization were affected by language and ethnicity. When participants' scores were reanalyzed with those items excluded, the rates of impairment across the Hispanic and non-Hispanic groups became similar (Escobar et al., 1986). In a related study, Bird, Canino, Rubio, Stipec, and Shrout (1987) found that Puerto Rican Hispanics demonstrated significantly higher rates of cognitive impairment on the MMSE than did non-Hispanics in the United States, even when the battery was modified to make the instrument more culturally and linguistically relevant. Both groups of authors suggested that when using the MMSE with Hispanics, clinicians may wish to consider eliminating or reweighing some items to reduce cultural and educational bias. However, these adjustment strategies imply that the existence of a difference is evidence of bias. Further research is needed to ensure that such adjustments enhance, rather than decrease, the validity of the tests.

Similarly, Loewenstein, Rubert, Argüelles, and Duara (1995) produced identical English and Spanish versions of the Direct Assessment of Functional Status, a test battery designed to assess the functional capabilities of patients with neurological damage through an extensive process of back translation and translation by committee. When scores on both versions of the battery were correlated with a standard battery of neuropsychological tests, however, different neuropsychological tests predicted different patterns of functional abilities in English- and Spanish-speaking patients. This finding is particularly striking in light of the fact that the Direct Assessment of Functional Status has been widely used in the assessment of both English- and Spanish-speaking patients (Loewenstein et al., 1995). It is clear that even when great care has been taken to develop linguistically appropriate assessment instruments, the ability to draw conclusions or make predictions about the performance of a minority client using majority culture norms is not guaranteed.

When administering timed tests, the assessor should be aware that examinees from different cultural groups may have an orientation to time that is different from the examiner's own. In traditional Native American culture, for example, the division of time into schedules and deadlines may be seen as artificial (D. W. Sue & Sue, 1990). In testing with some minority clients, the emphasis for the clients themselves may not be on the rapid completion of a task but on accuracy or deliberateness. The assessor working with minority clients should therefore be sensitive to cases in which slow performance or failure to complete a test under time constraints may represent the client's different orientation to the time demands of the task rather than an impairment in abilities.

Forensic Evaluation: Assessment of Trial Competency

Regardless of the setting, awareness of cultural issues in assessment is important. The experienced psychologist conducting diagnostic or neurological assessment in a familiar health setting may readily acknowledge the need for cultural sensitivity in the administration and interpretation of tests. However, the psychologist who is called on to apply these same skills in a forensic setting may be in unfamiliar territory. The unfamiliarity of the court procedures and the slightly different role of the psychologist as an advocate of the court as well as of the client may leave more room for social distance and misapplied base rates to interfere with the assessment process. It is therefore important for the assessor in a forensic setting to be especially aware of the impact of cultural factors on assessment.

In spite of the controversy surrounding the use of psychological testimony in determining competency (e.g., Faust & Ziskin, 1988), psychological assessment has come to play a large role in the determination of a defendant's competence to stand trial. Borum and Grisso (1995) reported that half of all psychologists and psychiatrists surveyed considered testing with standardized assessment instruments to be either essential or recommended in assessing trial competency. Arguing for the necessity of considering diversity issues in forensic assessment, Butcher and Pope (1993) cited the American Psychological Association's guideline that

> psychologists attempt to identify situations in which particular interventions or assessment techniques or norms may not be applicable or may require adjustment in administration or interpretation because of factors such as individuals' gender, age, race, ethnicity, national origin, religion, sexual orientation, disability, language, or socioeconomic status. (p. 278)

The authors likened the use of assessment techniques in a forensic evaluation without considering cultural factors to conducting an assessment in a clinic with a "Whites only" sign on the door. This may be particularly true in the assessment of trial competency, which requires a unique understanding of each defendant's situation as well as his or her psychological capacities.

Grisso (1986) suggested that determining competence is not simply a matter of assigning a diagnosis or assessing intellectual functioning. Rather, evaluating competency requires an understanding of the defendant's current functioning, the probable demands of the trial, and the role the defendant will be expected to play in his or her own defense. It is possible that two defendants with similar symptom profiles and levels of intellectual functioning might differ in their competence to stand trial depending on whether each would be required to testify on his or her own behalf, the length of the trial, and the availability of other witnesses. The difficulty of assessing the interaction between a defendant's functioning and the nature of a trial demands that the examiner be alert to issues of race, ethnicity, and SES, which may contribute to the defendant's overall functioning.

In a study by Roesch, Eaves, Sollner, Normandin, and Glackman (1981) comparing the characteristics of fit and unfit defendants, the average defendant referred for competency evaluation was "single, living alone, and unemployed at the time of arrest. The majority had not finished high school. In fact, fully 60% completed only junior high or less" (pp. 148–149). Furthermore, defendants who were found to be unfit were more likely to be transient or living in a hotel at the time of arrest. These findings suggest that an examiner who is called on to assess a defendant's competency is likely to encounter a person whose background and current situation are much different from those of the assessor.

In assessing trial competency, it is more common to use a specialized battery rather than the standard clinical tests described above. If the intellectual competence of a defendant is in question, the WAIS-R may be used, and the validity scales of the MMPI-2 are frequently examined to assess malingering (Berry, Wetter, & Baer, 1995). However, competency assessment often consists primarily of a thorough interview and the use of one or more of the screening instruments explicitly designed for the purpose of evaluating competency. The competency screening instruments designed to assess a defendant's fitness to stand trial may therefore be the only standardized source of information available to an examiner and, as such, warrants some discussion here.

Competency to Stand Trial Assessment Instrument

The Competency to Stand Trial Assessment Instrument (CAI; McGarry & Associates, 1973) was designed by a team of psychologists, psychiatrists, and lawyers for the purpose of "standardiz[ing], objectify[ing], and quantify[ing] the relevant criteria for competency to stand trial" (p. 99). The CAI is a semistructured clinical interview that addresses 13 functions thought to be necessary for a defendant to adequately meet the demands of a trial. They include understanding the court procedure, unmanageable behavior, and the capacity to testify relevantly. Although the CAI's manual includes a list of suggested questions, examiners use flexibility and individual judgment in interviewing. Each response is given a score from 1 (indicating total lack of ability to function) to 5 (indicating no impairment in that area), but no specific scoring criteria are provided.

Competency Screening Test

The Competency Screening Test (Lipsitt & Lelos, 1973) was designed for use as a brief screening instrument to determine whether a more extensive competency evaluation is necessary. It is often used in conjunction with the CAI and was designed by the same group of researchers for that purpose. The Competency Screening Test consists of 22 sentence stems that are thought to address three relevant dimensions of trial competency: the potential for a constructive lawyer–client relationship, understanding of the court process, and the ability to deal emotionally with the criminal process (Grisso, 1986). Each response is scored 0, 1, or 2 on the basis of the degree to which it demonstrates understanding of the relevant legal and psychological criteria. A total score of 20 or less is generally considered to be a sign that further assessment is needed to confirm the possibility of incompetence to stand trial.

Interdisciplinary Fitness Interview

In recognition of the fact that trial competency involves both legal and psychological factors, the Interdisciplinary Fitness Interview (Golding, Roesch, & Schreiber, 1984) combines items that evaluate the defendant's understanding of the legal process with those assessing psychological functioning. The instrument was designed to be administered jointly by an attorney and a mental health professional, with each administering and interpreting the section relevant to his or her profession. However, it also can be administered by one examiner with appropriate knowledge of both legal and psychological issues. Although questions may vary depending on the examiner and the nature of the defendant's situation, the authors provide an extensive list of possible questions in each category. Legal issues addressed by the interview include the quality of the defendant's relationship with his or her attorney and with attorneys in general as well as the capacity to disclose pertinent facts, events, and motives. The psychological section of the inventory is a symptom checklist in which the presence of symptoms such as thought disturbance, hallucinations, and severe mental retardation is noted by the examiner.

The competency screening instruments discussed earlier vary in the degree of structure in administration and scoring. Of the three instruments, only the Competency Screening Test guarantees that each defendant will be asked an identical series of questions. Although the flexibility afforded by these semistructured instruments allows for the gathering of information specific to each client's situation, the lack of standardization leaves ample room for examiner bias to interfere with scoring and interpretation.

The sensitive assessor should be attuned to responses on competency assessment instruments that may appear suspicious or paranoid but that in fact reflect genuine concerns for the minority defendant. Grisso (1986) provided an example of a Black defendant whose case was being handled by a court-appointed attorney. The defendant responded to a question on the CAI about his lawyer by saying that he did not think that the lawyer was interested in handling his case. The examiner interpreted this response as reflecting a lack of understanding of the lawyer–client relationship. However, the defendant may have been correct in assuming that his court-appointed attorney was not overly enthusiastic about representing him. For a minority client who may have experienced a series of negative encounters with representatives of the majority culture, seemingly irrational responses such as that of Grisso's (1986) defendant may represent a realistic appraisal of a familiar situation.

When assessing competency in defendants whose first language is not English, the careful selection of appropriate instruments becomes increasingly important. M. B. Johnson and Torres (1992) cited an example of a 35-year-old Cuban immigrant whose competency to stand trial was assessed using a WAIS-R that had been translated into Spanish by a bilingual examiner. His Full Scale IQ score was calculated to be 62, leading to a diagnosis of mild mental retardation. However, when the defendant's intellectual functioning was reassessed using the Escala de Intelligencia Wechsler para Adultos, a Spanish version of the WAIS-R that was normed on a Puerto Rican sample, he achieved a Full Scale IQ score of 105, a 43-point increase from the original assessment. In addition, a thorough interview with the defendant in his native language revealed that he understood the concepts of guilt, plea bargaining, and due process as they applied to his case.

M. B. Johnson and Torres (1992) suggested that the defense examiner underestimated the defendant's competency to stand trial for several reasons. The use of a translated assessment instrument whose norms did not apply to the defendant clearly resulted in an underestimation of the defendant's intellectual capabilities. Furthermore, a lack of appropriate rapport and thorough questioning in the interview by the defense examiner may have obscured the defendant's understanding of key legal concepts. Perhaps most significant, the authors proposed that the defense examiner's finding of incompetence was based largely on a stereotype about the Cuban Mariel immigrants, a group widely believed to be uneducated and of low social class. They cited as evidence the defense examiner's report, which stated that the defendant was "raised in a totalitarian society in which democratic concepts did not exist and absolute unquestioning obedience to authority was the norm" and that he was therefore incapable of appreciating his rights under democratic law (M. B. Johnson & Torres, 1992, pp. 70–71). That a culturally appropriate assessment provided evidence to the contrary is an indication of the bias and inaccuracy inherent in the defense examiner's assumptions.

Clearly, more research is required on the unique factors that affect the competency assessment of minority defendants. In recognition of this need, a conference titled Multicultural Issues in Forensic Mental Health Evaluations was recently sponsored by the Massachusetts Department of Mental Health's Division of Forensic Mental Health and the University of Massachusetts Medical Center. Presentations focused on cross-cultural issues in interviewing and diagnosis, demographics of the forensic mental health system, and promoting cross-cultural competence in forensic mental health services. We hope that with the growing interest in cross-cultural issues in forensic assessment that is evidenced by conferences such as this, psychologists will soon have access to a well-developed set of norms and guidelines to use in addressing issues of trial competency with culturally different defendants.

Forensic Evaluation: Assessment of Parenting Competency

In a study by Caplan and Wilson (1990), judges in the United States and Canada reported following recommendations from clinical assessments at least 92% of the time in reaching child custody decisions. Assessors in child custody cases play a large part in decisions that will ultimately affect the lives of many people, including children who may be too young to participate in decisions affecting their placement other than through assessment by a psychological examiner. It is therefore crucial that the clinician aiding in child custody decisions have a thorough understanding of the racial, ethnic, and socioeconomic factors that may affect performance on measures designed to assess parenting competency.

According to Brodzinsky (1993), four main types of instruments are typically used to assess parenting competency: intellectual assessment instruments, achievement tests for children, personality instruments, and instruments measuring parenting attitudes and beliefs. He also noted the importance of behavioral observations of parent–child interactions and of interviewing parents and children of an appropriate age. Bias in the interpretation of intellectual and personality assessment instruments has been discussed elsewhere throughout this book and applies equally to cases in which these instruments are used in child custody assessments. Although they were primarily designed for use as research instruments and may have questionable diagnostic and predictive utility in child custody cases (Grisso, 1986), measures of parenting attitudes and beliefs have sometimes been used to aid in custody decisions that involve assessing parental fitness or selecting the more appropriate of two competent parents.

The increasing diversity in the normative samples for instruments of parenting competency is encouraging. For example, the Adult-Adolescent Parenting Inventory (Bavolek, 1984), which attempts to identify high-risk adolescents in need of particular parenting skills, was normed on a sample of abused and nonabused Blacks and Whites and provides separate norms for each Age × Race × Gender combination. Similarly, various forms of the Parental Attitude Research Instrument (Schaefer & Bell, 1958) have included participants of stratified SES levels in their normative samples. However, much work remains to be done in this area. Particularly notable is the absence of Asian and Native American parents in the normative samples of many of these instruments. Additionally, an increased effort must be made to include both genders in the normative sample. Many of the instruments used to assess parenting competency were normed exclusively on mothers. For example, the Mother–Child Relationship Evaluation (Roth, 1980) was normed on a sample of middle-class mothers aged 25–35, all of whom resided in the same community. In using this instrument, the limited generalizability of the normative sample may leave custody assessors at a loss when interpreting the responses of lower SES, middle-aged, or male examinees.

On an individual item level, many of the research instruments that assess parental attitudes may reflect a bias toward the beliefs about parenting endorsed by the dominant culture. For example, an item on the Children's Report of Parental Behavior (Schaefer, 1965) asks the child to agree or disagree with the statement, "My mother often speaks of the good things I do." A response indicating that this behavior is uncharacteristic of a parent may appear to reflect a lack of positive reinforcement for a child's good behavior. However, parents from many cultures may choose not to speak publicly of a child's accomplishments for reasons as diverse as the belief among traditional Irish American families that excessive praise leads to a "swelled head" (McGoldrick, 1982), the value placed by Native Americans on not calling undue attention to oneself at the expense of the group (D. W. Sue & Sue, 1990), and the desire by traditional Jewish parents to avoid the "evil eye" that may befall a child who is too loudly and frequently praised (S. Zucker, personal communication, June 15, 1996).

It also is crucial to consider the effects of social desirability and acquiescence on examinees' responses to these instruments. For example, Marín and Marín (1991) suggested that among Hispanic participants, there may be a tendency to respond to the majority of questions in the affirmative or to endorse the seemingly correct response, independent of the content of the question or the participants' actual experiences. The tendency to produce these response sets may vary with the age, gender, education, SES, and acculturation level of the respondents. In cases of child custody, in which the examinees may perceive their responses as determining whether they are allowed to retain custody of their children, the tendency to provide socially desirable answers may be particularly apparent. This may lead to a profile that is invalid at best and that may bear little resemblance to the examinee's actual parenting behavior.

Marín and Marín (1991) suggested that examiners can partially compensate for socially desirable or acquiescent response sets by including a measure of social desirability in their assessment battery. This may alert the examiner to cases in which a respondent's approach to an inventory reflects a desire to appear socially appropriate rather than an accurate representation of his or her attitudes and behaviors. In addition, the authors recommended that multiple sources of data be gathered to validate an examinee's responses to a structured inventory. In the case of parenting competency, direct observations of parent–child interactions and consultation with members of the family or community who are familiar with the examinee's parenting style and capabilities may produce a more accurate picture than the use of a standardized assessment instrument alone.

When assessing parenting competency in many minority groups, it also is important for clinicians to consider the role of the extended family network in child rearing. The participation of the extended kinship network in the raising of a child is a well-documented practice among many minority families (e.g., McGoldrick, Giordano, & Pearce, 1996; Rubin, 1992). A biological parent's deficits in skills or resources may at times be compensated for by other family members, close friends, or members of the community who take an active role in caring for the child. In spite of its prevalence, this shared responsibility for child rearing may be misinterpreted. For example, Rubin suggested that among some urban Black families, the use of the extended kinship network in child care may result in a child's living with different relatives at different times according to the needs and abilities of various members of the extended family. This practice may be misinterpreted by the uninformed assessor as suggesting "a chaotic environment and even an attempt to keep the child away from [a] caseworker" (Rubin, 1992, p. 259). Such conclusions may reflect a lack of cultural awareness on the assessor's part and could conceivably lead to the child being removed without cause from a functional and nurturing family environment. Therefore, a thorough assessment of parenting competency may require that the examiner identify parties other than the biological parents who play a key role in the child's upbringing and include them in the formal assessment.

A striking example of the effects of sociocultural bias on the assessment of parenting competency can be found in the much-publicized case of Mary Beth Whitehead, a lower middle-class married mother of two. Mrs. Whitehead's attempt to gain custody of her biological daughter Sara Melissa (known to the press as Baby M) led to a heated court battle with the Sterns, the couple who had hired her as a surrogate mother. To determine the relative competencies of each couple, the court heard testimony from a clinical psychologist, a physician, and a social worker who had been chosen by Sara Melissa's court-appointed guardian to evaluate the Sterns and the Whiteheads. Although the couples were given similar test batteries, a careful examination of the expert testimony revealed a consistent bias in favor of the Sterns and against the Whiteheads on the basis of "prevailing middle-class beliefs about good mothers and good parenting" (Harrison, 1987, p. 300).

For example, both couples were given the Picture Arrangement subtest of the WAIS-R, a test that measures social judgment, planning ability, and sensitivity to part–whole relations. Neither of the Sterns scored higher than the low average range on this test, a finding that the examiners interpreted as an artifact of anxiety. However, similar deficiencies in scoring by the Whiteheads were interpreted as signs of psychopathology or low intellect (Harrison, 1987). Similarly, both Dr. Stern and Mrs. Whitehead scored high on a scale (presumably on the MMPI) that measures a person's tendency to present himself or herself as socially desirable. Nevertheless, Dr. Stern's testimony was judged by her assessors to be "generally sincere and honest as she understands and interprets the 'facts' of this case," whereas Mrs. Whitehead was believed to be "*frequently* covering up or selectively remembering past events'' (Brodzinsky, as quoted in Harrison, 1987, p. 304). Middle-class bias alone may not have been responsible for the eventual decision to grant the Sterns full custody of Sara Melissa; however, it unquestionably colored the assessment that contributed to the decision.

General Conclusions and Recommendations

Psychological tests are used to aid in diagnosis, treatment planning, and decision making in a wide range of situations. The psychologist who is called on to assess parenting competency will clearly need to be alert to issues that are slightly different from those involved in assessing psychiatric impairment. However, some general conclusions and recommendations can be made about the use of assessment devices with clients of diverse racial, ethnic, and socioeconomic backgrounds.

The most pressing need in the creation and use of clinical and forensic assessment instruments is for improved normative samples that include culturally diverse individuals. The scarcity of normative information on assessment instruments for Blacks, Hispanics, and clients of low SES, and the almost complete absence of such information for Asians and Native Americans, suggests the need to establish norms for clients from diverse backgrounds. This is especially true of competency assessment instruments, few of which include demographic descriptions of the samples on which they were normed. Including test norms for diverse groups would not eliminate the bias inherent in some tests. However, clinicians who assess minority clients would have a clearer framework within which to interpret the test performance of their clients.

The renorming of a test battery is, of course, a costly and time-consuming process, and progress in this area is likely to be slow. Until the necessary modifications to normative samples have been made, it may be most productive to take steps to compensate for the bias in commonly used instruments.

Some of the most important recommendations refer to good standard testing practices, but these standards take on special meaning in testing members of minority groups. The first is that there can be no substitute for a thorough familiarity with the instrument being used. Basic knowledge would include awareness of the groups on which the test was normed, and its appropriateness for the individual tested, as well as for the referral question.

Second, it is necessary to try to understand the client's background in order to place the interpretation of test results in a realistic context. General training in cultural sensitivity will be helpful in developing an overall approach to working with diverse populations, but it cannot be assumed that findings characterizing one minority group, such as Asian Americans, are applicable to other groups. Thus, information should be sought about the specific values and situation of the individual being tested. This may necessitate consultation with other professionals who are knowledgeable about the client's culture.

Whenever possible, multiple measures of the same construct should be used. Again, this is part of good standard practice and deserves special consideration in testing members of groups for whom there is limited information about test validity.

Consider the addition of an acculturation measure. Cervantes and Acosta (1992) and Okazaki and Sue (1995) recommended the use of acculturation measures for Hispanic and Asian American clients, respectively. Such tests would help to determine the extent to which the norms of a particular measure apply to the individual. Highly acculturated, middle-class clients may exhibit response patterns that approximate those of the normative group for many assessment instruments. For example, a third-generation, middle-class Mexican American may be more similar to the normative sample of the WAIS-R than to the predominantly lower class, island Puerto Rican sample used in developing the *Escala de Inteligencia Wechsler para Adultos* (the spanish version of the WAIS). There are several acculturation measures, and care needs to be exercised in selecting measures that are relevant to the assessment question. The difficulties of finding an appropriate measure of acculturation have been documented elsewhere (e.g., Moyerman & Forman, 1992; Rogler, Cortes, & Malagady, 1991) and are beyond the scope of this chapter. However, the addition of an acculturation measure to a test battery may be a valuable aid in test interpretation.

When interpreting responses on assessment devices, it is important to distinguish between incorrect or deviant responses that suggest intellectual deficiency or psychopathology and those that reflect a lack of familiarity with standardized testing procedures or knowledge about the area being assessed. For example, questions on forensic instruments that require defendants to describe the role of the prosecuting attorney may be answered incorrectly by a defendant who has had limited exposure to the legal system. Deficiencies on structured assessment devices that result from limited exposure to testing procedures or the content area of the assessment may be easily remedied and should be readily apparent to the examiner who has taken a thorough social history as part of the assessment.

Finally, as should be the case with all responsible test interpretation, we suggest that the assessor report all relevant race, gender, ethnicity, and SES information that may interfere with his or her ability to draw conclusions from the test data. Short of the currently unrealistic feat of selecting a test battery whose norms and cultural and linguistic demands are consistent with each client's personal cultural profile, this may be the best safeguard against misinterpreting test results or providing colleagues with incomplete or misleading information about a client's functioning.

References

Abel, T. M. (1973). *Psychological testing in cultural contexts*. New Haven, CT: College and University Press.

Adebimpe, V. R. (1979). Overview: White norms and psychiatric diagnosis of Black patients. *American Journal of Psychiatry, 138,* 279–285.

Aldwin, C., & Greenberger, E. (1987). Cultural differences in the predictors of depression. *American Journal of Community Psychology, 15,* 789–813.

Allen, A. M. (1992). Effects of race and gender on diagnostic judgments with the *DSM-III-R* [Doctoral dissertation, University of South Dakota, 1992]. *Dissertation Abstracts International, 53/05-A,* 1395.

Anastasi, A., & Urbina, S. (1997). *Psychological testing* (7th ed.). Upper Saddle River, NJ: Prentice-Hall.

Aronow, E., Reznikoff, M., & Moreland, K. (1994). *The Rorschach technique*. Needham Heights, MA: Allyn & Bacon.

Bailey, B. E., & Green, J. (1977). Black Thematic Apperception Test stimulus material. *Journal of Personality Assessment, 41,* 25–30.

Bavolek, S. J. (1984). *Handbook for the Adult–Adolescent Parenting Inventory*. Schaumberg, IL: Family Development Associates.

Beck, N. C., McRae, C., Hendrichs, T. F., Sneider, L., Horowitz, B., Rennier, G., Thomas, S., & Hedlund, J. (1989). Replicated item level factor structure of the MMPI: Racial and sexual differences. *Journal of Clinical Psychology, 45,* 553–560.

Bellak, L. (Ed.). (1993). *The TAT, CAT and SAT in clinical use* (5th ed.). Needham Heights, MA: Allyn & Bacon.

Bernard, L. C. (1989). Halstead-Reitan Neuropsychological Test performance of Black, Hispanic, and White young adult males from poor academic backgrounds. *Archives of Clinical Neuropsychology, 4,* 267–274.

Bernstein, I. H., Teng, G., Grannemann, B. D., & Garbin, C. P. (1987). Invariance in the MMPI's component structure. *Journal of Personality Assessment, 51,* 522–531.

Berry, D. T. R., Wetter, N. W., & Baer, R. A. (1995). Overreporting of closed-head injury symptoms on the MMPI-2. *Psychological Assessment, 7,* 517–523.

Betancourt, H., & López, S. R. (1993). The study of culture, ethnicity, and race in American psychology. *American Psychologist, 48,* 629–637.

Bird, H. R., Canino, G., Rubio, G., Stipec, M., & Shrout, P. (1987). Use of the Mini-

Mental State Examination in a probability sample of a Hispanic population. *Journal of Nervous and Mental Disease, 175,* 731–737.

Blatt, S. J. (1990). The Rorschach: A test of perception or an evaluation of representation. *Journal of Personality Assessment, 55,* 394–416.

Block, N. J., & Dworkin, G. (1976). *The IQ controversy.* New York: Pantheon Books.

Borum, R., & Grisso, T. (1995). Psychological test use in criminal forensic evaluations. *Professional Psychology: Research and Practice, 26,* 465–473.

Brodzinsky, D. M. (1993). On the use and misuse of psychological testing in child custody evaluations. *Professional Psychology: Research and Practice, 24,* 213–219.

Butcher, J. N., & Pope, K. S. (1993). Seven issues in conducting forensic assessments: Ethical responsibilities in light of new standards and new tests. *Ethics and Behavior, 3,* 267–288.

Butcher, J. N., Braswell, L., & Raney, D. (1983). A cross-cultural comparison of American Indian, Black, and White inpatients on the MMPI and presenting symptoms. *Journal of Consulting and Clinical Psychology, 51,* 587–594.

Calsyn, D. A., Saxon, A. J., & Daisy, F. (1991). Validity of the MCMI Drug Abuse scale varies as a function of drug choice, race, and Axis II subtypes. *American Journal of Drug and Alcohol Abuse, 17,* 153–159.

Campos, L. P. (1989). Adverse impact, unfairness, and bias in the psychological screening of Hispanic peace officers. *Hispanic Journal of Behavioral Sciences, 11,* 122–135.

Caplan, P. J., & Wilson, J. (1990). Assessing the assessor: Legal issues. *Canadian Family Law Quarterly, 6,* 179–226.

Cervantes, R. C., & Acosta, F. X. (1992). Psychological testing for Hispanic Americans. *Applied and Preventive Psychology, 1,* 209–219.

Chavez, E., & Gonzales-Singh, E. (1980). Hispanic assessment: A case study. *Professional Psychology, 11,* 163–168.

Chin, J. L. (1983). Diagnostic considerations in working with Asian-Americans. *American Journal of Orthopsychiatry, 53,* 100–109.

Choca, J. P., Shanley, L. A., Peterson, C. A., & Van Denburg, E. (1990). Racial bias and the MCMI. *Journal of Personality Assessment, 54,* 479–490.

Choca, J. P., Shanley, L. A., & Van Denburg, E. (Eds.). (1992). *Interpretative guide to the Millon Clinical Multiaxial Inventory.* Washington, DC: American Psychological Association.

Cogburn, M., Zalewski, C., Farrell, S., & Mendoza, M. (1993, April). *Comparison of Asian American and White college students on the MMPI-2.* Paper presented at the annual convention of the Western Psychological Association, Phoenix, AZ.

Constantino, G., Malagady, R. G., & Rogler, L. H. (1988). *TEMAS (Tell-Me-A-Story) manual.* Los Angeles, CA: Western Psychological Services.

Costello, R. M. (1977). Construction and cross-validation of an MMPI Black–White scale. *Journal of Personality Assessment, 41,* 514–519.

Craig, T., Goodman, A. B., & Hauglaund, G. (1982). Impact of *DSM-III* on clinical practice. *American Journal of Psychiatry, 139,* 922–925.

Cronbach, L. J. (1975). Five decades of public controversy over mental testing. *American Psychologist, 30,* 1–14.

Dahlstrom, W. G., Lachar, D., & Dahlstrom, L. E. (1986). *MMPI patterns of American minorities.* Minneapolis: University of Minnesota Press.

Dana, R. H. (1993). *Multicultural assessment perspectives for professional psychology.* Needham Heights, MA: Allyn & Bacon.

Davis, W. E., Greenblatt, R. L., & Pochyly, J. M. (1990). Test of MCMI Black norms for five scales. *Journal of Clinical Psychology, 46,* 175–178.

Escobar, J. I., Burnam, M. A., Karno, M., Forsythe, A., Landsverk, J., & Golding, J. A. (1986). Use of the Mini-Mental State Examination (MMSE) in a community population of mixed ethnicity. *Journal of Nervous and Mental Disease, 174,* 607–614.

Exner, J. Jr. (1986). *The Rorscach: A comprehensive system—Vol. 1: Basic foundations* (2nd ed.). New York: Wiley.

Fabrega, H., Mezzich, J., & Ulrich, R. F. (1988). Black–White differences in psychopathology. *Comprehensive Psychiatry, 29,* 285–297.

Fabrega, H., Rubel, A. J., & Wallace, C. A. (1967). Some social and cultural features of working class Mexican psychiatric outpatients. *Archives of General Psychiatry, 16,* 704–712.

Faust, D., & Ziskin, J. (1988). The expert witness in psychology and psychiatry. *Science, 241,* 31–35.

Finn, S. E., & Camphuis, J. H. (1995). What a clinician should know about base rates. In J. N. Butcher (Ed.), *Clinical personality assessment* (pp. 229–235). New York: Oxford University Press.

Flaskerud, J. H., & Hu, L. (1992). Relationship of ethnicity to psychiatric diagnosis. *Journal of Nervous and Mental Disorders, 180,* 296–303.

Garcia-Peltoniemi, R. E., & Azun, A. A. (1993). *Inventario multifascio de la personalidad-2-Minnesota (Version Hispana).* Minneapolis: University of Minnesota Press.

Golding, S. L., Roesch, R., & Schreiber, J. (1984). Assessment and conceptualization of competency to stand trial: Preliminary data on the Interdisciplinary Fitness Interview. *Law and Human Behavior, 8,* 321–334.

Goldman, V. J., Cooke, A., & Dahlstrom, W. G. (1995). Black–White differences among college students: A comparison of MMPI and MMPI-2 norms. *Assessment, 2,* 293–299.

Graham, J. R. (1993). *MMPI-2: Assessing personality and psychopathology* (2nd ed.). New York: Oxford University Press.

Gray-Little, B. (1995). The assessment of psychopathology in racial and ethnic minorities. In J. N. Butcher (Ed.), *Clinical personality assessment* (pp. 140–157). New York: Oxford University Press.

Greenblatt, R. L., & Davis, W. E. (1992). Accuracy of MCMI classification of angry and psychotic Black and White patients. *Journal of Clinical Psychology, 48,* 59–63.

Greene, R. L. (1987). Ethnicity and MMPI performance: A review. *Journal of Consulting and Clinical Psychology, 55,* 497–512.

Grillo, J. (1991). The influence on ethnicity of the validity and clinical scales of the MMPI-2 (validity scales). [Doctoral dissertation, Memphis State University, 1991]. *Dissertation Abstracts International, 52/07-B,* 3905.

Grisso, T. (1986). *Evaluating competencies: Forensic assessments and instruments.* New York: Plenum.

Gynther, M. D. (1972). White norms and Black MMPIs: A prescription for discrimination? *Psychological Bulletin, 78,* 386–402.

Gynther, M. D. (1989). MMPI patterns of Blacks and Whites: A review. *Journal of Clinical Psychology, 45,* 878–883.

Gynther, M. D., & Green, S. B. (1980). Accuracy may make a difference, but does difference make for accuracy? A response to Pritchard and Greenblatt. *Journal of Consulting and Clinical Psychology, 48,* 268–272.

Hamberger, L. K., & Hastings, J. E. (1992). Racial differences on the MCMI in an outpatient clinical sample. *Journal of Personality Assessment, 58,* 90–95.

Harrison, M. (1987). Social construction of Mary Beth Whitehead. *Gender and Society, 1,* 300–311.

Henry, W. E. (1987). *The analysis of fantasy.* New York: Wiley.

Holtzman, W. H. (1980). Projective techniques. In H. C. Triandis & J. W. Berry (Eds.), *Handbook of cross-cultural psychology* (Vol. 2, pp. 245–278). Boston: Allyn & Bacon.

Howes, R. D., & DeBlassie, R. R. (1989). Modal errors in the cross cultural use of the Rorschach. *Journal of Multicultural Counseling and Development, 17,* 79–84.

Johnson, D., & Sikes, M. (1965). Rorschach and T.A.T. responses of Negro, Mexican American, and Anglo psychiatric patients. *Journal of Projective Techniques, 29,* 183–188.

Johnson, M. B., & Torres, L. (1992). Miranda, trial competency, and Hispanic immigrant defendants. *American Journal of Forensic Psychology, 10,* 65–80.

Jones, B. E., & Gray, B. A. (1986). Problems in diagnosing schizophrenia and affective disorders among Blacks. *Hospital and Community Psychiatry, 37,* 61–65.

Kaplan, R. M., & Saccuzzo, D. P. (Eds.). (1993). *Psychological testing: Principles, applications and issues* (3rd ed.). Pacific Grove, CA: Brooks/Cole.

Kaplan, R. M., & Saccuzzo, D. P. (Eds.). (1997). *Psychological testing: Principles, applications, and issues* (4th ed.). Pacific Grove, CA: Brooks/Cole.

Karle, H. R., & Valasquez, R. J. (1996). *The comparability of the English and Spanish versions of the MMPI-2.* Manuscript submitted for publication.

Keefe, J., Sue, S., Enomoto, K., Durvasula, R., & Chao, R. (1994). Asian American and White college students' performance on the MMPI-2. In J. N. Butcher (Ed.), *Handbook of international MMPI-2 research* (pp. 204–235). New York: Oxford University Press.

Kleinman, A. (1986). *Social origins of distress and disease: Depression, neurasthenia, and pain in modern China.* New Haven, CT: Yale University Press.

Krall, V. (1983). Rorschach norms for inner city children. *Journal of Personality Assessment, 47,* 155–157.

Kuo, W. H. (1984). Prevalence of depression among Asian Americans. *Journal of Nervous and Mental Disease, 172,* 449–457.

Lang, W. S. (1992). Reviewing the TEMAS (Tell-Me-A-Story). In J. J. Kramer & J. C. Conoley (Eds.), *Eleventh mental measurements yearbook* (pp. 925–926). Lincoln: University of Nebraska, Buros Institute of Mental Measurement.

Lawson, W. B. (1986). Racial and ethnic factors in psychiatric research. *Hospital and Community Psychiatry, 37,* 50–54.

Lichtenberg, P. A., Ross, T., & Christensen, B. (1994). Preliminary normative data on the Boston Naming Test for an older urban population. *Clinical Neuropsychologist, 8,* 109–111.

Lipsitt, P., & Lelos, D. (1973). *Competency to stand trial and mental illness* (DHEW Publication No. ADM 77-103). Rockville, MD: U.S. Department of Health, Education, and Welfare.

Liss, J. L., Welner, A., Robins, E., & Richardson, M. (1973). Psychiatric symptoms in White and Black inpatients: I. Record study. *Comprehensive Psychiatry, 14,* 475–481.

Loewenstein, D., Rubert, M. P., Argüelles, T., & Duara, R. (1995). Neuropsychological test performance and prediction of functional capacities among Spanish-speaking and English-speaking patients with dementia. *Archives of Clinical Neuropsychology, 10,* 75–88.

López, S. R. (1989). Patient variable biases in clinical judgment: Conceptual overview and methodological considerations. *Psychological Bulletin, 106,* 184–203.

Loring, M., & Powell, B. (1988). Gender, race, and *DSM-III:* A study of the objectivity of psychiatric diagnostic behavior. *Journal of Health and Social Behavior, 29,* 1–22.

Lubin, B., Larsen, R. M., Matarazzo, J. D., & Seever, M. F. (1985). Psychological test usage patterns in five professional settings. *American Psychologist, 40,* 857–861.

Maduro, R. (1983). Curanderismo and Latino views of diseases and curing. *Western Journal of Medicine, 139,* 868–874.

Marín, G., & Marín, B. (1991). *Research with Hispanic populations.* Newbury Park, CA: Sage.

Marsella, A. J., Kenzie, D., & Gordon, P. (1973). Ethnic variations in the expression of depression. *Journal of Cross-Cultural Psychology, 4,* 435–458.

Marsella, A. J. Sanborn, K. O., Kameoka, V., Shizuru, L., & Brennan, J. (1975). Cross-validation of self-report measures of depression among normal populations of Japanese, Chinese, and Caucasian ancestry. *Journal of Clinical Psychology, 31,* 281–287.

Martin, T. W. (1993). White therapists' differing perception of Black and White adolescents. *Adolescence, 28,* 281–289.

McDonald, R. L., & Gynther, M. D. (1963). MMPI norms associated with sex, race, and class in two adolescent samples. *Journal of Consulting Psychology, 27,* 112–116.

McGarry, A. L., & Associates. (1973). *Competency to stand trial and mental illness.* Rockville, MD: U.S. Department of Health, Education, and Welfare.

McGoldrick, M. (1982). Irish families. In M. McGoldrick, J. K. Pearce, & J. Giordano (Eds.), *Ethnicity and family therapy* (pp. 310–339). New York: Guilford Press.

McGoldrick, M., Giordano, J., & Pearce, J. K. (Eds.). (1996) *Ethnicity and family therapy.* (2nd ed.). New York: Guilford Press.

McNulty, J. L., Graham, J. R., Ben-Porath, Y. S., & Stein, L. A. R. (1997). Comparative validity of MMPI-2 scans of African Americans and Caucasian mental health center clients. *Psychological Assessment, 9,* 464–470.

Megargee, E. (1966). A comparison of the scores of White and Negro male juvenile delinquents on three projective tests. *Journal of Projective Techniques, 30,* 530–535.

Millon, T. (1987). *Manual for the MCMI-II* (2nd ed.). Minneapolis, MN: National Computer Systems.

Moyerman, D. R., & Forman, B. D. (1992). Acculturaiton and adjustment: A meta-analytic study. *Hispanic Journal of Behavioral Sciences, 14,* 163–200.

Mukherjee, S., Shukla, S., Woodle, J., Rosen, A., & Olarte, S. (1983). Misdiagnosis of schizophrenia in bipolar patients: A multiethnic comparison. *American Journal of Psychiatry, 140,* 1571–1574.

Okazaki, S., & Sue, S. (1995). Cultural considerations in psychological assessment of Asian Americans. In J. N. Butcher (Ed.), *Clinical personality assessment: Practical approaches* (pp. 107–119). New York: Oxford University Press.

Park, B., & Rothbart, M. (1982). Perception of out-group homogeneity and levels of social categorization: Memory for the subordinate attributes of in-group and out-group members. *Journal of Personality and Social Psychology, 42,* 1051–1068.

Pavkov, T. W., Lewis, D. A., & Lyons, J. S. (1989). Psychiatric diagnoses and racial bias: An empirical investigation. *Professional Psychology: Research and Practice, 20,* 364–368.

Pedersen, P. (1987). Ten frequent assumptions of cultural bias in counseling. *Journal of Multicultural Counseling and Development, 5,* 17–25.

Phillips, L. (1992). A letter from Leslie Phillips. *SPA Exchange, 2,* 9.

Phillips, L., & Smith, J. G. (1953). *Rorschach interpretation: Advanced technique.* New York: Grune & Stratton.

Piotrowski, Z., & Keller, J. W. (1989). Psychological testing in outpatient mental health facilities. *Professional Psychology: Research and Practice, 20,* 423–425.

Piotrowski, Z., Sherry, D., & Keller, J. W. (1985). Psychodiagnostic test usage: A survey of the Society for Personality Assessment. *Journal of Personality Assessment, 49,* 115–119.

Pollack, D., & Shore, J. H. (1980). Validity of the MMPI with Native Americans. *American Journal of Psychiatry, 137,* 946–950.

Pritchard, D. A., & Rosenblatt, A. (1980). Racial bias in the MMPI: A methodological review. Journal of Consulting and Clinical Psychology, 48, 263–267.

Ritzler, B. A. (1996). Projective methods for multicultural personality assessment. In L. A. Suzuki, P. J. Meller, & J. G. Ponterotto (Eds.), *Handbook of multicultural assessment* (pp. 115–135). San Francisco: Jossey-Bass.

Ritzler, B. A., & Alter, B. (1986). Rorschach-teaching in APA-approved clinical graduate programs: Ten years later. *Journal of Personality Assessment, 50,* 44–49.

Roesch, R., Eaves, D., Sollner, R., Normandin, M., & Glackman, W. (1981). Evaluating fitness to stand trial: A comparative analysis of fit and unfit defendants. *International Journal of Law and Psychiatry, 4,* 145–157.

Rogler, L. H., Cortes, D. E., & Malagady, R. G. (1991). Acculturation and mental health status among Hispanics: Convergence and new directions for research. *American Psychologist, 46,* 585–597.

Rosenfield, S. (1984). Race differences in involuntary hospitalization: Psychiatric vs. labeling perspectives. *Journal of Health and Social Behavior, 25,* 14–23.

Roth, R. M. (1980). *The Mother–Child Relationship Evaluation: Manual.* Los Angeles, CA: Western Psychological Services.

Rubin, G. B. (1992). Multicultural considerations in the application of child protection laws. *Journal of Social Distress and the Homeless, 1,* 249–271.

Schaefer, E. (1965). Children's Reports of Parental Behavior: An inventory. *Child Development, 36,* 417–423.

Schaefer, E., & Bell, R. (1958). Development of a parental attitude research instrument. *Child Development, 29,* 339–361.

Scott, R. (1981). FM: Clinically meaningful Rorschach index with minority children? *Psychology in the Schools, 18,* 429–433.

Shondrick, D. D., Ben-Porath, Y. S., & Stafford, K. (1992, May). *Forensic assessment with the MMPI-2: Characteristics of individuals undergoing court-ordered evaluations.* Paper presented at the 27th Annual Symposium on Recent Developments of the MMPI (MMPI-2), Minneapolis, MN.

Simon, R. J., Fleiss, J. L., Gurland, B. J., Stiller, P. R., & Sharpe, L. (1973). Depression and schizophrenia in hospitalized Black and White mental patients. *Archives of General Psychiatry, 28,* 509–512.

Snowden, L., & Todman, P. (1982). The psychological assessment of Blacks: New and needed developments. In E. Jones & S. Korchin (Eds.), *Minority mental health* (pp. 193–226). New York: Holt, Rinehart & Winston.

Strawkowski, S. M., Lonczak, H. S., Sax, K. W., West, S. A., Crist, A., Mehta, R., & Thienhaus, O. J. (1995). The effects of race on diagnosis and disposition from a psychiatric emergency service. *Journal of Clinical Psychiatry, 56,* 101–107.

Strickland, T. L., Jenkins, J. O., Myers, H. F., & Adams, H. E. (1988). Diagnostic judgments as a function of client and therapist race. *Journal of Psychopathology and Behavioral Assessment, 10,* 141–151.

Sue, D. W., & Sue, S. (1990). *Counseling the culturally different: Theory and practice.* New York: Wiley.

Sue, S., & Morishima, J. K. (1982). *The mental health of Asian Americans.* San Francisco: Jossey Bass.

Sue, S., & Sue, D. W. (1974). MMPI comparisons between Asian-American and non-Asian students utilizing a student health psychiatric clinic. *Journal of Counseling Psychology, 21,* 423–427.

Thompson, C. E. (1949). The Thompson modification of the Thematic Apperception Test. *Rorschach Research Exchange and Journal of Projective Techniques, 13,* 469–478.

Timbrook, R. E., & Graham, J. R. (1994). Ethnic differences on the MMPI-2? *Psychological Assessment, 6,* 212–217.

Torgersen, S., & Alnaes, R. (1990). The relationship between the MCMI personality scales and the DSM-III Axis II. *Journal of Personality Assessment, 55,* 698–707.

Tsushima, W. T., & Onorato, V. A. (1982). Comparison of MMPI scores of White and Japenese-American medical patients. *Journal of Consulting and Clinical Psychology, 50,* 150–151.

Velasquez, R. J., & Callahan, W. J. (1990a). MMPIs of Hispanic, Black, and White *DSM-III* schizophrenics. *Psychological Reports, 66,* 819–822.

Velasquez, R. J., & Callahan, W. J. (1990b). MMPI comparisons of Hispanic- and White-American veterans seeking treatment for alcoholism. *Psychological Reports, 67,* 95–98.

Velasquez, R. J., & Callahan, W. J., & Carrillo, R. (1989). MMPI profiles of Hispanic-American inpatient and outpatient sex offenders. *Psychological Reports, 65,* 1055–1058.

Velasquez, R. J., & Callahan, W. J., & Young, R. (1993). Hispanic-White MMPI comparisons: Does psychiatric diagnosis make a difference? *Journal of Clinical Psychology, 49,* 528–534.

Weekes, J. R., Morison, S. J., Millson, W. A., & Fettig, D. M. (1995). A comparison of Native, Metis, and Caucasian offender profiles on the MCMI. *Canadian Journal of Behavioral Science, 27* 187–198.

Weisman, C. P., Anglin, M. D., & Fisher, D. G. (1989). The MMPI profiles of narcotics addicts. *International Journal of the Addictions, 24,* 881–896.

Westermeyer, J. (1987). Cultural factors in clinical assessment. *Journal of Consulting and Clinical Psychology, 55,* 471–478.

Wetzler, S., & Dubro, A. (1990). Diagnosis of personality disorders by the Millon Clinical Multiaxial Inventory. *Journal of Nervous and Mental Disease, 178,* 261–263.

Whitworth, R. H. (1988). Anglo- and Mexican-American performance of the MMPI administered in Spanish or English. *Journal of Clinical Psychology, 44,* 891–897.

Whitworth, R. H., & McBlaine, D. D. (1993). Comparison of the MMPI and MMPI-2 administered to Anglo- and Hispanic-American university students. *Journal of Personality Assessment, 61,* 19–27.

Widiger, T. A., & Sanderson, C. (1987). The convergent and discriminant validity of the MCMI as a measure of the *DSM-III* personality disorders. *Journal of Personality Assessment, 51,* 228–242.

Williams, R. L., & Johnson, R. C. (1981). Progress in developing Afrocentric measuring instruments. *Journal of Non-White Concerns, 9,* 3–18.

Part III

Dimensions of Diversity

Language

Jonathan Sandoval and Richard P. Durán

One of the more complex challenges for psychologists is the reliable and valid assessment of skills of people from non-English backgrounds who might be limited in their English proficiency and who communicate effectively in a language other than English. What inferences can be drawn from the use of tests with individuals limited in their command of English? What inferences can be drawn when the tests have been administered so that the instructions or the substance and content of the task may not have been completely understood by the examinee? All tests normed on native speakers of English, to some degree, are measures of English competency and proficiency. When used with English speakers, however, English proficiency usually does not account for significant variance in the total score. (An exception would be a test of English grammar or vocabulary.) When used with nonnative speakers, a test in English must be interpreted as measuring English proficiency in addition to the constructs it was designed to measure.

In this chapter, we outline some key issues that temper the use of tests with nonnative English speakers and offer guidelines for examiners to use to estimate the extent to which a test is measuring a construct of interest or English proficiency. Much of what we discuss applies to individuals whose first language is American Sign Language (ASL), or who have communication disorders in English, but our focus is on hearing individuals because deaf and hard-of-hearing individuals and others are discussed in later chapters.

We first consider the problem of assessing language proficiency or communicative competency. We then examine difficulties inherent in the available language proficiency tests in English and in the first language and note new horizons for the development of more adequate communication assessment strategies for nonnative speakers of English. Then, we examine common practices in assessing competencies other than language in nonnative English speakers. We discuss the use of English-language tests, the translation process, the adaptation of existing tests, the use of nonverbal tests, the use of foreign-normed tests, the use of adjustments to scores, and the use of performance tests. We conclude with a consideration of critical thinking about test interpretation for nonnative English speakers. Our intent is to provoke thought about what improvements might be made in assessment strategies enacted by psychological practitioners rather than to provide concrete assessment solutions that fit any circumstances faced by practitioners. We believe that our goal is prudent because assessments need to be grounded in the particular uses that are made of them. Furthermore, we recognize that tests are neutral and that difficulties arise from inappropriate inferences that are drawn from them by practitioners. Accordingly, our discussion centers on improving the validity of assessments and their interpretations with individuals for whom English is a second language (Messick, 1995).

Some authors have advocated not testing individuals who are speakers of a language other than English (e.g., Valdés & Figueroa, 1994). Although we acknowledge the many difficulties associated with assessing nonnative English speakers, we assume that the inferences drawn from assessments, if done thoughtfully using multiple measures of constructs, can lead to useful and valid decisions about individuals in a variety of contexts.

The Language Issue

The populations of interest in this chapter are people from non-English backgrounds who vary in their familiarity with English and who are in the process of learning English. We call such individuals "second-language learners" of English and presume that they are fluent for conversational purposes in a non-English first language acquired in infancy. We use the term *learner* loosely, not distinguishing between an individual pursuing formal instruction in a language and someone acquiring a second language through everyday contact with it. We also presume that the non-English language was or is a language spoken in the home or community, although English also may be a language used in these contexts. In policy discourse, such individuals in the United States are often referred to as a "language minority." Not all learners of English as a second language in the United States have been raised outside of the United States and its territories. Some English second-language learners were born in the United States and have lived here all their lives.

According to the 1990 U.S. Census (U.S. Bureau of the Census, 1990), there were 31,844,976 individuals above the age of 5 in the United States who spoke a language other than English at home (about 14% of the U.S. population). Of this group, 56% reported that they spoke English "very well" on a 4-point Likert-scaled question; 44% reported speaking English less than "very well." Included in this latter group were about 6% who reported not speaking English at all. (This 6% represents 0.008% of the total U.S. population.) Table 8.1 shows these numbers for the most common 25 spoken non-English languages whose speakers reported being the least competent in English. This table includes a Native American language, Navaho, languages of recent immigrants such as Mon-Khmer and Miao, and languages of groups who have long resided in this country, such as Pennsylvania Dutch. These figures do not include ASL. These self-reports may or may not be accurate, but they do provide some idea of the linguistic diversity in the United States. It should be obvious that individuals who speak other languages are not evenly spread around the country. In some areas there are a large number of particular types of language minorities. Given recent trends in immigration, there is reason to believe the number of people speaking a non-English home language has increased since 1990. As a result, the probability that psychologists will encounter someone with limited English is high and increasing.

High-Stakes Consequences of Assessment With Linguistically Different Individuals

In any testing situation, but particularly in high-stakes assessments, examinees must have an opportunity to demonstrate the competencies, knowledge, or attributes being measured. Comprehending directions and the content of items are clearly barriers to demonstrating competence. As a result, an assessment of individuals in a language they cannot

Table 8.1

Most Common 25 Languages Spoken at Home in the United States by Speakers Age 5 Years and Older

Language spoken at home	No. of speakers	% Speaking English less than "very well"	% Speaking English "not at all"
Spanish	17,339,000	47.9	8.4
French	1,702,000	28.0	0.5
German	1,547,000	33.2	0.3
Italian	1,308,000	24.9	1.3
Chinese	1,249,000	60.3	8.7
Tagalog	843,000	34.0	0.6
Polish	723,000	37.0	1.8
Korean	626,000	61.2	5.4
Vietnamese	507,000	63.3	4.9
Portuguese	430,000	45.3	6.9
Japanese	427,000	52.5	1.8
Greek	388,000	31.5	1.3
Arabic	355,000	33.7	1.7
Hindi (Urdu)	331,000	29.2	1.5
Russian	242,000	54.4	6.2
Yiddish	213,000	29.0	0.9
Thai (Laotian)	206,000	62.1	5.1
Persian	202,000	38.0	2.7
French Creole	188,000	52.5	3.3
Armenian	150,000	50.2	8.9
Navaho	149,000	44.6	5.1
Hungarian	148,000	35.0	0.8
Mon Khmer (Cambodian)	127,000	73.3	10.8
Pennsylvania Dutch	84,000	43.2	0.8
Miao (Hmong)	82,000	77.6	13.9

comprehend will almost always be a poor measure of the construct. Ideally, assessment for high-stakes decisions should be undertaken by an assessor who is bilingual and bicultural with respect to the language and culture of the examinee. An appropriate background and training will help, but critical thinking will still be important.

In many situations, a high-stakes assessment is used to predict future performance in a job or in a particular course of study in which English proficiency is required. Testing in English may be appropriate in this circumstance as long as the level of English proficiency demanded on the test is no higher than that needed to be successful on the job or in the classroom.

In other situations in which English competency is not needed to be successful, tests should not contain measures of irrelevant constructs such as English proficiency, or there should be an attempt to account for the influence of level of English proficiency on the test score. A first step in taking language proficiency into account is to evaluate it accurately.

Assessing Language Proficiency

Psychological practitioners first face the dilemma of assessing how well non-English speakers can communicate in English. This information will aid in decisions about whether nonnative speakers of English can participate in institutional settings and jobs requiring English as well as to consider the appropriateness of testing in English. An immediate next step in many instances is to assess how well the individuals can communicate in their first or home language. Before discussing the assessment of English competence and first-language competence, we examine the construct of language proficiency.

The Construct of Language Proficiency

Over the past 30 years or so, the notion of "language proficiency" has undergone a dramatic evolution (Spolsky, 1985, 1988). Many language proficiency experts still hold that language proficiency is a unitary mental trait that can be assessed accurately by carefully designed tests made up of numerous discrete item types or item types requiring integration of different forms of linguistic knowledge (Oller, Chesarek, & Scott, 1991). In large part this perspective has been fueled by the prominence of language theories emphasizing the grammatical and structural orderliness of language and the view that language is acquired or taught as a system of rules.

Most commercial language proficiency tests used in schooling, clinical settings, and job settings involve the use of discrete point types or integrative multiple-choice or short response item types. However, other assessment research has emerged suggesting that language proficiency is too narrowly conceived if it is restricted to such item types (see, e.g., Henning, 1987; Henning & Cascallar, 1992; Stansfield, 1986).

There is a growing trend toward a more complex characterization of the construct of language proficiency especially as it might be manifested in authentic everyday situations. These characterizations build on notions such as "communicative competence" (Canale & Swain, 1980; Hymes, 1974), "communicative language ability" (Candlin, 1986), and "communicative proficiency" (Bachman & Palmer, 1982).

Communicative Competence

Communicative competence is knowledge about the appropriateness of language form, content, and usage based on an understanding of the immediate purposes of communication and the social and cultural characteristics of communicative settings. This perspective holds that language proficiency is not well conceived if it postulates that there is a singular language ability encompassing all forms of knowledge about language and how to use it. Whereas traditional language proficiency tests have emphasized the "accuracy" of language form as the main issue for language assessment, communicative competence theory raises the importance of assessing the appropriateness of the functional uses of language in sociocultural contexts.

Language assessment researchers have proposed that communicative competence encompasses four major capacities: grammatical competence, discourse competence, sociolinguistic competence, and strategic competence (Canale & Swain, 1980). Each of these capacities is alleged to operate in a coordinated manner in everyday, authentic language use, but still each capacity is postulated as being distinguishable in terms of the underlying constructs represented and what they highlight about the ability to communicate in a language. Competence can also be examined orally or in writing, and a distinction is often made between expressive and receptive language.

Grammatical competence concerns knowledge about syntax, word structure, pronunciation, and other aspects of language structure at the word, phrase, and sentence levels of language. This is the form of language proficiency best captured by existing discrete point tests of language proficiency and many forms of integrative test items.

By contrast, discourse competence pertains to knowledge about appropriate language structure for the purpose of connecting meaning across phrase, clause, and sentence boundaries or adjacent spoken utterances; think, for example, of knowledge about how to use conjunctive terms such as "and," "oh," "but," and "because," although these are just one type of example. Discourse competence also pertains to knowledge about different genres of written and spoken language (e.g., a "newspaper editorial" vs. a "sermon"). Existing discrete and integrative tests of language proficiency can assess such skills, but usually only when they involve integrating meaning across sentences in abbreviated text passages or at most a few spoken utterances or turns of talk arising in test items.

Sociolinguistic competence, the third component of communicative competence, is the ability to speak or write, or to comprehend speech or writing, taking into account the social and cultural purposes of communication. Think, for example, of the knowledge required to address a physician as "doctor" as opposed to "mister." Discrete point and integrative language proficiency tests can assess sociolinguistic competence when they adequately simulate authentic socially and culturally embedded communication, but the social and cultural demands of simulated situations may not well represent the actual social and cultural characteristics of criterion settings encountered by examinees.

A fourth component of communicative competence is strategic competence. This term pertains to knowledge about how to adjust and regulate language production or comprehension so that it deals with immediate, and usually unforeseen, problems in communication. An example in reading comprehension would be rereading a passage to figure out the meaning of an unfamiliar word. An example in speech would be restarting an utterance to make a statement clearer. Some language assessment investigators (e.g., Bachman, 1990) argue that strategic competence is ubiquitous and always present in language assessment settings because it arises out of the need for examinees to carefully monitor and analyze the appropriateness of language in the assessment context. This point of view is not unlike that of Oller (1979), who argued that there is a close connection between the construct of intelligence and the capacity to use language appropriate to the pragmatic demands of communication.

Although communicative competence assessment researchers recognize that there may be necessary overlap among language skills, they nonetheless have found empirical evidence verifying the existence of separable facets of language ability consistent with accounts of communicative competence. These researchers have investigated assessments of communicative competence through the administration of batteries of multiple-choice and open-ended test items hypothesized to measure different facets of communicative competence. Follow-up factor analyses have confirmed the existence of separate but interrelated factors underlying communicative competence (Bachman & Palmer, 1982).

Testing Communicative Competence

The commercial development of communicative competence assessments of language proficiency have not yet emerged. Some reasons they have not appeared are the high demands that such assessments might make on time for assessment, the need for training of assessment administrators, and the need to develop defensible and reliable objective or rubric-based scoring procedures. Another limitation on the commercial development of tests of communicative competence has conceptual and practitioner bases. Even if it were possible to develop a test of communicative competence that might produce, say, "scores" on four dimensions of communicative competence, the information provided by the test scores would not necessarily be that much more useful for practitioners than a single score on a standardized language proficiency test. Practitioners are likely to want to know how well nonnative speakers of English can function in a specific institutional and sociocultural context given the nature of the context. Although a communicative competence test would provide more information, the practitioners would still need to infer the meaning of scores in light of the demands of the local context for people being assessed. This point is both practical and conceptual. Competence will vary depending on whether the individuals are at school, at work, at home, at church, playing sports, or watching TV.

Research in the fields of interactive sociolinguistics and sociocultural psychology provides evidence that communicative competence is strongly linked to the interactive demands of everyday settings and the roles and expectations guiding participants' actions in those settings. One suggestion is that practitioners and assessment specialists need to analyze the "scripts" and significant practices that constitute effective participation of language learners in authentic institutional and community settings (Adamson, 1993). Think, for example, about the communicative competence demands faced by a child whose first language is not English in understanding how to reply to questions raised by a teacher as a recurrent situation arising in the classroom. Or think about the communicative competence demands faced by a supply clerk in a warehouse or factory asked to find or order parts and materials. Every cultural context is a social context, and although some communicative skills apply across contexts, each context has its own specification of communicative demands. Analyses and reflections on what counts as effective participation in specific contexts yield insights on how language learners cope with the demands of language in those settings and how language learners acquire new competencies in a language. The insights and collaboration between practitioners and assessment specialists to understand the communicative demands of settings can assist them in the development of communicative assessment strategies that supplement, or even replace, the use of existing commercial language proficiency instruments.

Given the complexity of assessing communicative competence and the fact that an individual may be more competent in one language in a particular context than in another, it is still necessary to evaluate the competency of the individual vis-à-vis the testing situation. Existing language tests may be helpful until more sophisticated measures are developed.

Assessment of English Competence

Following the psycholinguistic convention, the second language for an individual will be called *L2* (Language 2); the first, native or home, language will be called *L1* (Language 1). Accordingly, we are concerned here with the assessment of L2 proficiency in English.

For synoptic reviews of widely available English-language proficiency tests, see Harris (1969), Alderson, Krahnke, and Stansfield (1987), and Zehler, Hopstock, Fleischman, and Greniuk (1993). Such tests typically do not require more than an hour or so and most commonly emphasize reading and oral comprehension in a multiple-choice item format, although some tests may include multiple-choice selection of responses that would be considered structurally and meaningfully appropriate in writing or speech. Actual writing or oral speech as part of most commercial language proficiency tests is somewhat rarer, and when it does arise it typically entails filling in at most a word or producing a relatively short statement in response to a test item prompt. The research of Oller (1979; Oller et al., 1991) has shown consistent evidence that performance across a range of test items, especially items integrating multiple language skills of the sort mentioned, correlates highly across items; this research also has shown moderately high to high correlations across different language proficiency tests. Factor analyses of performance on test items or across test batteries tend to produce a single common Language Proficiency factor. However, as Bachman and Palmer (1982) found, careful construction of test items to assess different facets of communicative competence can lead to evidence of different but related skills underlying language proficiency. As a result, good practice would require a selection of tests yielding relevant dimensions of proficiency.

English is one of the most commonly taught second languages in the world. As a result, tests of English proficiency abound. Different tests tend to focus on different language competencies, however. Some emphasize syntax and some morphology, phonology, semantics, or pragmatics. Receptive and expressive competence are often distinguished. This distinction may be helpful in that some tests may require only receptive language (listening comprehension), whereas others will require expressive language (writing or speaking). Receptive language is typically more advanced than expressive language, so that scores on receptive measures would be expected to be relatively higher than scores on tests requiring expression.

Perhaps the most common assessment used in higher education is the Test of English as a Foreign Language (TOEFL). This test was designed to measure beginning and intermediate English proficiency of nonnative speakers. It is used by colleges and universities to place students in English-as-a-second-language programs, to measure progress after instruction, and to determine whether students can function in an English-language instructional setting such as graduate school.

Several measures have been developed for use with children. Some of these include evaluations of English development as well as Spanish-language development. The Bilingual Syntax Measure is one example. This test was designed to measure children's oral proficiency in English or Spanish syntax using natural speech as a basis for making judgments (Burt, Dulay, & Hernandez-Chavez, 1978). Other tests examining English and Spanish include the Language Assessment Battery (New York City Board of Education, 1977), the Language Assessment Scales (DeAvila & Duncan, 1990), and the Basic Inventory of Natural Language (Herbert, 1971). Unfortunately, an examination of the psychometric properties of these tests by Merino and Spencer (1983) showed that these tests were different with respect to the area and variety of language assessed, the developmental difficulty of the items, the lexical domains tapped, and the psychometric qualities of the forms for each language (see also Ulibarri, Spencer, & Rivas, 1981). The norms are regional or limited, although the problem of norming these tests is incredibly complex. The scores on these tests may not be comparable, and any instrument used alone is not sufficient to determine relative proficiency in English and Spanish (Jitendra & Rohena-Diaz, 1996).

It is also useful to distinguish between normal language development and language problems such as aphasia or cleft palate. Speakers of two languages may also have language disorders that affect language competence over and above the interference resulting from exposure to two or more languages. Language loss and arrested language development are common in L2 learners and must not be confused with a language disorder. One means of assessing language disorders in children is the Clinical Evaluation of Language Fundamentals–Third Edition (Semel, Wiig, & Secord, 1997a), a normed test that covers ages 6 through 21. In addition to a direct test, a set of observational rating scales is available for this test. The test is available in a parallel Spanish version that has options for assessing children speaking dialects from areas such as South Texas, Puerto Rico, Mexico, Argentina, and Central America (Semel, Wiig, & Secord, 1997b).

Assessment of L1 Competence

Tests may be available from the country of origin of many non–English-language speakers to test competence in a particular language. Although many of the tests mentioned earlier have Spanish scales, tests of language competence in other languages that have been normed on U.S. populations are practically nonexistent. Tests developed in Canada may be useful for assessing French competence.

A psychologist must have an assessment of L1 competence to compare language development across languages and, if needed, to decide on appropriate accommodations to support work or learning. Sometimes it is important to distinguish between problems in language acquisition and language pathology as in individuals who have had a stroke. Assessing L2 is not sufficient.

One procedure for assessing speaking ability in a wide variety of languages was pioneered in the United States by the Defense Language Institute and is based on the pragmatics of language (Lowe & Clifford, 1982). Language pragmatics is the knowledge of linguistic codes and the appropriate use of language in different social contexts. The Oral

Language Interview is a face-to-face assessment of a person's language-speaking ability when talking to a trained native speaking tester for 10–40 min. The resulting speech sample is rated on a scale ranging from 0 (*no practical ability to function in the language*) to 5 (*ability equivalent to that of an educated native speaker*). Speech is elicited through a warm-up conversation and subsequent conversational topics (e.g., a personal experience on a trip) that are chosen to establish a ceiling level of performance. This procedure is used with foreign service officers in the State Department and has been adapted for use in industry. For this, and many other procedures, native language competence in the assessor and training is required.

Inferences From the Assessment of Language Proficiency

Bilingual is a term denoting the development of language skills in two languages. The term often implies that an individual has equal skills in both languages, but often there is a difference in the level of competence in the two languages. An individual is considered a "balanced bilingual" when the proficiency level in both languages is equivalent; otherwise, it is useful to indicate which language is dominant. A person's absolute level of proficiency in English may lead them to be called *limited English proficient*, but it is possible for such an individual to be considered English dominant if English skills surpass L1 skills. Because proficiency must be looked at across social, academic, and work domains, dominance of one language may not exist across all contexts.

The challenge is first to decide how much L2 English proficiency is necessary in a bilingual individual before a test may be properly administered in English and can be interpreted for an L2 English individual as for an L1 English individual. Many scholars argue that in most situations balanced, proficient bilingualism is an intellectual asset and that those who are highly English proficient are at no disadvantage on English-language tests. On the other hand, it is clear that for nonnative speakers with low levels of English proficiency, scores on most tests do not reflect the intended construct but rather limited proficiency in English. In some cases, that is all that they measure.

An obvious rule of thumb otherwise is to test the individual in his or her most proficient language if the means to do so are available. Ramos (1981), for example, found better performance from bilingual individuals assessed in their preferred language, either English or Spanish. If the most proficient language is not English, one might elect a translated and adapted test, a nonverbal test, or a test devised in L1. (These options are explored later in this chapter.) For many purposes it may be useful and is probably desirable to assess individuals in more than one language to gain a more complete picture of their capabilities and attitudes.

It is also the case that individuals may not score at the proficient level in either L1 or L2. Individual differences and language disabilities may be present in those functioning in two language environments as well as those who are monolingual. For example, some L2 learners will have special educational needs (Cloud, 1994). Others may not score well on either L1 or L2 tests because of poverty, lives disrupted by immigration, and lack of access to language stimulation.

Another variable that may influence performance in a second language is affect. Krashen (1982) hypothesized the existence of an affective filter in language learning and performance. Anxiety, motivation, and self-confidence may all influence how easily language is acquired and how commonly a second language is used in social and other situations. In high-stakes assessments, anxiety in particular may lead to restricted performance and, as a result, an underestimate of English-language proficiency. The personality and emotional state of the individual should be taken into account in the interpretation of language proficiency, particularly expressive proficiency.

In addition, on the basis of the outcomes of language proficiency assessments, there is always the logical possibility that the use of the non-English language in schools, in institutions, and on the job might be recommended as the most effective means to communicate. In this case, assessment of communication skills in the non-English language may be desirable but not always feasible or commensurate with institutional policies.

Using Tests in English Developed for English-Language Speakers

At what point on the continuum of bilingualism or proficiency in English as an L2 does one use with confidence a test with content or instructions in English? Unfortunately, there is little empirical evidence to guide the psychological professional, particularly in working with young children in whom language proficiency is developing.

Even if the individuals are proficient in English, if they have a different L1, there still may be a need to consider if the outcome of the test has been depressed by factors related to language, particularly for younger children with smaller vocabularies. Some work has been done to identify some of the transfer and interference effects of speaking more than one language. On verbal tests such as the Scholastic Assessment Test, items that have proven to be particularly difficult for Spanish–English bilinguals are homographs—words having more than one meaning (e.g., "bank" in English)—and false cognates—words similar in appearance or origin but with different meanings in English and L1 (e.g., the Spanish "enviable," which means "sendable" in English). On the other hand, true cognates may be easier for bilinguals, particularly when the word has a higher frequency of use in the L1 than in English (Schmitt, 1988). (Items with content of special interest to Hispanics were also easier in that study.)

There is some consensus that the extra time needed by bilingual individuals to process two languages also needs to be taken into account. The time and effort needed to process information from one language to another suggest that a reasonable accommodation in testing would be to extend time limits or give nonspeeded tests and to allow more frequent breaks in testing to recover from the mental effort. Of course, if the construct being measured involves speed, such an accommodation might not be appropriate.

Particular care must be taken if the responses to a test are given orally. Even if an individual is competent in English, the individual's speech may be highly accented. Accents are usually more pronounced in adults than in children. Comprehending accented English, even from an examinee who was reared in an English-speaking location such as Glasgow, Scotland, is no easy chore for most American psychologists. In the case of a test that yields a spoken response, the listening comprehension for the accent on the part of the examiner will be highly important for both rapport and understanding. If the psychologist is unable to understand an accent, it would be better to make a referral to a colleague who does. Practice with the particular accented English of the client will be necessary for full communication. The accented English of an L1 Chinese speaker is not the same as the accent of an L1 Spanish speaker.

An important factor, as mentioned earlier, is whether English proficiency is related to the reason for assessment. For example, if the assessment is to determine entrance into a college where English is the language of instruction, test scores in English usually correlate better with success in college humanities and social science course work than do test scores in another language.

One modification that is possible with the directions to a test is to give them bilingually. If the examiner is bilingual and a translation is available, the directions to the test might be given in both English and the examinee's first language. The effects of such a modification should be investigated empirically, however.

Alternatives to English-Language Testing

Translation of Tests or Other Assessment Devices Into L1

Perhaps the first option that comes to mind to psychologists as well as others (such as the courts) when faced with a nonspeaker or limited-English-proficient speaker is to have the test of interest translated into the language of the test taker and the examinee's response translated into English. It is best to take time and effort and translate the test before using it, but in many situations a translator, often a layperson competent in the non-English language, is drafted to translate questions or responses in situ. Both translating tests and the use of the translator in testing are fraught with hazards and issues. We examine each of these options in turn.

Test Translation or Adaptation

Translating a test from one language to another while preserving the content, difficulty level, reliability, and validity is a daunting undertaking. It is rarely done successfully at the local level. Nevertheless, tests developed in the United States are often adapted for use in other countries, and occasionally tests developed elsewhere have come to be used in this country (e.g., the original Binet–Simon scales, Raven Progressive Matrices).

An adaptation may be oriented to making the test suitable for use in a different culture, different language, or both. Geisinger (1994) pointed out that the term *test adaptation* has replaced the term *test translation* to emphasize the need to adapt to the culture of the examinee, to make changes in content and wording, and to translate the language itself.

Geisinger, in chapter 2 of this book and elsewhere (Geisinger, 1994), has developed a step-by-step approach to translation.

1. The test must be translated and adapted to the new language. In some instances, this can be done in an item-by-item fashion, but in others the concepts are freely translated. The usual approach is to use back translation. In back translation, the test is first converted by one translator into the target language and is then translated back into English by a second. Both translators must be fluent in both English and the target language. (We discuss the competencies of translators and interpreters in the next section.) The version translated back is then compared with the original. This process can be repeated to ensure accuracy. It is best that the translators do not know the purpose of the translation. If they are unaware of the reason for the translation, they will be less likely to choose wording that will back translate than to choose words that will best capture the meaning of the original. A flaw in the back translation process is that there may be too much emphasis on having the original language returned by the second translator so that a stilted and nonoptimal translation emerges.

    It is much easier to translate instructions and procedures than it is to translate test items or questions. Back translation does not easily allow the cultural and conceptual bases of the test to be transferred to the target language because the abstractions may be more variously translated. In addition, for some kinds of tests, such as ability tests, the relative difficulty of the vocabulary or word frequency is an important feature of the item, and finding a translated word with the same level of familiarity or commonality of usage can be difficult. For verbal items in particular, there must be an attempt to maintain the level of reading difficulty and word frequency in the two languages.

2. The new version of the translated or adapted test should be reviewed by a panel of expert bilingual and bicultural individuals serving like a focus group. Geisinger (1994) suggested that the panel members "(a) review the items and react in writing, (b) share their comments with one another, and (c) meet to consider the points made by each other and to reconcile any differences of opinion" (p. 306).

3. After the panel has deliberated without the original translator

present, the translator further adapts the draft instrument on the basis of the reviewer's comments.

4. The test is then given a pilot trial with a small group of typical examinees. Afterward, the test takers are interviewed to determine whether they understood the instructions, whether the time limit was appropriate, and whether the wording of the items made sense. The translation should be modified in response to the findings from these interviews.

5. At this point, the translated measure is ready for a field test. It should be administered to a large enough representative sample to yield data to examine reliability, to perform traditional or modern item analysis, and to examine differential item functioning. The test will probably be revised again using this information.

6. Few individual practitioners will be able to pursue these next few steps. They are presented in the interest of completeness and for practitioners to be able to recognize a competently adapted test. Once the test has emerged from its pilot testing, it is time to standardize the scores and, if desirable and appropriate, to equate the scores with those on the English original. To do a proper standardization, however, a representative sample of several hundred must be obtained. Geisinger (1994) pointed out that

> it would rarely, if ever, be appropriate to use the norms from the original instrument as calculated on the original population with the revised and adapted instrument. That is, one cannot simply translate a measure into a second language and use the norm tables for that measure based on the first language version of the instrument. (p. 307)

7. The necessary validation research must be performed. It is critical to determine whether the adapted instrument continues to measure the same construct as the original and whether the construct has meaning in the target culture. Such studies would include factor-analytic analyses and the prediction of relevant criteria as suggested by the construct in question.

8. A test developer should develop a manual and other documents for the users of the assessment device. This documentation should include a description of the appropriate use for the adapted test.

9. Geisinger (1994) pointed out that a test adapter also is obliged

to educate users in how to administer and interpret the adapted test. How the new test may differ from the original is an important aspect of this training.

10. A final step is to collect reactions from the test users after the test has been available for use. The information collected from users will help in future revisions and will determine whether there is misuse or misinterpretation that might warrant additional user training.

It should be obvious that adapting a test is a serious undertaking if done appropriately. Given the large number of Spanish speakers, it may be important to adapt tests for this group to achieve fairness in assessment. In fact, an increasing number of translated and adapted tests are available in Spanish.

Even when a test is translated into another language, it may be useful to give instructions in both languages spoken by the examinee. This practice will give the examinee an optimal chance to understand what is expected. This option will be particularly valid for children who are English learners and are used to such procedures in bilingual classrooms. Strictly speaking, a dual-language version of a test should also be standardized or at least shown to yield the same results as a single-language translation.

Working With Interpreters

Clearly, it would be best for an assessment of non-English speakers to be done by a psychologist who has demonstrated L2 proficiency. The availability of trained speakers in some languages, such as Spanish, may someday be sufficient, but given the large number of languages spoken in the United States, making it a requirement that individuals be assessed by native speakers of their language is impractical. Instead, psychologists need to be prepared to work with interpreters. This training can come from workshops or from consultation with an experienced psychologist.

The first task in working with interpreters is identifying a likely candidate for the role. In Europe and elsewhere, language interpreters are members of a recognized profession with training and licensure. In the United States, the courts are usually the only institutions using interpreters. As a result, in other contexts such as hospitals, native speakers with no special training are usually asked to serve in this capacity. Being a native speaker should not be the only qualification. "Interpreting is a cognitively demanding task. The best-educated native speaker is in all likelihood the best candidate to serve as an interpreter" (Figueroa, 1990, p. 101). On the other hand, selecting a well-educated person may result in class and dialect differences between the interpreter and the individual being assessed. In addition to linguistic competence, the personality of the potential interpreter will also have to be taken into account, with an emphasis on selecting someone who will be able to establish rapport with the individual being assessed. A final point to be explored is the dialects of the language spoken by the interpreter. Newcomers to the United States may speak unusual dialects that other speakers of the language may have difficulty comprehending. The working-class French Creole spoken by a Haitian immigrant may be difficult for a Parisian French speaker to understand. Checking to verify the dialect match between the examinee and the interpreter is important.

The second task is preparation of the psychologist. Before working with an interpreter, the assessor must learn about the dynamics of the interpretation process. Some of these dynamics include how to establish rapport with participants, how to anticipate the loss of information inherent in the interpretation procedure, how to use the authority position of the examiner, how to use appropriate nonverbal communication, what methods and techniques of interpretation are available, how to obtain accurate translations, and how to discourage personal evaluations by the translator (Figueroa, Sandoval, & Merino, 1984).

The third task is to prepare the interpreter. If translators are inexperienced, it will be necessary to educate the individuals in the techniques of translating in an assessment context. Interpreters must learn ethical concepts, particularly the importance of keeping information confidential, how not to elaborate responses or questions inappropriately, how to deal with physical gestures and other kinesthetic information, and how to establish and maintain rapport and motivation on the part of the examinee (Figueroa et al., 1984). The psychologist should go over any unusual terminology that might arise and should verify sensitivity to dialect variants and cultural differences. One important skill the translator must learn is how to refrain from reacting orally or physically to answers provided by the test taker. The test interpreter needs to keep from giving explicit feedback, instead offering neutral encouragement. The psychologist will be using the interpreter as a proxy and should feel confident that good professional practice will be followed.

The fourth task is to hold a preassessment conference with the interpreter where detailed planning for the assessment is carried out. The purpose of the assessment should be discussed and the material used reviewed so it can be presented naturally and efficiently. Figueroa (1990) made the following observations:

> During testing, an interpreter should never have to translate any part of the test being administered. Interpreters should only be used when there is a valid, normed translation of the test or when there are age-appropriate written instructions for a nonverbal test. There should be no problem in administering a test. The interpreter should know how to administer the test. The seating arrangements should be predetermined. And the pattern of communication(s) (who can talk to whom and when) should be set up before testing. (p. 102)

The objective is to allow the interpreter to concentrate on the responses of the person being assessed.

The fifth task in working with interpreters is conducting the assessment itself. The assessment should be a team effort to elicit the best performance or most honest response from the examinee. The psychologist should direct the process and monitor the situation for signs of distress or fatigue. It may be necessary to consult with the interpreter about the process, but long discussions in English in front of the examinee should be avoided.

A sixth task will be a postassessment conference with the interpreter to score the responses and to discuss the examinee's behavior during the assessment. It may be useful to audio- or videotape the assessment and to review the records jointly. The translator's impressions of the examinee may be recorded at this time but kept separate from the client's behavior or test results. The inferences from the assessment are the responsibility of the psychologist, not the interpreter.

After the conference, the interpreter will also be of assistance in relaying test feedback from the examiner to the test taker or other interested parties. The translator will work to ensure that the examinee understands the test results and will translate any questions about the results that the test taker may have.

Alternatives to Local Translation: Using Tests in L1

Tests may be available in the first language of the individual to be tested. Tests in languages other than English have been produced by publishers in the United States for the U.S. market. The most common non-English language spoken in the United States is Spanish, with more than 17 million speakers. Spanish versions of tests have become available, particularly tests designed for the school-age population, although employment tests and personality tests are also being developed or translated (Camara, 1992; Velasquez & Callahan, 1992). For example, the College Board has developed the Prueba de Aptitud Academica in Puerto Rico, Richard Woodcock has produced versions of his popular psychoeducational tests in Spanish, and there is a Spanish version of the Minnesota Multiphasic Personality Inventory (Garcia-Peltoniemi & Azun, 1993) that has been shown to give equivalent results in bilingual populations (Karle & Velasquez, 1997). Aside from Spanish, tests in other languages have not often been produced specifically for the U.S. population.

Spanish tests must be examined carefully for local usage, however. They may still be culturally determined because vocabulary and usage vary from place to place in the United States. There are vocabulary and other differences between the Spanish spoken in Puerto Rico, Mexico, Cuba, and other places in Latin America.

Non-U.S.-Normed Tests

Many individuals will have attended school in their country of origin or in bilingual programs in which they have had instruction in their home language and have gained academic competence in L1. If possible, it will be useful to assess their skills using tests developed in their country of origin.

If used with a U.S. population who has grown up in the United States, there may be problems in language and cultural context of the tests developed elsewhere. Chicanos in the Southwest do not necessarily share common referents with Mexican immigrants. This diversity will have to be taken into account in the interpretation.

Obviously, it would be a big advantage if the psychologist administering the test is highly competent in the test taker's L1. Not only will the test be more likely to be administered properly, but the responses, if it is not a simple paper-and-pencil test, will be understood. Fluency in the test taker's language will increase the likelihood that good rapport is established. If the psychologist is not a native or competent speaker, a referral may be necessary.

Adjusting Scores

A once common but inaccurate and ethically questionable procedure for drawing inferences from a score from a test administered in English to someone not proficient in English was to add points (e.g., 10 points, or 0.5 *SD*) to compensate for the lack of proficiency. The number of points added to a score was usually the result of folklore, but sometimes recommendations appear in the psychological literature. For example, Holland (1960) suggested using a language barrier score to adjust for bilingualism on the basis of the difference between an English-only administration and a home-language administration. Few attempts to validate these corrections or adjustments appear in the literature.

Adjusting scores for language proficiency has been attempted in research settings (Pennock-Roman, 1992). These studies have examined ways in which the prediction of college performance on aptitude tests may be improved by adding a measure of English proficiency such as the TOEFL to a prediction equation. Pennock-Roman concluded that at the higher levels of proficiency (e.g., 500–600 and above), there is little improvement in prediction. However, at lower levels of proficiency, there is improvement in prediction, although not for predicting success in all majors (e.g., mathematics vs. English literature) and not consistently for verbal and quantitative subtests (e.g., a quantitative test in Spanish may predict success in engineering as well as a quantitative test in English). Nevertheless, the concept of adjustment may be pursued. These adjustments will need to be done test by test and criterion by criterion.

One well-known attempt to adjust scores on a nonlinguistic basis was the System of Multicultural Pluralistic Assessment developed by Mercer (1979). In this system, a child's score on the Wechsler Intelligence Scale for Children is converted to Estimated Learning Potential on the basis of acculturation and other sociocultural variables. This adjustment has not been demonstrated to provide a more valid measure of language minority children's intelligence than the uncorrected score, however (Figueroa & Sassenrath, 1989).

Nonverbal Tests

Tests vary in the amount of language used in the directions and items. Items may be presented pictorially, symbolically, or numerically yet measure the same constructs as items presented verbally. A good nonverbal test begins with items so simple that test takers immediately realize what is being asked of them without being told. Among nonverbal tests, some are more culturally loaded than others. Picture tests such as the Peabody Picture Vocabulary Test are culturally loaded because they tap information associated with mainstream American culture; however, symbolic tests such as the Raven Progressive Matrices, Digit Span, and Maze tests are less culturally loaded because they tap information more neutrally associated with a particular culture. Table 8.2 shows dimensions on which tests may be culturally loaded. Examining this table, one may wish to find a test with the following characteristics: a nonverbal performance test with pantomime instructions that offers opportunities for practice, items that are abstract figural in nature but that require an oral response or gestural response, and a power test that reflects non-scholastic skills involving solving novel problems. Some such tests exist.

Language-reduced and less culturally loaded tests represent an op-

Table 8.2

Culture-Loaded and Culture-Reduced Dimensions on Which Tests Vary

Culture loaded	Culture reduced
Paper-and-pencil tests	Performance tests
Printed instructions	Oral instructions
Oral instructions	Pantomime instructions
No preliminary practice	Preliminary practice items
Reading required	Purely pictorial
Pictorial (objects)	Abstract figural
Written response	Oral response
Separate answer sheet	Answers written on the test itself
Language	Nonlanguage
Speed tests	Power tests
Verbal content	Nonverbal content
Specific factual knowledge	Abstract reasoning
Scholastic skills	Nonscholastic skills
Recall of past-learned information	Solving novel problems
Content graded from familiar to rare	All time content highly familiar
Difficulty based on rarity of content	Difficulty based on *complexity* of relation education

Note. From *Bias in Mental Testing* (p. 637), by A. R. Jensen, 1980, New York: Free Press. Copyright 1980 by Arthur R. Jensen. Reprinted with permission of The Free Press, a Division of Simon & Schuster.

tion for use with individuals who are limited English speakers. They have been explicitly designed for the purpose of assessing individuals with limited language. In addition, many yield comparable scores for linguistic minorities (Figueroa, 1990). Jensen (1980) has reviewed a number of the available nonverbal and culturally reduced measures of intellectual functioning.

In using a nonverbal test, it is most important that the instructions are understood and that they are meaningful to the examinee. This implies that examinees have had some experience with the test-taking process. Some coaching before the testing process may be useful. Gains from coaching have been shown to be greater for nonverbal and performance-type items than on verbal and information items and may even improve test validity (Jensen, 1980).

There is a long history of using nonverbal tests in the United States. In the cognitive domain, in addition to the Army Alpha test, the Army Beta test was developed during World War I to assess limited English speakers and illiterate English speakers. Both group tests and individual tests are available. For example, in individual tests, the Wechsler scales have long had performance tests that are language reduced, and most modern scales measuring intellectual functioning have nonverbal tests (the Differential Ability Scales, the Kaufman Assessment Battery for Children, the Stanford-Binet Intelligence Scale). Better measures are appearing all the time, with some requiring only gestural directions and permitting extensive practice and coaching before testing.

In personality assessment, many projective devices are nonverbal pictorial materials. Projective devices such as the Rorschach Inkblot Test may reveal useful information, but, as discussed in chapter 7 in this book, these measures still have high cultural loadings and little research has been done on norming responses by limited English speakers.

Note that there are several disadvantages to using nonverbal tests. It is almost always the case that verbal tests will predict verbal abilities and verbal performance better than nonverbal assessment. The ability to use language is an important feature of academic performance, job performance, and social competency in the mainstream culture. Nonverbal tests may not have the same degree of validity as verbal measures for many purposes.

Another problem is the abstract and symbolic nature of many nonverbal tests. The stimulus materials and tasks may be unfamiliar to examinees and represent an artificial testing context. Performance in authentic and context-rich environments may yield more valid results for some test takers.

Finally, there is the problem of norms. Nonverbal tests have usually been normed on groups who are monolingual, and there has been little attempt to establish validity for different limited English-speaking populations.

Performance Testing

A final option for assessing linguistic minorities is to examine performance in more naturalistic settings with assessments that authentically capture desired competencies. Achievement testing in classrooms has been discussed by Genesee and Upshur (1996; Genesee & Hamayan, 1994). They described the use of observation, informal objectives-referenced testing, conferencing, and portfolios to derive important information about achievement and other constructs.

Jitendra and Rohena-Diaz (1996) suggested the use of curriculum-based dynamic assessment with students who are linguistically diverse. Dynamic assessment involves determining improvement over time on tasks that are carefully taught to the examinee. Changes in performance when mediated in a one-to-one environment can be used to estimate ability, particularly when the mediation or training phase is conducted bilingually.

In employment settings, the use of assessment centers was explored by Ramos (1992). In those centers, candidates were observed over $2^{1}/_{2}$ days, during which they performed simulations and other tasks designed to reveal qualities such as decision making, organization and planning, and behavioral flexibility in work environments. Simulations included dealing with an in-basket of mail, memos, and reports and planning the manufacture of toys for the Christmas trade. Results from these tasks predicted fair and valid predictions of Hispanic participants.

The valid use of performance assessments with language minority individuals requires attention to the same concerns as for the valid use of standardized tests. Establishing the accuracy and reliability of scores and classifications on performance assessments is essential. Furthermore, it is important to ensure that the language competencies of the examinees as shown on performance assessments do not lead to inappropriate inferences regarding their competency in the construct areas under assessment. This can be a challenge. For example, in education, many of the new forms of performance assessment in subject matter areas, such as mathematics or science, include performance criteria requiring that examinees demonstrate their ability to communicate how they go about solving problems in writing. Fair and valid assessments in such circumstances may require accommodations such as allowing students more time to respond, writing responses in a non-English language, or giving oral responses in English or the non-English language. Note that assessment users have the responsibility for determining whether such accommodations alter the intended constructs under measurement. Further discussion of these issues and challenges in the assessment of language minority children and adults in light of the education reform movement and its increasing reliance on performance assessments are provided by LaCelle-Peterson and Rivera (1994) and August and Hakuta (1997).

Critical Thinking About Testing Linguistic Minorities

One hallmark of the professional is a reliance on self-reflection. Professionals, with the help of competent peers, must constantly examine their work, evaluate it for effectiveness, and judge whether they are living up to the standards of best practice. It is through this review process that critical thinking can occur. One guide to critical thinking is a set of questions to examine whether the clients' needs are being met in assessment when they are not native English speakers. We offer the following for self-reflection when considering work with limited English-proficient individuals:

1. Am I the best person to perform this assessment? Psychologists must balance their own training and skill against the availability of someone to whom they may refer an examinee. Other questions to ask include the following: Is there a native speaker available who is competent to do this assessment? Is there someone available to train as a translator or to interpret? Can I understand this individual's accent? Have I received sufficient training in the assessment of language proficiency and any testing materials I may use? Have I carefully selected an appropriate measure? Am I sufficiently aware of this individual's culture to establish rapport and to understand nonverbal behavior? Is there someone I can turn to for consultation who is experienced and competent?

2. In interpreting the results of this test or assessment, what are my attitudes about this person and language? Psychologists must consider how their preconceptions may sway their judgment. One must ask, What are my preconceptions? Will my biases, both favorable and unfavorable, about the reason for the testing or the examinee interfere with my judgment about the examinee? How can I guard against any biases I may have?

3. In evaluating the performance of this person on the test, have I made sure that this test is a measure of the construct in question as opposed to a test of English-language fluency? In test interpretation, psychologists want to draw accurate inferences about particular constructs. Self-questions may include the following: Have I reasonably and comprehensively assessed linguistic competence in L2 and L1? If English competence has also been measured, have I compensated for it appropriately in my interpretation?

4. In my evaluation, have I taken the acculturation of the test taker into account? Psychologists should be aware that culture and language are related but not perfectly correlated. It is important to ask, Are the testing process and the material familiar to the test taker? Has the examinee had an opportunity to learn the knowledge or skills called for by the test? Have I done sufficient training (as permitted) and coaching to reduce the influences of other irrelevant constructs, which may result from a lack of acculturation, contributing to performance?

5. Have I taken other cultural and language-related variables into account? Speed of response, for example, may be influenced by cultural norms and by the cognitive effort involved in dual-language processing. Has there been enough time for the examinee to demonstrate competency? Is there evidence of fatigue? Have the examinee and I established rapport?

6. Have I collected enough information? Assessors ideally have multiple measures and multiple sources of information about key constructs so that there is convergence and cross-validation. Psychologists might ask, Have I tested in both L1 and L2? Have I genuinely tested an alternative or competing hypothesis that might bear on the interpretation of test results and help render a more valid, professional judgment? Have I used multiple measures and found consistency? Am I incorrectly explaining away inconsistency in performance?

7. Have I included enough information in my written report or any conference with the examinee or the examinee's family to help others interpret the results fairly? Have I noted modifications made in the testing procedures? Have I been understood by all concerned when I have reported my inferences? Have I noted any limitations or reservations I have about my inferences?

Additional questions may be developed to guide a self-review or peer review. It is important to guard against stereotyped and simplistic thinking when assessing non-English-speaking individuals. So many factors may be involved in an interpretation, such as culture, poverty, and acculturation, not to mention the more usual irrelevant factors of emotion and developmental status, that drawing inferences about this population is especially difficult. Nevertheless, psychologists are usually charged with making judgments that affect lives and they cannot shirk their responsibility.

Conclusion

In the final analysis, in assessing individuals with limited English proficiency, psychologists must not only administer assessments of communicative abilities but they also must make sense of assessment test scores and performance assessing other constructs. Psychologists' sensitive interpretation of the meaning of communicative assessments of nonnative speakers of English requires attention to the background characteristics of examinees, the nature of criterion, the institutional and social contexts of the assessment, and the value of combining formal assessment strategies with informal but informative alternatives. In interpreting the meaning of assessments of other constructs such as aptitude, ability, personality, or mental competence, psychologists also must determine how much of what is being measured is English-language competence. There are ways to minimize the effect of irrelevant constructs, but they usually require sensitivity, training, and extra effort on the part of psychologists. Fairness, however, demands that extra care be taken with this growing segment of the population.

References

Adamson, H. D. (1993). *Academic competence: Theory and classroom practice—Preparing ESL students for content courses.* New York: Longman.

Alderson, J. C., Krahnke, K. J., & Stansfield, C. W. (1987). *Reviews of English proficiency tests.* Washington, DC: Teachers of English to Speakers of Other Languages.

August, D., & Hakuta, K. (Eds.). (1997). *Improving schooling for language-minority children: A research agenda.* Washington, DC: National Academy Press.

Bachman, L. F. (1990). *Fundamental considerations in language testing.* Oxford, England: Oxford University Press.

Bachman, L. F., & Palmer, A. S. (1982). The construct validation of some components of communicative proficiency. *TESOL Quarterly, 16,* 449–465.

Burt, M., Dulay, H., & Hernandez-Chavez, E. (1978). *Bilingual Syntax Measure II manual: English edition.* San Antonio, TX: Psychological Corporation.

Camara, W. J. (1992). Fairness and fair use in employment testing: A matter of perspective. In K. Geisinger (Ed.), *Psychological testing of Hispanics* (pp. 215–234). Washington, DC: American Psychological Association.

Canale, M., & Swain, M. (1980). Theoretical bases of communicative approaches to second language teaching and testing. *Applied Linguistics, 1,* 1–47.

Candlin, C. N. (1986). Explaining communicative competence: Limits of testability? In C. W. Stansfield (Ed.), *Toward communicative competence testing: Proceedings of the Second TOEFL Invitational Conference* (pp. 48–83). Princeton, NJ: Educational Testing Service.

Cloud, N. (1994). Special education needs of second language students. In F. Genesee (Ed.), *Educating second language children* (pp. 243–277). Cambridge, England: Cambridge University Press.

DeAvila, E. A., & Duncan, S. E. (1990). *Language Assessment Scale.* Monterey, CA: CTB/McGraw-Hill.

Figueroa, R. (1990). Best practices in the assessment of bilingual children. In A. Thomas & J. Grimes (Eds.), *Best practices in school psychology* (Vol. 2, pp. 93–106). Washington, DC: National Association of School Psychologists.

Figueroa, R. A. Sandoval, J., & Merino, B. (1984). School psychology with limited-English-proficient (LEP) children: New competencies. *Journal of School Psychology, 22,* 121–143.

Figueroa, R. A., & Sassenrath, J. M. (1989). A longitudinal study of the predictive validity of SOMPA. *Psychology in the Schools, 26,* 5–19.

Garcia-Peltoniemi, R. E., & Azun, A. A. (1993). *Inventario multifascio de la perrsonalidad-2-Minnesota (Version Hispana).* Minneapolis: University of Minnesota Press.

Geisinger, K. F. (1994). Cross-cultural normative assessment: Translation and adaptation issues influencing the normative interpretation of assessment instruments. *Psychological Assessment, 6,* 304–312.

Genesee, F., & Hamayan, E. V. (1994). Classroom-based assessment. In F. Genesee (Ed.), *Educating second language children* (pp. 212–239). Cambridge, England: Cambridge University Press.

Genesee, F., & Upshur, J. A. (1996). *Classroom-based evaluation in second language education.* Cambridge, England: Cambridge University Press.

Harris, D. P. (1969). *Testing English as a second language.* New York: McGraw-Hill.

Henning, G. (1987). *A guide to langauge testing.* New York: Newbury House.

Henning, G., & Cascallar, E. (1992). *A preliminary study of the nature of communicative competence* (TOEFL Research Rep. No. 36). Princeton, NJ: Educational Testing Service.

Herbert, C. H. (1971). *Basic Inventory of Natural Language.* San Bernardino, CA: CHECpoint Systems.

Holland, W. (1960). Language barrier as an educational problem of Spanish-speaking children. *Exceptional Children, 27,* 42–50.

Hymes, D. (1974). *Foundations in sociolinguistics: An ethnographic approach.* Philadelphia: University of Pennsylvania Press.

Jensen, A. R. (1980). *Bias in mental testing.* New York: Free Press.

Jitendra, A. K., & Rohena-Diaz, E. (1996). Language assessment of students who are linguistically diverse: Why a discrete approach is not the answer. *School Psychology Review, 25,* 40–56.

Karle, H. R., & Velasquez, R. J. (1997). *The comparability of the English and Spanish versions of the MMPI-2.* Manuscript submitted for publication.

Krashen, S. D. (1982). *Principles and practice in second language acquisition.* Oxford, England: Pergamon Press.

LaCelle-Peterson, M. W., & Rivera, C. (1994). Is it real for all kids? A framework for equitable assessment policies for English language learners. *Harvard Educational Review, 64,* 55–73.

Lowe, P., & Clifford, R. (1982). *Interagency language roundtable handbook on oral interview testing.* Monterey, CA: Defense Language Institute.

Mercer, J. R. (1979). *The System of Multicultural Pluralistic Assessment: Technical manual.* New York: Psychological Corporation.

Merino, B. J., & Spencer, M. (1983). The comparability of English and Spanish versions of oral language proficiency instruments. *NABE Journal, 8,* 1–4.

Messick, S. (1995). Validity of psychological assessment: Validation of inferences from persons' responses and performances as scientific inquiry into score meaning. *American Psychologist, 50,* 741–749.

New York City Board of Education. (1977). *Language Assessment Battery.* Chicago: Riverside.

Oller, J. W., Jr. (1979). *Language tests at school.* London: Longman.

Oller, J. W., Chesarek, S., & Scott, R. (1991). *Language and bilingualism: More tests of tests.* Lewisburg, PA: Bucknell University Press.

Pennock-Roman, M. (1992). Interpreting test performance in selective admissions for Hispanic students. In K. Geisinger (Ed.), *Psychological testing of Hispanics* (pp. 99–135). Washington, DC: American Psychological Association.

Ramos, R. A. (1981). Employment battery performance of Hispanic applicants as a function of English or Spanish test instruction. *Journal of Applied Psychology, 66,* 291–295.

Ramos, R. A. (1992). Testing and assessment of Hispanics for occupational and management positions: A developmental needs analysis. In K. F. Geisinger (Ed.), *Psychological testing of Hispanics* (pp. 173–194). Washington, DC: American Psychological Association.

Schmitt, A. P. (1988). Language and cultural characteristics that explain differential item functioning for Hispanic examinees on the Scholastic Aptitude Test. *Journal of Educational Measurement, 25,* 1–13.

Semel, E., Wiig, E. H., & Secord, W. A. (1997a). *Clinical Evaluation of Language Fundamentals – Third Edition: Technical manual.* San Antonio, TX: Psychological Corporation.

Semel, E., Wiig, E. H., & Secord, W. A. (1997b). *Clinical Evaluation of Language Fundamentals, Spanish version.* San Antonio, TX: Psychological Corporation.

Spolsky, B. (1985). What does it mean to know how to use a language? An essay on the theoretical basis of language testing. In A. Hughes & D. Porter (Eds.), *Language testing* (pp. 180–191). London: Edward Arnold.

Spolsky, B. (1988). Bilingualism. In F. J. Newmeyer (Ed.), *Linguistics: The Cambridge survey* (Vol. 4, pp. 100–118). Cambridge, England: Cambridge University Press.

Stansfield, C. W. (Ed.). (1986). *Technology and language testing.* Washington, DC: Teachers of English to Speakers of Other Languages.

Ulibarri, D., Spencer, M., & Rivas, G. (1981). Language proficiency tests and their relationship to school ratings as predictors of academic acheivement. *NABE Journal, 5,* 47–80.

U.S. Bureau of the Census. (1990). *Languages spoken at home and ability to speak English for United States, regions, and states.* (Publication No. CPH-L-133). Washington, DC: Government Printing Office.

Valdés, G., & Figueroa, R. A. (1994). *Bilingualism and testing: A special case of bias.* Norwood, NJ: Ablex.

Velasquez, R. J., & Callahan, W. J. (1992). Psychological testing of Hispanic Americans in clinical settings: Overview and issues. In K. Geisinger (Ed.), *Psychological testing of Hispanics* (pp. 253–266). Washington, DC: American Psychological Association.

Zehler, A., Hopstock, P. J., Fleischman, H. L., & Greniuk, C. (1993). *An examination of assessment of limited English proficient students: Special Issues Analysis Center, Task Order D070.* Arlington, VA: Development Associates.

9 Migration and Acculturation

Lillian Comas-Díaz and Julia Ramos Grenier

The assessment of culturally diverse clients can be an enigma to the diagnostician. The challenge to comprehensively evaluate them is compounded by clients' (im)migration status and subsequent acculturation level. The use of psychological testing with immigrants historically has been controversial. Cognitive testing has been used as a sociopolitical instrument to restrict immigration to the United States. Psychological tests were used at Ellis Island to restrict immigrants of color and those from southern and western Europe (Kraut, 1994). This historical reality provides an ironic backdrop to psychology's current mandate to evaluate immigrants effectively and ethically.

In this chapter we present a contextualized clinical assessment for individuals who have experienced migration, cultural dislocation, and concomitant adjustment. We first describe migration and acculturation and discuss the evaluation and assessment of migrants. We also present a contextualized assessment where the use of psychological tests is viewed as one of the multiple interacting sources informing behavior.

The Migration Experience

Migration and relocation involve a series of stressful experiences. The dislocations experienced because of migration and its sequelae can shape individuals' perceptions of reality. Indeed, migration is a psychological issue. The adjustment to a new culture is the dynamic product of multiple factors. In assessing clients who have experienced cross-cultural translocation, clinicians need to examine their clients' migration experiences. Migration generally involves three transitions: alterations in the bonding and reconstruction of interpersonal social networks, extraction from one socioeconomic system and insertion into another, and movement from one cultural system to a different one (Rogler, 1994). Migration can also be circular in that the migrants move back and forth between their country of origin and their host country, which affects their transition to the new culture. However, regardless of the migration process, it is important for clinicians to examine several areas. On the basis of the work of Adler (1975), Comas-Díaz (1996), Comas-Díaz and Jacobsen (1987), Comas-Díaz and Jacobsen (1998), Jacobsen (1988), and Lu, Lim, and Mezzich (1995) recommended the assessment of the areas outlined in Exhibit 9.1.

Premigration

The process of migration begins well before the actual physical move. In assessing the premigration history, clinicians need to examine the clients' country of origin within its historical and sociopolitical realities. The political relationship between the country of origin and the host country frequently determines the type and nature of migration. Was the migration planned or precipitous? Do the migrants have a legal or undocumented status? The type of migration, whether voluntary (e.g., job advancement, education, marriage, seeking adventure) or involuntary (e.g., lack of work, to escape political repression, wars, or prejudice) colors the migrants' subsequent adjustment. It is also important to examine the migrants' socioeconomic class, educational level, and proficiency in the language of the host society. These factors greatly affect the adjustment and functioning in the new country.

The provision of psychological services to migrant and refugee populations may be further complicated by previous trauma experienced in the country of origin as well as the psychosocial stress of cultural immersion (Marsella, Bornemann, Ekblad, & Orley, 1994). The refugee experience merits a closer examination. Some refugees receive institutional support from the host country, which makes their adjustment process different from that of other types of migrants. However, the refugees' journey to the host country is often terrifying (Tien, 1994). Therefore, clinicians need to examine the refugees' trauma history. Some of these experiences may be related to the premigration

Exhibit 9.1

Assessment of the Migration Experience

Premigration: Country of origin, sociopolitical context, education, socioeconomic status, gender, age at migration, beliefs system, religion, political ideology

Type of migration
  Reason for leaving: voluntary, involuntary
  Legal or undocumented status
  Refugee experience

Recent migration history: Separation, uprootedness, alienation, grief, bereavement

Previous migration history
  Intergenerational and individual adaptations
  Losses: material, family, and cultural

Traumatic experiences
  Torture, sexual abuse, imprisonment, witnessing violence
  Gender-specific trauma, domestic violence, forced prostitution

Relocation

Resources and stressors
  Physical resources and stressors
  Psychological resources and stressors
  Posttraumatic stress disorder
  Retraumatization
  Host country's attitude toward the migrant

Occupational and financial history: Original line of work, financial history, class displacements, current occupation, educational status

Psychological and medical history
  Individual and family history
  Culture-bound syndromes

Support systems: Current support systems: family, religion, ethnic and mainstream (sponsor) communities

Culture shock
  Stages of culture shock
  Contact, disintegration, reintegration, autonomy, independence

Postmigration

Level of acculturation
  Unacculturation, assimilation, biculturalism, transculturation
  Acculturative stress
  Generational status
  Language use and language preference

Impact on development
  Level of individual adjustment, family adjustment, family life cycle
  Gender and family roles

Impact on identity
  Host country's attitude toward the migrant
  Ethnocultural identity, ethnic minority-group membership
  Mainstream culture's reactions to the client's ethnicity and race

Note. From *Ethnocultural Psychotherapy* (1998), by L. Comas-Díaz and F. M. Jacobson, manuscript submitted for publication, Transcultural Mental Institute, Washington, DC.

period, as in the case of many refugees and politically displaced individuals. Torture, sexual abuse, political and religious repression, imprisonment, and the witnessing of violence are just a few forms of trauma. It is crucial to explore gender-specific trauma such as sexual abduction, forced prostitution, the inducement of abortion of pregnant imprisoned women (Comas-Díaz & Jansen, 1995), emasculation of male prisoners, domestic violence, and others. Traumatic experiences such as exploitation and abuse can occur during the journey to the host country as well as in the relocation process. Some male refugees resort to domestic violence as a reaction to witnessing traumatic events and as a means of reestablishing control and power (Friedman, 1992). Although posttraumatic stress disorder and issues of retraumatization require clinicians' vigilance when assessing refugee populations, they can also be present among other types of migrants.

Although migration is often mediated by the age of the migrants and gender (Rogler, 1994), other personal characteristics such as physical appearance, sexual orientation, and belief system such as attitudes toward health and illness, religion, and political ideology need to be explored. The assessment of the recent migration history aids in unfolding issues of separation, abandonment, uprootedness, alienation, and bereavement. The presence of a previous migration history often provides insight into material, family, and cultural losses as well as into intergenerational and individual adaptations to such losses.

Relocation

The experience of migration transcends the actual physical move. Relocation is a transitional experience that affects the individuals' behaviors, feelings, values, and cognitions. It is also a pervasive condition that influences the whole family system, even generations after the move (Sluzki, 1979). The relocation experience is often mediated by both physical and psychological resources and stressors. Therefore, exploring current support systems such as family, religious, ethnic, and mainstream community (such as sponsors for refugees) is essential for understanding the migrants' reality.

It is important to assess the migrants' occupational and financial history. Areas such as their original line of work, class displacements, current occupation, educational status, and aspiration can provide a blueprint for understanding their adjustment and functioning. Assessing their psychological and medical history is also crucial. Diagnosticians need to be familiar with culture-bound syndromes because these can surface as a result of adjustment difficulties. If clinicians are unfamiliar with culture-bound syndromes, they can consult the fourth edition of the *Diagnostic and Statistical Manual of Mental Disorders* (*DSM–IV*; American Psychiatric Association [APA], 1994), published information (e.g., Mezzich et al., 1993; Simons & Hughes, 1993), and cultural consultants. Migrants sometimes suffer from physical illnesses not familiar to Western-trained physicians, so consultation with specialists is required.

Culture Shock

Moving across cultures often causes culture shock because of unexpected problems in individual, family, and work adjustment. The shock of confronting a different cultural environment can be accompanied by depression stemming from isolation, lack of skills, loneliness, unfamiliar surroundings, a yearn for past objects and events, and a loss of social support from extended families. Paranoid tendencies can emerge as a result of feelings such as being stared at, mistreated, cheated, and talked about. Suspiciousness and distrust often lead to fears and phobias. Substance abuse can develop to cope with culture shock, leading to marital problems and sexual dysfunction as well as school and work difficulties.

Adler (1975) postulated a developmental sequence of culture shock, suggesting that specific psychological, cultural, and social dynamics emerge during the transition. This model also implies that a successful cross-cultural transition should result in the movement of personality adjustment and identity to a new consciousness of values, attitudes, and understanding through the stages of contact, disintegration, reintegration, autonomy, and independence. The contact stage describes migrants' functioning as still being integrated within their own culture. Although differences become increasingly noticeable in the disintegration stage, alienation, depression, and withdrawal give rise to disintegration of personality and confusion over individual identity. In the reintegration stage, the second culture is rejected through anger and rebellion, thus asserting oneself and increasing self-esteem. Those who have the choice may confront a turning point: either returning home or moving closer to a resolution of difficulties. The autonomy stage is characterized by the development of appropriate coping skills in the second culture, allowing migrants to culturally negotiate different situations. The last stage, independence, is marked by attitudes, emotions, and behaviors that are independent but not devoid of cultural influence. Thus, social, psychological, and cultural differences are accepted and enjoyed.

Consistent with these developmental stages, many adult migrants adapt to their experience of uprootedness using diverse psychological mechanisms. Piers and Piers (1982) described them as splitting, self-rejection and self-deprecation, rebuilding of the old homeland, and "passing," or pseudoassimilation. Migrants under stress tend to regress to a stage in which trust and mistrust are not yet fused, resulting in not being able to assess their homeland realistically and thus splitting the image of their homeland. Therefore, countries of origin are alternatively remembered as "all good" or "all bad." The splitting may be extended to the host country as well. Many migrants are also unable to see themselves as they really are, often resulting in self-rejection. Wanting to restore what they lost, several migrants create their own Chinatown or El Barrio and revive old ethnic elements such as costumes, menus, clothing, and so on. Many migrants tend to alternate between an intense desire to "belong" and a revulsion against such a desire. Passing reflects such a conflict, a betrayal of part of the self. A dilemma between the old and new ethnic identities develops. Although some individuals are more adept than others at combining aspects of both cultures, most of them cannot escape a period of distorted views of the self, of the new environment, and of the old one.

Adler's (1975) developmental model is complemented by Piers and Piers's (1982) discussion of the psychological dynamics present during the cross-cultural transition. For example, the psychological mechanism of splitting may occur during the contact stage. Living in the ethnic ghetto is an example of rebuilding the old homeland. During the stage of disintegration, the psychological dynamics of self-rejection, passing, and self-deprecation can emerge among some migrants. In general, the psychological mechanisms tend to be present during the Adlerian stages of contact, disintegration, and reintegration. The stages of autonomy and independence represent a movement toward and a sense of resolution of the cross-cultural transition, and thus the psychological mechanisms may no longer be required to function as coping devices.

Because cultures assign different values and expectations to developmental stages, it is important that clinicians understand the cultural meaning of migrants' developmental stages. A developmental–cognitive perspective can assist in culturally appropriate and contextual assessment. For instance, Ivey (1991) asserted that by exploring the cultural messages that the clients received at each state of development, clinicians can better understand migrants' worldview. To explore these messages, evaluators can use the Standard Cognitive Developmental Interview (Ivey, Rigazio-DiGilio, & Ivey, 1991), the Intospective Developmental Counseling Questions (Tamase & Ivey, 1991), or both.

Acculturation

As a central concept of understanding migrants' realities, the term *acculturation* refers to the adoption of beliefs, values, and practices of the host culture (Westermeyer, 1993). The level of acculturation can provide information about what sociocultural skills migrants have and what specific skills they must acquire to function effectively in a particular society (Lonner & Ibrahim, 1996). Defined as migrants' adaptation to a new culture, acculturation seems to have a fluid quality within a wide continuum (Berry, 1980). According to Paniagua (1994), the process of acculturation can be internal and external. Individuals can be unacculturated, assimilated, marginal, bicultural, and transcultural. Because living in an ethnic community tends to buffer acculturation, unacculturated migrants can remain immersed in their culture of origin. Moreover, some migrants may have extended visits to their country of origin, including family visits and vacations, thus interfering with their acculturation process.

As early as 1936, Redfield, Linton, and Herskovits defined acculturation as a process in which groups of individuals having different cultures come into continuous contact, with subsequent changes in the original cultural patterns of either or both groups. This definition is consistent with the concept of *transculturation*, which stipulates that a new hybrid culture develops out of both the original and the host ones (de Granda, 1968). Likewise, the term *assimilation* refers to migrants' loss of their original cultural identity as they acquire a new identity in a second culture (LaFromboise, Coleman, & Gerton, 1993).

There is a debate about measuring acculturation. As a complex process, acculturation appears to be poorly captured by current scales (Cortes, Rogler, & Malgady, 1994; Rogler, Cortes, & Malgady, 1991). Indeed, it is possible for acculturated migrants to show a complicated pattern of language preferences, such as preferring English for some activities and their mother tongue for others and having complex attitudes for both languages (Rogler, 1994). Nonetheless, several instruments have been developed to measure acculturation. Some scales tend to be culture general (see Berry, Trimble, & Olmedo, 1986), whereas others are more culture specific. The Acculturation Rating Scale for Mexican Americans I (Cuéllar, Harris, & Jasso, 1980), the Acculturation Rating Scale for Mexican Americans II (Cuéllar, Arnold, & Maldonado, 1995), the Short Acculturation Scale for Hispanics (Marín, Sabogal, Marín, Otero-Sabogal, & Pérez-Stable, 1989), the Behavioral Acculturation Scale for Cubans (Szapocznik, Scopetta, Arnalde, & Kurtines (1978), the Mexican American Children's Acculturation Scale (Franco, 1983), the Suinn–Lew Asian Self-Identity Acculturation Scale (Suinn, Richard-Figueroa, Lew, & Vigil, 1987), and the Acculturation Scale for American Indian Adolescents (King & Keane, 1992) are frequently used for research but are culturally specific and thus cannot be generalized to other ethnic groups. Paniagua (1994) has a listing of acculturation scales with their reference ethnic groups. Moreover, the concept of acculturation measurement is also relevant to those groups that are not considered traditional immigrants, such as African Americans. For example, Landrine and Klonoff (1994, 1995, 1996) have developed the African American Acculturation Scale, outlining the independent variables that predict not only who will acculturate and who will not but also the form (assimilated, blended, or bicultural) that the acculturation will take.

It is extremely important to examine the factors that are related to migrants' cultural adaptation and acculturation during assessment. Some of these factors include age at migration and generational status (including years of residence in the United States). Others include their occupational and educational status, frequency of visits to the original country, ethnic identification, gender roles, interactions with native-born Americans, and relationships with extended family and other ethnic support systems. Language preference is a crucial factor; indeed, younger migrants tend to acculturate and learn English faster than older migrants (Lu et al., 1995). The use of the Short Acculturation Scale (Marín et al., 1989), although originally developed for Hispanics, may be useful for assessing linguistic preference. The Short Acculturation Scale has four items assessing dominant language use in general, at home, for thinking, and for speaking with friends. For example, Latinos can rate themselves along a continuum (i.e., only Spanish, Spanish better than English, both English and Spanish equally, English better than Spanish, and only English), with an average score of 2.99 or higher suggesting a high level of acculturation.

On the basis of the work of Burnam, Hough, Karno, Escobar, and Telles (1987), Cuéllar et al. (1980), and Suinn et al. (1987), Paniagua (1994) described a brief scale for the clinical assessment of three central variables in the process of acculturation: generation, language preferred, and social activity. As an illustration, family members in the fifth generation are considered highly acculturated (obtaining a score of 5) when compared with members of the first generation (who obtain a score of 1). Regarding language preference, clinicians can use the Short Acculturation Scale or ask clients a general question covering most situations in which a language is preferred. Paniagua recommended that social activity be assessed in a similar fashion. Thus, Mexican migrants can be asked, When you go out to dinner, do you go out with Mexicans (or Latinos) only (score of 1), with Mexicans mostly (score of 2), with Mexicans and other racial groups (Whites, African Americans, Asians) mostly (score of 3), with a different racial group mostly (score of 4), or only with a different racial group (score of 5)? In assessing the acculturation scores, Burnam et al. (1987) suggested that low acculturation is reflected in scores between 1 and 1.75, medium acculturation by scores between 1.76 and 3.25, and high acculturation by scores between 3.26 and 5.

The *DSM-IV* has a category for "acculturation problem" in a section on other conditions that could require clinical attention. The diagnosis of an acculturation problem (V62.4) is used when the focus of clinical attention is a problem involving adjustment to a different culture following migration (APA, 1994, p. 685). Within this context, it is crucial to assess the migrants' vulnerability to acculturative stress. Some of the factors mediating acculturative stress include the attitude of the receiving host; the presence of other ethnic members; the presence of marketable skills; knowledge of or familiarity with the host culture and language; the type of immigration (voluntary or compulsory; involuntary immigrants are at a higher risk of developing psychopathology); personality traits conducive to successful acculturation such as the ability to develop interpersonal relationships; previous patterns of coping with crisis and stressful conditions; and similarity between the old and new culture.

It is essential to consider the migrants' acculturation status when evaluating them through psychological testing. Cuéllar et al. (1995) noted that acculturation indexes such as the Acculturation Rating Scale for Mexican Americans have been found to be moderator variables in the interpretation of the Minnesota Multiphasic Personality Inventory (MMPI), the Halstead–Reitan Neuropsychological Test Battery, the Mattis Dementia Rating Scale, the Psychological Screening Inventory, the Millon Clinical Multiaxial Inventory II, and other personality instruments influenced by culture for Mexican American populations. Similarly, Dana (1995) recommended a routine incorporation of an acculturation measure into the administration of the MMPI for Hispanic populations because they tend to receive higher MMPI profiles when acculturation is not considered in the profile interpretation. This recommendation could also be considered when working with other migrant groups. Furthermore, in making decisions about assessing migrants, clinicians need to contemplate a complex set of circumstances that change from individual to individual and across time for the same individual due to changes in acculturation status (Lonner & Ibrahim, 1996).

Developmental Issues

Cultural transition affects individuals differently according to their developmental stage. For example, many children who immigrate experience behavioral difficulties at home and at school. In school, new children often exhibit problems such as a disregard for regulations, ignorance of the mainstream customs, and overparticipation (e.g., too loud, too much) or underparticipation (inactive, not articulate enough) in classroom activities (Piers & Piers, 1982). The development of children who experience cross-cultural translocation is bound to suffer because of the distorted perception of reality that accompanies the adjustment to migration. The developmental stage in which individuals migrate has a definitive impact on their reaction and adjustment to the cross-cultural translocation.

Using Erikson's (1950) theory as a framework, we can further examine migration's impact on development. Migration will have limited impact on individuals who are in the developmental stages of basic trust versus basic mistrust, autonomy versus shame and doubt, and initiative versus guilt. These stages cover the oral–sensory, muscular–anal, and locomotor–genital developmental phases, in which the individuals are usually surrounded by family members and significant others and contact with the outside world is often limited. However, the individuals can be indirectly affected via the cultural transition's impact on their family.

Individuals whose transition occurs during their industry versus inferiority stage (latency) tend to be affected more directly. During this stage they are working on the developmental task of "entering into life." Thus, migration during this stage can affect their sense of mastery over the world. Dealing with two different cultures, one at home and a different one at school, could potentially create confusion, leading to emotional disturbances. The process of adaptation becomes complex with the dual adaptation to different, and at times conflicting, cultural contexts.

Likewise, migrants' translocation during the identity versus role confusion stage could have profound effects. This stage comprises puberty and adolescence, and its main developmental task is to integrate the accrued different kinds of experiences into the ego identity. As Erikson (1950) pointed out, the danger in this stage involves role confusion. Cultural translocation can result in role confusion, thus adding more pressure and complexity to an already-complicated task. This is the stage in which adolescents overidentify with the "group," at times to the point of apparent complete loss of identity. During migration, the group changes (from ethnic to American, or other), affecting adolescents' ethnic identity and thus the formation of their general identity.

Many adolescents migrating during this period face a myriad of different problems: linguistic, educational, cultural differences, and adjustment. In particular, for the girls who "travel" with a cultural baggage of traditional sex roles, dealing with the different sexual mores prevalent in United States mainstream society during their sexual development could cause additional complications in their achieving their developmental tasks and creating intergenerational conflicts. The Eriksonian stage of intimacy versus isolation covers the years of young adulthood. Here, individuals are emerging from their identity search and are eager to fuse their identity with others. According to Erikson (1950), prejudices develop during this stage, in which the struggle for identity sharply differentiates between the familiar and the foreign. The migratory experience during this stage could originate in the development of significant prejudice against other groups.

Erikson's (1950) work tends to emphasize child development more than adult development. However, following his model, when cultural translocation occurs during adulthood and maturity, the impact of cross-cultural translocation tends not to be as profound as when the transition occurs during earlier stages, as the previous discussion indicates, because these stages occur when the individual's sense of identity appears to be more defined. To illustrate, the generativity versus stagnation stage, which covers adulthood, has as its main developmental tasks the teaching and guiding of the next generation. Although the ego integrity versus despair stage, which covers maturity, is more concerned with the achievement of emotional integration by participation in followership as well as by accepting the responsibility of leadership. This suggests that older migrants experience their losses more profoundly than younger ones because they leave behind more memories and connections, are more prone to culture shock and culture-bound syndromes, may have more difficulty in learning a new language, and experience displacement because of the undervalued status accorded to elderly people in the United States (Lu et al., 1995).

Migration and Identity Transformation

The migrant's identity is affected by the individual and generational cross-cultural translocation and adjustment. The cognitive, behavioral, and affective restructuring created by acculturation affects the individuals' sense of self. Although some individuals are more adept than others at combining aspects of both cultures, most of them cannot escape a period of distorted self-views (Piers & Piers, 1982). Most migrants struggle to reconcile their previous cultural existence with their new ones and to achieve a new identity (Hoffman, 1989).

The host society's reaction to and attitude toward migrants is of paramount importance to the migrants' cultural adaptation and identity development. For example, many migrants of color become racial and ethnic minorities when they relocate to North America. Regardless of their motivation for migration, these migrants tend to be treated negatively by majority-group members, who perceive them as culturally, sociopolitically, and racially different from them. This socioecological context of discrimination often leads to the majority-group members' stereotyping of migrants of color as being inferior due to their lack of political power. Consequently, membership in a racial minority group requires constantly adjusting to being a North American and a person of color within an ethnocentric society. As members of a minority group, many migrants engage in certain coping strategies and behaviors developed by many minority groups to cope with oppressive environments. These strategies often revolve around issues of power and powerlessness. Thus, it is important for clinicians to differentiate between the strategies of powerless migrants and cognitive deficits.

Assessment of Migrants = Culture, Adjustment, and Context

Assessing individuals who are in the midst of the migration experience can be a major ordeal. For these clients, the picture provided by the assessment may be more reflective of the experience of migration, adaptation, and acculturation. Culture shock often produces cognitive disorientation (Jalali, 1988); therefore, the results of cognitive assessment need to be interpreted with extreme caution because they may not be an accurate estimation of the clients' potential functioning (Allen & Boykin, 1992; Armour-Thomas & Gopaul-McNicol, 1997). Even with individuals who have successfully undergone cultural translocation, assessment can still present diagnostic dilemmas to clinicians.

As discussed in other chapters of this book, traditional assessment methods may be limited and ineffective for many migrants and culturally diverse individuals. This applies to measures such as the Mental Status Examination, the Mini-Mental State Examination, and intellectual assessment instruments (Escobar, Burnam, & Karno, 1986; Lu et al., 1995; Valle, 1989). For example, the measure of orientation, commonly determined by asking clients the date, is affected by the use of different calendars by various cultures and the degree of attention or inattention to time (Escobar et al., 1986; Westermeyer, 1993). Likewise, the usefulness of general knowledge can vary because of educational differences. Even the relevance of asking clients their birthdate depends on the educational and geographical context. For example, for practical reasons, some Latin Americans from rural areas may be registered as being born at a later date. Seasons vary around the world, and the description of winter in one latitude will be different from another latitude (Westermeyer, 1993). Furthermore, interpreting proverbs as an index of abstraction, particularly if they are translated from English to another language, may be difficult because their meaning and wording vary between cultural groups. Moreover, short-term memory tests can be adversely affected if clinicians use culturally irrelevant items (Lu et al., 1995). Similarly, measures of semantic memory and language measures may be biased against clients for whom English is a second language (S. R. López & Taussig, 1991).

Developing culturally specific tests as a way of dealing with the problems inherent in traditional assessment instruments appears to be an ideal solution for the dilemma of testing migrants. Tell-Me-A-Story, a projective technique developed specifically for children of color (African Americans and Hispanics), is one example. Consisting of 23 chromatic pictures depicting African American and Hispanic characters, Tell-Me-A-Story was designed to elicit themes indicative of nine personality functions (Costantino, Malgady, Rogler, & Tsui, 1988). However, developing culture-specific tests standardized and validated for every migrant population is impractical and unrealistic, particularly because of the cost involved. We believe that as long as migrants' cultural, linguistic, and sociopolitical circumstances are taken into consideration, a contextual assessment (including psychological testing) can be a valuable tool for diagnosis and treatment.

Given that behavior is culturally situated, the assessment of migrants needs to follow Hilliard's (1996) recommendation that psychologists become experts in context. As an example of a contextual approach, Lonner and Ibrahim (1996) cited the use of constructivist approaches in cross-cultural assessment. Some of the constructivist tools include content analysis of clients' responses, journal work, and discourse analysis of clients' interactions. Lonner and Ibrahim argued that projective techniques are congruent with constructivist approaches because they require clients to interpret ambiguous stimuli, yielding responses suggestive of how clients construct reality. However, they warned that clinicians using projective techniques should be aware of the relevant cross-cultural literature on their use and misuse.

Another example of a contextual approach was provided by Nieves-Grafals (1995), who used a standard battery of psychological tests (i.e., the Wechsler scales or some of its subtests, the Bender–Gestalt Test, the Figure Drawings Test, and the Rorschach Inkblot Test) for diagnosing Latin American and African refugees. She used the 1993 Spanish version of the Wechsler Adult Intelligence Scale (Wechsler, 1993) with monolingual or Spanish-dominant migrants. She corrected culture-specific items by examining them and taking the refugees' culture into consideration when interpreting the results. When needed, Nieves-Grafals adapted cognitive measures by administering nonverbal cognitive tests (i.e., the Performance subscales of the Wechsler Adult Intelligence Scale–Revised) and projective measures, taking care to interpret cognitive results only as rough estimates of the respondents' intellectual functioning and aptitude. This is important because using only the Wechsler Adult Intelligence Scale–Revised Performance scale limits what can be said about the respondents' cognitive–intellectual abilities (S. R. López & Romero, 1988).

Language differences are also formidable barriers to assessing migrants. The literal translation of test items often leads to linguistic inequivalence, in which meanings, connotations, the level of difficulty, change, and idioms of expression differ between languages (Lu et al., 1995; Westermeyer, 1990). Back-to-back translations (translating a statement from Language A to Language B and then independently from Language B to Language A; Marín & Van Oss Marín, 1991) can provide viable alternatives to using clinical rating scales. For example, the Hopkins Symptom Checklist-25 has been back-to-back translated into Cambodian, Laotian, and Vietnamese (Mollica, Wyshak, Coelho, & Lavalle, 1985) and Amharic and Tigrigna (Giorgis, 1992). Notwithstanding their potential benefits, many translated tests are not necessarily standardized and validated for testing culturally diverse clients (Lu et al., 1995). Indeed, one must remember that some of the difficulties associated with assessing emotional and mental states among migrants arise from their cultural, linguistic, and subjective differences in expressing these experiences (Westermeyer, 1993).

Congruent with the recommendations of the American Psychological Association's (1993) Guidelines for Providers of Psychological Services to Ethnic, Linguistic, and Culturally Diverse Populations, the use and selection of interpreters in assessment requires special examination. Indeed, interpreters should be used as a last resort, and ideally they should be clinicians who are familiar to the clients (Nieves-Grafals, 1995). Tien (1994) provided guidelines for the use of interpreters when evaluating migrant and refugee populations. She identified the functions of an interpreter as a language specialist, a bilingual worker, and a bicultural–bilingual cotherapist. For a more detailed discussion of the use of interpreters in evaluating migrant and refugee populations, see Acosta and Cristo (1981), Marcos (1979), Mollica and Lavalle (1988), Paniagua (1994), Vasquez and Javier (1991), and Westermeyer (1990).

Culturally and linguistically appropriate translations are considered an important issue in computerized testing. For instance, bilingual (English and Spanish) computerized speech recognition applications have been developed to screen depression (Muñoz, González, & Strakeather, 1995). Furthermore, González, Costello, La Tourette, Joyce, and Valenzuela (1997) empirically evaluated a bilingual computer telephone program for screening depression with the Center for Epidemiological Studies Depression Scale. The findings generally support the viability of the automated Depression Scale as a culturally and linguistically appropriate instrument for screening depression in English and Spanish.

Considering culture-specific items, language and regionalisms, socioeconomic class, and historical and political realities of migrants' country of origin in administering and interpreting tests is an example of contextualizing assessment. The need to contextualize psychological testing is even more important when assessing migrant children. Many of these children face poverty, acculturation, and school-related problems (E. C. López, Lamar, & Scully-DeMartini, 1997). Migrant children in schools often require testing for classification, decision making, placement, and intervention (Cummins, 1984). Notwithstanding the controversy over cognitive testing, many parents of color intuitively accept the notion of individual differences and seem to be receptive to the practical use of the information provided by IQ tests in the educational and decision-making processes (Frisby, 1992). However, the cultural and linguistic problems arising when testing culturally diverse children with different levels of acculturation can be best addressed within a contextualized approach.

A Contextualized Assessment Approach

The cultural formulation diagnostic method is an example of a contextualized assessment approach (Lu et al., 1995). First, clinicians empathically elicit the clients' explanatory model, which consists of the clients' notions of their illness in terms of etiology, mode of onset, symptoms, severity, and care (Helman, 1990). Afterward, clinicians assess the symptoms in the context of the clients' family, workplace, belief systems, and community and then diagnose using the *DSM-IV* (Mezzich, Kleinman, Fabrega, & Parron, 1996). The *DSM-IV* has a cultural component (Mezzich et al., 1993). The *DSM-IV* now includes an introductory section placing cultural issues in a clinical context, a subsection per diagnostic category with relevant cultural treatment issues, and an appendix (Appendix I) with an outline for cultural formulations in diagnosis, along with a glossary of culture-bound syndromes recognized in other cultures that are not included in the main text (APA, 1994). The *DSM-IV*'s specific guidelines for cultural formulation include the clients' cultural identity; the clients' cultural explanation of their symptoms, including idioms of distress; cultural factors related to psychosocial environment and levels of functioning; cultural elements of the relationship between clients and clinicians; and an overall cultural assessment for diagnosis and care (APA, 1994). Notwithstanding the inclusion of this cultural component, Cervantes and Arroyo (1994) argued that the *DSM-IV* tends to pathologize Hispanics because the descriptions of disorders are limited in their cultural adequacy for these populations.

Dana (1993) described a contextual assessment combining a culturally sensitive approach with the careful use of traditional psychological testing. He suggested (a) assessing the clients' level of acculturation; (b) providing a culture-specific service delivery style (i.e., framing the interaction within the clients' cultural norms); (c) using the clients' (preferred) language; (d) selecting assessment devices that are culturally appropriate and syntonic to clients; and (e) providing culture-specific feedback on assessment results to clients.

On the basis of the suggestions of several experts on culturally relevant and gender-sensitive mental health assessment (Brown, 1986; Comas-Díaz, 1994; Jacobsen, 1988; Westermeyer, 1993), Comas-Díaz (1996) recommended gathering diverse contextual information. Exhibit 9.2 identifies the areas to be explored within a contextual assessment approach.

Ethnocultural Assessment

The ethnocultural assessment is a clinical procedure for contextually assessing clients' migration, acculturation level, and subsequent effects on identity. As described by Comas-Díaz and Jacobsen (1987, 1998) and Jacobsen (1988), the ethnocultural assessment is a diagnostic and treatment tool that examines migration and considers several stages that may have contributed to the development of clients' ethnocultural identity. These stages may differentially contribute to clients' presentation depending on the position in the continuum of cultural adaptation and identity development. This clinical procedure acknowledges the combined influence of external and internal factors, which may vary in their effects at different stages of migrants' life cycle.

As a contextualized approach, the ethnocultural assessment provides a format for assessing the different areas included in evaluating the clients' migration experience, as presented in Exhibit 9.1. More

---

Exhibit 9.2

Contextual Assessment Areas

1. Ethnocultural heritage
2. Racial and ethnocultural identities
3. Gender and sexual orientation
4. Socioeconomic status
5. Physical appearance, ability or disability
6. Religion when being raised and what now practicing, spiritual beliefs
7. Biological factors (genetic predisposition to certain illness, etc.)
8. Historical era, age cohort
9. Marital status, sexual history
10. History of (im)migration and generations from (im)migrations
11. Acculturation and transculturation levels
12. Family of origin and multigenerational history
13. Family scripts (roles of women and men, prescriptions for success or failure, etc.)
14. Individual and family life cycle development and stages
15. Client's languages and those spoken by family of origin
16. History of individual abuse and trauma (physical; emotional; sexual; political including torture, oppression, and repression)
17. History of collective trauma (slavery, colonization, Holocaust)
18. Gender-specific issues such as battered wife syndrome
19. Recreations and hobbies, avocations, and special social roles
20. Historical and geopolitical reality of ethnic group and relationship with dominant group (including wars and political conflict)

Note. From "Cultural Considerations in Diagnosis" (pp. 159–160) by L. Comas-Díaz, 1996, in F. W. Kaslow (Ed.), *Handbook on Relational Diagnosis and Dysfunctional Family Patterns*, New York: Wiley. Copyright 1996 by John Wiley & Sons, Inc. Adapted with permission by John Wiley & Sons, Inc.

specifically, the ethnocultural assessment is a practical tool to assess clients who are in cultural transition, adaptation, and acculturation. The assessment is composed of five stages. The first stage—ethnocultural heritage—involves obtaining a history of the clients' ethnocultural heritage, and the second—family myth—focuses on the circumstances that led to the clients' (and their family's) cultural translocations. The third stage—posttransition analysis—is based on the clients' intellectual and emotional perception of their family's ethnocultural identity in the host society since the migration. The fourth stage—self-adjustment—considers the clients' own perceived ethnocultural adjustment in the host culture as individuals, distinct from the rest of their family. The last stage —transference and countertransference—calls for consideration of clinicians' ethnocultural background to determine specific areas of real or potential overlap with that of their clients.

The ethnocultural heritage stage solicits contextual information about people's maternal and paternal cultures of origin, delineating ethnocultural heritage including countries of origin, religions, social class, gender and family roles, languages, and cultural translocations. Biological factors (i.e., genetic predisposition to certain illnesses, etc.) and sociopolitical factors are also examined. Assessing the family myth involves exploring the clients' migrations circumstances and sequelae. In this stage, clinicians explore clients' and their family's thoughts and feelings about the events that led to the migration. Family trees, genealogy, and or multigenerational genograms are used to elicit the contextual information.

The posttransition analysis explores what happened after the migration. It assesses the clients' cognitive and emotional perceptions of their family's ethnocultural saga. The family saga is learned by exploring the clients' perceptions of their family's ethnocultural identity in the host society since the migration. The self-adjustment stage explores the clients' views of their cultural adjustment distinct from the rest of the family. Exploration of these feelings frequently provides insights into the clients' acculturation status and ethnocultural identity. The transference and countertransference stage assesses the clients' feelings about their ethnicity and culture relative to clinicians' ethnocultural background. Features of the clinicians' own ethnicity may become apparent in the clients once the transference is established (Westermeyer, 1993). Because culture affects clinicians' diagnostic patterns (Mezzich et al., 1996), this stage requires clinicians to closely examine their own cultural background. This exploration helps to determine specific areas of real or potential overlap with that of their clients. Clinicians are better able to understand their clients' worldviews if they are aware of their own worldview (Lu et al., 1995). Acknowledging the confluence of both clients' and clinicians' realities further helps to contextualize the assessment process (Comas-Díaz, 1994).

In the language of the migration experience, the ethnocultural heritage and family myth stages assess the premigration history, whereas the posttransition analysis assesses the relocation experience. The self-adjustment stage examines the postmigration experience including cultural adaptation and acculturation. This stage also examines the effects of the migration on individual development and identity. The transference and countertransference stage explores overlapping areas with clinicians, thus acknowledging the pervasive influence of culture on mental health.

Clinical Application of the Ethnocultural Assessment

To assist readers in using the ethnocultural assessment, we provide a clinical example. First, the case is presented using a more "traditional" psychological testing approach, and the same case is then presented using the ethnocultural assessment approach. We must caution, however, that the example is not intended to be used as a "cookbook" for all such assessments. Rather, it is merely an example of how the assessment can be used. Clinicians are encouraged to add questions and areas that are of interest or that become important during assessment.

Dolores, a 25-year-old single Puerto Rican woman, presented to a community mental health clinic because of significant depression. She was assigned a therapist, who requested psychological testing to obtain a diagnostic impression and treatment recommendations. A White psychologist conducted the testing. During the first session, the psychologist discovered that Dolores was a schoolteacher who had moved from Puerto Rico to the continental United States to take a better paying job in the local school system. After being on the mainland for 6 months, she had sent for her parents, who relocated and jointly purchased a house with her. They had all been living on the mainland for approximately 4 years now. Dolores's depression began approximately 6 months ago, when she and her White boyfriend of 3 years broke up. The psychologist explored this event during the evaluation because she considered it to be a significant precipitating event in Dolores's current depression.

Psychological testing indicated that Dolores's intellectual functioning fell in the average range. The results of the Rorschach and the MMPI were consistent with significant depression, difficulty with concentration, and emotional lability. The psychologist diagnosed Dolores as suffering from dysthymia and recommended psychotherapy. The psychologist also suggested that Dolores see the clinic psychiatrist because the depression interfered with her work activities.

In psychotherapy, the sessions were spent working around the depression and issues of rejection and poor self-esteem. Although Dolores acknowledged that these were important issues in her case, she felt that the interventions provided were not bringing about any significant change in her depression. She discontinued therapy after 4 weeks, with her depression being somewhat alleviated by the medication, but it was still substantial enough to interfere with her daily activities. In writing the discharge summary, the therapist attributed Dolores's premature termination to her lack of experience with the therapeutic process and the difficulty she experienced in bringing up issues to talk about in the therapy sessions.

This case represents a fairly common scenario in many mental health clinics, where individuals of diverse ethnic–racial backgrounds are often treated. Although the psychologist and the therapist followed a fairly traditional method of obtaining information, diagnosing, and providing treatment, this traditional method did not lead to any significant understanding of, change, or improvement in the client. Thus, we present the same case again using an ethnocultural assessment process.

Ethnocultural Assessment

Dolores was assigned to a Spanish–English bilingual White psychologist who had been trained in conducting ethnocultural assessments with clients whose cultural background differed from his. As the first step, the psychologist used an IQ test in Spanish, which indicated that Dolores's intellectual functioning fell in the superior range compared with other Hispanics. In addition, the psychologist used the Rorschach and the MMPI but analyzed the results obtained on these tests in light of the information the psychologist received from the ethnocultural assessment.

For the first stage of the ethnocultural assessment, the psychologist began by asking Dolores about her family of origin and their own roots in Puerto Rico. The psychologist discovered that Dolores's mother and her family were from the Taíno Indian and Spanish cultures of the island and that her father's family represented Venezuelan and African cultures. This information provided rich material that could be developed further in the therapeutic sessions to discuss racial differences within the family.

For the second stage of the ethnocultural assessment, the psychologist obtained information about Dolores's parents and their decision to move to the mainland to be with her. This inquiry revealed a wealth of information about family dynamics, which included feelings of guilt on the part of the parents because of their feeling of having neglected

Dolores when she was a young child. Their move to the continental United States and helping Dolores purchase a house were ways to try to make up for this perceived neglect.

For the third stage, the psychologist also inquired about cultural clashes that the family had experienced when relocating to the mainland. Information was also obtained about family resources, including financial ones, to cope with the stresses that resulted from the relocation. A significant component of this stage was the information obtained about the family's perception of the host culture's (White) attitude toward Puerto Rican migrants. Here, the family's own racial issues were also important.

For the fourth stage of the ethnocultural assessment, the psychologist discussed Dolores's own level of acculturation to the mainland culture and her adjustment to this culture, including any cultural clashes she had experienced. The Brief Acculturation Scale yielded a score of medium acculturation for Dolores. Dolores informed the psychologist that her White boyfriend's family was not accepting of her because of her cultural background. This, she felt, had led to many of the difficulties she and her boyfriend had experienced in their relationship. Although racial prejudice was something that Dolores had encountered in Puerto Rico, the level of fear and hatred she experienced on the mainland went beyond her island experience. This clearly added to her level of stress and significantly attacked her self-esteem, which was already jeopardized by her boyfriend's rejection of her at a more personal level. This discussion revealed several other areas in which Dolores had been experiencing rejection by individuals from the mainland culture. For example, she believed that she had been passed over for promotions she had requested because of how she looked (dark skin) and spoke (with an accent).

For the fifth stage of the ethnocultural assessment, the psychologist offered suggestions for how the therapist assigned to Dolores could assess his or her own cultural–ethnic background to determine how the therapist's own patterns of beliefs, including prejudices, and lack of knowledge about Dolores's cultural background could affect the therapeutic relationship and the interventions provided. Suggestions about how the similarities between the therapist's cultural background and that of the client could be used to improve the therapeutic alliance and rapport were also made. Finally, the psychologist made recommendations about relevant articles and books about Puerto Rican history and culture that the therapist might find useful and included reference to workshops that would add to the therapist's knowledge base.

As can be seen from the descriptions of the two scenarios, although the first scenario provided clinically relevant information, which led to certain interventions, the second scenario provided much richer information, which helped delineate the therapeutic issues in a clearer way. Needless to say, the client will likely feel a sense of greater understanding by the therapist in the second scenario because the client's cultural translocation and personal issues were outlined and interwoven to form a more detailed profile of the clinical issues that existed. The treatment issues could then be embedded in a sociocultural context that would help the client with her personal, emotional, and cultural issues.

Conclusion

Many migrants and refugees enter the mental health system only after their symptoms have become severe (Westermeyer, 1993). Evaluating these populations can be complex, demanding, and challenging. As part of a comprehensive assessment process, psychological testing can provide useful information for diagnosis and treatment purposes. However, to be effective and ethical, it needs to used within a contextualized approach to assessment.

References

Acosta, F. X., & Cristo, M. H. (1981). Development of a bilingual interpreter program: An alternative model for Spanish speaking services. *Professional Psychology: Research and Practice, 12,* 475–482.

Adler, P. S. (1975). The transitional experience: An alternative view of culture shock. *Journal of Humanistic Psychology, 15*(4), 13–23.

Allen, B. A., & Boykin, W. A. (1992). African American children and the educational process: Alleviating cultural discontinuity through prescriptive pedagogy. *School Psychology Review, 21,* 586–596.

American Psychiatric Association. (1994). *Diagnostic and statistical manual of mental disorders* (4th ed.). Washington, DC: Author.

American Psychological Association. (1993). Guidelines for providers of psychological services to ethnic, linguistic, and culturally diverse populations. *American Psychologist, 48,* 45–48.

Armour-Thomas, E., & Gopaul-McNicol, S. (1997). Bioecological approach to cognitive assessment. *Cultural Diversity and Mental Health, 3*(2), 131–144.

Berry, J. W. (1980). Acculturation as varieties of adaptation. In A. M. Padilla (Ed.), *Acculturation: Theory, models, and some new findings* (pp. 9–26). Boulder, CO: Westview Press.

Berry, J. W., Trimble, J. E., & Olmedo, E. L. (1986). Assessment of acculturation. In W. J. Lonner & J. W. Berry (Eds.), *Field methods in cross cultural research* (pp. 291–324). Newbury Park, CA: Sage.

Brown, L. S. (1986). Gender-role analysis: A neglected component of psychological assessment. *Psychotherapy, 23,* 243–248.

Burnam, M. A., Hough, R. L., Karno, M., Escobar, J. I, & Telles, C. A. (1987). Acculturation and lifetime prevalence of psychiatric disorders among Mexican Americans in Los Angeles. *Journal of Health and Social Behavior, 28,* 89–102.

Cervantes, R. C., & Arroyo, W. (1994). *DSM-IV:* Implications for Hispanic children and adolescents. *Hispanic Journal of Behavioral Sciences, 16,* 8–27.

Comas-Díaz, L. (1994). An integrative approach. In L.Comas-Díaz & B. Greene (Eds.), *Women of color: Integrating ethnic and gender identities in psychotherapy* (pp. 287–318). New York: Guilford Press.

Comas-Díaz, L. (1996). Cultural considerations in diagnosis. In F. W. Kaslow (Ed.), *Handbook on relational diagnosis and dysfunctional family patterns* (pp. 152–168). New York: Wiley.

Comas-Díaz, L., & Jacobsen, F. M. (1987). Ethnocultural identification in psychotherapy. *Psychiatry, 50,* 232–241.

Comas-Díaz, L., & Jacobsen, F. M. (1998). *Ethnocultural psychotherapy.* Manuscript submitted for publication, Transcultural Mental Institute, Washington, DC.

Comas-Díaz, L., & Jansen, M. (1995). Global conflict and violence against women. *Peace and Conflict: Journal of Peace Psychology, 1,* 315–331.

Cortes, D. E., Rogler, L. H., & Malgady, R. G. (1994). Biculturality among Puerto Rican adults in the United States. *American Journal of Community Psychology, 22,* 707–721.

Costantino, G., Malgady, R. G., Rogler, L. H., & Tsui, E. C. (1988). Discriminant analysis of a clinical and public school children by TEMAS: A Thematic Apperception Test for Hispanics and Blacks. *Journal of Personality Assessment, 52,* 670–678.

Cuéllar, I., Arnold, B., & Maldonado, R. (1995). Acculturation Rating Scale for Mexican Americans: 2. A revision of the original ARSMA scale. *Hispanic Journal of Behavioral Sciences, 17,* 275–304.

Cuéllar, I., Harris, L. C., & Jasso, R. (1980). An acculturation scale for Mexican American normal and clinical populations. *Hispanic Journal of Behavioral Science, 2,* 199–217.

Cummins, J. (1984). *Bilingualism and special education.* Clevedon, England: Multilingual Matters.

Dana, R. H. (1993). *Multicultural assessment perspectives for professional psychology.* Needham Heights, MA: Allyn & Bacon.

Dana, R. H. (1995). Culturally competent MMPI assessment of Hispanic populations. *Hispanic Journal of Behavioral Sciences, 17,* 305–319.

de Granda, G. (1968). *Transculturación e interferncia lingüística en el Puerto Rico contemporáneo* [Transcultration and linguistic interference in contemporary Puerto Rico]. Bogotá, Colombia: Ediciones Bogotá.

Erikson, E. H. (1950). *Childhood and society.* New York: Norton.

Escobar, J. I., Burnam, M. A., & Karno, M. (1986). Use of the Mini-Mental State Examination (MMSE) in a community population of mixed ethnicity: Cultural and linguistic artifacts. *Journal of Nervous and Mental Disease, 174,* 607–614.

Franco, J. N. (1983). An acculturation scale for Mexican American children. *Journal of General Psychology, 108,* 175–181.

Friedman, A. R. (1992). Rape and domestic violence: The experience of refugee women. *Women and Therapy, 13,* 65–78.

Frisby, C. L. (1992). Issues and problems in the influence of culture on the psychoeducational needs of African American children. *School Psychology Review, 21,* 532–551.

Giorgis, T. (1992). *Ethiopian version of the Hopkins Symptom Checklist-25.* Washington, DC: National Institute of Mental Health.

González, G. M., Costello, C. R., La Tourette, T. R., Joyce, L. K., & Valenzuela, M. (1997). Bilingual telephone-assisted computerized speech recognition assessment: Is voice activated computer program a culturally and linguistically appropriate tool for screening depression in English and Spanish? *Cultural Diversity and Mental Health, 3,* 93–111.

Helman, C. G. (1990). *Culture, health and illness: An introduction for health professionals.* London: Wright.

Hilliard, A. (1996). Either a paradigm shift or no mental measurement: The nonscience of the bell curve. *Cultural Diversity and Mental Health, 2,* 1–20.

Hoffman, E. (1989). *Lost in translation: A life in a new language.* New York: Penguin Books.

Ivey, A. E. (Ed.). (1991). *Developmental strategies for helpers.* Pacific Grove, CA: Brooks/Cole.

Ivey, A. E., Rigazio-DiGilio, S. A., & Ivey, M. B. (1991). The standard cognitive-developmental interview. In A. E. Ivey (Ed.), *Developmental strategies for helpers* (pp. 289–299). Pacific Grove, CA: Brooks/Cole.

Jacobsen, F. M. (1988). Ethnocultural assessment. In L. Comas-Díaz & E. E. H. Griffith (Eds.), *Clinical guidelines in cross-cultural mental health* (pp. 135–147). New York: Wiley.

Jalali, B. (1988). Ethnicity, cultural adjustment and behavior: Implications for family therapy. In L. Comas-Díaz & E. E. H. Griffith (Eds.), *Clinical guidelines in cross-cultural mental health* (pp. 9–32). New York: Wiley.

King, J., & Keane, E. (1992). *Acculturation Scale for American Indian Adolescents: Voices of Indian teens project.* Denver: University of Colorado Health Sciences Center.

Kraut, A. M. (1994). *Silent travelers: Germs, genes, and the "immigrant menace."* New York: Basic Books.

LaFromboise, T., Coleman, H. L. K., & Gerton, J. (1993). Psychological impact of biculturalism: Evidence and theory. *Psychological Bulletin, 114,* 395–412.

Landrine, H., & Klonoff, E. A. (1994). The African American Acculturation Scale: Development, reliability, and validity. *Journal of Black Psychology, 20,* 104–127.

Landrine, H., & Klonoff, E. A. (1995). The African American Acculturation Scale II: Cross validation and short form. *Journal of Black Psychology, 21,* 124–152.

Landrine, H., & Klonoff, E. A. (1996). African American Acculturation Scale: Origin and current status. In R. L. Jones (Ed.), *Handbook of tests and measurements for Black populations* (Vol. 2, pp. 119–138). Hampton, VA: Cobb & Henry.

Lonner, W. I., & Ibrahim, F. A. (1996). Appraisal and assessment in cross-cultural counseling. In P. B. Pedersen, J. G. Draguns, W. J. Lonner, & J. E. Trimble (Eds.), *Counseling across cultures* (pp. 293–322). New York: Guilford Press.

López, E. C., Lamar D., & Scully-DeMartini, D. (1997). The cognitive assessment of limited-English-proficient children: Current problems and practical recommendations. *Cultural Diversity and Mental Health, 3,* 117–130.

López, S. R., & Romero, A. (1988). Assessing the intellectual functioning of Spanish-speaking adults: Comparison of the EIWA and the WAIS. *Professional Psychology: Research and Practice, 19,* 263–270.

López, S. R., & Taussig, F. M. (1991). Cognitive-intellectual functioning of Spanish-speaking impaired and nonimpaired elderly: Implications for culturally sensitive–psychological assessment. *Journal of Consulting and Clinical Psychology, 3,* 448–454.

Lu, F. G., Lim, R. F., & Mezzich, J. E. (1995). Issues in assessment and diagnosis of culturally diverse individuals. In J. M. Oldham & M. B. Riba (Eds.), *Review of psychiatry* (pp. 477–510). Washington, DC: American Psychiatric Press.

Marcos, L. R. (1979). Effects of interpreters on the evaluation of psychopathology in non-English speaking patients. *American Journal of Psychiatry, 136,* 171–174.

Marín, G., Sabogal, F., Marín, B. V., Otero-Sabogal, R., & Pérez-Stable, E. J. (1989). Development of a short acculturation scale for Hispanics. *Hispanic Journal of Behavioral Sciences, 9,* 183–205.

Marín, G., & Van Oss Marín, B. (1991). *Research with Hispanic populations* (Applied Social Research Methods Series, Vol. 23). London: Sage.

Marsella, A. J., Bornemann, T., Ekblad, S., & Orley, J. (Eds.). (1994). *Amidst peril and pain: The mental health and well-being of the world's refugees.* Washington, DC: American Psychological Association.

Mezzich, J. E., Kleinman, A., Fabrega, H., Good, B., Johnson-Powell, G., Lin, K.-M., Manson, S., & Parron, D. (Eds.). (1993). *Cultural proposals and supporting papers for DSM-IV.* Rockville, MD: National Institute of Mental Health.

Mezzich, J. E., Kleinman, A., Fabrega, H., & Parron, D. L. (1996). (Eds.). *Culture and psychiatric diagnosis: A DSM-IV perspective.* Washington, DC: American Psychiatric Press.

Mollica, R. F., & Lavalle, J. P. (1988). Southeast Asian refugees. In L. Comas-Díaz & E. E. H. Griffith (Eds.), *Clinical guidelines to cross-cultural mental health* (pp. 262–304). New York: Wiley.

Mollica, R. F., Wyshak, G., Coelho, R., & Lavalle, J. (1985). *Hopkins symptom Checklist-25 manual: Cambodian, Laotian, and Vietnamese versions.* Washington, DC: U.S. Office of Refugee Resettlement.

Muñoz, R. F., González, G. M., & Strakeather, J. (1995). Automated screening for depression symptoms: Toward culturally and linguistically appropriate uses of computerized speech recognition. *Hispanic Journal of Behavioral Sciences, 17,* 194–208.

Nieves-Grafals, S. (1995). Psychological testing as a diagnostic and therapeutic tool in the treatment of traumatized Latin American and African refugees. *Cultural Diversity and Mental Health, 1,* 19–27.

Paniagua, F. A. (1994). *Assessing and treating culturally diverse clients: A practical guide.* Thousand Oaks, CA: Sage.

Piers, G., & Piers, W. W. (1982). On becoming a newcomer. *Annual of Psychoanalysis, 10,* 369–378.

Redfield, R., Linton, R., & Herskovits, M. (1936). Memorandum for the study of acculturation. *American Anthropologist, 38,* 149–152.

Rogler, L. H. (1994). International migrations: A framework for directing research. *American Psychologist, 49,* 701–708.

Rogler, L. H., Cortes, D. E., & Malgady, R. G. (1991). Acculturation and mental health status among Hispanics. *American Psychologist, 46,* 585–597.

Simons, R. C., & Hughes, C. C. (1993). Culture-bound syndromes. In A. Gaw (Ed.), *Culture, ethnicity and mental illness* (pp. 75–99). Washington, DC: American Psychiatric Press.

Sluzki, C. E. (1979). Migration and family conflict. *Family Process, 18,* 379–390.

Suinn, R. M., Richard-Figueroa, K. S., Lew, S., & Vigil, P. (1987). The Suinn–Lew Asian Self-Identity Acculturation Scale. *Psychological Measurement, 47,* 401–407.

Szapocznik, J., Scopetta, M. A., Arnalde, M., & Kurtines, W. (1978). Cuban value structure: Treatment implications. *Journal of Consulting and Clinical Psychology, 46,* 961–970.

Tamase, K., & Ivey, A. E. (1991). Tamase's introspective-developmental counseling questions. In A. E. Ivey (Ed.), *Developmental strategies for helpers* (pp. 313–415). Pacific Grove, CA: Brooks/Cole.

Tien, L. (1994). Southeast Asian American women. In L. Comas-Díaz & B. Greene (Eds.), *Women of color: Integrating ethnic and gender identities in psychotherapy* (pp. 479–503). New York: Guilford Press.

Valle, R. (1989). Cultural and ethnic issues in Alzheimer's disease family research. In E. Light & B. D. Lebowitz (Eds.), *Alzheimer's disease treatment and family stress: Directions for research* (DHHS Publication No. ADM-89-1569). Washington, DC: U.S. Government Printing Office.

Vasquez, C., & Javier, C. A. (1991). The problem with interpreters: Communicating with Spanish-speaking patients. *Hospital and Community Psychiatry, 42,* 163–165.

Wechsler, D. (1993). *Escala de Inteligencia de Wechsler para Adultos* (rev. ed.). (Available from Fray Bernardino de Sahagún, 24, 28036, Madrid, Spain).

Westermeyer, J. J. (1990). Working with an interpreter in psychiatric assessment and treatment. *Journal of Nervous and Mental Disease, 178,* 745–749.

Westermeyer, J. J. (1993). Cross-cultural psychiatric assessment. In A. Gaw (Ed.), *Culture, ethnicity and mental illness* (pp. 125–144). Washington, DC: American Psychiatric Press.

10 Poverty and Socioeconomic Status

Craig L. Frisby

Attempts to identify the effects of poverty and social class on testing and assessment performance are fraught with several challenges. Under laboratory conditions, there are sure strategies that researchers can use to test the effects of an independent variable on a dependent variable. In group designs, researchers can randomly assign participants to two or more groups and apply the treatment to one group but not the others (making sure to keep all other relevant variables controlled). In a single-subject design, researchers can observe the baseline frequency of a naturally occurring behavior, observe changes in frequency when a treatment is introduced, and then observe what happens when the treatment is discontinued.

Poverty and social class are variables that are not amenable to such straightforward experimental manipulations. In real life, participants can never be randomly assigned to groups, and many other important variables are hopelessly confounded with poverty and social class. Poverty and social class, as these terms are understood in the social sciences, are rarely "administered" and "discontinued" according to the whims of an experimenter because researchers know that many individuals spend their entire lives under the same life circumstances. This has caused researchers to grapple with certain fundamental questions: Do poverty and socioeconomic status (SES) reflect conditions that merely "happen" to people who are basically the same? Or are there preexisting differences inherent in people that cause their life circumstances? If people were not in poverty or came from a higher social class position, would their test and assessment results be different? If so, how are diagnosticians to interpret test and assessment results of people whose life circumstances differ widely? Although there are no easy answers to these questions, the various issues relevant to these questions are discussed in this chapter.

What Is Poverty?

Poverty is not a unidimensional concept, nor is it considered to be synonymous with low SES (Huston, McLoyd, & Coll, 1994). Poverty also is not synonymous with economic hardships that are transient (e.g., a job loss), nor is it the same as voluntary sacrifices that lead to conditions of low earnings (e.g., the lifestyle of young college students; people who choose a modest lifestyle over conspicuous consumption for religious, philosophical, or ideological reasons).

Citro and Michael (1995) defined poverty as "a circumstance, defined by a set of specific conditions that are considered to reflect economic deprivation" (p. 21). Poverty manifests itself in people's lack of economic resources necessary for the securing of basic needs such as food, clothing, and shelter. According to this definition, individuals can be said to be living in poverty when their personal resources do not enable them to maintain a minimally adequate standard of living as determined by the standards of the country in which they live. Yet, there are still unresolved questions, such as the lack of agreement about the specific level of consumption that distinguishes a state of poverty from a state of adequacy (Citro & Michael, 1995).

There is a range of difficult conceptual and statistical issues involved in defining and measuring poverty as well as setting standards for governmental assistance programs (Citro & Michael, 1995). Nevertheless, the official poverty level established by the U.S. government has been the most widely used index of poverty for the past three decades (Huston, 1991). It was originally based on the estimated cost of an "economy food budget" multiplied by 3, on the assumption that food should constitute one-third of a family's budget after taxes. It is adjusted for family size, the age of the head of the household, and the number of children under the age of 18. Annual adjustments to the poverty index are made for the cost of living on the basis of the Consumer Price Index (Huston, 1991).

Poverty in the United States

According to the U.S. Bureau of the Census (1996), the current official poverty definition is based only on pretax money income, excluding capital gains, and does not include the value of noncash benefits such as employer-provided health insurance, food stamps, Medicaid, Medicare, or public housing. In 1995, the number of people (including children) below the official government poverty level was 36.4 million, representing 13.8% of the nation's population.

Breakdown by Race and Ethnicity

In 1995, 8.5% of all non-Hispanic Whites lived in poverty (U.S. Bureau of the Census, 1996). These figures were 29.3% for Blacks, 30.3% for Hispanics (who may be any race), 14.6% for Asians and Pacific Islanders, and 14.3% for Native Americans. Although non-White groups have a larger proportion of members who live in poverty, the majority of Americans living in poverty (in absolute numbers) are Whites who may or may not be of Hispanic origin.

The foreign-born population is disproportionately poor compared with natives of the United States. Although foreign-born individuals represent only 9% of the total population, they make up 15% of poor people. In 1995, 40% of all poor people lived in the South, which continues to have a disproportionate share of the nation's poverty population (U.S. Bureau of the Census, 1996).

Urban and Rural Poverty

The poverty rate for people living in metropolitan and outside-metropolitan areas was 13.4% and 15.6%, respectively. Urban poverty is primarily concentrated within America's inner cities. Urban neighborhoods with poverty rates of 40% or more are often termed *ghetto neighborhoods* (Jargowsky & Bane, 1990). Such areas are characterized by a high percentage of publicly operated and often substandard housing (e.g., housing projects in violation of building codes). Many of these neighborhoods have deteriorated rapidly because of large population changes within a relatively short time period (e.g., working and middle-class people abandon areas, leading to divestment and isolation of poor people). Urban poverty areas are also characterized by high rates of out-of-wedlock births, low birth weight babies, infant deaths, juvenile delinquency rates, and crime (e.g., Coulton & Pandey, 1992).

In contrast to urban poverty, rural poverty is a problem that is often invisible to most Americans (Deavers & Hoppe, 1992). Although rural poverty is most heavily concentrated in the South, isolated pockets of poverty can be found in the Southwest, Midwest, and Northeast. These groups include, but are certainly not limited to, rural Blacks in the South; Appalachians in the coal fields; Native Americans on scattered reservations, and low-wage, part-time migrant farm workers.

What Is Socioeconomic Status?

In industrial societies, an individual's status (prestige ascribed by the community), power (influence in political contexts), and class (economic level) have provided the main foundation on which the measurement of social stratification has proceeded (Keeves & Saha, 1994). The most commonly used single indicator of an individual's relative standing with respect to the concepts of status, power, and class is that of occupational status (Keeves & Saha, 1994). A person's occupational status varies as a function of the level of skill required, the level of education necessary to engage in the occupation, and the income received from regular employment in the occupation (Keeves & Saha, 1994). Attempts to objectively measure occupational status in industrialized societies typically yield the following six subcategories (ranked from high to low): professional, managerial, clerical, skilled, semiskilled, and unskilled. The first three represent "white-collar" occupations, and the last three represent "blue-collar" occupations. The first usage of the term *socioeconomic status* came from Edwards's (1938) early attempt to use education and income to generate 10 hierarchically ordered classes of occupations.

Educational researchers have felt the need to supplement the concept of SES with measures that take into account the quality of the home environment that reinforces the intellectual values of schools. These measures are viewed as measuring the "sociocultural" level of the home. Variables that measure sociocultural background involve the following three components: (a) a cultural component such as the number of books in the home, visits to the theater or museum, or use of the public library; (b) a social component that comprises the parents' educational and occupational status; and (c) an economic component that refers to the family income and possessions (Bloom, 1976; Comber & Keeves, 1973; Postlethwaite & Ross, 1992).

Herrnstein and Murray (1994) studied the relationship between SES background and current poverty among Whites by using longitudinal data from 12,686 youths (aged 14–22 years) followed from 1979 to 1990 (the National Longitudinal Survey of Youth [NLSY]). They created an index of SES background in which the highest category (within a total of five) reflected advanced education, affluence, and prestigious occupations, whereas the lowest scores reflected poverty, meager education, and the most menial jobs. Herrnstein and Murray (1994, p. 131) discovered an obvious inverse relationship between a hierarchy of social class backgrounds and the percentage of individuals at each level who were below the poverty line in their late 20s and 30s. Their data showed that 13% of the sample from the three highest SES backgrounds (middle, high, and very high) were below the poverty line in their late 20s and 30s, whereas 36% of the sample from the two lowest SES backgrounds (low and very low) ended up below the poverty line in their early adult years.

Correlates of Poverty and Low SES for Children

The word *correlate* is a conceptually neutral term that carries no assumptions about the direction of causality. There is considerable debate about whether economic deprivation by itself causes certain problems or whether problems occur with greater frequency among poor people because of a more robust unknown variable (Egbuonu & Starfield, 1982). A brief summary of these correlates in the lives of poor children that may have relevance for the interpretation of school-related tests and assessments is discussed below.

Health

Poor children are much more likely than middle-class children to be victims of child abuse and neglect, maternal drug use, malnutrition, intrauterine infections, lead poisoning, failure to thrive, otitis media, and other infectious diseases (Parker, Greer, & Zuckerman, 1988). Because minority children make up a disproportionate share of poor people, they are much more likely than White children to be affected with these conditions (Newman & Buka, 1990). For example, African American children have been found to be much more likely to have blood lead levels high enough to be linked to significant physical damage, including damage to the central nervous system. Urban African American children from low-income families are especially likely to have elevated lead levels, reflecting in part the fact that many such children live in substandard houses or apartments with peeling lead-based paint (Needleman, 1990).

Language

The most persistent theme that runs throughout the poverty literature, particularly from the 1960s and early 1970s, is that the language skills of lower-class (particularly African American) children are deficient in significant areas. For example, disadvantaged children have less access to and proficiency with formal, elaborated language (e.g., vocabulary, syntactic structure); are more prone to use nonstandard English; are more deficient in auditory discrimination skills; and are less able to understand word meanings (see reviews by Williams, 1970; Williams & Naremore, 1970). Although many deficiencies have been identified from this research, some researchers have argued that a large portion of the language characteristics of lower-class children could be more appropriately interpreted as different but not deficient (Baratz, 1970; Labov, 1970). Some take a middle ground and argue that children from poverty environments do not have deficits in language skills but just use certain important language functions less frequently than middle-class children (Farran, 1982). Johnson (1974) speculated that when language researchers do not control for nonverbal intelligence in social class and racial group comparisons, findings of language differences may actually reflect differences in broad cognitive functioning.

School Learning, Behavior, and Special Education Eligibility

Zill, Moore, Smith, Stief, and Coiro (1991) analyzed the results from a large national survey of poor families who received Aid to Families With Dependent Children, poor families who did not receive such aid, and families who were not poor. The researchers found that children from poor families (regardless of whether they received such aid) were more likely to fail in school, were more likely to present serious conduct and discipline problems to their teachers and parents (some of which required suspension or expulsion), and were more likely to have repeated a grade. Parents who received such aid were more likely than nonpoor parents to have been called in for a school conference because of their child's behavior problems. Finally, researchers have used multiple regression procedures to demonstrate significant positive relationships between SES and children's eligibility for mentally handicapped and learning-disabled special education services (Barona & Faykus, 1992; McDermott, 1994).

Home Environment

Many scholars have focused their research efforts on discovering specific environmental process variables that are most likely to be the actual links in the causal chain that contributes to the well-known positive correlations among SES, school achievement, and intelligence tests (e.g., see studies by Marjoribanks, 1972; Portes, 1991).

According to Christenson (1990), optimal home environments for school success can be described by the following qualities:

> There is predictability and a basic routine to daily and weekly life. The physical environment of the home exhibits some order and organization conducive to the development of organizational skills relevant in the school environment. The child's life has not been a stressful one. The family provides a secure environment for the child, and the child is encouraged to develop initiative and take responsibility for specific tasks. Parents hold high, but reasonable expectations for their child's educational and employment possibilities. There is an emphasis on the value of education within the home and practical support is available for academic progress. Parents are supportive of the child's school. (adapted from Christenson, 1990, p. 511)

Caveats in Interpreting the Effects of Poverty and SES on Test Performance

The literature on the effects of poverty and SES on test results must be interpreted in light of the following interrelated caveats. First, research has shown that poverty is not uniform in its impact on children (Escalona, 1982; Korbin, 1992). Many research efforts have been directed at the identification of traits that characterize "resilient" children and adolescents. Resilience has been given many definitions (see the review by Henderson & Milstein, 1996) but can generally be defined as "successful adaptation despite risk and adversity" (Masten, 1994, p. 3). Resilience can refer to both the characteristics of people or characteristics of environments. Personal characteristics of resilient children include strong intellectual and interpersonal skills, the ability to set goals, the belief that life has meaning, a capacity to be responsive to others, and the tendency to perceive experiences constructively (Wang, Haertel, & Walberg, 1994). In addition, resilient children are able to constructively distance themselves from troubled family members and friends in order to accomplish goals and safeguard healthy personal development (Chess, 1989). Peng, Lee, Wang, and Walberg (1991) identified 9.2% of low-SES urban students who achieved combined reading and math achievement test scores in the highest quartile of national norms. They found that these "resilient" students had higher levels of internal control and self-concept, interacted more often with their parents, and were more likely to attend schools that were perceived as more learning oriented. Although the concept of resiliency sensitizes professionals about the wide variety of developmental outcomes of poor children, there are problematic methodological and validity issues related to the concept of resilience that have not been resolved (Bartelt, 1994; McCord, 1994; Rigsby, 1994).

Second, the impact of poverty on children is ordinarily understood to be mediated by the behavior of adults. How adults react to inadequate financial resources structures the consequences of poverty for children (e.g., see Dorris, 1989; Elder, 1974; McLoyd, 1990; Mingione, 1991). This last statement is not intended to suggest, however, that childhood poverty problems are synonymous with bad parenting. Bradley and Caldwell (1984) have shown that the quality of parenting children receive is only moderately correlated with economic status and that there are several other ecological and organismic factors associated with the quality of parenting.

Third, many environmental and organismic variables that are isolated and studied separately by researchers more than likely interact synergistically to influence a dependent variable. Characteristics of the child (e.g., genetic endowment, temperament, health) shape his or her responses to the environment, and the modified environment shapes the child's responses. In a low-SES environment, more risk factors for adverse developmental and behavioral outcomes are likely to be present. The most pertinent of these include increased stress, diminished social support, and maternal depression. These risk factors in turn exert an influence on the child through the quality of the home environment and the parent–child interactions. Parker et al. (1988) called this the *transactional view of child development.*

Fourth, SES is not a conceptually "pure" category in the United States. Class is highly correlated with race, ethnicity, religion, geographical location, immigration or refugee status, and age. To study the "pure" effects of SES, it is necessary to remove the effects of the other variables. Researchers have had varying degrees of success in doing this. Even if researchers are successful at controlling for other confounding variables, this does violence to the phenomenology of social class, which in "real life" always occurs in the context of the other sociocultural variables (Ehrenreich, 1990). The very act of isolating what is in social reality found only in combination may both minimize and falsify the significance of that which is isolated (Ehrenreich, 1990).

Fifth, most social science research tends to ignore the effects of genetic components in explaining SES differences in outcomes (e.g., test scores). Jensen (1987) labeled this the *sociologist's fallacy*, which is defined as the attribution of environmental causation without controlling for the causal effects of genetic factors. Lines of evidence that point to the important role of genetic factors, using IQ scores as an example, are well established in the social sciences. For example, purely environmental arguments cannot explain the presence of high-IQ offspring of average- or below-average parents, as well as the presence of average-IQ children from high-IQ parents. In addition, children of both low and high SES show regression from the parental IQ toward the mean of the general population. However, both findings are completely predictable from a polygenic theory of intelligence (Burt, 1961; Gottesman, 1963). Identical twins separated in the first year of life and reared in widely different social classes show greater resemblance in IQ than unrelated children reared together (Burt, 1961). The IQs of children adopted in early infancy show a much lower correlation with the SES of the adopting parents than do the IQs of children reared by their own parents (Leahy, 1935). The IQs of children reared in orphanages from infancy, who have not known their parents, show approximately the same correlation with their biological father's occupational status as do children reared by their own parents (.23 vs. .24; Lawrence, 1931). The correlations between the IQs of children adopted in infancy and the education of their biological mother is close to that of children reared by their own mothers (.44), whereas the correlation between children and their adopting parents is close to zero (Honzik, 1957). When full siblings (who have, on the average, at least 50% of their genetic inheritance in common) differ significantly in intelligence, those who are above the family average tend to move up the SES scale, and those who are below it tend to move down (Young & Gibson, 1965). For a summary of recent studies showing a significant genetic influence within

SES (occupational status) and educational level, see Plomin (1994). Ideally, the optimal method for truly understanding the relationship between environmental variables (poverty, SES) and its effects on a particular outcome would be to study samples of children adopted at birth who are randomly assigned to different homes, such that the children's genotypes and environments are uncorrelated.

The Effects of Poverty and SES on Personality and Behavior

The "Culture of Poverty" Thesis

Although many authors have written extensively about the characteristics of poverty and poor people in the United States during the 1960s (e.g., Harrington, 1962), Oscar Lewis (1966) is generally credited with popularizing the concept of a "culture of poverty" (COP). According to Lewis's earliest writings on the subject, the lack of adequate economic means is a necessary but not sufficient condition for the COP to exist. In other words, people can be in poverty, but not show personality and behaviors characteristic of the COP.

According to Lewis (1966), the COP refers to a way of life that is characteristic of the "abject poor" regardless of regional, rural–urban, and national differences. The COP is much more than an attempt to adapt to a set of transient external conditions but instead is hypothesized to perpetuate itself from generation to generation through basic values and attitudes that are absorbed by the children. The COP is characterized by these general characteristics (Lewis, 1966): (a) the lack of effective participation and integration in the major institutions of the larger society (e.g., marriage, schools, banks, hospitals, department stores, political parties, museums); (b) a minimum level of social organization beyond the level of nuclear and extended families, which is exacerbated by poor housing conditions and overcrowding; (c) the absence of childhood as a prolonged and protected developmental stage, which is compromised by early initiation into sex, "common law" marriages, male abandonment of children, and the proliferation of female-headed households; and (d) personal traits that reflect feelings of marginality, helplessness, weak ego structure, lack of impulse control, a strong "present-time" orientation, weak ability to defer gratification and plan for the future, and a high tolerance for psychological pathology.

Some writers in the mid- to late 1960s accepted the COP thesis uncritically and used the concept as a robust explanation for a variety of psychological, linguistic, and behavioral traits of poor people (e.g., Hess, 1970; Sarbin, 1970). For others, Lewis's COP thesis sparked much critical scrutiny and debate (della Fave, 1974; Leacock, 1971; Massey, 1975; Valentine, 1968). In addition, numerous empirical tests of the COP thesis (using survey and interview methodology) were conducted across a variety of ethnic–racial groups living in the United States and abroad. Generalizations across studies were inconclusive because each study showed various degrees of support for (or opposition to) the COP thesis (e.g., Billings, 1974; Coward, Feagin, & Williams, 1974; Davidson & Gaitz, 1974; Graves, 1974; Kutner, 1975; Safa, 1970; Salling & Harvey, 1981).

SES and Personality Assessment

Some researchers have asked whether there are different personality structures or configurations within social classes that may cause different responses to test stimuli (Levy, 1970). Because SES and race–ethnicity are positively correlated, a straightforward answer to this question is confounded by researchers' primary interest in identifying the effects of race–ethnicity in the results of psychological assessments (Gray-Little, 1995; Okazaki & Sue, 1995; Velasquez, 1995). For example, Greene (1987) attempted to identify differential Minnesota Multiphasic Personality Inventory (MMPI) score patterns among five ethnic–racial groups within normal participants, psychiatric patients, prisoners, and substance abusers. Greene found that when the effects of social class, education, and type of setting were statistically controlled, reliable relationships between ethnic–racial group and MMPI profiles could not be found.

There are few studies with the primary objective of isolating the effect of SES on test and assessment results. For example, some research reviewers have suggested that social class has a more profound effect than ethnicity in psychiatric symptomatology (Dohrenwend & Dohrenwend, 1974; Eaton, 1980; Kohn, 1973).

Ehrenreich (1990) analyzed the written responses to five Thematic Apperception Test cards of 70 White female college students who were classified as "working class" or "middle class" according to the characteristics of their families of origin. He found significant differences in the pattern of dependency and locus of control, but not for the number of drive expressions, intensity of drive expressions, or level of defenses used.

Long, Graham, and Timbrook (1994) examined differences in MMPI-2 scores between individuals in the normative sample who differed in educational (i.e., no high school diploma, high school diploma, some college, college diploma, and postgraduate) and family income levels (less than $15,000, $15,000–$24,999, $25,000–$34,999, $35,000–$44,999, and $45,000 or more). Participants were 1,138 men and 1,462 women in the normative sample and a subset of 841 couples who provided ratings of each other in terms of symptoms and problems. Long et al. found that for some scales, participants from lower income levels scored significantly higher than did those from higher income levels. However, Long et al. also found that some MMPI-2 scales underpredicted symptoms and problems for people from the lowest levels of education and family income and overpredicted symptoms and problems for people from the highest levels. Many of these errors of prediction had no easily interpretable linear pattern, leading Long et al. (1994) to conclude that "MMPI-2 differences between persons of varying socioeconomic levels, as assessed by education and family income, are minimal and probably not clinically meaningful" (p. 176).

SES and Test Anxiety

Endler and Bain (1966) found a significant correlation between social class and interpersonal anxiety for male participants in the personality testing situation. However, Beutler and Harwood (1995) reviewed studies suggesting that similarities between patients and therapists (in the context of a personality assessment) in gender, ethnicity, and SES increases the likelihood that therapeutic outcomes will be perceived favorably.

Zeidner (1990) studied sex and sociocultural group differences in the level and pattern of test anxiety among 361 Israeli college students taking college entrance scholastic aptitude tests. Zeidner found no significant differences in test anxiety scores by ethnicity or social class.

Turner, Beidel, Hughes, and Turner (1993) studied the relationship between test anxiety and non-test-related fears, academic achievement, and self-concept in low-SES African American schoolchildren between the ages of 8 and 12 years. Turner et al. found that the academic achievement of test-anxious students was significantly lower than that of the non-test-anxious group. Although the researchers found that the prevalence of test anxiety in the low-SES African-American sample was 41%, this figure was not significantly different from prevalence rates obtained in a middle-to-high SES district serving predominantly White students.

Sapp, Durand, and Farrell (1995) studied the effects of test anxiety, as measured by the Test Anxiety Inventory, among 101 academically at-risk and ethnically diverse low-SES college students in a natural testing situation. Using a randomized pretest–posttest design, Sapp et al. found that respondents reported a statistically significant level of heightened posttest anxiety after taking a battery of standardized writing, mathematical, and reading ability tests.

Findings such as these are ambiguous in their interpretation of the direction of causality. Although it may be argued that test anxiety negatively influences test performance, it can also be argued that respondents who have extensive histories of performing poorly on achievement tests find subsequent test situations to be anxiety provoking (Jensen, 1980).

Relationships Among Poverty, SES, Academic Achievement, and Intelligence

Herrnstein and Murray (1994) found an inverse relationship between poverty status and the percentage of individuals in five hierarchical categories of cognitive ability. In their NLSY data set, 11% of those in the top three cognitive categories (i.e., normal, bright, and very bright) lived below the poverty line in 1989, compared with 46% of those in the bottom two cognitive categories.

Estimates are that mild mental retardation (IQs = 2–3 SDs below the mean) constitutes 75–90% of all people classified as mentally retarded (Stein & Susser, 1992). Children living below the poverty level are at increased risk for mild mental retardation, although the vast majority of poor children develop with normal intelligence (Duncan & Rodgers, 1991). Mild mental retardation is usually relatively common and strongly associated with lower SES, whereas severe mental retardation is rarer and less strongly or not at all associated with lower SES (McDermott & Altekruse, 1994; Stein & Susser, 1992).

Health Problems and IQ

Poverty is associated with a variety of health problems that may have a deleterious effect on IQ. According to Kushlick (1996), prematurity has the strongest known relation to brain dysfunction of any reproductive factor, and many of the complications of pregnancy are strongly associated with prematurity. The crucial factor in prematurity is the problem of low birth weight. Although the incidence of babies weighing less than 5.5 lb increases from higher to lower social classes, only about 1% of the total variance of birth weight is accounted for by socioeconomic variables (Jensen, 1969).

Low birth weight acts as a threshold variable with respect to intellectual impairment (Jensen, 1969). That is, the mean IQ is lowered only among children having birth weights under 3 lb, particularly among boys (Kushlick, 1966). When extreme cases (IQs below 50) are not counted, the effects of prematurity or low birth weight (even as low as 3 lb) have a very weak relationship to children's IQs by the time they are of school age (Jensen, 1969; Kushlick, 1966).

It is not surprising that prenatal and infant nutrition can have significant effects on brain development because the human brain attains 70% of its maximum adult weight in the first year after birth (Krassner, 1986; Rosovski, Novoa, Aberzua, & Monkeberg, 1971). Data collected in Third World countries show that severe undernutrition before 2–3 years of age, especially a lack of the proteins, vitamins, and minerals essential for their anabolism, results in lowered intelligence (Monkeberg, Tisler, Toro, Gattas, & Vegal, 1972; Stoch & Smythe, 1963).

The effects of lead poisoning on cognitive functioning have been described in detail by Angle (1993), Dyer (1993), Evans, Daniel, and Marmor (1994), and Huber (1991). However, the effects of blood lead levels on cognitive test scores are confounded with maternal IQ and other home environmental variables (Dietrich, Berger, Succop, Hammond, & Bornschein, 1993; Dietrich, Succop, Berger, & Keith, 1992). The deleterious effects of abnormal doses of iodine, zinc, and vitamin A on human development was described by Huber (1991). Numerous studies conducted in Latin America (Lozoff, 1990; Walter, 1989) and Asia (Seshadri & Gopaldas, 1989) have consistently shown that infants and young children with iron-deficiency anemia score lower than iron-replete control children on a wide range of psychological tests (e.g., developmental scales, intelligence tests, tasks of specific cognitive function).

Infants suffering from cytomegalovirus infection from poor families have lower IQ scores and 2.7 times more school failure than do matched control children (Hanshaw, Scheiner, & Moxley, 1976). By contrast, these outcomes were not found for infected infants of middle- or upper-class backgrounds.

SES and IQ

The substantial correlation, averaging .4–.6 in various studies, between indexes of SES and phenotypic intelligence is one of the most consistent and firmly established findings in psychological research, and it holds true in every modern industrial society in which it has been studied (Jensen, 1969). Because of assortive mating (the tendency for humans to bear offspring with partners of similar intelligence), intelligence differences between social classes (within racial groups) are the one type of subpopulation difference in which there is a substantial genetic component (Eckland, 1967; Gottesman, 1968; Tyler, 1965). When a population is stratified into four or more SES levels, mean IQ differences of 1 or 2 *SD*s are generally found between the extreme groups. Despite intensive efforts by psychologists, educators, and sociologists to devise tests intended to eliminate SES differences in measured intelligence, none of these efforts have succeeded (Jensen, 1980; Lambert, 1964).

At the same time, intelligence variation *within* social class categories is great, particularly among the offspring of the parents on whom the SES classification is based (Jensen, 1969). Variability in IQ across social classes is influenced by genetic, environmental, and interaction effects. The substantial contribution of the environment is illustrated by the finding that, absent any conscious intervention efforts, identical twins who have been reared apart can manifest an average IQ difference of about 8–14 points (Gottesman, 1968). Practically the entire range of abilities can be found within each broadly defined social class level (although the average overlap between the lowest and highest SES levels may be small).

Interactions Among Race, SES, and Cognitive Tasks

Yando, Seitz, and Zigler (1979) studied a sample of 304 Black and White second and third graders who were evenly distributed among both economically advantaged and disadvantaged social class groupings. They studied 23 dependent variables using various measures of children's creativity, self-confidence, dependency, frustration threshold, curiosity, autonomy, self-concept, and teacher ratings of these traits. When the effects of IQ and mental age were controlled (both statistically and experimentally in two separate studies), Yando et al. found no racial group differences but significant SES differences among the outcome variables studied. The specific nature of the SES differences was extremely complex, nuanced, and task specific, so convenient generalizations cannot be made. However, Yando et al. (1979) concluded that

> perhaps the clearest finding of the present investigation is that no one group of children performed uniformly better than any other group when their performance was examined across a wide variety of problem-solving situations. Furthermore, when group differences did emerge, they were more likely to reflect stylistic patterns rather than capacity differences. . . . Even though the present investigation was not conducted within a naturalistic setting, the examination of a wide array of behaviors, the use of a large number of measures, and the emphasis on nonconventional rather than traditional academic problem-solving tasks revealed important information about the variations in problem-solving strategies of children from different SES backgrounds. (p. 107)

Interactions Among Race, SES, and IQ

In major early studies based on large-scale samples (Coleman et al., 1966; Scarr-Salapatek, 1971; Shuey, 1966), the mean mental test scores of the lowest SES White group exceeded the mean IQ of the highest SES Black group. In newer data (Herrnstein & Murray, 1994), when the mean IQ score for both races was plotted within different levels of SES, the magnitude of the Black–White difference in standard deviations did not decrease. In fact, the Black–White difference stayed at 1 *SD*, even at the highest parental SES level (Herrnstein & Murray, 1994). In other studies, the gap has continued to increase throughout the range of SES status (Jensen & Figueroa, 1975; Reynolds, Chastain, Kaufman, & McLean, 1987).

SES and Achievement Tests

The first large-scale American study to establish the relationship between family background and school achievement tests is the Coleman report (Coleman et al., 1966). Such relationships are consistent to the present day, as reflected in large-scale achievement test data. For example, the National Education Longitudinal Study of 1988 examined the academic performance of a nationally representative sample of eighth graders. Substantial differences among eighth graders in the ed-

ucation levels of their parents were associated with dramatically different likelihoods that students would be among the highest or lowest
scorers on the standardized tests used in the study. Fully 56% of the
eighth graders with a parent who had a graduate degree were in the
top achievement test score quartile, and only 7% of this group were in
the bottom quartile. The situation was virtually reversed for eighth graders who had parents with relatively little formal education. About 51%
had test scores in the bottom quartile, whereas only 5% scored in the
top quartile (Miller, 1995).

School district administrators are faced with a variety of options in
deciding whether to take into account student background characteristics (e.g., SES) in reporting achievement test results. There are four
major approaches to account for student background in reporting assessment results (Selden, 1990):

1. *Adjusting scores.* Scores can be statistically adjusted to eliminate
   the effects of background variables once those effects are
   known. The interpretation is as follows: This is what the average
   score for School X would be if the effects of this background
   variable did not exist. The disadvantage of this method is that
   the consumer has no way of knowing if a high score reflects
   high performance or substantial "adjustment."

2. *Reporting by comparison bands.* A school's mean raw scores are
   displayed in the context of other schools that are similar in SES.
   The interpretation is as follows: School X did very well (or very
   poorly) relative to schools that are similar to School X. The
   disadvantage of this method is that it is vulnerable to criticism
   from groups who feel that it diminishes expectations for low-
   SES students.

3. *Evaluating actual versus predicted performance.* A school's predicted score is calculated on the basis of students' prior performance and background characteristics. This is then compared
   with the school's actual performance. The interpretation is as
   follows: School X did better (or worse) than what would be
   predicted on the basis of its background characteristics. This
   method suffers the same criticisms as the previous method.

4. *Desegregating results and other methods.* A school's scores are broken down by student subgroups, or other statistics (such as percentage of minority or low SES students) are reported along
   with the actual scores. The interpretation is as follows: Within
   School X, the mean for Subgroup 1 was "a," the mean for Sub-

group 2 was "b," and so on. The disadvantage of this method is the potential for stigmatizing subgroups on the basis of sensitive characteristics such as race or ethnicity.

Interpretation of Low Cognitive Test Scores for Poverty and Low-SES Test Takers

The significant correlation between low cognitive test scores and lower SES is well established in the literature. However, in many settings, psychological practitioners and researchers may suspect that factors inherent in poverty and low-SES status may artificially depress a test taker's performance, such that the score is an underestimate of what the test taker is optimally capable of.

Nutritional Deficiencies

Cravioto (1966) reported gains of as much as 18 IQ points from nutritional improvements in a group of extremely undernourished children when the improvements were implemented as late as 2 years of age. After 4 years of age, however, nutritional therapy effected no significant change in IQ (Cravioto, 1966). The earlier the age at which nutritional therapy is instituted, the more beneficial are its effects.

The most consistent results can be found in nutritional intervention studies in Third World countries. Many studies have been conducted that were designed to identify the consequences of early supplementary feeding with samples of children in Latin America, the Caribbean, and Asia to test the effects of protein and energy supplements on mental and motor development during the first 24 months of life. In particular, nutritionally at-risk children who receive a high-calorie and protein supplement obtain higher scores in motor development scales than children without supplements in the first years of life. Similar beneficial effects are observed on mental development during the second year of life (see the reviews by Idjradinata & Pollitt, 1993; Pollitt, 1994).

Enriching Environments

Jensen (1969) discussed the concept of an "environmental threshold," above which efforts to improve environmental conditions (short of adoption) for low-SES children yield little lasting IQ gains. According to Jensen (1969), reports of large and lasting IQ gains as a result of altered environments usually involve children under 6 years of age (e.g., Infant Health and Development Program, 1990; Rauh, Achenbach, Nurcombe, Howell, & Teti, 1988) or children who have been reared under the most extreme conditions of social and sensory deprivation (Davis, 1947; Skeels & Dye, 1939). By contrast, low-SES "culturally disadvantaged" children (who have not experienced extreme social or sensory deprivation) usually show a slight initial gain in IQ after their first few months of exposure to the environmental enrichment afforded by school attendance or compensatory education program. However, they soon lose this gain, and in a sizable proportion of children the initial IQ gain is followed by a gradual decline in IQ throughout the subsequent years of schooling. These results have been confirmed in reviews by Spitz (1986) and Herrnstein and Murray (1994).

Test Wiseness

Test wiseness (TW) is widely recognized as a source of additional variance in test scores and as a possible depressor of test validity. Millman, Bishop, and Ebel (1965) defined TW as a participant's ability to use the characteristics and formats of the test and the test-taking situation to receive a high score. This ability is logically independent of the examinee's knowledge of the subject matter that the items supposedly measure. Synonyms of TW include "test sophistication," "testmanship," and "test insight" (see the reviews by Benson, 1989; Jensen, 1980; Sarnacki, 1979). TW is a construct that includes many subcomponents. According to the taxonomy proposed by Millman et al. (1965), TW includes but is not limited to (a) time management strategies to implement on tests with restrictive time limits; (b) "rules of thumb" to avoid minor mistakes, so that the test taker is not penalized for carelessness; (c) proficiency with guessing techniques that allow the test taker to gain points beyond those attained on the basis of knowledge of the subject matter; (d) deductive reasoning strategies, which depend on some knowledge of the tested material; and (e) knowledge of the test maker's idiosyncrasies and patterns in test construction that may aid in maximizing scores. TW appears to be composed of many specific skills rather than a general trait (Benson, 1989; Diamond & Evans, 1972). Benson (1989) reviewed the literature on TW measures and found low-to-moderately high reliability estimates across numerous TW scales for school-age children and adults.

Measurement experts suspect that individual differences in TW may contribute to reduced true score variance due to individual differences in the trait that the tests are originally designed to measure. Hence, it is logical to conclude that the best method of reducing this possible source of variance is to train students who are low in TW (rather than attempt to inhibit the skills of individuals who are high in TW). Several researchers have shown that training in various TW skills will improve test scores on individual and group-administered standardized cognitive tests (see the reviews by Bond, 1989; Jensen, 1980; Powers, 1993; Sarnacki, 1979; Scruggs, White, & Bennion, 1986).

Bond (1989) defined "coaching" as instruction in TW, highly specific instruction on the types of knowledge and skill required of a specific test, and general instruction across broad vocabulary and mathematics domains. The term *practice* refers to a testee taking the same or similar tests two or more times at various intervals without any special instructions. Jensen (1980) summarized findings from several literature reviews before 1980 on the effects of coaching and practice on cognitive test scores. The subset of generalizations relevant to coaching and practice on IQ tests is as follows:

1. Both practice and coaching effects are greatest for respondents who have never been tested before (naive respondents). There are more examples of large practice effects in young children because fewer of them have had prior experience with tests when compared with older children or adults. Coaching is ineffective unless it is accompanied by practice at taking complete tests under regular test conditions. However, coaching effects tend to diminish with prior test-taking experience.

2. When test score gains are expressed as standard scores with a standard deviation of 15, the retesting of naive respondents on an identical test, after a short interval, shows gains of about 2–8 points, with an average of about 5 points. The typical gain from several hours of coaching plus practice gain on a similar test is about 9 IQ points. However, practice effects show little transfer of training. Practice gains are largest when identical tests are used and get progressively smaller when researchers move from the use of parallel forms to similar (but no parallel) tests to different types of tests.

3. There is considerable variability in practice effects among individual, in which high-ability respondents tend to gain more from practice than low-ability respondents. Even with equal

prior testing experience, there are substantial individual differences in gains from coaching.

4. Practice gains between the first and second test experiences is usually as great or greater than the total of all further gains from subsequent practice trials.

5. The gain from both coaching and practice effects is smallest on verbal tests and largest for performance and nonverbal tests. Numerical reasoning and arithmetic problems are more susceptible to coaching gains than are items based on verbal knowledge and reasoning.

6. For naive respondents, the practice effects are greater on group-administered paper-and-pencil tests than on individually administered tests.

7. Practice effects can last significantly, with half of the gains from practice remaining as long as 1 year. However, the effects of coaching seem to fade considerably faster than the effects of practice. (adapted from Jensen, 1980)

Jensen (1980) reviewed several studies in which race and social class interaction effects were tested in test practice and coaching. Although some effects were reported, these effects were minimal and did not approximate the size of well-established social class and racial group differences on such tests. In a more recent meta-analysis, Scruggs et al. (1986) found that elementary school-age students from low-SES backgrounds benefited more than twice as much as students who were not from low-SES backgrounds when training in test-taking skills exceeded 4 hr.

"Dynamic" Assessment

These discouraging results do not warrant the conclusion that practice and coaching should be abandoned. Currently, the most systematic and focused research effort related to the effects of coaching and practice on individually administered cognitive test performance comes from the "dynamic" or "interactive" assessment movement (Haywood & Tzuriel, 1992; Lidz, 1991; Palincsar & Winn, 1992). Dynamic–interactive assessment is a generic label given to a number of distinct approaches that are concerned with: the strategies children use to achieve a given test score and how well a child performs (and why) once given assistance (Palincsar & Winn, 1992). Reuven Feuerstein, a major figure in the dynamic assessment movement, developed many of his ideas in the context of extensive experience with poor immigrant subgroups to Israel who were experiencing cultural disorientation and significant life disruptions (Feuerstein, Rand, & Hoffman, 1979). As the movement progressed, dynamic assessment research spread to poor minority children in the United States (Haywood & Tzuriel, 1992). Dynamic assessment approaches are built on the assumption that disadvantaged or low-performing children often lack the dispositional, problem-solving, or verbal mediational skills to successfully master items such as those found on standardized intelligence tests. Measurement focuses on the degree of change that occurs on a task from guided assistance and the extent to which change is facilitated from examiner behaviors (Lidz, 1991).

The dynamic–interactive assessment movement is not without its critics (e.g., Frisby & Braden, 1992). Critics have argued that this research is undermined by the lack of resemblance of many dynamic assessment tasks to schoollike tasks (Reynolds, 1986), the unreliability of gain scores (Glutting & McDermott, 1990), the significant correlation between IQ and the size of pretest–posttest gains (Glutting & McDermott, 1990), and unimpressive results from intervention studies based on dynamic assessment theory (Savell, Twohig, & Rachford, 1986). In addition, dynamic–interactive assessment proponents essentially argue that children's individualized choices of cognitive strategies (either good or bad) are a significant source of variance in "traditional" test scores. However, this idea is inconsistent with all the evidence showing high positive correlations between different populations in the rank order of item difficulty on nonverbal tests such as the Raven Progressive Matrices. Different Raven's items require different strategies for solution. Dynamic assessment theory would predict that certain items would be relatively more difficult for "disadvantaged" groups than more advantaged groups (as a result of their strategy demands). Despite the fact that low-SES test takers produce lower mean scores than high-SES groups on such tests, strategy differences among items to not produce significant differences in the rank order of item difficulty across high–low SES or racial groups. It is unlikely that this condition would exist if strategy factors were a main source of group differences (Jensen, 1987). If it can be shown that strategy differences interact with subgroup differences, then these differences do not appear to be independent of item difficulty rank orderings.

Although subgroups may demonstrate similar rank orderings of item difficulties on cognitive tests, there is some evidence that the same tests may not be yielding similar factor patterns when administered to widely different SES and ethnic groups. For example, Cattell and Horn (1978) found that "fluid *g*" (i.e., problem-solving ability with novel tasks) was not as highly correlated with "crystallized *g*" (i.e., problem-solving ability dependent on prior learning) in a sample of poor rural Black children compared with an affluent (mostly White) sample.

Supporters of the dynamic–interactive assessment approach may continue to argue that there are populations who are so environmentally disadvantaged that dynamic assessment is a more accurate indication of cognitive potential compared with traditional tests. Such groups might include recent immigrants to America, people attending unusual schools who are largely unfamiliar with standardized testing, or others who have had little or no formal schooling. Although this is a reasonable argument, the acid test of the proper use of coaching, practice, or dynamic assessment methods with a specific subpopulation is if their effects significantly and consistently improve the test's concurrent and predictive validity with the subpopulation in question (e.g., Ortar, 1960).

Conclusion

Disentangling the effects of poverty and social class on test and assessment performance is no easy task, as shown in this chapter. Because poverty does not affect all test takers in the same way, clinicians need to supplement their test interpretations with in-depth developmental histories and the analysis of trends in prior test data. In some instances, conditions associated with poverty detrimentally influence test scores, and appropriate intervention (i.e., practice, coaching, dynamic assessment) has been shown to improve performance. At the same time, there are subpopulation differences in test performance that have been shown to be enduring and intractable. The information presented in this chapter will hopefully assist clinicians in making appropriate test interpretations for clients whose economic circumstances are significantly different from their own.

References

Angle, C. R. (1993). Childhood lead poisoning and its treatment. *Annual Review of Pharmacology and Toxicology, 33,* 409–434.

Baratz, J. C. (1970). Teaching reading in an urban Negro school system. In F. Williams (Ed.), *Language and poverty* (pp. 11–24). Chicago: Markham.

Barona, A., & Faykus, S. P. (1992). Differential effects of sociocultural variables on special education eligibility categories. *Psychology in the Schools, 29,* 313–320.

Bartelt, D. W. (1994). On resilience: Questions of validity. In M. C. Wang & E. W. Gordon (Eds.), *Educational resilience in inner-city America: Challenges and prospects* (pp. 97–108). Hillsdale, NJ: Erlbaum.

Benson, J. (1989). The psychometric and cognitive aspects of test-wiseness: A review of the literature. In L. W. Barber (Ed.), *Test wiseness* (pp. 1–14). Bloomington, IN: Phi Delta Kappa.

Beutler, L. E., & Harwood, T. M. (1995). How to assess clients in pretreatment planning. In J. N. Butcher (Ed.), *Clinical personality assessment: Practical approaches* (pp. 59–77). New York: Oxford University Press.

Billings, D. (1974). Culture and poverty in Appalachia: A theoretical discussion and empirical analysis. *Social Forces, 53,* 315–323.

Bloom, B. S. (1976). *Human characteristics and school learning.* New York: McGraw-Hill.

Bond, L. (1989). The effect of special preparation on measures of scholastic ability. In R. L. Linn (Ed.), *Educational measurement* (pp. 429–444). New York: Macmillan.

Bradley, R. H., & Caldwell, B. M. (1984). The HOME Inventory and family demographics. *Developmental Psychology, 20,* 315–320.

Burt, C. (1961). Intelligence and social mobility. *British Journal of Statistical Psychology, 14,* 3–24.

Cattell, R. B., & Horn, J. L. (1978). A cross-social check on the theory of fluid and crystallized intelligence with discovery of new valid subtest designs. *Journal of Educational Measurement, 15,* 139–164.

Chess, S. (1989). Defying the voice of doom. In T. Dugan & R. Coles (Eds.), *The child in our times* (pp. 179–199). New York: Brunner/Mazel.

Christenson, S. L. (1990). Differences in students' home environments: The need to work with families. *School Psychology Review, 19,* 505–517.

Citro, C. F., & Michael, R. T. (1995). *Measuring poverty: A new approach.* Washington, DC: National Academy Press.

Coleman, J. S., Campbell, E. Q., Hobson, C. J., McPartland, J., Mood, A. M., Weinfeld, F. D., & York, R. L. (1966). *Equality of educational opportunity.* Washington, DC: U.S. Government Printing Office.

Comber, L. C., & Keeves, J. P. (1973). *Science education in nineteen countries: An empirical study.* New York: Wiley.

Coward, B. E., Feagin, J. R., & Williams, J. A. (1974). The culture of poverty debate: Some additional data. *Social Problems, 21,* 621–634.

Coulton, C. J., & Pandey, S. (1992). Geographic concentration of poverty and risk to children in urban neighborhoods. *American Behavioral Scientist, 35,* 238–257.

Cravioto, J. (1966). Malnutrition and behavioral development in the pre-school child. *Pre-school malnutrition* (National Health Science Publications, No. 1282).

Davidson, C., & Gaitz, C. M. (1974). "Are the poor different?" A comparison of work behavior and attitudes among the urban poor and nonpoor. *Social Problems, 22,* 229–245.

Davis, K. (1947). Final note on a case of extreme isolation. *American Journal of Sociology, 57,* 432–457.

Deavers, K. L., & Hoppe, R. A. (1992). Overview of the rural poor in the 1980s. In C. M. Duncan (Ed.), *Rural poverty in America* (pp. 3–20). New York: Auburn House.

della Fave, L. R. (1974). The culture of poverty revisited: A strategy for research. *Social Problems, 21,* 609–621.

Diamond, J. J., & Evans, W. J. (1972). An investigation of the cognitive correlates of test-wiseness. *Journal of Educational Measurement, 9,* 145–150.

Dietrich, K. N., Berger, O. G., Succop, P. A., Hammond, P. B., & Bornschein, R. L. (1993). The developmental consequences of low to moderate prenatal and postnatal lead exposure: Intellectual attainment in the Cincinnati lead study cohort following school entry. *Neurotoxicology and Teratology, 15,* 37–44.

Dietrich, K. N., Succop, P. A., Berger, O. G., & Keith, R. W. (1992). Lead exposure and the central auditory processing abilities and cognitive development of urban children: The Cincinnati lead study cohort at age 5 years. *Neurotoxicology and Teratology, 14,* 51–56.

Dohrenwend, B. P., & Dohrenwend, B. S. (1974). Social and cultural influences on psychopathology. *Annual Review of Psychology, 25,* 417–452.

Dorris, M. (1989). *The broken chord.* New York: HarperCollins.

Duncan, G. J., & Rodgers, W. (1991). Has children's poverty become more persistent? *American Sociological Review, 56,* 538–550.

Dyer, F. J. (1993). Clinical presentation of the lead-poisoned child on mental ability tests. *Journal of Clinical Psychology, 49,* 94–101.

Eaton, W. W. (1980). *The sociology of mental disorders.* New York: Praeger.

Eckland, B. K. (1967). Genetics and sociology: A reconsideration. *American Sociological Review, 32,* 173–194.

Edwards, A. (1938). *A social-economic grouping of the gainful workers of the United States, gainful workers of 1930 in social-economic groups, by color, nativity, age, and sex, and by industry, with comparative statistics for 1920 and 1910.* Washington, DC: U.S. Government Printing Office.

Egbuonu, L., & Starfield, B. (1982). Child health and social status. *Pediatrics, 69,* 550–557.

Ehrenreich, J. H. (1990). Effect of social class of subjects on normative responses to TAT cards. *Journal of Clinical Psychology, 46,* 467–471.

Elder, G. H., Jr. (1974). *Children of the Great Depression.* Chicago: University of Chicago Press.

Endler, N. S., & Bain, J. M. (1966). Interpersonal anxiety as a function of social class. *Journal of Social Psychology, 70,* 221–227.

Escalona, S. K. (1982). Babies at double hazard: Early development of infants at biologic and social risk. *Pediatrics, 70,* 670–676.

Evans, H. L., Daniel, S. A., & Marmor, M. (1994). Reversal learning tasks may provide rapid determination of cognitive deficits in lead-exposed children. *Neurotoxicology and Teratology, 16,* 471–477.

Farran, D. C. (1982). Mother-child interaction, language development, and the school performance of poverty children. In L. Feagans & D. C. Farran (Eds.), *The language of children reared in poverty: Implications for evaluation and intervention* (pp. 19–52). New York: Academic Press.

Feuerstein, R., Rand, Y., & Hoffman, M. B. (1979). *The dynamic assessment of retarded performers: The learning potential assessment device, theory, instruments, and techniques.* Baltimore: University Park Press.

Frisby, C., & Braden, J. P. (1992). Feuerstein's dynamic assessment approach: A semantic, logical, and empirical critique. *Journal of Special Education, 26,* 281–301.

Glutting, J. J., & McDermott, P. A. (1990). Principles and problems in learning potential. In C. R. Reynolds & R. W. Kamphaus (Eds.), *Handbook of psychoeducational and educational assessment of children: Intelligence and achievement* (pp. 296–347). New York: Guilford Press.

Gottesman, I. I. (1963). Genetic aspects of intelligent behavior. In N. Ellis (Ed.), *Hand-*

book of mental deficiency: Psychological theory and research (pp. 253–296). New York: McGraw-Hill.

Gottesman, I. I. (1968). Biogenetics of race and class. In M. Deutsch, I. Katz, & A. R. Jensen (Eds.), *Social class, race, and psychological development* (pp. 11–52). New York: Holt, Rinehart & Winston.

Graves, T. D. (1974). Urban Indian personality and the "culture of poverty." *American Ethnologist, 1,* 65–86.

Gray-Little, B. (1995). The assessment of psychopathology in racial and ethnic minorities. In J. N. Butcher (Ed.), *Clinical personality assessment: Practical approaches* (pp. 140–157). New York: Oxford University Press.

Greene, R. L. (1987). Ethnicity and MMPI performance: A review. *Journal of Consulting and Clinical Psychology, 55,* 497–512.

Hanshaw, J., Scheiner, A., & Moxley, A. (1976). School failure and deafness after silent congenital cytomegalovirus infection. *New England Journal of Medicine, 295,* 468–470.

Harrington, M. (1962). *The other America: Poverty in the United States.* New York: Macmillan.

Haywood, H. C., & Tzuriel, D. (Eds.). (1992). *Interactive assessment.* New York: Springer-Verlag.

Henderson, N., & Milstein, M. M. (1996). *Resiliency in schools: Making it happen for students and educators.* Thousand Oaks, CA: Corwin Press.

Herrnstein, R. J., & Murray, C. (1994). *The bell curve: Intelligence and class structure in American life.* New York: Free Press.

Hess, R. D. (1970). The transmission of cognitive strategies in poor families: The socialization of apathy and underachievement. In V. L. Allen (Ed.), *Psychological factors in poverty* (pp. 79–92). Chicago: Markham.

Honzik, M. P. (1957). Developmental studies of parent-child resemblances in intelligence. *Child Development, 28,* 215–228.

Huber, A. M. (1991). Nutrition and mental retardation. In J. L. Matson & J. A. Mulick (Eds.), *Handbook of mental retardation* (2nd ed., pp. 308–326). Elmsford, NY: Pergamon Press.

Huston, A. C. (1991). Children in poverty: Developmental and policy issues. In A. C. Huston (Ed.), *Children in poverty: Child development and public policy* (pp. 1–22). Cambridge, England: Cambridge University Press.

Huston, A. C., McLoyd, V. C., & Coll, C. G. (1994). Children and poverty: Issues in contemporary research. *Child Development, 65,* 275–282.

Idjradinata, P., & Pollitt, E. (1993). Reversal of developmental delays in iron-deficient anaemic infants treated with iron. *The Lancet, 341,* 1–4.

Infant Health and Development Program. (1990). Enhancing the outcomes of low-birth weight, premature infants. *Journal of the American Medical Association, 263,* 3035–3042.

Jargowsky, P. A., & Bane, M. J. (1990). Ghetto poverty: Basic questions. In L. E. Lynn, Jr., & G. H. McGeary (Eds.), *Inner-city poverty in the United States* (pp. 235–280). Washington, DC: National Academy Press.

Jensen, A. R. (1969). How much can we boost IQ and scholastic achievement? *Harvard Educational Review, 39,* 1–123.

Jensen, A. R. (1980). *Bias in mental testing.* New York: Free Press.

Jensen, A. R. (1987). Differential psychology: Towards consensus. In S. Modgil & C. Modgil (Eds.), *Arthur Jensen: Consensus and controversy* (pp. 353–396). New York: Falmer Press.

Jensen, A. R., & Figueroa, R. A. (1975). Forward and backward digit span interaction with race and IQ: Predictions from Jensen's theory. *Journal of Educational Psychology, 67,* 882–893.

Johnson, D. L. (1974). The influences of social class and race on language performance and spontaneous speech of preschool children. *Child Development, 45,* 517–521.

Keeves, J. P., & Saha, L. J. (1994). Measurement of social background. In T. Husen & T. N. Postlethwaite (Eds.), *The international encyclopedia of education* (Vol. 7, 2nd ed., pp. 3715–3722). New York: Elsevier Science.

Kohn, M. L. (1973). Social class and schizophrenia: A critical review and a reformulation. *Schizophrenia Bulletin, 7,* 60–79.

Korbin, J. E. (1992). Child poverty in the United States. *American Behavioral Scientist, 36,* 213–219.

Krassner, M. B. (1986). Diet and brain function. *Nutrition Reviews, 44,* 12–15.

Kushlick, A. (1966). Assessing the size of the problem of subnormality. In J. E. Meade & A. S. Parkes (Eds.), *Genetic and environmental factors in human ability* (pp. 121–147). New York: Plenum.

Kutner, N. G. (1975). The poor vs. the non-poor: An ethnic and metropolitan-nonmetropolitan comparison. *Sociological Quarterly, 16,* 250–263.

Labov, W. (1970). The logic of nonstandard English. In F. Williams (Ed.), *Language and poverty* (pp. 153–189). Chicago: Markham.

Lambert, N. (1964). The present status of the culture fair testing movement. *Psychology in the Schools, 1,* 318–330.

Lawrence, E. M. (1931). An investigation into the relation between intelligence and inheritance. *British Journal of Psychology* monograph supplement, 16(5).

Leacock, E. (1971). *The culture of poverty: A critique.* New York: Simon & Schuster.

Leahy, A. M. (1935). Nature-nurture and intelligence. *Genetic Psychology Monographs, 17,* 241–305.

Levy, M. R. (1970). Issues in the personality assessment of lower-class patients. *Journal of Projective Techniques and Personality Assessment, 34,* 6–9.

Lewis, O. (1966). The culture of poverty. *Scientific American, 215,* 19–25.

Lidz, C. S. (1991). *Practitioner's guide to dynamic assessment.* New York: Guilford Press.

Long, K. A., Graham, J. R., & Timbrook, R. E. (1994). Socioeconomic status and MMPI-2 interpretation. *Measurement and Evaluation in Counseling and Development, 27,* 158–177.

Lozoff, B. (1990). Has iron deficiency been shown to cause altered behavior in infants? In J. Dobbing (Ed.), *Brain, behaviour, and iron in the infant diet* (pp. 107–131). London: Springer-Verlag.

Marjoribanks, K. (1972). Environment, social class, and mental abilities. *Journal of Educational Psychology, 63,* 103–109.

Massey, G. (1975). Studying social class: The case of embourgeoisement and the culture of poverty. *Social Problems, 22,* 595–608.

Masten, A. S. (1994). Resilience in individual development: Successful adaptation despite risk and adversity. In M. C. Wang & E. W. Gordon (Eds.), *Educational resilience in inner-city America: Challenges and prospects* (pp. 3–26). Hillsdale, NJ: Erlbaum.

McCord, J. (1994). Resilience as a dispositional quality: Some methodological points. In M. C. Wang & E. W. Gordon (Eds.), *Educational resilience in inner-city America: Challenges and prospects* (pp. 109–118). Hillsdale, NJ: Erlbaum.

McDermott, S. W. (1994). Explanatory model to describe school district prevalence rates for mental retardation and learning disabilities. *American Journal on Mental Retardation, 99,* 175–185.

McDermott, S. W., & Altekruse, J. M. (1994). Dynamic model for preventing mental retardation in the population: The importance of poverty and deprivation. *Research in Developmental Disabilities, 15,* 49–65.

McLoyd, V. C. (1990). The impact of economic hardship on Black families and children: Psychological distress, parenting, and socioemotional development. *Child Development, 61,* 311–346.

Miller, L. S. (1995). *An American imperative: Accelerating minority educational advancement.* New Haven, CT: Yale University Press.

Millman, J., Bishop, C. H., & Ebel, R. (1965). An analysis of test-wiseness. *Educational and Psychological Measurement, 25,* 707–726.

Mingione, E. (1991). *Fragmented societies: A sociology of economic life beyond the market paradigm.* Cambridge, MA: Basil Blackwell.

Monkeberg, F., Tisler, S., Toro, S., Gattas, V., & Vegal, L. (1972). Malnutrition and mental development. *American Journal of Clinical Nutrition, 25,* 766–772.

Needleman, H. L. (1990). The long-term effects of exposure to low doses of lead in childhood: An 11-year follow-up report. *New England Journal of Medicine, 322,* 83–88.

Newman, L., & Buka, S. L. (1990). *Every child a learner: Reducing risks of learning impairment during pregnancy and infancy.* Denver, CO: Education Commission of the States.

Okazaki, S., & Sue, S. (1995). Cultural considerations in psychological assessment of Asian-Americans. In J. N. Butcher (Ed.), *Clinical personality assessment: Practical approaches* (pp. 107–119). New York: Oxford University Press.

Ortar, G. R. (1960). Improving test validity by coaching. *Educational Research, 2,* 137–142.

Palincsar, A. S., & Winn, J. (1992). Dynamic assessment. In M. C. Alkin (Ed.), *Encyclopedia of educational research* (Vol. 1, 6th ed., pp. 346–350). New York: Macmillan.

Parker, S., Greer, S., & Zuckerman, B. (1988). Double jeopardy: The impact of poverty on early child development. *Pediatric Clinics of North America, 35,* 1227–1240.

Peng, S. S., Lee, R. M., Wang, M. C., & Walberg, H. J. (1991). *Resilient students in urban settings.* Unpublished manuscript, Temple University Center for Research in Human Development and Education, Philadelphia.

Plomin, R. (1994). *Genetics and experience.* Thousand Oaks, CA: Sage.

Pollitt, E. (1994). Poverty and child development: Relevance of research in developing countries to the United States. *Child Development, 65,* 283–295.

Portes, P. R. (1991). Assessing children's cognitive environment through parent-child interactions. *Journal of Research and Development in Education, 24*(3), 30–37.

Postlethwaite, T. N., & Ross, K. N. (1992). *Effective schools in reading: Implications for educational planners.* Hamburg, Germany: International Education Association.

Powers, D. E. (1993). Coaching for the SAT: A summary of the summaries and an update. *Educational Measurement Issues and Practice, 12*(2), 24–39.

Rauh, V. A., Achenbach, T. M., Nurcombe, B., Howell, C. T., & Teti, D. M. (1988). Minimizing adverse effects of low birthweight: Four-year results of an early intervention program. *Child Development, 59,* 544–553.

Reynolds, C. R. (1986). Transactional models of intellectual development, yes: Deficit models for process remediation, no. *School Psychology Review, 15,* 256–260.

Reynolds, C. R., Chastain, R. L., Kaufman, A. S., & McLean, J. E. (1987). Demographic characteristics and IQ among adults: Analysis of the WAIS-R standardization sample as a function of the stratification variables. *Journal of School Psychology, 25,* 323–342.

Rigsby, L. C. (1994). The americanization of resilience: Deconstructing research practice. In M. C. Wang & E. W. Gordon (Eds.), *Educational resilience in inner-city America: Challenges and prospects* (pp. 85–94). Hillsdale, NJ: Erlbaum.

Rosovski, J., Novoa, F., Aberzua, J., & Monkeberg, F. (1971). Cranial transillumination in early and severe malnutrition. *British Journal of Nutrition, 25,* 107–111.

Safa, H. T. (1970). The poor are like everyone else, Oscar. *Psychology Today,* pp. 26–32.

Salling, M., & Harvey, M. E. (1981). Poverty, personality, and sensitivity to residential stressors. *Environment & Behavior, 13,* 131–163.

Sapp, M., Durand, H., & Farrell, W. (1995). Measures of actual test anxiety in educationally and economically disadvantaged college students. *College Student Journal, 29,* 65–72.

Sarbin, T. R. (1970). The culture of poverty, social identity, and cognitive outcomes. In V. L. Allen (Ed.), *Psychological factors in poverty* (pp. 29–46). Chicago: Markham.

Sarnacki, R. E. (1979). An examination of test-wiseness in the cognitive test domain. *Review of Educational Research, 49,* 252–279.

Savell, J. M., Twohig, P. T., & Rachford, D. L. (1986). Empirical status of Feuerstein's "instrumental enrichment" (FIE) technique as a method of teaching thinking skills. *Review of Educational Research, 56,* 381–409.

Scarr-Salapatek, S. (1971). Race, social class, and IQ. *Science, 174,* 1285–1295.

Scruggs, T. E., White, K. R., & Bennion, K. (1986). Teaching test-taking skills to elementary grade students: A meta-analysis. *Elementary School Journal, 87,* 69–82.

Selden, R. (1990). Should test results be adjusted for socioeconomic differences? *The School Administrator, 47*(5), 14–18.

Seshadri, S., & Gopaldas, T. (1989). Impact of iron supplementation on cognitive functions in preschool and school-aged children: The Indian experience. *American Journal of Clinical Nutrition, 50,* 675–686.

Shuey, A. M. (1966). *The testing of Negro intelligence* (2nd ed.). New York: Social Science Press.

Skeels, H. M., & Dye, H. B. (1939). A study of the effects of differential stimulation on mentally retarded children. *American Association of Mental Deficiency, 44,* 114–136.

Spitz, H. H. (1986). *The raising of intelligence: A selected history of attempts to raise retarded intelligence.* Hillsdale, NJ: Erlbaum.

Stein, Z. A., & Susser, M. (1992). Mental retardation. In J. Last & R. B. Wallace (Eds.), *Public health and preventive medicine* (13th ed., pp. 963–972). Norwalk, CT: Appleton & Lange.

Stoch, M. B., & Smythe, P. M. (1963). Does undernutrition during infancy inhibit brain growth and subsequent intellectual development? *Archives of Disabilities in Childhood, 38,* 546–552.

Turner, B. G., Beidel, D. C., Hughes, S., & Turner, M. W. (1993). Test anxiety in African American school children. *School Psychology Quarterly, 8,* 140–152.

Tyler, L. E. (1965). *The psychology of human differences* (3rd ed.). New York: Appleton-Century-Crofts.

U.S. Bureau of the Census. (1996). *Poverty in the United States: 1995.* Washington, DC: U.S. Government Printing Office.

Valentine, C. A. (1968). *Culture and poverty: Critique and counterproposals.* Chicago: University of Chicago Press.

Velasquez, R. J. (1995). Personality assessment of Hispanic clients. In J. N. Butcher (Ed.), *Clinical personality assessment: Practical approaches* (pp. 120–139). New York: Oxford University Press.

Walter, T. (1989). Infancy: Mental and motor development. *American Journal of Clinical Nutrition, 50,* 655–664.

Wang, M. C., Haertel, G. D., & Walberg, H. J. (1994). Educational resilience in inner cities. In M. C. Wang & E. W. Gordon (Eds.), *Educational resilience in inner-city America: Challenges and prospects* (pp. 45–72). Hillsdale, NJ: Erlbaum.

Williams, F. (Ed.). (1970). *Language and poverty.* Chicago: Markham.

Williams, F., & Naremore, R. C. (1970). An annotated bibliography of journal articles. In F. Williams (Ed.), *Language and poverty* (pp. 416–456). Chicago: Markham.

Yando, R., Seitz, V., & Zigler, E. (1979). *Intellectual and personality characteristics of children: Social-class and ethnic-group differences.* Hillsdale, NJ: Erlbaum.

Young, M., & Gibson, J. B. (1965). Social mobility and fertility. In J. E. Meade & A. S. Parkes (Eds.), *Biological aspects of social problems.* Edinburgh, Scotland: Oliver & Boyd.

Zeidner, M. (1990). Does text anxiety bias scholastic aptitude test performance by gender and sociocultural group? *Journal of Personality Assessment, 55,* 145–160.

Zill, N., Moore, K. A., Smith, E. W., Stief, T., & Coiro, M. J. (1991). *The life circumstances and development of children in welfare families: A profile based on national survey data.* Washington, DC: Child Trends.

Visual Impairments

Sharon Bradley-Johnson and Ruth Ekstrom

Compared with many impairments such as mental retardation and learning disabilities, visual impairment appears infrequently, with only 0.4% of students between the ages of 6 and 21 years receiving special education services because of a visual impairment (U.S. Department of Education, 1992). The majority of visually impaired individuals are adults; only 9% are younger than 45 years (Vander Kolk, 1981).

In 1879 the federal Act to Promote the Education of the Blind was passed. Under this act, the American Printing House for the Blind (APH) conducts the Federal Quota Registration annually to determine the number of students enrolled in schools and agencies so that funds can be allocated for procuring books and educational materials APH produces (Poppe, 1996). As of January 1995, there were 54,763 students registered. About 15% were in programs for adults, 32% in primary through secondary grades, 3% in kindergarten, 11% in preschools, 8% in programs for infants, and 28% were "other." The mean age of the adult group was 40 years, consisting of those enrolled in rehabilitation programs, in programs for people with multiple handicaps, and in residential schools. Other registrants usually had handicaps in addition to visual loss, and many were in nonacademic multihandicapped programs. The majority of students (84%) were enrolled in state department of education programs, 8% were in residential schools, 5% were in rehabilitation programs, and 3% were in multihandicapped programs. The mean age of students in primary through secondary grades tended to be approximately 2 years older than the expected mean age of sighted students, ranging from 8 years 6 months in Grade 1 to 19 years 7 months in Grade 12 (Poppe, 1996).

Definitions

Numerous terms are used to describe the various types of severe visual loss. The terms *visually impaired* and *visually handicapped* refer to individuals who require more than corrective lenses to function adequately. Those who are partially sighted as well as those who are blind fall into these categories.

Individuals who are functionally blind must rely primarily on senses other than sight to learn. They use auditory (e.g., readers and tape recorders) and tactile means (e.g., braille) to acquire information.

The term *legally blind* is used in determining eligibility for government benefits. The term applies to those with central visual acuity of 20/200 or less in the better eye with correction or to those with visual acuity of greater than 20/200 but who have a defect of the visual field for which the widest diameter is 20° or less. This classification does not necessarily mean that an individual is totally blind because more than 75% of people classified as legally blind have some usable vision (American Foundation for the Blind, n.d.; Vander Kolk, 1981). For planning instructional programs, this classification is not helpful because many legally blind individuals can use visual materials. Some organizations describe individuals who must rely on nonprint materials, such as audiotapes and braille, as "print disabled."

Terms used to describe visually impaired individuals who are not functionally blind include *low vision, limited vision*, and *partially sighted*. For these individuals, vision is used for learning, but more than corrective lenses is needed to do so. In this chapter, we use the term *low vision*. These individuals may use regular or large-type material, some may require magnifiers, and some may need auditory and tactile material as well.

In the educational system, definitions for eligibility for special education services because of a visual impairment are based on federal regulations, but they vary somewhat from state to state. According to the Individuals With Disabilities Education Act (IDEA; 1990), a visual impairment is one that, "even with correction, adversely affects a child's educational performance." The definition for a particular state can be obtained from either a state department of education or a local education agency.

Etiology and Types of Visual Impairment

The etiology of severe visual losses may be a result of either congenital or adventitious factors. Congenital factors involve inherited conditions, prenatal damage, or trauma at birth. Examples include congenital cataracts, which can be associated with problems such as photophobia (i.e., abnormal sensitivity to light), strabismus (i.e., muscle imbalance that results in failure of the eyes to gaze at the same object simultaneously), and nystagmus (i.e., rapid, involuntary movement of the eyeball); retinitis pigmentosa, which involves a gradual deterioration of the receptor cells in the eyes that can result in total blindness or a restricted visual field; anophthalmos, which is the absence of the eyeball; and optic nerve hypoplasia, a condition occurring in utero involving the underdevelopment of the optic nerve.

Adventitious factors causing visual loss involve accidents or diseases. An example is optic atrophy resulting from head trauma or tumors of the brain or eye. This condition may result in a loss of the peripheral field, a decrease in acuity, and photophobia. Corneal disease involves scarring of the cornea due to injury, allergies, or infections. Diseases such as diabetes, hydrocephalus, and multiple sclerosis may also cause visual loss. For a more detailed discussion of types of visual loss, see Happe and Koenig (1987).

There is considerable heterogeneity in terms of the types of visual loss. Hazekamp and Huebner (1989) noted that there is a continuum of visual impairment ranging from mild losses to functional blindness. Furthermore, a visual loss may be stable, fluctuating, improving, or slowly or rapidly deteriorating. Thus, an individual's instructional needs will be affected by the cause of the condition and the type of loss.

Besides etiology and type of loss, age at onset also affects functioning and instructional needs. Individuals who lose their vision after the age of 5 usually retain visual memories. These memories can facilitate the acquisition of certain language concepts, especially concepts that are difficult to teach to those who have never had vision. For example, the concepts of "castle," "cow," and "color" are difficult to comprehend without visual images. Individuals who do not have a complete understanding of these concepts may still use them correctly at times because they have learned the concepts by rote. Thus, when assessing individuals whose visual loss occurred before the age of 5, it is important to probe questionable responses to determine whether the individual understands the concepts adequately. Also, an emphasis on assessment of vocabulary for young children with a visual loss is advisable so that misconceptions or inadequate concept development can be remediated as soon as possible.

Many visually impaired individuals have other impairments in addition to visual loss. Kirchner (1983) suggested that 30–50% of visually impaired children have one or more additional impairments. Silberman (1981) estimated that more than 60% of visually impaired students have additional impairments resulting in delays in gross motor, fine motor, perceptual, language, cognitive, and self-help skills.

Assessment of Visual Impairment: Eye Specialists' Reports

To understand an individual's visual loss, information from the eye specialist's report is necessary. This report may include information relevant to planning assessment as well as intervention. Hence, this report should be considered before administering psychological tests.

There are several types of eye specialists. Ophthalmologists are medical doctors who diagnose and treat eye defects and diseases. They also prescribe medication and lenses as well as perform surgery and other medical treatments. Optometrists are licensed nonmedical specialists who prescribe lenses and measure refractive errors and muscle disturbances. Opticians grind lenses according to prescriptions and adjust eyeglass frames, for example.

Ophthalmologists' or optometrists' reports usually contain information related to the etiology of vision loss, age at onset, prognosis, required medical interventions and prescriptions, and restrictions on activities or use of the eyes. Information regarding the etiology of visual loss may help in understanding what, if any, useful vision the individual may have. For example, as noted previously, the age at onset has implications for concept development. The prognosis can have implications for instruction. If the prognosis indicates a changing condition, for example, there may be a need for supportive counseling to help the individual understand and adjust to the changes in vision. If the prognosis is for a gradual deterioration, it may be beneficial to begin braille instruction while the individual still has some useful vision to aid instruction.

Because eye conditions can change rapidly, the report from eye specialists should be up to date. To be useful, the visual assessment should have been completed within the past year.

The following abbreviation information should help in interpreting results of eye specialists' reports. Visual acuity and field of vision are measured separately for each eye. The abbreviation *OD* stands for ocular dexter (Latin for "right eye"), *OS* stands for ocular sinister (Latin for "left eye"), and *OU* stands for oculi unitis or both eyes. *Visual acuity* refers to the sharpness of vision. Acuity is measured with and without correction (lenses) and for both near and distant vision. It is measured with a Snellen chart, in which 20/20 indicates normal vision. If acuity is described as 20/200, this means that the individual can see at 20 ft what a person with normal vision can see at 200 ft. If the loss is so severe that it cannot be measured with a Snellen chart (greater than 20/400), it may be measured in terms of the ability to count fingers held at varying distances. This result is abbreviated CF for "counts fingers." If the loss is such that the individual cannot count fingers, then acuity may be measured in terms of ability to see hand movements at varying distances. This is abbreviated HM. The abbreviation NLP indicates that an individual has no awareness of external light (no light perception), whereas awareness of light is abbreviated as LP (light perception). If acuity is within normal limits, it is abbreviated WNL.

Some individuals may have good central vision but poor peripheral vision. This loss of visual field can occur in one or both eyes. The eye report will illustrate the degree of loss and where the fields are restricted. This information has implications for the most useful direction of gaze. Individuals with a significant loss of visual field must be attentive to auditory input and learn to move their head and eyes to explore their environment.

Assessment of Visual Impairment: Functional Vision Assessment

Because clinic conditions used by eye specialists are not the same as those in other settings, recommendations in eye specialists' reports may or may not apply to a classroom or work situation. Thus, a functional visual assessment may be carried out to ensure that appropriate environmental accommodations are made. This assessment typically is completed in the classroom or work setting by a teacher of the visually impaired or an orientation and mobility (O&M) specialist. Such assessments are not required in all states. Results from a functional vision assessment describe how individuals use their vision. Because of the heterogeneity in the population of visually impaired individuals, two visually impaired individuals with the same visual acuity may vary greatly in ability to use their vision. Different visual problems, such as different visual fields or the presence or absence of nystagmus or photophobia, is one variable responsible for differences in the ability to use residual vision. A second factor is individual differences in motivation to use vision (Blind Children's Center, 1993). Results from a functional vision assessment can provide important information for planning both assessments and interventions. For example, the reports may indicate the type of lighting needed to optimize the use of vision, the appropriate size print, the best posture (for those with a limited visual field), the optimal distance for viewing material, and recommendations for using low-vision equipment. An environmental assessment (i.e., the assessment of the compatibility of the environment with an individual's capabilities) also may be included (Kelley, Davidson, & Sanspree, 1993). Because of the important implications of this information for the administration of psychological tests, results from functional vision assessments should be sought before beginning a psychological assessment.

Preparing for an Assessment

Organizing Background Information

A comprehensive, useful psychological assessment of an individual with a visual impairment requires considerable planning before the administration of tests. Because of the quantity of different types of information involved, it is usually more time-consuming to gather, organize, and interpret background information than it is for sighted individuals.

To assist examiners working in school systems, Bradley-Johnson (1994) provided information organizing checklists for this purpose. One checklist is for use with infants or preschoolers, and another is designed for school-age students who are visually impaired.

Besides obtaining information from school and clinic records and from interviews with others who know the individual well, input from several specialists is needed to plan a psychological assessment. Clearly, a multidisciplinary effort is critical if test results and recommendations are to be useful for visually impaired individuals. Because individuals with severe visual losses must rely to a considerable extent on auditory input, the report from a recent hearing evaluation should be obtained along with the eye specialist's report. If these reports are not current, the psychological assessment may need to be postponed until such information is available. The report from a functional vision assessment, if available, also should be reviewed.

If relevant, a report from a qualified O&M specialist also should be obtained. An O&M evaluation can be carried out even for infants. Assessment and intervention for O&M is critical for those with little or no vision to enable them to move about the environment independently. Examples of skills taught include the use of public transportation; safe travel within the home, school, and work environments; and appropriate walking stride and gait. Information describing other handicaps or health issues also will require consideration in planning a psychological assessment.

Classroom and Workplace Observations

Observing the individual functioning in a natural environment before administering tests can be highly informative. For examiners with little or no experience working with visually impaired individuals, this observation should help prepare them for what to expect during testing. Valuable information can be obtained from this observation for planning realistic and relevant intervention as well. Such observation is particularly important for school-age students. The more systematic the observational method, however, the more likely the data are to be objective. Procedures for systematic direct observation are described by Alessi and Kaye (1983) and Gelfand and Hartman (1984).

One aspect of functioning that is especially useful to note when observing in the natural environment is the individual's organizational skills. Individuals who have little usable vision and poor organizational skills have a difficult time functioning efficiently and independently. Much time is wasted searching for lost items and requesting help from others when materials are not well organized and not returned to their original location when no longer needed. Unnecessary and frustrating searches can be avoided if visually impaired individuals are taught organizational skills early in life. Teaching organizational habits to young children can begin by having a specific place where toys are stored and requiring children to return toys to their storage spot when children have finished playing with them. If organization is a problem, this is an important area to target for intervention.

Test Selection: Areas to Consider

Because most tests normed on individuals who are visually impaired are dated, lack technical adequacy, and have little instructional relevance, use of additional information sources is important, including records review, interviews, systematic observation, rating scales, and individually or group-administered tests. Different types of tests should be considered, including norm- and criterion-referenced measures and curriculum-based measurement, to obtain enough data to support conclusions. Furthermore, a comprehensive assessment is needed to provide a well-integrated picture of an individual's functioning in various areas of development. It is not wise to base conclusions on assessment of only one or two areas, especially when technically adequate measures are limited. Areas to consider for assessment include daily living skills, play skills for young children, social skills, intellectual development, behavior and emotions, vocational skills, language skills, and other areas of achievement.

Adaptive behavior measures that consist of numerous items requiring vision will penalize individuals who are visually impaired and should be avoided when possible. An example of a measure that requires little if any adjustment for visually impaired school-age students is the Adaptive Behavior Inventory (L. Brown & Leigh, 1986). If a visually impaired individual uses adaptive devices to complete daily living activities, such as a braille watch or a slicing guide, the individual should be given credit on an adaptive behavior scale for performing these skills independently.

Because of their contribution to all areas of development, play skills are important to assess for visually impaired infants and preschoolers. For descriptions of tests for this purpose and special considerations for intervention in this area, see Bradley-Johnson (1994).

Social skills are particularly important to assess for visually impaired preschoolers through adults: "Appropriate social interaction is the logical prerequisite to social acceptance" (Raver-Lampman, 1990, p. 70).

Many visually impaired individuals have difficulty in this area because they do not have the opportunity to learn some of the social skills that their sighted peers learn through observation of others' behavior. Examples of difficulties include lack of certain gestures and not orienting to a speaker. Furthermore, the emotions of individuals with visual impairments may be misunderstood because these individuals do not use the type of nonverbal communication used by their sighted peers.

Although observation in the natural environment and interviews with others may provide useful information on social skills, more comprehensive assessment is often warranted. Students with disabilities were included in the norm sample for the Social Skills Rating Scale (Gresham & Elliott, 1990), and the items on this rating scale do not penalize students with a visual loss. The age range for the scale is from preschool through high school.

Assessment of receptive and expressive language also should be considered. Visually impaired preschoolers may be delayed in concept development, and individuals without visual memories may not have a complete understanding of some concepts. Some visually impaired students use words in a meaningful way in one context but not in another context, suggesting an incomplete understanding of the concepts (Higgins, 1973). Thus, results from verbal tests should be interpreted cautiously, especially for young children. Questionable verbal responses from visually impaired individuals of any age should be probed to ensure valid results.

When vision is severely impaired, reliance on verbal directions is more often necessary. Thus, a good understanding of concepts describing position and relationships such as *down, over,* and *right* is important. Such concepts aid O&M training and enable more independent functioning. Some of these concepts are especially difficult to learn for individuals with little or no useful vision and take longer to acquire. An emphasis on these concepts in assessment, especially with young children, seems appropriate.

Listening skills are especially useful when vision is limited. Results from observation of the individual functioning in the natural environment as well as during the assessment should provide useful information on the development of listening skills. For individuals with difficulties in this area, however, an assessment of receptive vocabulary and syntax, attending behavior, hearing, motivation to perform requested tasks, and memory may be needed to determine which areas require intervention.

Test Selection: Issues To Consider

When selecting norm-referenced measures, timed tests should be avoided whenever possible. If an individual reads braille, additional time will be required because braille reading takes longer than regular-size print. Duckworth and Caton (1986) suggested that braille requires about $2\frac{1}{2}$ times longer to read than regular print, but this time varies as a function of the reader's experience with braille and on the use of additional materials such as audiotapes to augment braille text. Reading large print takes more time also. In addition, the use of limited vision is tiring. If timed tests are used, a visually impaired individual may be penalized because of the additional time necessitated by the visual loss. Also, if frequent breaks are not used during testing, the individual may become more fatigued than sighted individuals, resulting in an underestimate of performance.

To circumvent a visual impairment, if only a portion of a test is used, such as the Verbal section of a Wechsler scale, this restricts the range of skills assessed. Results would be based on a limited sample of skills and should be interpreted accordingly. Every effort should be made to use multiple measures for each area tested, especially when only portions of tests are given.

Tests in the appropriate medium for the individual being tested will be needed. If an individual's primary reading medium is braille, then braille materials will be required for testing. Large print or magnifiers will be needed by individuals who use primarily large print. Other individuals may need audiotapes or speech synthesizers. Many individually administered and group administered tests have been transcribed into braille and are available through the APH (P.O. Box 6085, Louisville, KY 40206). Large-print and audio materials also are available through the APH.

There are few tests normed on a visually impaired sample, and few have been published within the past 15 years. Although the response requirements in these tests should be appropriate, the visually impaired norm sample may or may not be an appropriate comparison group. Because of the many factors affecting visual loss and its manifestation, such as age at onset, type of loss, and amount of usable vision, this population is highly heterogeneous. A relatively large norm sample would be required to ensure adequate representation of the many types of visual loss. Simeonsson (1986) noted that when tests have some norms specific to visually impaired individuals, this may involve small, biased samples (e.g., students in residential institutions), or the information may be confounded by individuals with varying amounts of useful vision.

Using tests normed on a sighted sample also is problematic. If the individual has the enabling behaviors required to respond to the test items, and if comparison to sighted peers is desirable, such a test might be useful. Using such a measure assumes, however, that the individual has had experiences similar to those of the sighted sample. This cannot be the case because of the visual loss. If, for example, the visually impaired woman had attended a residential school and was overprotected by her parents because of the handicap, then her background would be much different from that of the sighted norm group.

To help address problems with appropriate norm groups, conclusions about visually impaired individuals should be based on multiple sources of information, assessment of various areas of development, and periodic reevaluation. An extensive list of measures, and discussion of their technical characteristics, for use with infants through adolescents was provided in Bradley-Johnson (1994). Tobin (1994) provided similar information, along with information on the assessment of blind and visually impaired adults, based on practices in Great Britain.

The importance of using multiple sources of information when selecting college students was also addressed in the Rehabilitation Act of 1973. It stated that a college would not be out of compliance in requiring the submission of test scores "even though there is a strong possibility that these tests do not reflect a handicapped applicant's ability. However, ... the institution must guarantee that admissions decisions take into account other factors such as high school grades, recommendations, etc." (p. 22).

Appropriate norm groups are not an issue with criterion-referenced tests. Furthermore, flexible administration procedures and various materials can be used. For braille readers, the APH has tactile supplements for both the Revised Brigance Diagnostic Inventory of Early Development (Brigance, 1991), covering skills typically learned between birth and 7 years of age, and the Brigance Diagnostic Comprehensive Inventory of Basic Skills (Brigance, 1983), covering skills typically taught from kindergarten to 10th grade. These criterion-referenced tests are extensive and cover areas such as daily living, language, play, reading, mathematics, written language, and general knowledge. Valuable information for instructional planning can be obtained with these measures.

For monitoring progress in braille reading, a modification of the curriculum-based measurement procedure described by Shinn (1989) was examined by Morgan and Bradley-Johnson (1995). Because braille takes longer to read than regular print, a 2-min sample (rather than 1 min) was used, and 6 s (rather than 3 s) were allowed for error correction. Morgan and Bradley-Johnson found that the reliability and validity of this modified procedure for braille readers was highly similar to that of the original procedure used with sighted individuals. The curriculum-based measurement procedure can be used to monitor individual progress in braille reading frequently and efficiently and to compare an individual's performance with peers at any grade level.

Appropriate Accommodations: Special Equipment and Materials

Tests are standardized to ensure that identical conditions are provided for everyone taking a particular test. The purpose of standardization is to ensure fair testing of all participants and aid in the interpretation of test scores. However, the use of many standardized testing conditions for individuals with visual impairments is often impossible. To ensure that tests are fair for these individuals, various comparable testing conditions, referred to as accommodations, are used. For visually impaired individuals, these accommodations could include (a) provision of special lighting; (b) changes in test scheduling such as allowing extra time or administering the test over several days; (c) revision of test directions such as reading print directions aloud; (d) revision of test format such as use of braille, large print, or an audiotape; and (e) revision of response methods such as dictating answers or using low-vision aids such as magnification devices, tactile graphs, an abacus, or a computer. Appropriate accommodations may be described in a functional vision report.

Individuals with low vision may read regular or large-type materials. Some require low-vision equipment. If this is the case, arrangements to use this equipment during testing will be necessary. Examiners should become familiar with the use of this equipment before an assessment.

There is a wide variety of low-vision equipment, including magnifiers mounted on a headband, on glasses, or on a stand, or some may be hand held. Book stands are often used to decrease fatigue caused by holding reading materials close to the eyes.

Some individuals with little or no functional vision use computer systems to scan printed materials to produce braille or speech output. They also may use computers to produce written output. A device similar to a typewriter, a braille writer, can also be used to produce braille.

The slowest method for writing braille is to use a hand-held slate and stylus. The slate holds the paper and the stylus is used to press braille dots into the paper.

Equipment that enables individuals to respond easily and efficiently in the school or work environment should be used during testing as well. Talking calculators, however, may be an exception. Even though these calculators are used in the school or work environment, they would invalidate test results on norm-referenced arithmetic or mathematics tests. Examples of other equipment that would be appropriate for use during testing include a braille watch or clock, a braille ruler, an abacus for calculations, and a signature guide (i.e., a metal plate with a space within which individuals write their name). Some individuals will need to use bold-line or raised-line paper to make a written response. According to the Federal Quota Registration for the APH, 26% of visually impaired students were visual readers, 10% braille readers, 8% auditory readers, 24% prereaders, and 32% nonreaders (i.e., they lacked a functional reading mode; Poppe, 1996).

During Assessment

Fairness in testing includes ensuring that the individuals are comfortable in the testing situation and familiar with the setting. Whenever individuals with disabilities are assessed, accessibility of the testing site should be considered.

Stress can negatively affect the ability of some visually impaired individuals to use their residual vision. A tense examiner may miss important observations and nonverbal messages from the examinees. Hence, establishing adequate rapport is important.

To assist examiners in making visually impaired individuals and themselves comfortable, Eyde, Nester, Heaton, and Nelson (1994) offered the following suggestions:

a. Speak directly to the person. Identify yourself and let the person know you are speaking to him or her. When you are leaving the person who is blind, say so.
b. Do not avoid using works like "look" or "see." There are not any reasonable substitutes. Briefly describe the physical layout of the examining room, especially the furniture arrangement.
c. Do not pet or otherwise distract a guide dog without permission. The dog is responsible for the safety of the blind person and is not a pet.

d. When assisting the person to a chair, simply guide his or her hand to the back or arm of the chair for location.

e. Do not push or pull the person. Let the person take your arm and walk about half a step ahead of him or her. Identify stairs, curbs, or other obstacles as you approach them. (p. 15)

The following suggestions also may be useful: (a) Before handing materials to the person, indicate that you will be doing so and place the material so that it touches his or her hand; (b) when you are recording responses or arranging materials, explain what you are doing so that the person does not wonder what is happening if you are not administering test items; and (c) be sensitive to fatigue, using several testing sessions and frequent breaks.

After Assessment: Interpretation Issues

To provide a comprehensive picture of an individual's abilities and difficulties, results from testing should be integrated with information obtained from interviews, records review, and direct observation. Furthermore, the validity of information from norm-referenced tests should be evaluated in light of results obtained from criterion-referenced and curriculum-based assessment when possible.

Because of the limitations of norm-referenced tests for visually impaired individuals, conclusions should be based on an integration of information from the assessment of various areas important for development including social skills, adaptive behavior, play skills for young children, emotions and behavior, intellectual development, vocational skills for older individuals, language development, and skills in other academic areas. Finally, repeated assessment of progress over time is a better basis for conclusions than a single assessment.

Assessment for Special Education Eligibility

The mandates of the IDEA (1990) apply to assessment for eligibility for special education services. Among other requirements, the IDEA requires a multidisciplinary team and use of tests and other evaluation materials besides those designed to provide only a general IQ score. With regard to test selection, the IDEA (1990) requires that tests are selected and administered so as best to ensure that when a test is administered to a child with impaired sensory, manual, or speaking skills, the test results accurately reflect the child's aptitude or achievement level or whatever other factors the test purports to measure, rather than reflecting the child's impaired sensory, manual, or speaking skills (except where those skills are the factors which the test purports to measure). (p.42496)

Monitoring Student Progress

To enhance accountability in education, the National Assessment of Educational Progress (NAEP) and many state programs attempt to document what typical students at various grade levels are able to do. The IDEA (1990) requires that most students with disabilities be included in district, state, and national assessments. Despite this requirement, many students with disabilities have been excluded from these testing programs. In 1994, for example, the NAEP included only 50% of 4th-grade students, 38% of 8th-grade students, and 36% of 12th-grade students identified as having an individualized education plan (IEP) for special education services.

The NAEP has recently implemented new procedures to include more students with disabilities. Under the old procedure, such students were excluded if they were mainstreamed less than 50% of the time in academic subjects or if the IEP team determined that the student was incapable of participating meaningfully in the assessment. Under new procedures, students with an IEP will be included unless the IEP team determines that the student cannot participate or if the student's cognitive functioning is so severely impaired that he or she cannot participate even with accommodations (Olson & Goldstein, 1996).

The National Center for Educational Outcomes has been pressing for the inclusion of students with disabilities in national and state accountability assessments. They stated that

the ability to extract useful national and state policy-relevant information on the outcomes of students with disabilities from national and state data collection programs is seriously hampered by the extensive exclusion of portions of this population. . . . The categorical exclusion of students with disabilities perpetuates the myth of inherent differences. (McGrew, Thurlow, Shriner, & Spiegel, 1992, pp. iii–iv)

Siskind (1993b) provided an extensive summary of the types of modifications made in 30 statewide criterion-referenced testing programs to accommodate students with disabilities. All 30 states provided large-print versions of the test and permitted use of visual magnification devices; 28 states provided a braille transcription and permitted braille writers. Twenty-three states permitted devices to transform print into tactile form. Electronic readers, such as voice synthesizers, were permitted in 19 states, and the same number of states provided answer documents with enlarged type. Only 9 states provided audiocassette versions of the test. In a related article, Siskind (1993a) noted that statewide criterion-referenced tests administered to students who are visually impaired are not always instructionally valid. She urged that attempts be made to introduce additional accommodations so that no student is tested in an unfamiliar mode, especially when test results are part of promotion or graduation requirements.

Siskind (1993c) surveyed 60 South Carolina classroom teachers' knowledge of approved modifications for students with disabilities on state-mandated tests. She concluded that the teachers were not well informed on this issue and stated that

> if teachers are unaware of the accommodations they can make when testing children, it is unlikely that allowable accommodations are employed. Hence, some students are not being tested in the most appropriate and valid manner, and perhaps more problematic, there is inequality in the treatment of students with disabilities. (p. 155)

Performance assessment is becoming a part of many state assessment programs. In 1994, 38 states were considering or using some form of performance assessment (Thurlow, 1995). Some issues regarding the inclusion of students with disabilities in performance assessments have been described by McLaughlin and Warren (1995):

1. Outcomes-based systems present special educators with a difficult conceptual switch from believing that each student with a disability should have individualized outcomes to accepting the notion of a common set of outcomes across students.
2. There is still ambiguity among assessment experts regarding how much accommodation should be provided within an assessment program.
3. When one set of scoring standards is defined for all students, with no modifications made for students with disabilities, students with disabilities may be denied diplomas or otherwise penalized.
4. When results are used for high stakes accountability, there may be greater pressure to exempt students with disabilities. Once

the decision to exempt students with disabilities has been made, there may also be pressure to identify more students as having disabilities in order to exempt more students from the assessment. (p. 3)

Assessment for Admission to College, Graduate, or Professional School

Students with visual impairments face the same college and graduate school admissions tests as sighted students. Organizations administering these tests provide a variety of accommodations including braille transcriptions, large-print versions, and audiotapes. Before testing, students who wish to have an accommodation must identify themselves to the testing organization, request an accommodation, and provide documentation of their disability. Arrangements can then be made for appropriate accommodations. In a few circumstances, testing organizations are unable to provide a requested and preferred accommodation. Voice synthesizers, for example, currently are not commonly available. In such cases, an alternative accommodation must be used for the assessment; this may negatively affect the validity of the results.

Bennett, Rock, Kaplan, and Jirele (1988) examined results on the Scholastic Aptitude Test (SAT; now known as the Scholastic Assessment Test) for three groups of visually impaired students: 203 using a braille transcription, 984 using a large-type version, and 398 using a regular-type version (in some cases with adaptive devices such as magnifiers). All groups were given extra time. The mean verbal scores for the three groups were essentially comparable to those of sighted students. Similar results were found for students using the large-print and regular-type versions for the mathematics test, but students using a braille transcription scored lower. Certain mathematical item types were more difficult for students using the braille transcription. Differential item function techniques showed that these students had lower scores than would have been expected on the basis of their total mathematics test score on items containing graphics and on items intended to assess "relatively novel content." Bennett et al recommended that caution be used in transcribing tests into braille and emphasized the importance of pilot testing braille items.

Braun, Ragosta, and Kaplan (1988) examined the predictive validity of the SAT for 6,255 nondisabled students and 35 visually impaired individuals who took a regular edition of the test and 171 individuals who took "special" versions such as braille transcriptions or large-print versions. The SAT results, combined with high school grade point averages, were used to predict standardized freshman-year averages. Correlations for visually impaired students who took the regular, and those who took the special versions, were both .37. The correlation for nondisabled students was .49. Low but positive residuals indicated that the visually impaired students performed slightly better than their predicted scores.

The predictive validity of the Graduate Record Examination (GRE) was examined for 105 visually impaired individuals using special administration (Braun et al., 1988). The difference between actual first-year average in graduate education and the first-year average predicted from a combination of GRE results and undergraduate grade point average was greater for visually impaired students for whom higher grades were predicted and less for those for whom lower grades were predicted. Correlations between actual and predicted first-year averages were .29 for visually impaired students and .63 for nondisabled students.

The construct validity of the GRE for visually impaired students was examined by Bennett et al. (1988). They concluded that the three-factor model (verbal, quantitative, and analytical) provided a moderately good fit for visually impaired students using regular type and a less adequate fit for visually impaired students taking the large-type, extended-time administrations. The analytical factor behaved differently for visually impaired students taking the large-type version than for most other GRE examinees with the item types that compose it. Logical reasoning and analytical reasoning appeared to fit better as separate factors. In addition, the analytical scores of these students showed different relationships with other factors. There were considerably lower intercorrelations between the verbal and quantitative factors for visually impaired students who took the large-type version of the test. Bennett et al. emphasized the importance of using these two scores separately rather than as part of a composite.

Willingham (1988) examined the college admissions process for students with visual disabilities. Compared with other applicants to the same colleges, visually impaired students were found to be slightly below average with respect to their academic qualifications. The selection process for visually impaired students and other students with disabilities was similar to that for other applicants. Overall admissions rates were slightly but not significantly lower than would be predicted from the

SAT and high school grade point average. In smaller institutions, how-ever, this difference was significant, suggesting "that students with dis-abilities [who] require special equipment or resources may be less likely to be admitted in smaller institutions that are perhaps less able to pro-vide those resources" (Willingham, 1988, p. 79).

In advising students with visual disabilities who will be taking stan-dardized tests for college or graduate school admission, it is important that they (a) learn about the test (e.g., what the test is designed to measure, what the test scores mean, and what kinds of testing accom-modations are available); (b) register early for special administrations, making known their need for accommodations; (c) obtain information about the required documentation to support any accommodation they request; and (d) obtain practice materials from the testing company and use them to familiarize themselves with typical test items.

An important issue in admissions testing is "flagging" of test scores to indicate that a test was given under nonstandard conditions. The policy is consistent with the *Standards for Educational and Psychological Testing* (1985), as suggested by the American Educational Research As-sociation, American Psychological Association, and National Council on Measurement in Education. Standard 15.4 reads as follows: "In school situations involving admissions . . . any modification of standard test ad-ministration procedures or scoring should be described in the testing reports with appropriate cautions regarding the possible effects of such modifications on validity" (pp. 83–84). In 1979 the Office of Civil Rights established an interim policy allowing the flagging of test scores in college admissions. Although this interim policy remained after the passage of the Americans With Disabilities Act (ADA) in 1990, there are increasing concerns about this practice because it may violate portions of the ADA. According to D. C. Brown (1996), "most agree that ad-missions counselors and committees assume the individual has a dis-ability when they see a flagged score" (p. 16). A concern is that testing organizations often flag scores without providing information to assist in interpretation. Those who use test results need to know whether the accommodation affects the validity of the results. It is important to con-sider, however, that the examinee with a visual impairment or other disability probably will use the same accommodation for test taking as they will in their college or graduate school work. Thus, the test score should reflect how the individual will perform the kinds of tasks rep-resented by the test items.

The decision regarding which accommodations to flag varies considerably not only between testing organizations but also within organizations and their various testing programs. Students with visual impairments may want to inquire about a testing organization's flagging policies when they register for admissions tests to determine which accommodations are and are not flagged. This information may influence their choice of testing accommodations.

Although many with disabilities feel that flagging is a violation of privacy, there are circumstances in which flagging can be useful. This would be the case, for example, if an individual with a visual impairment took a test using a nonpreferred and less familiar accommodation. Under such circumstances, the flagging, with an appropriate explanation, might alert the recipient of the test results to the fact that the individual was placed at a disadvantage because the preferred and usual accommodation was not available and the result might therefore have been higher under the preferred conditions.

Employment Testing

The Guide for Administrating Written Employment Examinations to Persons With Disabilities (Eyde et al., 1994) is the key resource for assessment in this area. This guide contains a summary of legal requirements, physical accessibility issues, and advance preparation and detailed suggestions for testing job applicants who are visually impaired. Suggestions are also presented for interacting with people with disabilities.

The ADA requires employers to provide accommodations when testing individuals with disabilities and to administer tests in accessible locations. The ADA forbids the use of employment tests or other hiring criteria that screen out individuals with disabilities unless the test or hiring criteria are shown to be job-related for the position under consideration. It is also required that tests be selected and administered to applicants with a disability in such a manner that the results reflect the skills or aptitude of the applicant rather than the impaired sensory skills, except when such skills are the factors the test purports to measure.

The employment examination of visually impaired individuals begins with determining whether the applicant qualifies as an individual with a disability as defined in the Rehabilitation Act of 1973 or the ADA. For applicants deemed disabled, the next step is to determine whether they can perform the essential job functions, either with or without reasonable accommodations as defined by law. This requirement may call into question the use of tests of general ability for employment screening purposes. Employers may be asked to demonstrate that general-ability instruments are relevant for specific job functions. Reasonable accommodations include adjusting or modifying examinations. Eyde et al. (1994) stated that "testing accommodations should level the playing field for persons with a disability. Accommodations facilitate a person's capacities, usually through providing a mechanical or other kind of substitute for the disability" (p. 2).

Key considerations when testing individuals with visual impairments with written employment examinations are as follows:

- Provide individual testing to meet the necessary accessibility, procedural, and time requirements.
- Provide accessible materials such as braille transcriptions, large print, or audiotapes. In some cases the examiner may act as a reader. Eyde et al. (1994) provided suggestions about reading a test to a visually impaired examinee.
- Provide information in advance about permitted aids, such as a slate and stylus, braille writer, or tape recorder for taking notes, computational aids such as an abacus, and low-vision aids.
- Explain the method to be used to mark answers. Eyde et al. (1994) suggested that when visually impaired individuals use a braille writer to record answers or mark them directly in a large-print test booklet, the answers should then be transferred to a regular answer sheet.
- Provide appropriate time limits. As previously noted, braille, for example, takes longer to read than regular print. Eyde et al. (1994) suggested giving nonspeeded (power) tests without any time limit. They noted that individuals with diabetes (a major cause of blindness in adults) may experience numbness in the fingers after an hour or so of reading braille and will need either a break or a change to another test format. They also noted that speeded tests are usually omitted for applicants with visual impairments.

Performance tests for employment present additional problems. The best solution may be to determine the type of accommodation the job applicant would require to perform such tasks and administer the test using that accommodation. The law does not require employers to provide accommodations if this would cause the employer unusual hardship.

The assessment of older adults presents special problems because many of them have not learned to use assistive devices, as many younger people have. Because many older people have experienced hearing losses that accompany aging, their use of audiotapes also may be limited. Older adults who are hard of hearing or deaf and who lose their vision also may no longer be able to use their lipreading or sign language skills. Furthermore, mental health problems in older people that may accompany loss of vision, hearing, or both may also require assessment.

Conclusion

A multidisciplinary effort is necessary to carry out a valid assessment of visually impaired individuals. Reports from other professions (e.g., eye specialists, O&M specialists) should be reviewed before psychological testing for implications regarding testing procedures. Interviews and observations in the natural environment are valuable, especially for examiners who are unfamiliar with visual impairment.

Before assessment, the examiner must arrange for, and become familiar with, any special equipment and materials needed for testing. To ensure valid results, special procedures before and during assessment have been described. Issues regarding assessment for special education, monitoring student progress, college, graduate, or professional school admissions, and work assessment also are noted.

Assessment is changing considerably, including introduction of computer-based testing and the use of alternatives to standardized tests, especially performance tests. Accommodations with the computer can sometimes be better for visually impaired individuals than with paper-and-pencil tests, or they may make appropriate accommodations more difficult.

Performance tests seem to be less problematic. They often provide a more representative work sample than a paper-and-pencil test. However, the tasks used may have to be adapted so that they can be performed by individuals with visual disabilities. Such adaptations raise questions of validity, similar to those posed for paper-and-pencil tests. Research is needed to determine whether performance tests and work samples have as good or better construct or predictive validity.

Publishers of standardized tests, and organizations offering major testing programs, should provide normative and interpretative information about examinees with visual impairments. Few currently provide this type of assistance. Part of the problem is small samples, in that the population of individuals with visual impairments is not homogeneous. There is wide variation in impairments and a wide range of accommodations used by visually impaired examinees. Providing normative information will require the accumulation of data over a period of several years, or across similar tests provided by different publishers.

A related problem is the need for more consistent criteria from test publishers when flagging test scores. Professional organizations such as the American Psychological Association may have to take the lead in bringing measurement professionals together to consider whether a particular accommodation may affect the validity of a test and, if so, the kind of information about the score that should be provided to users of test results. Perhaps flagging should be eliminated in most assessments of individuals with visual impairments if the same type of accommodation is used to answer the test questions that will be used in college, graduate, or professional school examinations.

As Frisby, Reynolds, and Wang (1996) noted, "the actual practice of giving a person a test is in and of itself an equity issue." If equity in assessment is to be provided to individuals with visual impairments, much work is needed.

References

Alessi, G., & Kaye, J. (1983). *Behavior assessment for school psychologists.* Silver Spring, MD: National Association of School Psychologists.

American Foundation for the Blind. (n.d.). *Facts about blindness.* New York: Author.

Bennett, R. E., Rock, D. A., Kaplan, B. A., & Jirele, T. (1988). Psychometric characteristics. In W. W. Willingham, M. Ragosta, R. Bennett, H. Braun, D. A. Rock, & D. E. Powers (Eds.), *Testing handicapped people* (pp. 83–97). Needham Heights, MA: Allyn & Bacon.

Blind Children's Center. (1993). *First steps.* Los Angeles: Author.

Bradley-Johnson, S. (1994). *Psychoeducational assessment of students who are visually impaired or blind: Infancy through high school* (2nd ed.). Austin, TX: Pro-Ed.

Braun, H., Ragosta, M., & Kaplan, B. (1988). Predictive validity. In W. W. Willingham, M. Ragosta, R. Bennett, H. Braun, D. A. Rock, & D. E. Powers (Eds.), *Testing handicapped people* (pp. 109–132). Needham Heights, MA: Allyn & Bacon.

Brigance A. (1983). *Brigance Diagnostic Comprehensive Inventory of Basic Skills.* North Billerica, MA: Curriculum Associates.

Brigance, A. (1991). *Revised Brigance Diagnostic Inventory of Early Development.* North Billerica, MA: Curriculum Associates.

Brown, D. C. (1996, July). Flagging test scores. *The Score Newsletter.* pp. 16–17.

Brown, L., & Leigh, J. (1986). *Adaptive Behavior Inventory.* Austin, TX: Pro-Ed.

Duckworth, B., & Caton, H. (1986). *Braille Reading Rate Scale*. Louisville, KY: American Printing House for the Blind.

Eyde, L. D., Nester, M. A., Heaton, S. M., & Nelson, A. V. (1994). *Guide for administering written employment examinations to persons with disabilities* (PRDC-94-11). Washington, DC: U.S. Office of Personnel Management, Personnel Research and Development Center.

Frisby, C. L., Reynolds, M. C., & Wang, M. C. (1996, August). *Equity issues in educational testing*. Paper presented at the 104th Annual Convention of the American Psychological Association, Toronto, Ontario, Canada.

Gelfand, D., & Hartman, D. P. (1984). *Child behavior analysis and therapy* (2nd ed.). Elmsford, NY: Pergamon Press.

Gresham, F. M., & Elliott, S. N. (1990). *Social Skills Rating Scale*. Circle Pines, MN: American Guidance Service.

Happe, D., & Koenig, A. (1987). Children and vision. In A. Thomas & J. Grimes (Eds.), *Children's needs* (pp. 658–667). Washington, DC: National Association of School Psychologists.

Hazekamp, J., & Huebner, K. M. (1989). *Program planning and evaluation for blind and visually impaired students: National guidelines for educational excellence*. New York: American Foundation for the Blind.

Higgins, L. C. (1973). *Classification in the congenitally blind*. New York: American Foundation for the Blind.

Individuals With Disabilities Education Act. (1990). Public Law 101-476, §1401.

Kelley, P., Davidson, R., & Sanspree, M. J. (1993). Vision and orientation and mobility consultation for children with severe multiple disabilities. *Journal of Visual Impairment and Blindness, 87*, 397–401.

Kirchner, C. (1983). Special education for visually handicapped children: A critique of data on numbers served and costs (Statistical Brief #23). *Journal of Visual Impairment and Blindness, 77*, 217–223.

McGrew, K. S., Thurlow, M. L., Shriner, J. G., & Spiegel, A. N. (1992). *Inclusion of students with disabilities in national and state data collection programs* (Tech. Rep. No. 2). Minneapolis: MN: University of Minnesota, National Center on Educational Outcomes.

McLaughlin, M. J., & Warren, S. H. (1995). *Using performance assessment in outcomes-based accountability systems*. Reston, VA: Council for Exceptional Children.

Morgan, S., & Bradley-Johnson, S. (1995). Technical adequacy of curriculum-based measurement for braille readers. *School Psychology Review, 24*, 21–103.

Olson, J. G., & Goldstein, A. A. (1996). Increasing the inclusion of students with disabilities and limited English proficiency students in NAEP (NCES 96-894, monograph). *Focus on NAEP, 2*(1).

Poppe, K. J. (1996). *Distribution of quota registrants in 1995: Program type, grade placement, visual acuity, reading medium, and age*. Louisville, KY: American Printing House for the Blind.

Raver-Lampman, S. A. (1990). Effect of gaze direction on evaluation of visually impaired children by informed respondents. *Journal of Visual Impairment and Blindness, 84*, 64–70.

Shinn, M. R. (1989). *Curriculum-based measurement: Assessing special children*. New York: Guilford Press.

Silberman, R. K. (1981). Assessment and evaluation of visually handicapped students. *Journal of Visual Impairment and Blindness, 75*, 109–114.

Simeonsson, R. J. (1986). *Psychological and developmental assessment of special children*. Boston: Allyn & Bacon.

Siskind, T. G. (1993a). The instructional validity of statewide criterion-referenced tests for students who are visually impaired. *Journal of Visual Impairment & Blindness, 87,* 115–117.

Siskind, T. G. (1993b). Modifications in statewide criterion-referenced testing programs to accommodate students with disabilities. *Diagnostique, 18,* 232–249.

Siskind, T. G. (1993c). Teachers' knowledge about test modification for students with disabilities. *Diagnostique, 18,* 145–157.

Standards for educational and psychological testing. (1985). Washington, DC: American Psychological Association.

Thurlow, M. L. (1995). *National and state perspectives on performance assessment and students with disabilities.* Reston, VA: Council for Exceptional Children.

Tobin, M. J. (1994). *Assessing visually handicapped people: An introduction to test procedures.* London: Fulton.

U.S. Department of Education. (1992). *Fourteenth Annual Report to Congress on the implementation of the Individuals With Disabilities Education Act.* Washington, DC: Author.

Vander Kolk, C. J. (1981). *Assessment and planning with the visually impaired.* Baltimore: University Park Press.

Willingham, W. W. (1988). Admission decisions. In W. W. Willingham, M. Ragosta, R. Bennett, H. Braun, D. A. Rock, & D. E. Powers (Eds.), *Testing handicapped people* (pp. 71–81). Needham Heights, MA: Allyn & Bacon.

Deaf and Hard of Hearing People

Barbara A. Brauer, Jeffery P. Braden,
Robert Q Pollard, and Steven T. Hardy-Braz

The purpose of this chapter is to sensitize psychologists to the importance of familiarizing themselves with key assessment issues pertaining to individuals who are deaf or hard of hearing. A thorough historical review of the development of psychological services, including testing and personality assessment, provided to deaf people in the United States can be found in Levine (1977) and Pollard (1993).

Deaf individuals make up a linguistic minority in the United States, approximately 1 half million to 1 million, who use a particular minority language: American Sign Language (ASL; Commission on Education of the Deaf, 1988, p. 9; Lane, 1984). Until the 1950s, however, to our knowledge, no psychologist had studied the sign language used by deaf people, a language considered to be the first language for a large percentage of this population (Johnson, Liddell, & Erting, 1989). To this day, few psychologists have mastered ASL. Given the typical deaf test taker's limited mastery of the English language and the typical test giver's ignorance of ASL, issues involving test selection, test administration, and test interpretation become complicated. There is still a general undercurrent of querulousness on the part of many employers, team colleagues from other disciplines, and consumers with the quality of psychological services given to deaf individuals and with the manner in which they are administered (Levine, 1977, p. 6).

Fortunately, the more recent legislative events such as the passage of the Americans With Disabilities Act (ADA) and Section 504 of the Rehabilitation Act of 1973, together with a number of litigations and ADA rulings across the country, have encouraged the rapid evolution of psychology's view and treatment of deaf people. The American Psychological Association's Division 22 (Rehabilitation Psychology) recognized the first special-interest section in 1990 that focuses on a specific population, people who are deaf or hard of hearing. Since then, the numbers of new deafness professionals have grown and their efforts in practice, science, and education are arguably transforming the field of psychology and deaf people into a discipline in its own right (Pollard, 1996). There is agreement among increasing numbers of deafness professionals that competence in psychology and deafness implies sign language fluency, knowledge about deafness from many perspectives, and a solid background in mental health as well.

The Deaf Population

It is critical to understand some fundamental issues about this linguistic minority. There are various subgroups of the American deaf population who are well noted for their heterogeneous character. This heterogeneity exists on at least four levels: medical and audiological, communication abilities and preferences, educational setting and achievement, and sociocultural characteristics and behaviors.

Medically and audiologically, consideration must be given to the etiology (cause), the onset (timing), the severity, and the type of deafness. The two major causes of deafness are genetic or chromosomal conditions and disease or trauma. Depending on certain deafness etiologies (e.g., meningitis, rubella, anoxia, prematurity), a neuropathological sequelae requires medical, educational, and psychological attention. Despite years of repeated evaluation in the school system, it is not unusual for neuropathology to have escaped detection by school psychologists and other professionals. Knowledge of learning disabilities, and particularly the expertise to assess them, remains limited in most deaf education settings. Adding to assessment complications, the etiology of deafness is undiagnosed in almost half of all deaf children (Brown, 1986). Deafness present at birth, whether caused by genetic conditions or prenatal trauma, is termed *congenital*. Deafness that occurs after birth, whether caused by progressive genetic conditions, diseases, or trauma, is termed *adventitious*. Deafness is measured in terms of the decibel level (sound intensity) needed to recognize the presence of a sound at a given frequency (in Hertz). The degree of deafness ranges from mild (25–40 dB; difficulty with only faint speech), moderate

(40–55 dB; frequent difficulty with normal speech), moderately severe (55–70 dB; frequent difficulty with loud speech), severe (70–90 dB; understands only shouted speech), and profound (90–110 dB; cannot understand speech at all; Salvia & Ysseldyke, 1995). Deafness can be consistent over the frequency range or vary greatly at different frequency levels. The nature of deafness is critical for prescribing amplification because hearing aids can be programmed to amplify sounds at certain frequencies more than others.

Regarding communication abilities, deaf people's written English may range from functional illiteracy to mastery. Deaf people's speech intelligibility also varies greatly; psychologists may require good listening skills or a sign language interpreter to understand a deaf client. Deaf people's communication preferences range from spoken English to total communication (spoken English simultaneously with signed English) to ASL, with a combination of speech, speech reading, and writing falling anywhere in between. All assessment sessions should begin with a discussion of communication preferences. The mastery of the English language, spoken and written, remains the major developmental challenge confronting deaf individuals. About 95% of deaf people are reared in hearing families that use oral and vocal native languages (Schildroth & Karchmer, 1986). Because they lack hearing to sufficient degrees, deaf children's English proficiency is frequently limited.

Where previously sign language was widely assumed to be an unsophisticated communication pattern of mimed pictures in the air or a crude visual representation of English, it is now understood to have evolved anthropologically through the social intercourse of deaf people living in any given area, primarily in the schools, clubs, and organizations of deaf people. Sign language can now be characterized on a multidimensional continuum encompassing numerous styles, lexical variants, syntactic structures, dialects, and approximations to or departures from English word ordering (Stokoe, 1960). ASL structure, however, is not derived from English, and its syntax and grammar differ markedly from English. ASL takes advantage of the particular capabilities of physical communication in 3-D space.

Here, emphasis must be given to the fact that there is much greater variability in ASL and English fluency in the deaf population as compared with the variability of English fluency in the hearing population. This does not reflect on the deafness itself or on the deaf person's intelligence but on the frequent inadequacies in family and school nurturance of linguistic and cognitive development.

The ways in which deafness affects the educational development of deaf people depend primarily on the onset, or timing, of the deafness as well as the degree of the deafness. Deafness that occurs before the child acquires language fundamentals (generally before the age of 4 years) is considered prelingual, and deafness that occurs after the child acquires language fundamentals is considered postlingual. Thus, children with severe or profound bilateral postlingual deafness have markedly better educational prognoses than children with similar prelingual deafness (Allen, 1986; Braden, 1994).

Because prelingual deafness inhibits the usual acquisition of speech, deaf preschoolers generally have limited spoken English (Litowitz, 1987). For example, a typical hearing 4-year-old child has a vocabulary of about 2,000–3,000 words, whereas a typical prelingually deaf child of the same age has a vocabulary of about 25 words (Vernon & Andrews, 1990). Even if early intervention programs attempt to improve deaf children's English development, the most successful programs, however, rarely close the gap. Deaf children's syntactical and grammatical English usage lags behind their vocabulary acquisition (Quigley & Paul, 1989). Whether this is a linguistic difference (Litowitz, 1987) or a linguistic deficiency (Quigley & Paul, 1989) is debatable; the fact is that deaf children's limited English vocabularies and mastery of standard English's oral and vocal syntax do limit their acquisition of reading, writing, spelling, and mathematical skills. These lags in English vocabulary acquisition and English syntactical and grammatical usage usually continue into adulthood. One must remember, however, that while these lags are occurring, the mastery of ASL on the part of some may be as advanced as hearing people's mastery of English.

There are different ways to educate deaf children. Those with mild deafness may need only supplementary support to succeed in regular classrooms. Such support includes speech therapy, the use of closed-loop amplification systems, audiological services to monitor and maintain hearing aids, note takers, or tutoring. Those with more severe deafness, however, require more intensive educational support. The three distinct approaches to the education of deaf children are the oral method, the total communication method, and the bilingual–bicultural (bi-bi) method. The oral method emphasizes the acquisition of speech reading and production skills and discourages the use of sign language. The total communication method emphasizes language development through English signs and speech (i.e., signing and speaking simultaneously). The bi-bi method rejects spoken and signed English as a primary language and instead emphasizes the use of ASL, introducing written and signed forms of English after the children have mastered ASL. In the education of deaf children, there is much controversy over the virtues of these methods. Basically, oralists value speech competence in English, bi-bi educators value the acquisition of ASL and a deaf identity,[1] and total communication adherents value any communication regardless of language and modality.

The educational outcomes of the three educational approaches are still ambiguous. Evaluation studies have revealed inconsistent or small differences among methods (Geers, Moog, & Schick, 1984; Moores, 1987). Large gaps in general academic achievements continue to be found between deaf and hearing peers, with gaps increasing with age. Mainstream programs yield slightly better academic outcomes, but slightly worse social outcomes, than residential or segregated programs. One reason for this is the differences in the population of deaf children who enroll in mainstream versus residential school environments. The mainstream children are those with lesser degrees of deafness and fewer additional disabilities. Bi-bi programs have yet to be evaluated. Individual outcomes vary widely within programs, with advocates of each approach pointing to outstanding successes as well as dismal failures. Despite the best efforts of today's systems of education of deaf children, "over half of deaf students graduating from high school in America are functionally illiterate" (Gjerdigen, 1987, p. 3).

From the sociocultural perspective, deaf people generally object to the term *hearing impaired* and some to the term *hearing loss*. They object because the term *hearing impaired* emphasizes abnormality, also the term *hearing loss* suggests that something is lost when, from the perspective of congenitally deaf people, nothing has ever been lost. There are also those who call themselves "Deaf"; use ASL as their primary mode of communication; base their identity on the sharing of linguistic, historical, cultural traditions based on ASL; are active in the social and civic events of the Deaf community; and identify themselves as members of the Deaf community (Lane, Hoffmeister, & Bahan, 1996). There are also those who are audiologically deaf but not necessarily Deaf (in the sociocultural sense); may identify themselves as "hard of hearing"; use speech as their primary mode of communication; and base their identity on the sharing of linguistic, historical, and cultural traditions of the so-

---

[1]As proposed by Woodward (1972) and discussed by Padden and Humphries (1988), the lowercase *deaf* is used to refer to the audiological condition of not hearing, and the uppercase *Deaf* to refer to a particular group of deaf people who share a language (ASL) and a culture.

called "normal" hearing community. Thus, the broadly defined deaf population subsumes at least three sociocultural groups: hard of hearing people who typically have mild or moderate deafness and who identify with "normal" hearing society; deaf people who typically have severe or profound deafness; and Deaf people who are typically deaf and who identify with the Deaf community. Finally, there are people who are "late deafened" (i.e., those who lose their hearing later in life), who generally experience severe-to-profound deafness, who experience postlingual onset by definition, who may obtain some benefit from assistive listening devices, who may know sign language, who may affiliate with the Deaf community, and who are active in the Association of Late Deafened Adults.

Deafness is unique among disabilities because it is the only disability in which most members share a common language not shared by the dominant hearing society and in which most members do not learn their native language and cultural identity from their parents. Although many hearing parents of deaf children learn some form of sign language, they rarely become proficient in ASL and rarely become involved in the Deaf community. An exception that makes for another level of heterogeneity (i.e., parental hearing status) are genetically deaf individuals whose parents and, often, whose siblings are also deaf; they make up about 5% of the deaf population. By learning their native language and cultural identity from their parents, deaf children of deaf parents generally have a head start in their language and cognitive developments (Braden, 1994; Schlesinger & Meadow, 1972). Another level of heterogeneity involves different geographic and ethnic groups in which deaf members communicate in their own sign language dialects, a situation that complicates the provision of psychological services. These members than become even more underserved.

Understanding all these variations that make up the deaf population is critical for undertaking test selection, test administration, and test interpretation procedures. It is necessary for psychologists to obtain more realistic and accurate psychological test portrayals of the various subgroups of the American deaf population. Research findings to date (Altshuler, 1962, 1963; Baroff, 1963; Levine, 1956; Myklebust, 1960; Pintner, Fusfeld, & Brunschwig, 1937; Schlesinger & Meadow, 1972; Springer & Roslow, 1938), based on untranslated instruments and conducted by nondeaf and largely nonsigning researchers, have resulted in psychological test portrayals of personality deviancy that are at variance with objective observations by researchers who are knowledgeable and experienced with deafness and deaf people. Vestberg (1988) pointed to the Rosenthal effect operative among the former: They "only seek and find confirmation of their own prejudices in their studies" (p. 7). In a review of the literature on the "psychology of the deaf," such mismeasures of deaf people are attributed to examiner biases that stem from paternalistic attitudes prone to the pathologizing of cultural differences and the interpretation of differences as deviancies (Lane, 1988).

Assessment Issues

First Considerations

For those who are not deafness professionals, what are psychologists to do when handling referrals for the assessment of deaf people? The first issue to confront is one's own expertise as a psychologist. There is also the need to confront one's own sensitivity to, and appreciation for, the normality in deaf people and the heterogeneity in the deaf population. As previously mentioned, today's expert deafness professionals agree that competence in the deafness field, including competence in psychological assessments, implies sign language fluency and knowledge about deafness from audiological, developmental, educational, vocational, legal, social, and cultural perspectives (in addition to a solid background in mental health; Pollard, 1996). One especially needs a thorough understanding of the implications of deafness and the use of sign language for making diagnoses for people who are deaf. Few hearing psychologists have these skills. The push is for specialized training programs in deafness and psychology, a need that has been recognized for decades (Elliot, Glass, & Evans, 1988; Levine, 1977; Pollard, Gutman, DeMatteo, & Stewart, 1991; Sussman, 1989).

If such skills are lacking, then the assessment referral should be given to a psychologist who has the requisite skills and expertise. The Special Interest Section on Deafness of the American Psychological Association's Division 22 (Rehabilitation Psychology) and the Special Interest Section on Deafness of the National Association of School Psychologists can be contacted for a list of such experts and for overall guidance. In addition, most states in the United States have residential schools for deaf people that may be willing to share expertise. When planning, conducting, and reporting an assessment, consultation with experts may assist in making decisions about whether to assess or to refer.

If, however, the decision is made to conduct the assessment, then to break away from the typical preoccupation with psychopathology, which lends a distorted view of deaf individuals, the first order of business should be familiarization with the psychological and behavioral characteristics of the well-adjusted, healthy deaf person (Sussman, 1991). Familiarization with the relevant literature should follow. The mental health and deafness field is one with an existing knowledge base, one that has grown substantially during the past 2 decades (Braden, 1994; Brauer, 1992, 1993; Elliott et al., 1988; Lane, 1992; Pollard, 1993, 1996; Vernon & Andrews, 1990; Zieziula, 1982).

The Use of Sign Language Interpreters

Another step to consider is the option to obtain the services of a certified sign language interpreter. Such services may be an option if the referred client is deaf, particularly when the examiner is not proficient in the client's primary mode of communication. The assumption that an interpreter is not needed if the client uses spoken language should never be made: Some clients use supplemented oral communication, and others simply may not understand the psychologist. Significant others (e.g., a child's parents and teachers) may assist in making decisions about whether an interpreter is needed and, if so, what kind of interpreter will be needed. Parents, relatives, and teachers must not serve as interpreters. The impact of any accommodation on test results must be considered. Deaf people who sign achieve higher IQs with signed directions than with oral or written directions (Braden, 1992, 1994; Sullivan, 1982). Whatever procedures are followed will influence the test results. Such factors must be considered when interpreting the assessment results of deaf clients.

The use of the services of certified sign language interpreters is controversial. The presence of sign language interpreters does not substitute for psychologists who have the necessary skills and expertise because the professional education of interpreters does not involve mental health training. For example, certified sign language interpreters are not trained to recognize and distinguish between variations in ASL use and psychotic distortions in deaf people's responses to test items.

The Test Selection Procedure and the Normative Sample

A thorough review of the complexities and recommended procedures in the psychometric assessment of deaf individuals is beyond the scope of this chapter. Reports of psychological testing can be found in the literature. Before we offer suggestions, however, the following three caveats are in order.

One needs to consider the bias of the assessment. First, some cognitive tests are likely to elicit the fund of information bias. These tests assume exposure to and familiarity with common knowledge. The restricted access to deaf individuals of information from the printed page, radio programs, overheard conversations, and so on leaves most with some limitations in factual knowledge that may be attributed to limited intellectual ability. Second, in tests of personality, there is the reading and cultural bias, in which, for example, deaf individuals have restricted knowledge of the sociocultural norms of people who hear, thus, they may not give valid responses to test items. The point is that tests frequently require or assume reading proficiency, knowledge of (hearing) sociocultural norms, and a sizable fund of information that may not be found in the average deaf test taker. Thus, careful thought must be given to the test selection procedure.

Third, one needs to consider the normative sample on which the test findings will be based and its appropriateness for deaf individuals. One must be cautioned against the current demand for deaf norms. Although there may be times when a comparison of deaf people's scores to a nondeaf normative sample may be appropriate (e.g., when using tests that do not require English proficiency or an assumed fund of information of average size), there are many times when norms developed with deaf samples would be more appropriate.

General Purposes of Testing

Generally, two questions are asked when assessing deaf clients: What skills do deaf clients have at this time? Do deaf clients have a disability other than deafness that contributes to linguistic, academic, vocational, or social problems? The first question can be addressed through structured observation, interviews, adaptive behavior checklists, responses to teaching probes, curriculum-based assessment, work skill samples, and other criterion-referenced measures. The second question requires the use of norm-referenced measures such as IQ tests, standardized achievement tests, behavioral inventories, and so on. With deaf adults, the purposes of testing are varied and include the assessment of general and specific cognitive functions, the identification of psychopathology, the documentation of educational achievement or any form of change (e.g., symptoms), the identification of vocational aptitudes and interests, and so forth. In forensic settings, there are assessments of mental status and competence to stand trial.

It is imperative that psychologists think through the entire administration of the desired test, from instructions to the item content to the response modality to scoring procedures and normative base. If English knowledge, deafness, the fund of information, or typical deaf sociocultural experiences and values play an undesirable role, the test's utility is suspect.

Neuropsychological Assessments

Some studies in the literature recommend screening for neuropathology. Although several tests can be used for such screening, a combination of the Symbol Digit Modalities Test (Smith, 1982), reportedly the most sensitive instrument for this purpose, and the Rey–Osterrieth Complex Figure Test (Lezak, 1983), might be considered. When indicated, negative findings can be followed up with additional instruments in accordance with the Boston or process model of neuropsychological assessment (Lezak, 1983).

Intellectual Assessments

The Wechsler (1993, 1997) performance scales are the most popular tools to assess deaf people's intelligence (Braden & Hannah, 1998). Other nonverbal tests, such as the Raven Progressive Matrices (Raven, Court, & Rave, 1983) are also used. The most recent edition of the adult Wechsler scales has a formal ASL translation developed and disseminated by the test publisher (Kostrubala & Braden, 1998).

With deaf children, an example of an important question to be addressed is whether the child has a cognitive disability. Many deaf children exhibit characteristics similar to children with mental retardation, such as delayed speech and language, inconsistent attention to the environment, and delayed linguistic and academic skills. Thus, their cognitive functioning must be estimated independent of their deafness. The best way to separate intellectual ability from language acquisition is to use language-reduced or nonverbal tests of intelligence (Braden, 1994).

There are two types of nonverbal tests: performance tests that require children to manipulate objects (e.g., the Wechsler Performance Scale [WPS]) and motor-free tests that do not allow children to manipulate objects (e.g., the Matrix Analogies Test or Raven Progressive Matrices). Deaf children's IQs on performance tests and from motor-free nonverbal intelligence tests are usually in the average range, although they score lower on motor-free nonverbal tests than they do on performance tests (Braden, 1994; Braden, Kostrubala, & Reed, 1994).

The WPS is the most popular IQ test with deaf children. In samples of deaf children, the WPS consistently shows good reliability (Hirshoren, Hurley, & Kavale, 1979; Maller & Braden, 1993) and good correlations with other nonverbal IQ tests (Braden, 1992, 1994; Braden & Paquin, 1985). Its correlations with achievement tests, however, have been found to be less consistent. Because the discrepant findings are attributed to the metric used for expressing achievement scores, however, IQ–achievement correlations support the validity of the WPS when appropriate achievement score metrics are used (Braden, Wollack, & Allen, 1995; Kishor, 1995). Deaf children have a WPS subtest score profile that is often characterized by low Coding subtest scores. Those with additional disabilities often reveal abnormal WPS profiles, especially very low Coding subtest scores (Braden, 1990). Research on the WPS and most other nonverbal intelligence tests suggests that, altogether, they are reliable and valid when appropriately administered to deaf individuals.

Although the nonverbal IQs of deaf people are typically average, their scores on verbal IQ tests are usually well below average; these low IQs are attributed to linguistic deficits. Analogous to an English-speaking person scoring low on a foreign-language intelligence test, deaf people score low on intelligence tests that are based on the English language. Because there are no intelligence tests normed in ASL that we know of, it is not known whether deaf people have verbal reasoning deficits or simply lack a knowledge of English (Braden, 1994). Moreover, because verbal items do not function the same way for deaf and hearing people, they may be statistically biased when used with deaf people (Maller, 1997). Even though verbal IQs predict academic performance better than do nonverbal or performance tests for hearing people, verbal tests of intelligence are never to be used to estimate deaf individuals' intelligence. If verbal intelligence tests are administered to deaf people, scores are to be reported as measures of "incidental learning" (i.e., to reflect language and information that deaf individuals acquire through social interactions and not to be used to estimate cognitive abilities).

Regarding the intellectual assessment of deaf clients, the controversy continues about the use of special norms. Here, special norms are not recommended. On practical grounds, scores derived from special norms differ little from regular norms. On clinical grounds, special norms flatten abnormal psychometric profiles that may obscure psychological differences in deaf children (Braden, 1990). On psychometric grounds, there is no evidence of the need for special norms because most tests reveal similar reliability and validity for deaf and hearing people. Another controversy concerns whether deaf children's intelligence is qualitatively different from that of hearing children (Myklebust, 1964; Tomlinson-Keasey & Kelly, 1978). Although some neuropsychological differences have been found between deaf and hearing peers, the preponderance of evidence reveals strong neuropsychological similarities (Poizner, Klima, & Bellugi, 1987). Although the results vary by age, the intellectual organization for deaf and hearing children converges with age so that the structure of intelligence in both groups of children is highly similar by the time they reach adolescence.

Academic Assessments

With some modifications, the same instruments used with hearing children can be used with deaf children. There is the need to ensure that deaf children understand test directions; they may have good mathematics skills but may not understand directions or word problems. Clinicians should recognize that deaf children do not master academic material in a consistent sequence; whereas hearing children progress through the curriculum in logical sequences, deaf children often fail to master subordinate skills. Finally, clinicians must understand that deaf children often develop precocious guessing strategies. Because they often act without complete information (e.g., not fully understanding what has been said to them), they may develop exceptional guessing strategies (e.g., reading nonverbal cues), thus yielding achievement test raw scores that may overestimate the child's actual skill level (Moores, 1970). The Stanford Achievement Test offers special norms and technical adequacy data from large, nationally representative samples of deaf children (Holt, Traxler, & Allen, 1992). Because deaf children's achievement test scores are much lower than those of hearing peers, the use of regular and special norms have strong practical utility. Regular norms reveal how the deaf child's performance compares with normative (grade- or age-level) expectations, whereas special norms reveal how well the child is doing relative to deaf peers.

Social—Emotional Assessments

The Minnesota Multiphasic Personality Inventory (MMPI; Hathaway & McKinley, 1943) has been used to evaluate personality and social—emotional functioning in many outcome studies (Myklebust, 1960; Rosen, 1967). Its utility is greatly limited by its eighth-grade reading level and its deafness content biases. The Personality Assessment Inventory (Morey, 1991), a test that addresses a range of common Axis I and Axis II psychopathology symptoms and related treatment planning concerns, may be more useful. Its fourth-grade reading level and considerably shorter length are also advantages over the MMPI (Pollard, 1996). Although the Rorschach Inkblot Test (Rorschach, 1921/1942) is highly recommended by a few deafness professionals, it is repudiated by many because of the scoring issues this test presents when used with deaf people. Its greatest limitation is its psychologist bias, such that the written English protocols of client responses as "translated" by nondeaf psychologists via sign language interpreters do not seem to capture the conceptual meaning of the client's original responses.

Of all assessments, the social—emotional assessment of deaf people is probably the most difficult. First, few tests in this area are nonverbal. Behavior rating scales, which bypass deaf children's difficulties with the English language by using English-speaking respondents, nonetheless implicitly assume average English-language skills. Thus, poor peer interaction, due to poor spoken-language skills, may reflect a deaf client's English-language rather than social difficulties. Second, research on social—emotional assessments of deaf people is practically nonexistent. Third, whether a particular behavior is abnormal, dysfunctional, or functional is difficult to decide. At younger ages, deaf children tend to be aggressive to achieve control over their environment, whereas at older ages, they may isolate themselves from peers to avoid difficult, spoken-language social interactions. Thus, such difficult behaviors may serve either functional or dysfunctional purposes.

Given such difficulties, current deafness professionals suggest the cautious use of three types of social—emotional assessment approaches: nonverbal projective techniques, structured response techniques, and interviews or rating scales. Projective and structured response techniques, or personality inventories, are controversial with deaf clients because deaf clients lack English skills to understand the items and because many test items are irrelevant to the real-life situations of deaf people. Recently, however, the revised MMPI (MMPI-2) has been translated into ASL and, with the bilingual retest technique, reveals adequate linguistic equivalencies of the ASL MMPI-2 (Brauer, 1992, 1993). Before the ASL MMPI-2 can be used to supplement other approaches, however, it requires further pilot and field testing as well as validation research to ensure that its items assess the same constructs in the language and culture of deaf people (Geisinger, 1994). Finally, most deafness professionals rely on information obtained from interviews with deaf clients and others to assess social–emotional adjustment. Test items in the Social–Emotional Assessment Inventory were specifically designed with an understanding of the implications of deafness on normal developmental behavior, and the test has shown good reliability (Schlesinger & Meadow, 1972). The School Behavior Checklist demonstrates adequate conceptual validity and diagnostic utility with deaf children (Miller, 1977). The Maladaptive Behavior subscale of the Vineland Adaptive Behavior Scale also shows adequate validity for assessing deaf children's behavior problems (Sparrow, Balla, & Cicchetti, 1984).

Test Interpretation Issues

As is the case for all culturally diverse groups, the interpretation of test scores is the most important consideration in the testing of the deaf population. Interpretation is the process of assigning meaning to assessment results. The meaning of any particular result (e.g., a test score, biodata, responses to projective stimuli) is determined by the validity of the data source for deaf people. In many instances, clinicians may presume the meaning of a result to be similar for both deaf and nondeaf individuals. However, there are many instances in which this assumption is inappropriate or misleading, that is, there are instances in which deafness alters the meaning of the result.

Messick (1995) identified two threats that invalidate or alter assessment results: construct underrepresentation and construct-irrelevant variances. The term *construct underrepresentation* refers to the inappropriate narrow sampling of the domain of interest. For example, psychologists who evaluate the communication skills of deaf people by using only spoken language proficiency are narrowing the domain of interest inappropriately, that is, by overlooking ASL fluency and other nonverbal skills. The term *construct-irrelevant variance* refers to the inclusion of task characteristics that are unrelated to the relevant domain but increase the difficulty (or easiness) of the task for individuals or groups. For example, the assessment of intelligence with verbal tests increases the difficulty of the task for deaf individuals by including a task characteristic, knowledge of and fluency in English, which is unrelated to the domain of interest (i.e., intelligence).

In reviewing the history of psychological assessments with deaf people, construct-irrelevant variance is recognized as a significant problem in the psychological testing of the deaf population. Construct-irrelevant difficulties may be introduced by test biases or method biases. With test biases, as discussed earlier, there is the fund of information bias on tests of innate ability or reading and cultural bias on tests of personality. With method biases, for example, there is the misadministration of instruments by the psychologist's use of a language and mode incongruous with the deaf person's ability or preference or by the psychologist's translation from English to ASL that can alter the item difficulty of a test. There is ample evidence that in most cases, a construct-irrelevant variance lowers, depresses, or increases the abnormality of deaf people's responses. For example, word problems in mathematics contain construct-irrelevant difficulty (knowledge of English) that depresses scores (i.e., the deaf person understands the math but not the problem). Another example is the administration of projective tests during which deaf people (especially children) may think the psychologist wants them to name an image rather than to elaborate a response (i.e., they overgeneralize school vocabulary-building exercises to the assessment context and give "primitive" or "impoverished" single-word responses).

The issue of construct underrepresentation is less recognized and controversial when assessing deaf clients. For example, adaptive behavior scales assess whether clients can use the telephone independently. Some psychologists may delete this item when assessing deaf clients, claiming that this introduces construct-irrelevant difficulty. Others may argue that adaptive behavior in contemporary society includes the newest technologies in telecommunications and will include the item after some alterations (e.g., the deaf person can get an interpreter to act as a telephone go-between, the deaf person can provide a telephone number, or the deaf person can use a telecommunications device for deaf people). However, such adaptations may alter task difficulty, that is, most people can use the telephone before they can type; thus, the use of a telecommunications device for deaf people is harder than using a telephone. The impact of testing accommodations must be considered carefully, both in terms of whether accommodations could lead to construct underrepresentation and with respect to whether accommodations introduce construct-irrelevant variances (i.e., make the task too easy or too difficult).

There is also the need to be sensitive to other aspects of interpretation, particularly the consequential validity of assessment (Messick, 1995). That is, the consequences stemming from an assessment must be considered when interpreting the results. Decisions about client status must be considered more cautious as the stakes increase. Psychological assessments may guide effective dispositions for deaf clients by identifying or ruling out cognitive or affective disorders. However, there is little knowledge of many forms of validity for psychological assessment methods and tools when used with deaf clients. A recommendation is that psychologists supplement traditional in vitro psychological assessment (e.g., in the psychologist's office) with in vivo assessment (e.g., direct observations and interviews with people in relevant settings). To be especially encouraged is the use of trial placements when making decisions about eligibility for particular programs (e.g., special education, inpatient therapy) or occupational opportunities (e.g., new jobs, advancement). A brief but sufficient trial placement often defines the relative costs, benefits, and prognoses far more accurately and with less bias than traditional psychological testing and assessment alone.

Conclusion

In this chapter we have provided a framework for taking into consideration not only test interpretation issues but also test selection and test administration concerns. Because language is a critical aspect of psychiatric presentation and symptomatology, as well as of assessment and research methodology, any discussion of psychological assessments with deaf people cannot be separated from matters of ASL fluency and the consequences of dysfluency. Deaf people differ from hearing people in their language, cultural identity, and hearing acuity; these linguistic and cultural differences are most important for guiding psychological assessment.

References

Allen, T. E. (1986). Patterns of academic achievement among hearing impaired students: 1974 and 1983. In A. N. Schildroth & M. A. Karchmer (Eds.), *Deaf children in America* (pp. 161–206). San Diego, CA: College Hill Press.

Altshuler, K. A. (1963). Sexual patterns and family relationships. In J. D. Rainer, K. Z. Altshuler, & F. J. Kallmann (Eds.), *Family and mental health problems in a deaf pop-*

ulation (pp. 92–112). New York: Columbia University, New York State Psychiatric Institute.

Altshuler, K. Z. (1962). Psychiatric considerations in the adult deaf. *American Annals of the Deaf, 107,* 560–561.

Baroff, G. S. (1963). Rorschach data and clinical observations. In J. D. Rainer, K. Z. Altshuler, & F. J. Kallmann (Eds.), *Family and mental health problems in a deaf population* (pp. 177–181). New York: Columbia University, New York State Psychiatric Institute.

Braden, J. P. (1990). Do deaf persons have a characteristic psychometric profile on the Wechsler Performance Scales? *Journal of Psychoeducational Assessment, 8,* 518–526.

Braden, J. P. (1992). Intellectual assessment of deaf and hard of hearing people: A quantitative and qualitative research synthesis. *School Psychology Review, 21,* 82–94.

Braden, J. P. (1994). *Deafness, deprivation, and IQ.* New York: Plenum.

Braden, J. P., & Hannah, J. M. (1998). Assessment of hearing impaired and deaf children with the WISC-III. In D. Saklofske & A. Prifitera (Eds.), *Use of the WISC-III in clinical practice* (pp. 175–201). New York: Houghton-Mifflin.

Braden, J. P., Kostrubala, C., & Reed, J. (1994). Why do deaf children score differently on performance v. motor-reduced nonverbal intelligence tests? *Journal of Psychoeducational Assessment, 12,* 357–363.

Braden, J. P., & Paquin, M. M. (1985). A comparison of the WISC-R and WAIS-R Performance Scales in deaf adolescents. *Journal of Psychoeducational Assessment, 3,* 285–290.

Braden, J. P., Wollack, J. A., & Allen, T. E. (1995). Reply to Kishor: Choosing the right metric. *Journal of Psychoeducational Assessment, 13,* 250–265.

Brauer, B. A. (1992). The signer effect on MMPI performance of deaf respondents. *Journal of Personality Assessment, 58,* 380–388.

Brauer, B. A. (1993). Adequacy of a translation of the MMPI into American Sign Language for use with deaf individuals: Linguistic equivalency issues. *Rehabilitation Psychology, 38,* 247–260.

Brown, S. C. (1986). Etiological trends, characteristics, and distributions. In A. N. Schildroth & M. A. Karchmer (Eds.), *Deaf children in America* (pp. 33–54). San Diego, CA: College Hill Press.

Commission on Education of the Deaf. (1988). *Toward equality: Education of the deaf.* A report to the President and the Congress of the United States. Washington, DC: U.S. Government Printing Office.

Elliott, H., Glass, L., & Evans, J. W. (Eds.). (1988). *Mental health assessment of deaf clients: A practical manual.* Boston: Little, Brown.

Geers, A. J., Moog, M. P., & Schick, J. (1984). Acquisition of spoken and signed English by profoundly deaf children. *Journal of Speech and Hearing Disorders, 49,* 378–388.

Geisinger, K. F. (1994). Cross-cultural normative assessment: Translation and adaptation issues influencing the normative interpretation of assessment instruments. *Psychological Assessment, 6,* 304–312.

Gjerdigen, D. (1987). Language acquisition and reading scores. *Newsounds, 12,* 3.

Hathaway, S. R., & McKinley, J. C. (1943). *Minnesota Multiphasic Personality Inventory.* New York: The Psychological Corporation.

Hirshoren, A., Hurley, O. L., & Kavale, K. (1979). Psychometric characteristics of the WISC-R Performance scale with deaf children. *Journal of Speech and Hearing Disorders, 44,* 73–79.

Holt, J. A., Traxler, C. B., & Allen, T. E. (1992). *Interpreting the scores: A user's guide to the 8th edition Stanford Achievement Test for educators of deaf and hard of hearing students.* Washington, DC: Gallaudet Research Institute.

Johnson, R. E., Liddell, S. K., & Erting, C. J. (1989). *Unlocking the curriculum: Principles for achieving access in deaf education* (Gallaudet Research Institute Working Paper 89-3). Washington, DC: Gallaudet University, Department of Linguistics and Interpreting, and the Gallaudet Research Institute.

Kishor, N. (1995). Evaluating predictive validity: A rejoinder to Braden et al. (1995). *Journal of Psychoeducational Assessment, 13,* 266–270.

Kostrubala, C. E., & Braden, J. P. (1998). *The American sign language translation of the WAIS-III.* San Antonio, TX: The Psychological Corporation.

Lane, H. (1984). *When the mind hears: A history of the deaf.* New York: Random House.

Lane, H. (1988). Is there a "psychology of the deaf?" *Exceptional Children, 55,* 7–19.

Lane, H. (1992). *The mask of benevolence: Disabling the deaf community.* New York: Knopf.

Lane, H. L., Hoffmeister, R., & Bahan, B. J. (1996). *A journey into the deaf-world.* San Diego, CA: Dawn Sign Press.

Levine, E. S. (1956). *Youth in a soundless world.* New York: New York University Press.

Levine, E. S. (1977, July). The preparation of psychological service providers to the deaf: A report of the Spartanburg conference on the functions, competencies and training of psychological service providers to the deaf. *Journal of Rehabilitation of the Deaf* (PRWAD Monograph No. 4).

Lezak, M. D. (1983). *Neuropsychological assessment* (2nd ed.). New York: Oxford University Press.

Litowitz, B. E. (1987). Language and the young deaf child. In E. D. Mindel & M. Vernon (Eds.), *They grow in silence: Understanding deaf children and adults* (2nd ed., pp. 111–147). Boston: College Hill Press.

Maller, S. M. (1997). Deafness and WISC-III item difficulty: Invariance and fit. *Journal of School Psychology, 35*(3), 299–314.

Maller, S. M., & Braden, J. P. (1993). The criterion validity of the WISC-III with deaf adolescents. In B. A. Bracken & R. S. McCallum (Eds.), *Wechsler Intelligence for Children: Third edition. Journal of Psychoeducational Assessment. Advances in psychoeducational assessment* (pp. 105–113). Brandon, VT: Clinical Psychology.

Messick, S. (1995). Validity of psychological assessment: Validation of inferences from persons' responses and performances as scientific inquiry into score meaning. *American Psychologist, 50,* 741–749.

Miller, L. C. (1977). *School Behavior Checklist manual.* Los Angeles: Western Psychological Services.

Moores, D. F. (1970). An investigation of the psycholinguistic functioning of deaf adolescents. *Exceptional Children, 36,* 645–652.

Moores, D. F. (1987). *Educating the deaf: Psychology, principles, and practices* (3rd ed.). Boston: Houghton Mifflin.

Morey, L. C. (1991). *Personality assessment inventory: Professional manual.* Odessa, FL: Psychological Assessment Resources.

Myklebust, H. R. (1960). *The psychology of deafness.* New York: Grune & Stratton.

Myklebust, H. R. (1964). *The psychology of deafness* (2nd ed.). New York: Grune & Stratton.

Padden, C., & Humphries, T. (1988). *Deaf in America: Voices from a culture.* Cambridge, MA: Harvard University Press.

Pintner, R., Fusfeld, I. S., & Brunschwig, L. (1937). Personality tests of deaf adults. *Journal of Genetic Psychology, 51,* 305–327.

Poizner, H., Klima, E. S., & Bellugi, U. (1987). *What the hands reveal about the brain.* Cambridge, MA: MIT Press.

Pollard, R. Q. (1993). 100 years in psychology and deafness: A centennial retrospective. *Journal of the American Deafness and Rehabilitation Association, 26,* 32–46.

Pollard, R. Q. (1996). Professional psychology and deaf people: The emergence of a discipline. *American Psychologist, 51,* 389–396.

Pollard, R. Q., Gutman, V. A., DeMatteo, A. D., & Stewart, L. G. (1991, August). *Training in deafness and mental health: Status and issues.* Paper presented at the 99th Annual Convention of the American Psychological Association, San Francisco.

Quigley, S. P., & Paul, P. V. (1989). English language development. In M. C. Wang, M. C. Reynolds, & H. J. Walberg (Eds.), *Handbook of special education: Research and practice* (Vol. 3, pp. 3–21). Elmsford, NY: Pergamon Press.

Raven, J. C., Court, J. H., & Raven, J. (1983). *Manual for Raven's Progressive Matrices and vocabulary scales.* London: Oxford Psychologists Press.

Rorschach, H. (1942). *Psychodiagnostik* (H. Huber Verlag, Trans.). Bern, Switzerland: Bircher. (Original work published 1921)

Rosen, A. (1967). Limitations of personality inventories for assessment of deaf children and adults as illustrated by research with the Minnesota Multiphasic Personality Inventory. *Journal of Rehabilitation of the Deaf, 1,* 47–52.

Salvia, J., & Ysseldyke, J. E. (1995). *Assessment* (6th ed.). Boston: Houghton Mifflin.

Schildroth, A. N., & Karchmer, M. A. (Eds.). (1986). *Deaf children in America.* San Diego, CA: College Hill Press.

Schlesinger, H. S., & Meadow, K. P. (1972). *Sound and sign: Childhood deafness and mental health.* Berkeley: University of California Press.

Smith, A. (1982). *Symbol Digit Modalities Test manual* (Rev. ed.). Los Angeles, CA: Western Psychological Services.

Sparrow, S. S., Balla, D. A., & Cicchetti, D. V. (1984). *Vineland Adaptive Behavior Scales.* Circle Pines, MN: American Guidance Service.

Springer, N. N., & Roslow, S. (1938). A further study of the psychoneurotic responses of deaf and hearing children. *Journal of Educational Psychology, 29,* 590–596.

Stokoe, W. C. (1960). *Sign language structure: An outline of the visual communication systems of the American deaf* (Studies in Linguistics: Occasional Papers 8). Buffalo, NY: University of Buffalo.

Sullivan, P. M. (1982). Administration modifications on the WISC-R Performance scale with different categories of deaf children. *American Annals of the Deaf, 127,* 780–788.

Sussman, A. E. (1989). Training in mental health services. In R. G. Brill (Ed.), *Proceedings of the national conference on deaf and hard of hearing people* (pp. 31–32). Silver Spring, MD: T. J. Publishers.

Sussman, A. E. (1991). *Characteristics of a well adjusted deaf person or: The art of being a deaf person.* Unpublished manuscript, Gallaudet University, Washington, DC.

Tomlinson-Keasey, C., & Kelly, R. R. (1978). The deaf child's symbolic world. *American Annals of the Deaf, 123,* 452–458.

Vernon, M., & Andrews, J. F. (1990). *The psychology of deafness: Understanding deaf and hard-of-hearing people.* New York: Longman.

Vestberg, P. (1988). *Deaf personality: Myths and reality.* Unpublished manuscript, Gallaudet University, Washington, DC.

Wechsler, D. (1993). *Wechsler Intelligence Scale for Children–Third edition.* San Antonio, TX: The Psychological Corporation.

Wechsler, D. (1997). *Wechsler Adult Intelligence Scale–Third edition.* San Antonio, TX: The Psychological Corporation.

Woodward, J. (1972). Implications for sociolinguistics research among the deaf. *Sign Language Studies, 1,* 1–7.

Zieziula, F. R. (1982). *Assessment of hearing impaired people.* Washington, DC: Gallaudet College Press.

Learning Disabilities

Jacqueline L. Cunningham

The category *learning disabilities* (LDs) differs from the other categories discussed in this book as dimensions of diversity. Although individuals can be assigned to the other categories on a self-evident basis, assignment to the LDs category depends on using criteria that are not self-evident but empirically derived. Such criteria are based on hypothetical constructs (e.g., IQ) and are subject to the limitations inherent in the psychological measurement of these constructs. The resulting ambiguities, controversies, and inconsistencies that characterize LDs make it possible to even deny that the category actually exists (Coles, 1987). By contrast, how could one deny the reality of hearing impairment, poverty, immigration status, and the other dimensions of diversity under consideration in this book?

To avoid the circularity that could develop from considering test interpretation issues with regard to a category that, itself, is operationalized within the context of testing technology, in this chapter I focus on specific decision factors that need to be considered when using psychological tests as valid and reliable sources of information. Therefore, I use a decision-making model developed by Keogh (1994), which she described as a "matrix of decision points in the measurement of learning disabilities," as a framework for grounding discussions.

The process of drawing inferences about individuals with LDs has been described by Kavale and Forness (1985) as a "disorganized mass

This chapter was prepared with the cooperation of Children's Hospital, Washington, DC, while I was completing a postdoctoral fellowship appointment in pediatric neuropsychology awarded by the Children's National Medical Center and the George Washington University Medical Center. I thank Thomas D. Oakland for his helpful review of this chapter.

of justification, assumption, and incantation'' (p. 100). I begin the discussion with an overview of conceptualizations of LDs to give readers a sense of the problems inherent in defining the term. This is followed by an application of Keogh's (1994) model to show how it can guide decision making with regard to four main objectives: (a) deciding when LDs are reflected in test performance; (b) deciding when to use standardized tests with individuals with LDs and interpreting them in a straightforward way, and when not to do so; (c) deciding when to risk an impact on test validity by using special accommodations; and (d) deciding when examiner bias is likely to affect test interpretation. A systematic approach to relating the context of testing to specific decision points may provide a useful heuristic for taking control over the interpretative process and thus arrive at conceptualizations of LDs that are internally consistent and reflect the reality of this pervasive condition.

Overview of Conceptualizations of LDs

Since the term *learning disability* was initially introduced in 1963 by Samuel Kirk (1975) at an organizational meeting of the Association for Children with Learning Disabilities, it has remained a source of controversy as parents, professionals, organizations, and governmental agencies have tried to develop a valid and widely accepted definition. The term emerged because of the need to identify and serve in the schools a group of children who were performing poorly in academic areas but who did not fit into any existing category of exceptionality (Doris, 1993). In 1963, the term was accepted as a name for children who manifest a variety of learning problems (Kirk, 1975). Its most widely used and legally accepted definition is one devised originally by the National Advisory Committee on Handicapped Children (U.S. Office of Education, 1968) and later reconfirmed by the passage of the Education for All Handicapped Children Act (EAHCA; 1977). This definition states the following:

> "Specific learning disability" means a disorder in one or more of the basic psychological processes involved in understanding or in using language, spoken or written, which may manifest itself in an imperfect ability to listen, think, speak, read, write, spell, or to do mathematic calculations. The term includes such conditions as perceptual handicaps, brain injury, minimal brain dysfunction, dyslexia, and developmental aphasia. The term does not include children

who have learning problems which are primarily the result of visual, hearing, or motor handicaps, of mental retardation, of emotional disturbance, or of environmental, cultural, or economic disadvantage. (EAHCA, 1977)

From its inception, the EAHCA was designed to guide funding practices associated with federal school legislation. This law provides students with LDs with a legal guarantee to special services. Thus, although it promotes the most commonly used definition of LDs, the intent of the law was to provide a procedural definition rather than a comprehensive theoretical statement about the nature of the disorder (Doris, 1993).

Other definitions also vie for legitimacy. In 1987, the Interagency Committee on Learning Disabilities proposed a revision of the prevailing definition to include disorders of social skills. The recognition that LDs are not limited to academic achievement but may affect many aspects of living seems reasonable. However, because the proposed revision blurs the boundaries between LDs and other problem conditions, particularly behavior disorders and mild emotional conditions, it has not gained broad support. Nonetheless, in 1988, the National Joint Committee for Learning Disabilities supported the position that LDs are a heterogeneous group of disorders; that they are concomitant with other handicapping conditions; and that they are a result of central nervous system damage, dysfunction, or structural irregularity (Keogh, 1993).

Because there is no consensus about identification, it is difficult to estimate the number of people who are diagnosed with LDs. Although incidence figures have varied from 1% to 40% (Keogh, 1982), most screening surveys have indicated that approximately 5–15% of school-age children have some form of an LD. A report by the United States Department of Education in 1988 indicated that 46% of all students identified for special education services in the schools were classified as learning disabled. During the 1986–1987 school year, students so classified made up 4.8% of the total school-age population and 44% of all students receiving special education services (Myers & Hammill, 1990).

In addition to being the largest field of special education, LDs have also been the fastest growing over the past two decades. From 1977 until 1989, there was a 152% increase in the number of students with LDs who received special education services (Frankenberger & Fronzaglio, 1991). LDs are more common in boys than girls, with incidence ratios typically ranging from 2:1 to 5:1 (Finucci & Childs, 1991).

Although the field of LDs, as it is known today, did not emerge until the 1960s, research investigating LDs began around 1800. In its earliest phase (i.e., 1800–1929), researchers formulated theoretical speculations about LDs on the basis of disorders in spoken language, written language, and perceptual–motor processes (Doris, 1993). Beginning in the 1930s and 1940s, investigators began to discuss LDs as having a neurological basis and suggested that these problems were caused by brain damage (e.g., Strauss & Lehtinen, 1947). Thus, the terms *minimal brain damage* and later *minimal brain dysfunction* (MBD) were used as diagnostic labels (Mercer, 1991).

During the 1960s, to further characterize children with MBD, a document by Clements (1966) was published by the U.S. Department of Health, Education, and Welfare that described such children as having difficulties in school despite being of average intelligence. In this work, MBD was defined as a variety of learning and behavioral difficulties attributed to functional deviations in the central nervous system. In trying to create a conceptualization of MBD that reflected the diverse manifestations of the syndrome while also not implicating any particular localized insult to the brain, Clements created confusion in the way the syndrome was viewed within the medical, psychological, and educational professions (Doris, 1993).

It was also in the 1960s that differences developed among physicians, psychologists, and educators that resulted in the evolution of two distinct but overlapping classification systems relating to LDs. Educators focused on the learning difficulties of children with MBD and, during that decade, the learning disabilities movement was born. The medical and psychological fields focused more on the behavioral difficulties, specifically hyperactivity, distractibility, and impulsivity—a trend that gained momentum with the advent of stimulant medication and an emphasis on hyperactivity as the basis for treatment (Wender, 1971). The term *minimal brain dysfunction* was later replaced with the term *hyperkinetic reaction of childhood,* which is now called *attention deficit hyperactivity disorder* (ADHD) in the fourth edition of the *Diagnostic and Statistical Manual of Mental Disorders* (American Psychiatric Association, 1994). Despite the emergence of LDs as an entity separate from ADHD, there is still confusion and controversy about the relationship between the two disorders (Denckla, 1989). From a historical perspective, much of this current confusion and controversy can be traced directly to the inextricable link between learning difficulties and behavioral disturbance in MBD (Fletcher, Francis, Rourke, Shaywitz, & Shaywitz, 1993).

To understand and explain difficulties that people with LDs encounter, and to provide a framework for the classification of the heterogeneous groups of LDs, various theoretical models have been proposed in the development of the field. These include neuropsychological, cognitive- and information-processing, and achievement–behavioral models.

Originating from a medical perspective, neuropsychological models attempt to explain certain types of academic failure in terms of damage to specific brain functions (Rourke, 1994). On the other hand, cognitive- and information-processing models focus on the psychological and cognitive processes that underlie and are prerequisites to academic learning. In such models, LDs are assumed to be deficits in information processing or cognitive processing, and proponents attempt to understand how people with LDs think and learn rather than what they learn (Swanson, 1993; Torgesen, 1994).

Despite the predominance of cognitive theoretical models in the LDs field, their ecological validity has been questioned. Critics argue that ecologically invalid tasks and measures, which tap various cognitive-processing abilities, may produce valuable information about cognitive-processing deficits in people with LDs but that correlations between these cognitive measures and academic performance measures may not be large enough to be meaningful. Furthermore, training and remediation for students with LDs based on presumed cognitive-processing deficits are not always effective and do not necessarily translate into improved academic performance in the classroom (Meltzer, 1994).

A third type of conceptual model from which to view LDs is an achievement model (Berninger & Abbott, 1994). Such models are based on the assumption that people with LDs experience academic failure in one or more academic skill areas. These models do not attempt to explain the deficits that underlie the academic failure but instead focus on the creation and validation of ways to remediate them. Such models are also referred to as "behavorial models" because they avoid the use of hypothetical constructs referring to disruptive neuronal mechanisms and deficient psychological processes, and instead concentrate on observable academic behavior for the purposes of remediation (Greenwood, 1996).

There is much support for the achievement model of LDs as evidenced by the salience of empirical research devoted to identifying students with LDs on the basis of academic achievement patterns. In contrast to cognitive-processing models, much of the value of achievement models resides in their potential ecological validity. Because of the relevance of research on interventions promoting academic achievement, the achievement model has been widely adopted in educational settings. This is evidenced in the conventional assessment, identification, and treatment procedures regarding people with LDs in the schools as well as in the legislative regulations that mandate these procedures (Zigmond, 1993).

Despite some convergence on viewing LDs from the perspective of achievement models in school settings, the ongoing controversy and debate about the definition of LDs have perpetuated confusion about this condition and its operational diagnostic criteria. This, in turn, has confounded identification and classification issues. Definitional criteria used in the identification of LDs vary as a function of the purpose of identification. For the most part, selection criteria used for the delivery of educational services and for research are different. Because one of the main purposes of research is to identify intrinsically homogeneous, not "systems-identified" subtypes, selection for research purposes is more optimally based on various cognitive and neuropsychological assessment procedures than on achievement-based ones (Keogh, 1993).

In the schools, the identification and classification of students with LDs have been driven primarily by the federal definition of LDs undergirding the EAHCA. The most fundamental criterion used to identify LDs, relative to this landmark law, focuses on the presence of a severe discrepancy between intellectual ability and academic achievement (Stanovich, 1993). However, because the federal definition does not specifically quantify the degree of underachievement required to define LDs, individual states have to make this decision themselves, thus creating additional sources of confusion about identification and classification issues (Ross, 1995).

It is not surprising that the states' criteria for procedures used in identifying students with LDs vary greatly on the basis of their interpretation of the federal regulation (Martin, 1993). Although most states agree on the inclusion of an aptitude–achievement discrepancy in the identification of LDs, there is little consensus among states about how to quantify this discrepancy. Cone and Wilson (1981) found that most states used one of the following methods: an expectancy formula, a standard score comparison, deviation from grade level, and regression analysis. As a result of the different methods used in quantifying the aptitude–achievement discrepancy, the number and characteristics of students identified as learning disabled in schools vary greatly across states (Schuerholz et al., 1995).

Criticism abounds regarding the widespread adoption of the federal definition by states for identifying students as learning disabled. Some believe that too much emphasis has been placed on the statistical formulas used in determining the aptitude–achievement discrepancy that underscores that definition and that the presence or absence of a severe discrepancy is not diagnostic by itself (Morris, 1994a). There is also concern about the correlation between the intelligence and achievement measures used to determine the discrepancy (Stanovich, 1993). Finally, critics propose that severity should not be the sole criterion if the field is to further its understanding about unique and homogeneous deficits in LDs and homogeneous subtypes (Blashfield, 1993). Nonetheless, despite the limitations of and the compelling criticism aimed at the definition of LDs promoted by the EAHCA, the aptitude–achievement discrepancy remains the standard by which people in school are diagnosed for special education services under the LDs classification (Ross, 1995). In view of the variety of disciplines and perspectives, and wide range of constructs and variables that undergrid conceptualizations of LDs , the standard definition fuels rather than abates the controversy. Consequently, the status quo in LDs remains one of enduring definition and classification problems, an inconsistent research literature, diverse treatment and intervention approaches, and strongly held and divisive advocacy positions (Oakland & Cunningham, 1990).

The Need for Decision-Making Models for Identifying LDs

In an insightful discussion, Keogh (1993) pointed out that the circularity that characterizes conceptualizations of LDs basically relates to the failure to distinguish between "classification" and "identification." *Classification* is theory driven and measurement free, whereas *identification* refers to assignment to a category and is necessarily measurement bound. Accordingly, conceptualizations of LDs have remained hopelessly inconsistent and fragmented because definitions of LDs emerged from characteristics of clinically or educationally identified (i.e., "measured") individuals or groups rather than from a coherent theory.

Given researchers' limited knowledge, Keogh (1993) believed that a "constructionist" (i.e., relativist) position needs to be advocated with regard to understanding LDs. This is not to negate the reality of this problem condition but to "underscore the need for a more powerful conceptual system of classification and more precise operational definitions and measures" (Keogh, 1993, p. 312). Because a constructionist position stems from the assumption that "we do not discover scientific facts; we invent them" (Scarr, 1985, p. 499), its merit resides in its enhancing objectivity by taking into account the context in which a condition becomes identified (Kavale, 1993).

According to Keogh (1994), identifying people with LDs is necessarily an interpretative process. Therefore, decision-making models are needed to guide this process. To that end, Keogh offered her own matrix of decision points in the measurement LDs. The model essentially demands that a series of decision points, relating to the purpose, domain, target variables, techniques, and methods of testing, be incorporated into the measurement process to arrive at identifications and diagnoses that are both intrinsically and extrinsically sound. I consider each of four main objectives by focusing on the model's decision points as guideposts for reaching informed judgments about knowing when (a) LDs are reflected in test performance; (b) to use standardized tests with individuals with LDs; (c) to use special accommodations; and (d) to expect a potential for bias in test interpretation.

Deciding When LDs Are Reflected in Test Performance

Purpose of Testing

The need to identify and serve in the schools those students who are unexpectedly performing poorly in academic areas remains the primary purpose for identifying LDs. The important point is that identification is bound to an external (i.e., social–contextual referent), not necessarily to an internal (i.e., theoretical), one. Under these conditions, LDs are reflected in test performance when tests are able to identify the students who are intended to be served. From a social–contextual perspective, the aptitude–achievement discrepancy formulas that most states use to identify LDs are appropriate to the extent that they meet extrinsic sociopolitical contingencies as well as those that are more intrinsic (i.e., theoretically sound).

The problem is that systems-identified LDs may be associated with particular selection processes that the systems themselves do not intend to create. For example, Stanovich (1993) pointed to "Matthew effects," which refer to the commonplace occurrence that students with reading disabilities graduate to the status of "slow learner" as they get older. Such students no longer qualify for services when their IQ does not remain high enough to allow them to meet the aptitude–achievement discrepancies required to obtain special education placement. Matthew effects occur because reading stimulates the development of other related cognitive abilities; accordingly, the associated intercorrelations between IQ and achievement measures reflect the impact of reading disability on cognitive development. School-based decisions to graduate students with reading disabilities from special education are not intended to allow their disability to have an even greater detrimental impact on their cognitive functioning, yet that is what usually happens. When deciding whether LDs are reflected in the test performance of an older student with a reading disability, it is best to keep in mind the likelihood of finding Matthew effects.

As another caution against unintended systems-level processes associated with using aptitude–achievement discrepancy formulas for selecting students for LDs services, it is best to consider differences in the characteristics of students who are selected by one type of formula over another. Two common discrepancy-based models used in identifying LDs are regression and reliability models. The regression model corrects for statistical regression to the mean of the achievement score relative to the ability score, whereas the reliability method accounts for the reliability of the measurement instruments, which are most reliable at the extreme lower and upper limits of their frequency distributions. One correlate of these differences is that fewer children and, more specifically, fewer bright children, are likely to be identified as learning disabled by the regression method than they are by the reliability method. Thus, systems that seek to contain the numbers of identified children to more manageable limits will do so by using the regression method. However, these systems probably do not intend to select a different type of LD over another by using one or the other model. In effect, research by Schuerholz et al. (1955) suggests that they do so nonetheless.

In the study by Schuerholz et al. (1995), brighter students with reading disabilities, matched for IQ and selected by the regression method, tended to represent classic reading disabilities characterized particularly by poor phonological processing skills. On the other hand, brighter students with reading disabilities who were selected by the reliability method tended to be less classically reading disabled and to have a broader based language disorder, executive dysfunction, attention deficits, and hyperactivity; their attention deficits also appeared to affect reading comprehension. Implications of the study are that systems that use the regression formula likely fail to identify bright students who exhibit one type of reading disability but not another. Whereas the results of the study point to the limitations of aptitude–achievement discrepancy formulas, I do not cite the study to dispute them as much as to indicate that measurement practices guided by sociopolitical forces are unlikely to yield authoritative classification taxonomies of LDs. Instead, such taxonomies are likely to come from concerns that are driven by science. As Morris (1994b) aptly stated, with specific reference to LDs, "If we improve the scientific basis of our measurements, we also will improve their sociopolitical impact" (p. 616).

Testing Domains

Outcomes such as Matthew effects allude to the importance of examining the domain in which a disability is expressed (or not expressed), as a second decision point, when deciding whether LDs are reflected in test performance. In prevailing methods of diagnosing LDs, measured cognitive ability (i.e., IQ) is treated as a predictor variable that establishes expectancies for academic achievement. Yet, Matthew effects implicate a bidirectional relationship between the acquisition of academic skills and the development of intellectual ability. Such a relationship requires that assessment be directed at characteristics of instructional settings, as an important domain of testing, if LDs are to be appropriately identified.

Because the bidirectional relationship underlying learning problems cannot be represented by aptitude–achievement discrepancy formulas, supplanting them with interactional and transactional assessment models is widely advocated; in addition, the recommended models consider treatment conditions to be essential components of the evaluation process (Berninger & Abbott, 1994). These models, also known as "dynamic assessment models," are contiguous with the achievement and behavioral frame of reference, in that they are designed to identify failure to respond to validated treatment protocols as the preferred method of diagnosing LDs.

Although a method of diagnosing LDs on the basis of failure to benefit from instruction may seem parsimonious and intuitively plausible, dynamic assessment methods are highly complex in that they demand repeated within- and between-subjects analyses of change over time. That is, instead of relying on static measures such as IQ, individual and group growth trajectories need to be continuously plotted to determine the probabilities for successfully responding to treatment protocols as a basis for differentiating LDs from other types of learning difficulties. Furthermore, because perplexing scale-of-measurement problems hinder progress in the development of such methods, the merit of dynamic assessment cannot be determined. That is, despite staunch advocacy to the contrary, such methods are insufficiently validated to consider them viable alternatives to conventional assessment procedures (Oakland & Cunningham, 1990).

Despite the problematic nature of dynamic assessment models, their value resides in their acknowledgment of the power of social–psychological influences on behavior and achievement. Accordingly, recognition of the significance of the domains of testing (i.e., whether evaluation should be of individuals or conditions in their environment) is critical to determining how LDs may be reflected in test performance. At the least, before concluding that a given person has an LD, it is important to decide how much of his or her problem may be due to inadequate pedagogy, disorganized and inadequate classrooms, and inappropriate instructional methods as opposed to how much may be attributable to his or her neurological status (Keogh, 1994).

Target Variables

As a third decision point, knowing which variables need to be assessed, is important when determining whether LDs are reflected in test performance. The study by Schuerholz et al. (1995), cited earlier, makes a compelling case for increasing awareness of the variables needing systematic consideration when selecting students for services under the LDs classification. If school systems that use regression models were intent on identifying disorders of reading comprehension in their brighter students, they would need to scrutinize specific target variables to do so. Moreover, the 1995 study is informative with regard to specifying the nature of relevant variables because it showed that bright students' disabilities in reading comprehension, identifiable by the reliability model but not the regression model, were associated with broad-based language disorder, executive dysfunction, attention deficits, and hyperactivity.

The kinds of variables associated with some forms of reading disability point to the arbitrariness of separating LDs from ADHD, as these entities have been conceptualized following their evolution from earlier notions of MBD. Denckla (1989) addressed such arbitrariness by keying in on "executive function" as the "overlap zone between deficit hyperactivity disorder and learning disabilities" (p. 155). According to Denckla, LDs and ADHD are frequently accompanied by (a) difficulty with planning and sequencing complex behaviors; (b) paying attention to several components at once; (c) grasping the gist of a complex situation; (d) resisting distraction and interference; (e) inhibiting inappropriate response tendencies; and (f) sustaining behavioral output for relatively prolonged periods. Because these executive functions depend on the integrity of the frontal lobes and their subcortical connections, their disturbance in LDs and ADHD suggests a congruent neurodevelopmental etiology for both disorders.

The frequency with which developmental dyslexia (i.e., a reading disability) is accompanied by attention deficits and executive dysfunction led Hughes and Denckla (1978) to distinguish between "dyslexia-pure" and "dyslexia-plus," with the latter condition involving comorbid reading and attentional deficits. According to them, dyslexia-plus is far more common than dyslexia-pure and may not yield test data that allow a discrepancy-based diagnosis of a reading disorder, especially in the case of people who are older and brighter. Hughes and Denckla proposed that the most common ingredients in dyslexia, in varying proportions, are language and attentional inefficiency, with the more subtle cognitive elements applying to that group of people who do not necessarily meet discrepancy-based criteria.

Denckla and Rumsey (1992) also pointed out that a reason for older and brighter people's failure to meet discrepancy-based criteria is that their verbal IQ scores usually surpass specific constituent spoken language competencies, thus yielding a score that reflects "a whole that is more than the sum of its parts" (p. 638). Moreover, a higher IQ reduces the likelihood of meeting discrepancy criteria in states that use a regression model to stipulate in standard deviation units the aptitude–achievement discrepancy needed to be classified as learning disabled. For example, in these cases, a person with an IQ in the 130–139 range usually requires a discrepancy of 2.0–2.3 *SD*s to meet criteria, whereas a person with an IQ in the 90–99 range requires only a discrepancy of 0.9–1.5 *SD*s to do so (Schuerholz et al., 1995, p. 22, Table 3).

Because the basal level IQ may render discrepancy-based formulas to be of limited value in identifying some forms of reading disabilities, decisions about which variables to target for the identification of LDs may need to include those that are not usually assessed in conventional evaluations (e.g., spoken language variables). The decision to include such variables is encouraged by Denckla's (1989) observation that youngsters who obtain respectable average verbal IQ scores routinely score as much as 5 years below age expectations on one or more of the basic elements of language, including phonology, semantics, syntax, and pragmatics, when assessed by language tests.

Furthermore, the findings of the Schuerholz et al. (1995) study imply that, in addition to language-related variables, those pertaining to attention deficits and executive dysfunction need to be scrutinized when testing for LDs. These findings are reminiscent of the debate about MBD, with a modern version of the controversy now relating to whether, or to what extent, ADHD is an LD or its comorbid condition (Silver, 1990). Such enduring controversy points to the limitation of the knowledge and the likelihood that discrepancy formulas will be misused when the diagnosis of LDs is approached too narrowly.

Techniques and Methods

Information on the many variables that should be addressed when diagnosing LDs suggests, at least at face value, that the prevailing techniques and methods for identifying LDs (i.e., those based on aptitude–achievement discrepancies) are inadequate. However, it must be remembered that under the EAHCA, final judgments about the eligibility of a student for school classification purposes are the responsibility of a multidisciplinary evaluation team. That is, professional specialists are charged with weighing all pertinent variables so that decisions are not the result of one or more arbitrary test procedures (Dangel & Ensminger, 1988). Unfortunately, however, parents and other advocates for students frequently report that certain school districts, and perhaps entire states, have established a rigid discrepancy criterion (e.g., a 50% gap between achievement and ability, as measured by intelligence tests). Overly rigid testing approaches appear to be illegal under the EAHCA (Martin, 1993), requiring their replacement by assessment methods and techniques that can provide enough information on pertinent variables to allow sound decision making.

Keogh's (1994) decision-making matrix is particularly useful as a heuristic for broadening the scope of assessment. According to the model, decisions about which evaluation methods to use need to consider qualitative methods as viable additions or alternatives to quantitative methods when formulating a comprehensive assessment. The model encourages broadening parameters even more widely by considering both indirect and direct observation techniques as options that may be used when evaluating variables that are elusive but that can provide critical evidence of some subtle forms of LDs.

For example, when evaluating an older, brighter individual suspected of having a reading disability, one would decide whether to include qualitative methods and indirect assessment techniques as part of interpreting the psychometric data obtained. Given what is known about the coexistence of spoken language, attentional, and self-organizational deficiencies in people with reading disabilities (i.e., in dyslexia-plus; Denckla & Rumsey, 1992), the likelihood of finding comordid deficits would make at least an informal and indirect examination of such deficits relevant components of a multifaceted evaluation. Accordingly, careful interviewing to gather naturalistic case history data would be considered critical to obtaining the information needed to make a formal diagnosis. Ultimately, a personal history of preschool language inefficiency and a family history of disorders of language and achievement could form the convergent evidence needed to accurately diagnose a reading disability.

Given the life-long at-risk status of an individual whose biobehavioral disabilities would readily escape detection when focusing too narrowly on psychometric data, the importance of systematically attending to a broad set of decision factors when interpreting psychological tests cannot be overemphasized. In the section that follows, I focus on Keogh's (1994) five decision points (i.e., those relating to the purpose, domains, target variables, and methods and techniques of testing) as aids in arriving at a sound clinical judgment when addressing thorny issues relating to the use and interpretation of standardized tests when LDs are a dimension of diversity.

Deciding on the Use and Interpretations of Standardized Tests

Purpose of Testing

Decisions about the use and interpretation of standardized tests for people with LDs are particularly compelling when high-stakes outcomes hinge on their ability to show their qualifications through their test performance. Because LDs are frequently accompanied by language disorders, executive dysfunction, attention deficits, and hyperactivity residing alongside at least average intellectual abilities, a strong potential for bias in testing practices makes decisions about test selection, administration, and interpretation especially consequential. (See chapter 14 in this book for a comprehensive discussion relating to this topic.)

Although the issue of unfair test practices receives much legal scrutiny, existing court rulings are equivocal and reflect the prevailing confusion in conceptualizing LDs. For example, such confusion was evidenced in the opposing sides that were taken in 1997 proceedings about whether to allow medical or law licensing candidates with purported LDs to take their licensing examinations under test accommodations (*Disability Compliance Bulletin*, 1997).

In a 1997 West Virginia proceeding involving three medical students as the plaintiffs and the National Board of Medical Examiners as the defendant (*Price v. National Board of Medical Examiners*, as cited in *Disability Compliance Bulletin*, 1997), the conflict centered on whether to consider these students' alleged ADHD to be a qualifying disability under the Americans With Disabilities Act (ADA) and thus allow them to take their licensing examination under special accommodations. The requested accommodations included a quiet testing room and more time than allowable by standardized test directions, accommodations to which people with disabilities are commonly entitled under Title III of the ADA (Eyde, Nester, Heaton, & Nelson, 1994). The presiding U.S. district judge denied the right to such accommodations, stating that, given the students' outstanding achievement, they did not show an impairment that substantially limited one or more major life activities, an earmark of a disability under the ADA. The decision was a victory for the National Board of Medical Examiners, which has received a steadily increasing number of requests for accommodations over the past few years. However, according to the plaintiffs' attorney, the judge's decision failed to consider that the students had had to compensate for their learning disability to achieve their academic success and that they had been "penalized for their being successful in overcoming adversity" (as cited in *Disability Compliance Bulletin*, 1997, p. 11).

In a departure from *Price v. National Board of Medical Examiners* (as cited in *Disability Compliance Bulletin*, 1997) a U.S. district judge in New York ruled in favor of a 49-year-old college professor with dyslexia against the New York State Board of Bar Examiners (*Bartlett v. New York*

State Board of Bar Examiners, cited in *Disability Compliance Bulletin*, 1997) to permit her to be examined with more time than allowed by test directions after having failed her bar examination five times. In a 131-page ruling, the judge stated that dyslexia substantially limited the plaintiff's major life activities, relative to those of her professional peers, and that failing to pass the bar examination would disqualify her from "thousands of jobs and hundreds of employers" (cited in *Disability Compliance Bulletin*, 1997, p. 10).

Under the ADA, showing an impairment that substantially limits one or more of a person's major life activities is only one of the criteria used for identifying a disability. Having a record of impairment and being regarded by the covered entity as having such an impairment are the second and third criteria (Equal Employment Opportunity Commission & U.S. Department of Justice, 1992; Eyde et al., 1994). However, unlike other disabilities, the confusion relating to classification and identification issues in the case of LDs prevents the authoritative use of the third criterion. That is, a fruitless tautology develops when LDs as the "covered entity" are expected to dictate assignment to that entity. The result is widespread variation in national and state testing programs with regard to providing test accommodations for this invisible condition (National Center on Educational Outcomes, 1993). Moreover, testing programs can be too stringent to account for the subtle forms of LDs, which may easily elude school identification (Denckla, 1989). For example, the Educational Testing Service in Princeton, New Jersey, requires that three conditions be satisfied for an untimed test taking of the Scholastic Assessment Test (SAT): letters obtained from two professionals not working together on the same team, each of whom must state that the individual has a diagnosis of LDs, and guidelines met for LDs in the state in which the person resides (National Center for Learning Disabilities, 1989). (Only one letter is needed when a diagnosis of LDs is made in a school-based evaluation that meets state requirements.)

Testing Domains

Decisions about whether and how to use standardized tests with people with LDs are different from those involving people with visible handicapping conditions, such as sensory or motor disorders. The difference makes the need to attend to the greater subtlety of the possible sources of bias in the testing environment critical to the decision-making process.

The overlap and heterogeneity of impaired cognitive processes that can form part of an LD (Denckla & Rumsey, 1992) make an evaluation of the particular setting characteristics of a testing situation important. Assurance is needed that such a setting will not aggravate problems with attention, sensory integration, visual discrimination, and motor processes and thus prevent people from exhibiting their qualifications equitably through their test performance (Bennett, Rock, & Kaplan, 1987).

Setting characteristics that have received much consideration, although insufficient research scrutiny, include those relating to time pressure or distracting surroundings as sources of undue hardship for test takers with LDs (Sattler, 1988). There is a professional and legal consensus that potentially debilitating demand characteristics, such as time constraints, should be eliminated unless such elimination would significantly alter the assessment of the skills a test is intended to measure (see chapter 14 in this book). However, the unsettling outcome in *Price v. National Board of Medical Examiners* (cited in *Disability Compliance Bulletin*, 1997) points to the complexity of deciding what is relevant to a psychological construct as well as to the fact that sociopolitical expediency, rather than construct validation, is the prevailing mode of legitimizing high-stakes decisions made on the basis of scores obtained on standardized examinations (Haladyna, 1994; Kane, 1992, 1994).

Target Variables

In a challenging approach to addressing the issue of construct validation, Kane (1992, 1994) and Haladyna (1994) proposed that the target variables of interest are those relating to *interpretations* assigned to scores rather than to the scores themselves when judging the merits of standardized testing. With regard to licensure and certification examinations, an argument-based approach to construct validation demands that the inferences underlying test interpretations be made so explicit that operational definitions of professional competence may be derived from them. Applied to *Price v. National Board of Medical Examiners* (as cited in *Disability Compliance Bulletin*, 1997), an argument-based approach to judging the merits of standardized testing would have required that the medical students' licensing examination scores be interpretable enough to explain the implications of their compensatory skills on their future professional performance.

A focus on the importance or interpretations assigned to test scores, rather than the test scores themselves, also figured prominently in the work of Barnett and Macmann (1992) with regard to clinical decision making in the school setting. In their criticism of widespread misinterpretation of aptitude–achievement discrepancies in qualifying students for special education services, Barnett and Macmann contended that testing practices should be geared toward collaborative problem solving. Such practices promote multifaceted analyses of problem situations, and those analyses furnish their own impetus for evaluating intervention objectives as a means of securing construct validation.

In a similar vein, Rizzo (1993) focused on the interpretative argument as a framework for making clinical judgments in the medical setting. According to Rizzo (1993), qualitative methods, including "foraging for consensus by expert panels" (p. 1451), need to be encouraged in medical decision making because data gathered from quantitative evaluations are frequently inconclusive.

With regard to LDs, the proposal for emphasizing interpretations of scores, rather than the scores themselves, is a frank acknowledgment that LDs are a stipulative entity whose meaning is defined by the shared perceptions of particular reference groups. Presently lacking robust taxonomies of homogeneous deficits and homogeneous subtypes of the disorder, the importance of interpretative approaches resides in the potential for construct development through the validating input of shared knowledge (Kavale, Forness, & Lorsbach, 1991).

Methods and Techniques

An emphasis on interpretation is consistent with the need for test users to include multiple measures of functioning whenever high-stakes decisions are made on the basis of test performance. When situations demand that a person with a disability take a standardized test so that educational, intervention, employment, or other important decisions can be made, it is imperative that the measurement process be geared toward providing the most accurate picture of that person's qualifications (American Psychological Association, 1992). To that end, results of qualitative methods and indirect techniques of assessment, possibly involving a multidisciplinary evaluation team, should be incorporated into the test interpretations. Such methods and techniques include record reviews, interviews, and informal observations in various settings and by various sources.

Following the outcome in *Price v. National Board of Medical Examiners* (as cited in *Disability Compliance Bulletin*, 1997), clinical inferential methods may become increasingly important aspects of standardized testing. Given that the courts are presently less likely to allow subtle forms of LDs to qualify as disabilities under the ADA, as they have been in the past (*Disability Compliance Bulletin*, 1997), test users (e.g., universities and licensing boards) may be increasingly pressured to interpret scores in terms of whether they accurately represent the qualifications needed by test takers to achieve their individual goals. Thus, decisions about using standardized tests will inevitably be tempered by the challenge imposed in making ideographic (i.e., clinical interpretative) analyses of a person's functioning relative to the objectives of testing.

The divergent outcomes in *Price v. National Board of Medical Examiners* (as cited in *Disability Compliance Bulletin*, 1997) and *Bartlett v. New York State Board of Bar Examiners* (as cited in *Disability Compliance Bulletin*, 1997) reflect the difference in determining a disability with regard to one form of LD versus another in that the request to accommodate a test taker's dyslexia was less refutable than the request to accommodate more subtle impairments in those respective cases. Nonetheless, in any given situation, complex sociopolitical factors make decisions about the provision of special accommodations inherently problematic (Hishinuma, 1995). This issue is addressed next, again using Keogh's (1994) decision points to frame the discussion.

Deciding on Provision of Test Accommodations

Purpose of Testing

Because special accommodations involve the risks of obtaining meaningless scores and producing an unfair advantage to people with disabilities, test users find themselves in a "catch-22" position whenever they consider providing them to eliminate discriminatory practices (Hishinuma, 1995; also see chapter 14 in this book). However, by relating the degree of risks imposed by accommodations to the particular purpose of testing, it may be possible to arrive at a method of judging the reasonableness of using them under given conditions. Klimoski and Palmer (1993) suggested such a method by underscoring the fact that the different types of accommodations vary greatly in the risks they impose on the psychometric integrity of standardized tests. Therefore, according to Klimoski and Palmer, accommodations should be placed on a continuum to form three levels of their potential psychometric impact. Level 1 accommodations would have no appreciable impact. Adapting table height and extending time limits for power tests are two examples because, in these cases, there is relatively little concern about the effects of deviating from standardized procedures. Level 2 accommodations would have a possible psychometric impact (e.g., extending time limits for speeded tests). Waiving one or more tests in a test battery represents the risks involved at Level 3, the level at which accommodations would have their most significant impact.

By relating the purpose of testing to Klimoski and Palmer's (1993) classification arrangement, a decision-making matrix can be developed for weighing the risks imposed by special accommodations in given instances. Using such a matrix, competitive conditions requiring high-stakes decisions by test users (e.g., examinations for professional licensure) would be rated as being incompatible with the high-level risks to test validity associated with Level 2 and Level 3 accommodations, whereas Level 1 accommodations would be rated as being more acceptable. Conditions suitable for Level 2 and Level 3 accommodations would include those that allow supplemental tests of the same or related construct, as, for example, the comprehensive evaluations conducted by collaborative decision-making teams for identifying LDs. The compatibility of risk factors in the latter situation would be due to the fact that the high risks imposed by specific accommodations would be offset by the relatively low level of risks involved in fulfilling the purpose of testing (i.e., accurately diagnosing LDs).

Domains of Testing

A consideration of setting characteristics is another important decision factor when judging the compatibility of risks whenever special test accommodations are used. As the preceding discussion implies, the format of testing may affect the risks imposed by Level 2 and Level 3 accommodations. Accordingly, because these types of accommodations should be used with extreme caution, their implementation is most defensible when used with multiple measures from the same conceptual domain and multifaceted data analyses conducted by multidisciplinary teams.

Target Variables

Although the consideration of risks to test validity is consistent with sound decision making, there is virtually no research knowledge on the psychometric effects of accommodations when used with specific exceptionalities (American Educational Research Association, American Psychological Association, & National Council on Measurement in Education, 1985; Nester, 1993; Tenopyr, Angoff, Butcher, Geisinger, & Reilly, 1993). The lack of research evidence is particularly disturbing when LDs are the handicapping condition because the target variables (e.g., measures of academic achievement) that are scrutinized in competitive high-stakes situations are usually those that are most problematic for people with LDs. More specifically, measures of academic achievement demand intact verbal processing skills, and tests of verbal processing, particularly those with reading components, pose particular difficulty for people with LDs because of their problems in organizing sensory information, visual discrimination, and attention (Bennett et al., 1987; Eyde et al., 1994). Although Level 1 accommodations are commonly used to address these processing difficulties, the heterogeneity and complexity of dysfunction that characterize LDs prevent the systematic removal of sources of test bias and thus provide no assurance that the use of accommodations will result in improved assessment (Bennett, 1995).

Methods and Techniques

Special accommodations for people with LDs commonly include extending or suspending time limits, printing test questions in large type, and putting test items on an audiotape (Bennett et al., 1987; Rock, Bennett, & Kaplan, 1987). However, given the lack of research, Hishinuma (1995) reminded test users that they may be able to select standardized tests that furnish their own accommodations, as a way of minimizing threats to test validity, when having to meet the needs of people with LDs. For example, the Wechsler Intelligence Scale for Children–Third Edition (WISC-III; the Psychological Corporation, 1991) already provides some accommodations via its test items and administration protocol. No reading or decoding is required of examinees, with the negligible exception of the last six questions of the Arithmetic subtest, which can be read by examiners if examinees cannot read them. Nor is any written expression (such as an essay) required. Furthermore, the WISC-III is administered one on one, which allows examiners to control problematic behaviors, including inattention, distractibility, and impulsivity. Moreover, examiners may assess such behaviors as sources of bias in test taking using the *Guide to the Assessment of Test Session Behavior for the WISC-III and the WIAT* (Wechsler Individual Achievement Test; the Psychological Corporation, 1992b), a test that provides scoring criteria for these behaviors, as demonstrated during a WISC-III or other standardized test administration.

In addition to the WISC-III, other commonly used standardized tests provide built-in accommodations, either by design or coincidence. For instance, the Reading Comprehension subtest of the Woodcock–Johnson Psychoeducational Battery–Revised (WJ-R; Woodcock & Mather, 1989–1990) imposes no time constraints for reading and responding to test items other than the direction given in the manual that examiners maintain a "brisk administration" (p. 25). Accordingly, examiners concerned with the confounding impact of ADHD characteristics on reading comprehension may decide to use this subtest rather than one that does impose time specifications. For example, directions for the Reading Comprehension subtest on the Wechsler Individual Achievement Test (the Psychological Corporation, 1992a) specifically state in the manual that 15 s are allowed to respond to each orally presented question and also state that, after about 1 min, if the examinee is not making progress in reading a passage, the examiner is to move to the next item by saying, "Let's go on" (p. 47).

However, examiners selecting the WJ-R subtest, for example, to remove the confounding impact of attentional inefficiency on reading comprehension, need be wary of overestimating the reading abilities of intellectually proficient people who lack rapid reading recognition skills—the hallmark of dyslexia—but have acquired the compensatory skill of using contextual clues to decipher the meaning of a written passage. Moreover, by eliminating time constraints, examiners also may underestimate difficulties in the development of study skills. The latter possibility was suggested by Willingham (1988), who found that a nonstandard administration of the SAT overpredicted grades obtained in the first year of college by 0.39 *SD*s for individuals with LDs. Such overprediction has been interpreted as having been the result of the nonstandard administration's failure to account for the time management, organization, and other study skills needed to be successful in college (Hishinuma, 1995). Similar conclusions have also been reported in other research on the predictive validity of college entrance examinations for special-tested students (e.g., Wightman, 1993; Ziomek & Andrews, 1996).

The problematic issue of overprediction noted in the aforementioned studies suggests that a more useful approach to accommodations than one that allows only generous timing for examinees with disabilities may be one that also allows such timing for those without them. Moreover, as has been pointed out by Bennett (1995), generalized accommodations are both feasible and forthcoming through major design changes in testing programs based on the computer testing of everyone.

Because decision making in the case of LDs is a particularly vexing process, bias in test interpretation is an ever-present threat to the valid and reliable use of psychological tests as sources of needed information. I now discuss this issue.

Deciding When To Expect Bias in Test Interpretation

Purpose of Testing

Bias in test interpretation occurs because test-taker needs, professional standards, federal legislation, psychometric theory, and empirical research represent divergent perspectives that lack the synthesis needed to guide decision making (Sherman & Robinson, 1982). As indicated in the preceding section, the issue of bias especially relates to controversies about the methods of interpreting scores obtained under nonstandard testing conditions by people with disabilities to demonstrate their qualifications in competitive, high-stakes situations. In particular, the controversy about "flagging" is characteristic of the professional discord on this issue. The position taken by the ADA is that any "preadmission inquiry" is prohibited under law to avoid providing information on the nature of a person's disability that could be discriminatory (Equal Employment Opportunity Commission & U.S. Department of Justice, 1992). A competing position, derived from psychometric theory, is that scores obtained under modified conditions need to be flagged because their comparability to those obtained under standardized procedures is questionable (Bennett, 1995). However, because of the ban imposed by the ADA on divulging information that could be prejudicial, flagging usually occurs without noting the specific modifications used or providing guidelines for interpreting results relative to research conducted on these modifications (Mehrens, 1997). Thus, although the ban protects the right to confidentiality, it also undermines the professional obligation to understand the unique characteristics of test takers to make unbiased interpretative judgments. Although resolving the "comparability" issue by finding ways to equate scores obtained with and without modifications may be the only logical solution to the dilemma created by the ban against preadmission inquiry, such a goal is almost impossible to attain (Mehrens, 1997).

Mehrens (1997) discussed the unresolvable nature of the comparability issue in a paper prepared to facilitate discussion at a planning meeting on test score flagging policies sponsored by the Board on Testing and Assessment at the National Academy of Sciences. One of Mehren's (1997) main conclusions was that "there are serious problems in doing definitive research on the comparability question because of the numerous types and degrees of disabilities and types of accommodations" (p. 4). More specifically regarding LDs, the fundamental problem relates to the issue that there is no robust classification system of types and subtypes of the disorder (Morris, 1993).

Although competitive, high-stakes situations create the most compelling challenges to maintaining objectivity, the lack of a valid classification system in LDs promotes a potential for bias in most situations in which testing technology is used for selection purposes. Reasons to test individuals with LDs are to determine eligibility, plan for services, assess outcomes, conduct research, and promote advocacy (Keogh, 1994). Regulations concerning each of these purposes are different. For example, the criteria adopted by schools to identify LDs result in groupings that lack the homogeneity required of subject pools to be used for research (Keogh, 1993). Moreover, internecine battles rage over the selection criteria (e.g., aptitude–achievement discrepancy formulas) needed for meeting any of these objectives (e.g., determining eligibility). Thus, because political squabbles tend to characterize professional dialogue and relationships, the potential for ideological and confirmatory biases threatens even the most routine situations for which test interpretations will be used to guide selection decisions (Kavale, 1993).

There are many sources of bias in test interpretations. Some stem from the rigid adherence to a theoretical orientation (e.g., neuropsychological, cognitive- and information-processing, achievement and behavioral), to collegial opinions, or to personal values (Rabinowitz, 1993). Additionally, the inadequate understanding and application of statistical principles by many psychological examiners is a frequent impediment to the reliability of selection processes (Ross, 1995). Stereotypical expectancies regarding client variables, including ethnicity, race, gender, and intellectual achievement, also undermine objectivity. For example, Payette and Clarizio (1994) found that being White, male, older, and of higher ability and achievement reduced the likelihood of the school identification of LDs despite meeting the state-regulated aptitude–achievement discrepancies required for such identification. More general biases and constraints that contribute to selection errors include overconfidence in one's judgments, underestimation of performance variability, and overemphasis on salient cues (Kleinmuntz, 1990); overreliance on impressive computer printouts has been singled out as a common example of the noncritical acceptance of the face validity of misleading test interpretations to guide selection decisions (Butcher, 1994).

Test users need be wary of the many sources of potential bias. The overall formulation of an assessment plan can be seriously hampered by ignorance about the many pitfalls biases impose on the validity of psychological measurement.

Testing Domains and Target Variables

With specific regard to LDs, decisions pertaining to the domains of testing (i.e., focus on the individual or the setting) and the specific target variables within these domains (e.g., attentional skills, ability to use problem-solving strategies, etc.) reflect test users' views about the nature of LDs. Thus, such views undermine objectivity unless they are taken to be hypotheses that compete with other hypotheses that may better explain the specific contingencies of a given situation. For example, the overexpectation of the neurological basis of LDs could result in underestimating classroom climate as an important variable needing consideration in a comprehensive assessment. A consequence could be attributing neurologically based deficits to a student whose learning problems stem mainly from disruptive peer models and an overcrowded classroom.

Techniques and Methods

Similar to decisions about domains of testing and target variables, decisions pertaining to indirect versus direct assessment techniques and qualitative versus quantitative observational methods present potentials for bias unless such decisions are related to the particular context of testing. Although the direct, quantitative approach associated with the psychometric tradition holds the greatest appeal for psychologists, it represents only a portion of the instruments and systems, for both direct and indirect measurement, that have utility and power under particular conditions (Evertson & Green, 1986). Importantly, a qualitative, indirect approach may provide better examples of behaviors and abilities that represent an individual's competencies or problems than one that is psychometrically flawed or used inappropriately (Keogh, 1994). Thus, the need for fair-mindedness requires that test users familiarize themselves with documentation in support of nontraditional assessment procedures provided by authoritative sources (e.g., the *12th Mental Measurements Yearbook;* Conoley & Impara, 1995), so that they may use them confidently. A full armamentarium is needed when attempting to assess the complexities and realities of LDs.

Conclusion

A discussion of test interpretation issues underscores the fact that improved frames of reference for assessing LDs depend on their improved conceptualizations. Unfortunately, such understanding is seriously hindered by counterproductive influences that are both intellectual and political. Nonetheless, despite the subjectivity of professional dialogue and relationships, and the diversity of sociopolitical forces, the field of LDs is not necessarily prevented from building the knowledge base needed to make it more scientific. Consistent with a constructionist perspective, Kavale (1993) proposed that this is the case because the process of knowledge accumulation is akin to the process of natural selection. As such, it involves negotiations and arguments among those who hold competing ideas and the marshaling, often selectively, of the evidence to bear on a position vying for dominance over others. Eventually, this sociopolitical and theoretical process results in a synthesis of competing vantage points and the building of a consensual body of knowledge. Accordingly, Kavale (1993) emphasized the importance of building a metatheoretical frame of reference on LDs to consolidate intellectual thought on the subject. Similarly, Morris (1994b) argued for working toward dialectic synthesis by developing a macrolevel theory that could coordinate individual theories into a comprehensive and unified perspective about the LD phenomenon. Moreover, Morris (1994b) challenged government agencies (e.g., the National Institutes of Health) to provide the necessary infrastructure to enlist expert working groups who could help LD researchers better define their constructs and measure these constructs. If this clarion call heralded by Kavale,

Morris, and others is heeded, the field of LDs should be able to build the classification taxonomies needed for it to become more scientific.

Test users should feel encouraged by the theory development that leading scholars believe is lying ahead for LDs. More definitive frameworks for assessing LDs should follow this envisioned theoretical integration. The paradox remains, however, that an entity that defines itself as a "disability" is necessarily subject to the social, political, and legal ramifications that decide whether problem conditions may be considered "disabilities." It follows that, with regard to LDs, test interpretations will always demand more than the assignment to a predetermined category.

References

American Educational Research Association, American Psychological Association, & National Council on Measurement in Education (1985). *Standards for educational and psychological testing* (Rev. ed.). Washington, DC: American Psychological Association.

American Psychiatric Association. (1994). *Diagnostic and statistical manual of mental disorders* (4th ed.). Washington, DC: Author.

American Psychological Association. (1992). *Ethical principles and code of conduct.* Washington, DC: Author.

Barnett, D. W., & Macmann, G. M. (1992). Aptitude-achievement discrepancy scores: Accuracy in analysis misdirected. *School Psychology Review, 21,* 494–508.

Bennett, R. E. (1995). *Computer-based testing for examinees with disabilities: On the road to generalized accommodation* (Research Memo 95-1). Princeton, NJ: Educational Testing Service.

Bennett, R. E., Rock, D. A., & Kaplan, B. A. (1987). SAT differential item performance for nine handicapped groups. *Journal of Educational Measurement, 24,* 41–55.

Berninger, V. W., & Abbott, R. D. (1994). Redefining learning disabilities: Moving beyond aptitude-achievement discrepancies to failure to respond to validated treatment protocols, In G. R. Lyon (Ed.), *Frames of reference for the assessment of learning disabilities: New views on measurement issues* (pp. 163–184). Baltimore: Brookes.

Blashfield, R. K. (1993). Models of classification as related to a taxonomy of learning disabilities. In G. R. Lyon, D. B. Gray, J. F. Kavanagh, & N. A. Krasnegor (Eds.), *Better understanding learning disabilities: New views for research and their implications for education and public policies* (pp. 17–26). Baltimore: Brookes.

Butcher, J. N. (1994). Psychological assessment by computer: Potential gains and problems to avoid. *Psychiatric Annals, 24,* 20–24.

Clements, S. D. (1966). *Minimal brain dysfunction in children: Terminology and identification* (PHS Pub. No. 141). Washington, DC: U.S. Department of Health, Education, and Welfare.

Coles, G. S. (1987). *The learning mystique: A critical look at learning disabilities.* New York: Pantheon Books.

Cone, T. E., & Wilson, L. R. (1981). Quantifying a severe discrepancy: A critical analysis. *Learning Disability Quarterly, 4,* 163–174.

Conoley, J. C., & Impara, J. D. (1995). *The twelfth mental measurements yearbook.* Lincoln, University of Nebraska, Buros Institute of Mental Measurements.

Dangel, H. L., & Ensminger, E. E. (1988). The use of a discrepancy formula with LD students. *Learning Disability Focus, 4,* 24–31.

Denckla, M. B. (1989). Executive function, the overlap zone between attention deficit hyperactivity disorder and learning disabilities. *International Pediatrics, 4,* 155–160.

Denckla, M. B., & Rumsey, J. M. (1992). Developmental dyslexia. In A. K. Asbury, G. M. McKhann, & W. I. McDonald (Eds.), *Diseases of the nervous system: Clinical neurobiology* (pp. 636–645). Philadelphia: W. B. Saunders.

Disability Compliance Bulletin. (1997, July 31). Medical students with learning disabilities not entitled to accommodations, court rules. *LRP Publications,* pp. 1, 10–11.

Doris, J. L. (1993). Defining learning disabilities: A history of the search for consensus. In G. R. Lyon, D. B. Gray, J. F. Kavanagh, & N. A. Krasnegor (Eds.), *Better understanding learning disabilities: New views from research and their implications for educational and public policies* (pp. 97–116). Baltimore: Brookes.

Education of All Handicapped Children Act of 1977, 20 U.S.C. 1401 *et seq.,* 42 Fed. Reg. 65082.

Equal Employment Opportunity Commission and U.S. Department of Justice. (1992). *Americans With Disabilities Act handbook* (EEOC Publication No. 92-19). Washington, DC: U.S. Government Printing Office.

Evertson, C. M., & Green, J. L. (1986). Observation as inquiry and method. In M. C. Wittrock (Ed.), *Handbook of research on teaching* (3rd ed., pp. 162–213). New York: Macmillan.

Eyde, L. D., Nester, M. A., Heaton, S. M., & Nelson, A. V. (1994). *Guide for administering written employment examinations to persons with disabilities* (PRDC Publication No. 94-11). Washington, DC: U.S. Office of Personnel Management, Personnel Research and Development Center.

Finucci, J., & Childs, B. (1991). Are there really more dyslexic boys than girls? In A. Ansara, N. Geschwind, A. Galaburda, M. Albert, & N. Gartrell (Eds.), *Sex differences in dyslexia* (pp. 1–9). Towson, MD: Orton Dyslexia Society.

Fletcher, J. M., Francis, D. J., Rourke, B. P., Shaywitz, S. E., & Shaywitz, B. A. (1993). Classification of learning disabilities: Relationships with other childhood disorders. In G. R. Lyon, D. B. Gray, J. F. Kavanagh, & N. A. Krasnegor (Eds.), *Better understanding learning disabilities: New views from research and their implications for education and public policies* (pp. 18–27). Baltimore: Brookes.

Frankenberger, W., & Fronzaglio, K. (1991). A review of states' criteria and procedures for identifying children with learning disabilities. *Journal of Learning Disabilities, 24,* 495–500.

Greenwood, C. R. (1996). The case for performance-based instructional models. *School Psychology Quarterly, 11,* 283–296.

Haladyna, T. M. (1994). A research agenda for licensing and certification testing validation studies [Special Issue]. *Evaluation and the Health Professions, 17,* 242–256.

Hishinuma, E. S. (1995). WISC-III accommodations: The need for practitioner guidelines. *Journal of Learning Disabilities, 28,* 130–135.

Hughes, J. R., & Denckla, M. B. (1978). Outline of a pilot study of electroencephalographic correlates of dyslexia. In A. L. Benton & D. Pearl (Eds.), *Dyslexia: An appraisal of current knowledge* (pp. 112–122). New York: Oxford University Press.

Interagency Committee on Learning Disabilities. (1987). *Learning disabilities: A report to the U.S. Congress* (ICLD Publication No. 87-47/2). Washington, DC: Author.

Kane, M. T. (1992). An argument-based approach to validity. *Psychological Bulletin, 112,* 527–535.

Kane, M. T. (1994). Validating interpretive arguments for licensure and certification examinations [Special Issue]. *Evaluation and the Health Professions, 17,* 133–159.

Kavale, K. A. (1993). A science and theory of learning disabilities. In G. R. Lyon, D. B. Gray, J. F. Kavanagh, & N. A. Krasnegor (Eds.), *Better understanding learning disabilities: New views from research and their implications for education and public policies* (pp. 171–196). Baltimore: Brookes.

Kavale, K., & Forness, S. (1985). *The science of learning disabilities.* Boston: College Hill Press.

Kavale, K. A., Forness, S. R., & Lorsbach, T. C. (1991). Definition for definitions of learning disabilities. *Learning Disability Quarterly, 14,* 257–266.

Keogh, B. K. (1982). Research in learning disabilities: A view of status and need. In J. P. Das, R. F. Mulcahy, & A. E. Wall (Eds.), *Theory and research in learning disabilities* (pp. 27–44). New York: Plenum.

Keogh, B. K. (1993). Linking purpose and practice: Social-political and developmental perspectives on classification. In G. R. Lyon, D. B. Gray, J. F. Kavanagh, & N. A. Krasnegor (Eds.), *Better understanding learning disabilities: New views from research and their implications for educational and public policies* (pp. 311–324). Baltimore: Brookes.

Keogh, B. K. (1994). A matrix of decision points in the measurement of learning disabilities. In G. R. Lyon (Ed.), *Frames of reference for the assessment of learning disabilities: New views on measurement issues* (pp. 15–26). Baltimore: Brookes.

Kirk, S. A. (1975). Behavioral diagnosis and remediation of learning disorders. In S. A. Kirk & J. M. McCarthy (Eds.), *Learning disabilities: Selected ACLD papers* (pp. 7–10). Boston: Houghton Mifflin.

Kleinmuntz, B. (1990). Why we still use our heads instead of formulas: Toward an integrative approach. *Psychological Bulletin, 107,* 296–310.

Klimoski, R., & Palmer, S. (1993). The ADA and the hiring process in organizations. *Consulting Psychology Journal, 45,* 10–36.

Martin, E. W. (1993). Learning disabilities and public policy: Myths and outcomes. In G. R. Lyon, D. B. Gray, J. F. Kavanagh, & N. A. Krasnegor (Eds.), *Better understanding learning disabilities: New views from research and their implications for educational and public policies* (pp. 325–342). Baltimore: Brookes.

Mehrens, W. A. (1997). *Flagging test scores: Policy, practice, and research.* Unpublished manuscript.

Meltzer, L. J. (1994). Assessment of learning disabilities: The challenge of evaluating the cognitive strategies and processes underlying learning. In G. R. Lyon (Ed.), *Frames of reference for the assessment of learning disabilities: New views on measurement issues* (pp. 571–606). Baltimore: Brookes.

Mercer, C. D. (1991). *Students with learning disabilities* (4th ed.). New York: Merrill Press.

Morris, R. (1993). Issues in empirical versus clinical identification of learning disabilities. In G. R. Lyon, D. B. Gray, J. F. Kavanagh, & N. A. Krasnegor (Eds.), *Better understanding learning disabilities: New views from research and their implications for educational and public policies* (pp. 73–95). Baltimore: Brookes.

Morris, R. (1994a). Multidimensional neuropsychological assessment models: Potential and problems. In G. R. Lyon (Ed.), *Frames of reference for the assessment of learning disabilities: New views on measurement issues* (pp. 515–522). Baltimore: Brookes.

Morris, R. (1994b). A review of critical concepts and issues in the measurement of learning disabilities. In G. R. Lyon (Ed.), *Frames of reference for the assessment of learning disabilities: New views on measurement issues* (pp. 615–626). Baltimore: Brookes.

Myers, P. I., & Hammill, D. D. (1996). *Learning disabilities: Basic concepts, assessment practices, and instructional strategies* (4th ed.). Austin, TX: Pro-Ed.

National Center on Educational Outcomes. (1993). *Accommodating students with disabilities in national and state testing programs* (Brief Rep. No. 9). Minneapolis, MN: Author.

National Center for Learning Disabilities. (1989). *The General Educational Development Testing Service and the American Council on Education: The Center for Adult Learning and Educational Credentialing.* New York: Author.

Nester, M. A. (1993). Psychometric testing and reasonable accommodation for persons with disabilities. *Rehabilitation Psychology, 38,* 75–85.

Oakland, T., & Cunningham, J. L. (1990). Advocates for educational services for all children need improved research and conceptual bases. *School Psychology Quarterly, 5,* 66–77.

Payette, K. A., & Clarizio, H. F. (1994). Discrepant team decisions: The effects of race, gender, achievement, and IQ on LD eligibility. *Psychology in the Schools, 31,* 40–48.

The Psychological Corporation. (1991). *Wechsler Intelligence Scale for Children–Third Edition: Examiner's manual.* San Antonio, TX: Harcourt Brace Jovanovich.

The Psychological Corporation. (1992a). *Guide to the assessment of test session behavior for the WISC-III and the WIAT: Examiner's manual.* San Antonio, TX: Harcourt Brace Jovanovich.

The Psychological Corporation. (1992b). *Wechsler Individual Achievement Test: Examiner's manual.* San Antonio, TX: Harcourt Brace Jovanovich.

Rabinowitz, J. (1993). Diagnostic reasoning and reliability: A review of the literature and a model of decision-making. *Journal of Mind and Behavior, 14,* 297–315.

Rizzo, J. A. (1993). Physician uncertainty and the art of persuasion. *Social Science and Medicine, 37,* 1451–1459.

Rock, D. A., Bennett, R. E., & Kaplan, B. A. (1987). Internal construct validity of a college admissions test across handicapped and nonhandicapped groups. *Educational and Psychological Measurement, 47,* 193–205.

Ross, R. P. (1995). Impact on psychologists of state guidelines for evaluating underachievement. *Learning Disability Quarterly, 18,* 43–56.

Rourke, B. P. (1994). Neuropsychological assessment of children with learning disabilities: Measurement issues. In G. R. Lyon (Ed.), *Frames of reference for the assessment of learning disabilities: New views on measurement issues* (pp. 475–514). Baltimore: Brookes.

Sattler, J. M. (1988). *Assessment of children* (3rd ed.). San Diego, CA: Author.

Scarr, S. (1985). Constructing psychology: Making facts and fables for our times. *American Psychologist, 40,* 499–512.

Schuerholz, L. J., Harris, E. L., Baumgardner, T. L., Reiss, A. L., Freund, L. S., Church, R. P., Mohr, J., & Denckla, M. B. (1995). An analysis of two discrepancy-based models and a processing-deficit approach in identifying learning disabilities. *Journal of Learning Disabilities, 28,* 18–29.

Sherman, S., & Robinson, N. (1982). *Ability testing and handicapped people: dilemma for government, science, and the public.* Washington, DC: National Academy Press.

Silver, L. B. (1990). Attention deficit hyperactivity disorder: Is it a learning disability or a related disorder? *Journal of Learning Disabilities, 23,* 394–397.

Stanovich, K. E. (1993). The construct validity of discrepancy definitions of reading disability. In G. R. Lyon, D. B. Gray, J. F. Kavanagh, & N. A. Krasnegor (Eds.), *Better understanding learning disabilities: New views from research and their implications for educational and public policies* (pp. 273–308). Baltimore: Brookes.

Strauss, A. A., & Lehtinen, L. E. (1947). *Psychopathology and education of the brain injured child*. New York: Grune & Stratton.

Swanson, H. L. (1993). Learning disabilities from the perspective of cognitive psychology. In G. R. Lyon, D. B. Gray, J. F. Kavanagh, & N. A. Kasnegor (Eds.), *Better understanding learning disabilities: New views from research and their implications for education and public policies* (pp. 199–228). Baltimore: Brookes.

Tenopyr, M. L., Angoff, W. H., Butcher, J. N., Geisinger, K. F., & Reilly, R. R. (1993). Psychometric and assessment issues raised by the Americans With Disabilities Act (ADA). *The Score Newsletter, 15*, pp. 1–2, 7–15.

Torgesen, J. K. (1994). Issues in the assessment of executive function: An information-processing perspective. In G. R. Lyon (Ed.), *Frames of reference for the assessment of learning disabilities: New views on measurement issues* (pp. 143–162). Baltimore: Brookes.

U.S. Office of Education. (1968). *First annual report of the National Advisory Committee on Handicapped Children* (OE Publication No. 68-969). Washington, DC: U.S. Department of Health, Education, and Welfare.

Wender, P. H. (1971). *Minimal brain dysfunction in children*. New York: Wiley.

Wightman, L. F. (1993). *Test takers with disabilities: A summary of data from special accommodations of the LSAT* (Res. Rep. No. 93-03). Newton: PA: Law School Admission Council and Law School Admission Services.

Willingham, W. W. (1988). Testing handicapped people: The validity issue. In H. Wainer & H. I. Braun (Eds.), *Test validity* (pp. 89–103). Hillsdale, NJ: Erlbaum.

Woodcock, R. W., & Mather, N. (1989–1990). WJ-R Tests of Achievement: Examiner's manual. In R. W. Woodcock & M. B. Johnson (Eds.), *Woodcock–Johnson Psycho-Educational Battery–Revised*. Allen, TX: DLM Teaching Resources.

Zigmond, N. (1993). Learning disabilities from an educational perspective. In G. R. Lyon, D. B. Gray, J. F. Kavanagh, & N. A. Krasnegor (Eds.), *Better understanding learning disabilities: New views from research and their implications for educational and public policies* (pp. 273–308). Baltimore: Brookes.

Ziomek, R. L., & Andrews, K. M. (1996). *Predicting the college grade point averages of special-tested students from their ACT assessment scores and high school grades* (Res. Rep. No. 96-7). Iowa City, IA: American College Testing.

14 Individuals With Other Characteristics

Sarah I. Pratt and Kevin L. Moreland

The issue of fairness in testing has received considerable attention in the past 2 decades in the courts, legislatures, schools, and employment settings. Test developers, users, and interpreters are bound by legal mandates and professional obligations that require them to consider and account for the unique characteristics of individuals to whom tests are administered. Much of the debate about fairness in testing has been centered on the issue of bias in item content. There is an additional dimension to the issue of fairness in testing individuals with handicapping conditions because testing conditions often must be altered to accommodate the limitations imposed by disabilities (Willingham, 1988). Therefore, testers must not only consider the characteristics of test takers in terms of potential bias created by item content but also the potential bias in terms of the skills and abilities that are required to complete test items.

Individuals who perform poorly on an assessment device simply because they lack the skills required to respond to test items have not been afforded an equal opportunity to demonstrate their abilities. Testing individuals with handicapping conditions requires careful consideration of test selection, method of administration, and score interpretation. Testers should strive to select assessment devices that are commensurate with the abilities of the test taker. Inevitably, though, individuals with handicapping conditions may at some point be tested using assessment devices that require skills that they do not have. In these instances, it is important for testers to ensure that individuals with handicapping conditions are not penalized for the detrimental effects of limitations imposed by a disability, assuming that the limitations are irrelevant to the abilities assessed by the test. Testers may sometimes need to provide several special accommodations to enable test takers to respond to test items. Although such accommodations permit testers to evaluate individuals with handicapping conditions by removing the deleterious effects of disabilities that are irrelevant to the abilities being assessed, special test administrations give rise to a number of important considerations. Testers must determine whether a modified version of a test or test administration measures the same abilities in essentially the same manner as the unmodified version or administration. Furthermore, some modifications may preclude the use of standardized norms or affect the interpretation of scores. This poses a problem because norms for individuals with disabilities, particularly those who require nonstandard administration, are often not available. Finally, testers must decide whether to "flag" scores obtained from nonstandard administrations (i.e., to report that the standard administration procedures were modified).

Professional Obligations and Legal Mandates Regarding Fairness in Testing

There are several professional standards and legal mandates for protecting people with handicapping conditions from discrimination on the basis of their disability. The issue of fairness in testing individuals with disabilities is one that has been included with increasing frequency during the past 2 decades in major legislation as well as professional standards, ethical principles, and codes of conduct (Fremer, Diamond, & Camara, 1989). The purpose of establishing regulations and standards of fairness in testing is to ensure that individuals with handicapping conditions are not wrongly penalized for limitations in the skills and abilities they have. The ultimate goal of fair testing is to facilitate the assessment of skills and abilities by eliminating any deleterious effects of limitations imposed by a disability that are irrelevant to the skills and abilities being evaluated.

Legal Mandates

Several laws designed to protect the rights of people with handicapping conditions have been enacted in the past 20 years (Geisinger, 1994).

Section 504 of the Rehabilitation Act of 1973, which applied to federal agencies and private institutions receiving federal funding, granted protection to people with disabilities from discrimination in employment practices, accessibility of physical facilities, education, and social services (Anastasi, 1988). The Americans With Disabilities Act of 1990 (ADA), which extends to both private and public entities, has provisions that safeguard against discrimination on the basis of disability in public accommodations, transportation, state and local government services, telecommunications, and employment. With respect to the workplace, the ADA prohibits discrimination in all employment-related activities by requiring that all employment decisions be based on an individual's capabilities rather than on preconceptions about the limitations imposed by a disability (Eyde, Nester, Heaton, & Nelson, 1994). This includes activities that may conceivably require testing, such as job application procedures, advancement, compensation, recruitment, layoff, and fringe benefits. Title II of the ADA, which applies to public entities (i.e., state and local government agencies), prohibits discrimination on the basis of disability in the granting of licenses or certification. With respect to testing, Title III specifically mandates that private test-taking entities administer assessments in a manner that reasonably accommodates limitations imposed by disabilities (Geisinger, 1994).

Professional Obligations

Professional organizations with a stake in testing have promulgated numerous professional standards and obligations with regard to the testing of individuals with handicapping conditions. These standards are embodied in documents such as the American Psychological Association's (APA; 1992) Ethical Principles and Code of Conduct, the *Standards for Educational and Psychological Testing* (1985), the Code of Professional Responsibilities in Educational Assessment (National Council on Measurement in Education [NCME], 1995), and the interdisciplinary Joint Committee on Testing Practices' (JCTP; 1988) Code of Fair Testing Practices in Education. For example, Section 2.04 of the APA ethics code requires psychologists to consider an individual's disability among the factors that may preclude particular assessment techniques or mandate modifications of standard administration or interpretation of an assessment. The Code of Professional Responsibilities in Educational Assessment (NCME, 1995) reminds educational testers of their obligation to conduct assessments in a manner that is free of potential bias and to make "allowable accommodations for the administration of the assessment to persons with disabilities or special needs" (Section 4.8). The Code of Fair Testing Practices in Education (JCTP, 1988) requires test users to consider the characteristics of the individual or population tested, including handicapping conditions, that may affect the selection, administration, and interpretation of tests (Sections A8, B10, and C16). The Rights and Responsibilities of Test Takers (JCTP, 1996) informs examinees of their rights with respect to use of appropriate assessment devices, manner of testing, and accommodations for special needs (Section 2).

Although the technical recommendations of psychological tests and diagnostic techniques (APA, 1954), the precursor to the *Standards for Educational and Psychological Testing* (1985), made no specific reference to individuals with disabilities, Sections F.6 and F.7 allude to the issue of fairness in testing by emphasizing the importance of developing norms on "defined and clearly described populations" who are representative of the groups to whom test users will compare the people tested. Subsequent iterations of these test standards, published in 1974 and 1985, contain sections that explicitly mandate obligations of test users with regard to practices designed to prevent discrimination on the basis of handicapping conditions in test development, selection, and interpretation. Although the 1974 *Standards* were primarily concerned with warning against ethnic and gender bias, this version acknowledged, in the following example, the potential for "inappropriate discrimination" in the administration of tests to individuals with special physical conditions: "Placing a hand-dexterity test on a low table may unfairly bias the test against tall people" (Standard E.9). The 1974 version also advised test users about their responsibility to anticipate potential sources of bias in testing while admitting that sources of bias "are neither well understood nor easily avoided" (Standard G.4). Test users were also encouraged to inform themselves about the most current literature and developments regarding bias in testing (Standard G.4). By 1985, the *Standards* included an entire chapter on testing people with handicapping conditions, providing suggestions for various modifications of tests or test procedures to enable individuals with disabilities to take tests developed for nondisabled populations. The 1985 *Standards* also outlined obligations for test users regarding validation of standardized and modified versions of tests and interpretation of scores obtained for people with handicapping conditions.

Test Selection

Testing individuals with handicapping conditions can be problematic because individuals with disabilities may not have the skills required to perform the tasks associated with a particular assessment device. Most commonly administered psychological, educational, and occupational tests, for example, require skills such as reading, turning pages, writing, and concentration. Widely used tests of cognitive functioning and intellectual abilities developed for use with nondisabled populations often also require manipulating objects with the hands (Cohen, Montague, Nathanson, & Swerdlik, 1988). Testing individuals with disabilities using assessment devices that require skills that they do not have seriously confounds the measurement of the individuals' actual abilities (Bennett, Rock, & Kaplan, 1987).

Faced with this dilemma, test administrators have several options, including elimination from a test those tasks that cannot be performed by examinees with disabilities. For example, a possible solution to the problem of assessing nonverbal as opposed to verbal skills on an intelligence test, particularly with regard to individuals with physically handicapping conditions, is to eliminate subtests that require motor skills. Some have suggested, for example, that the Vocabulary subtest of the Wechsler Adult Intelligence Scale correlates highly enough with the rest of the test to serve as a rough estimate of both verbal and nonverbal intelligence. Others have argued that eliminating such tasks results in an overassessment of verbal skills and underassessment of nonverbal skills (Cohen et al., 1988). Cohen et al. stated that some examiners choose to eliminate performance tasks from IQ tests for test takers with disabilities because the verbal tests (vocabulary in particular) correlate higher with the rest of the test. They have warned that the IQ obtained from such an administration should only be considered a "rough estimate" (p. 509) and should not be used as part of a placement decision.

Another option for test users is to modify the administration procedures, response format, or, in extreme cases, the content of a test to accommodate the limitations imposed by a test taker's disability (Geisinger, 1994). Many traditional tests of intelligence, for example, may be altered for use with individuals with disabilities. For instance, subtests on the Stanford–Binet Intelligence Scale and the Wechsler Adult Intelligence Scale–Revised (WAIS-R) that require verbal responses may be changed to a written format for individuals who have speech deficits. Or an examiner could perform random trials of a task requiring motor abilities for individuals with physical disabilities who might indicate their response choice by winking an eye. Because modifications of standardized procedures can create problems in terms of reliability, validity, and comparison with established norms, it is advisable for test users to select tests for individuals with disabilities that will require the least amount of deviation from standardized procedures (Cohen et al., 1988). Finally, in assessing individuals with disabilities who are unable to perform the tasks required for a traditional, standardized measure, test users have the option of selecting a test whose format is consistent with the particular abilities of the test taker.

Tests That Accommodate Handicapping Conditions

Providing appropriate accommodations in the area of ability testing is more problematic than testing other psychological variables such as personality or interests. Tests of ability more often include unwanted confounds such as a motor component complicating the assessment of perception. Many tests permit the measurement of abilities assessed by traditional tests without requiring skills that people with handicapping conditions may not have (Kaplan & Saccuzzo, 1989). We briefly note some of the most popular tests.

In the area of intelligence testing, the Columbia Mental Maturity Scale, Third Edition (Burgemeister, Blum, & Lorge, 1972) requires neither reading, verbal responses, nor fine motor skills. The examiner presents the test taker with a number of 6 × 9 in. (15.24 × 22.86 cm) cards containing three to five drawings of objects that are expected to be commonly recognizable to most Americans (Anastasi, 1988). The test taker then indicates which drawing does not belong with the others on the card. Although this assessment device essentially measures only visual discrimination and vocabulary, it is easily administered to individuals with speech impairments, and even individuals with severe physical limitations could use "eye pointing" to complete this test (Cohen et al., 1988).

Similar in format, the Peabody Picture Vocabulary Test–Revised (Dunn & Dunn, 1981) requires the test taker to choose which of four pictures printed on a large card is best related to a word read by the examiner. This test also has the advantage of requiring neither reading, writing, verbal responding, nor manipulating objects with the hands. However, inherent in the multiple-choice format of both the Columbia Mental Maturity Scale and the Peabody Picture Vocabulary Test is a significant percentage of random error attributable to guessing. Sole reliance on scores obtained from these tests as measures of intelligence is inadvisable. Examiners should attempt to supplement them with subtests of traditional assessment devices that the test taker is able to perform (Kaplan & Saccuzzo, 1989). Although IQ scores with a mean of 100 and a standard deviation of 15 may be generated from raw scores on these tests, these scores are not interchangeable with IQ scores obtained from more comprehensive tests of intelligence such as the Stanford–Binet Intelligence Scale or the Wechsler Adult Intelligence Scale (Sattler, 1988).

Finally, the Raven Standard Progressive Matrices (Raven, 1947a) and the Coloured Progressive Matrices (Raven, 1947b) are tests that measure some of the abilities assessed by traditional intelligence tests such as spatial aptitude, visual discrimination, and perceptual accuracy, and they can be performed easily by individuals with many handicapping conditions. The Raven tests require examinees to select which design elements most logically fit into a blank space on a larger design pattern. Other tests of abilities that are often useful with people with disabilities include the Pictorial Test of Intelligence (French, 1964), the Full-Range Picture Vocabulary Test (Ammons & Ammons, 1948), the Quick Test (Ammons & Ammons, 1962), the Motor-Free Visual Perception Test (Colarusso & Hammill, 1972), and the Expressive One-Word Picture Vocabulary Test (Gardner, 1979).

Alternate Forms of Traditional Assessment Devices

Several modified versions of traditional assessment devices have been developed, among other reasons, to accommodate individuals with handicapping conditions. For example, the modified WAIS (WAIS-M) (Vincent, 1979) is a modification designed to reduce the time required to complete the WAIS-R. The WAIS-M may be used when the first 10 items of the Information subtest of the WAIS-R are answered correctly and allows higher starting points on five of the WAIS-R subtests, which reduces administration time by 25%. A study of the relationship between the WAIS-M scores and the WAIS-R scores of a group of elderly patients concluded that WAIS-M scores were comparable to WAIS-R scores because correlations between the two test forms were significant and agreement in IQ classifications made on the basis of the two forms was high (Cargnello & Gurekas, 1987). The Split-Half Short Form of the Wechsler Intelligence Scale for Children–Revised (WISC-R) also allows for the expeditious evaluation of intellectual ability by reducing administration time. A study of the usefulness of the short form as a substitute for the full-length WISC-R indicated that the short form over-estimated Verbal, Performance, and Full Scale IQs, resulting in consistent shifts from the low-average to the average classification for a sample of youngsters with neurological impairments (Bawden & Byrne, 1991). Note that in the studies by Cargnello and Gurekas (1987) and Bawden and Byrne (1991), the scores on the short forms were not derived from actual administrations of the full-length versions of the WAIS-R and the WISC-R, respectively. Therefore, the effects of reduced administration time on actual item responses is unknown. Other examples of special forms of traditional assessment devices include the Improved Readability Form of the Minnesota Multiphasic Personality Inventory (Dillon & Ward, 1989) and Form E of the Sixteen Personality Factor Questionnaire (Spirrison, 1992), both of which were designed to accommodate low-literacy populations.

Test Administration

Although there are currently several tests available that accommodate the limitations of individuals with handicapping conditions, there are occasions when individuals with disabilities will have to be tested with instruments designed for use with nondisabled populations. For example, many colleges and universities require applicants to take nationally administered, standardized tests such as the Scholastic Assessment Test (SAT) or the American College Test (ACT) as part of their admissions process. Also, some employers require job applicants to take standardized paper-and-pencil personality tests as part of their hiring process. When test takers do not have the skills required to perform the tasks of an examination, they may request modifications to standardized administration procedures. Such modifications may include transforming the actual format of a test, transforming the method of responding to test items, or changing the method of interpreting scores (Cohen et al., 1988). Note that most of the accommodations suggested in this section represent unvalidated "clinical wisdom."

Legal Mandates

Title III of the ADA requires that private testing agencies provide the following to test takers with disabilities: (a) testing in an accessible place and manner or alternative accessible arrangements; (b) test selection and administration that accurately reflect an individual's aptitude and achievement rather than reflecting impairments caused by a disability; (c) changes in the length of time allowed to complete a test or other adaptation of the usual manner of test administration, when necessary, unless use thereof would significantly alter the assessment of the skills the test is intended to measure. In the context of the hiring process, the ADA (Section 101 [9]) also requires that employers make reasonable accommodations to the known physical or mental limitations of qualified applicants, including adjusting or modifying examinations and providing qualified readers, unless the employer can demonstrate that special accommodations would cause undue hardship on the operation of its business (Eyde et al., 1993).

The Amendments to the Architectural Barriers Act of 1968 outline several requirements with respect to amenities and handicapped accessibility for buildings designed, built, or altered after 1968 or leased after 1977. For example, with respect to rooms in which testing occurs, doorways must be at least 32 in. (81.28 cm) wide, tables and chairs must be at least 30 in. (76.20 cm) high, and aisles between tables and rows of chairs must be at least 36 in. (91.44 cm) wide (Eyde et al., 1993).

Professional Obligations

Professional organizations have recommended several specific accommodations that may be made in the testing of individuals with disabilities. The *Standards* (1985), for example, recommend modification of the medium in which test items are presented. For example, test instructions and questions may be printed in extra-large type, presented on an audiocassette recording, or read by an individual appointed to assist the test taker. The *Standards* (1985) also suggest that the method of recording responses to test items may be modified. For example, an individual assigned to assist a test taker with physical limitations may record the examinee's responses on the answer sheet. Testers may also change the time limits or the number of rest periods, test content, or testing locations to accommodate individuals with disabilities. Finally, testers may simply need to provide amenities in the testing room or area, including tables, chairs, lighting, or space that ensure the comfort and optimal functioning of test takers with disabilities (*Standards*, 1985). The Code of Fair Testing Practices in Education (JCTP, 1988) specifically advises testers to use appropriately modified forms of tests or administration procedures for examinees with handicapping conditions (Section C.16). The APA ethics code likewise reminds psychologists of their obligation to consider adjustments to assessment devices that may be necessitated by several factors, including disability (Section 2.04 [c]).

Special Accommodations for Particular Handicapping Conditions

Several specific adaptations to the procedures for the administration and recording of responses are commonly made to accommodate many disabilities. One fairly simple accommodation that can be made for individuals with disabilities is the relaxation or elimination of time limits (Ekstrom & Lenke, 1995; Geisinger, 1994; *Standards*, 1985). Appointing a nondisabled individual to assist with the administration and recording of responses is another accommodation that enables the use of tests designed for use with nondisabled populations without requiring changes in test content (Ekstrom & Lenke, 1995; Geisinger, 1994; *Standards*, 1985). Other adaptations that are frequently made to promote the optimal performance of individuals with a variety of disabilities include modification from group to individual administration, large-type editions of tests, tape-recorded administration, adaptation of worktables to accommodate wheelchairs, and a change of testing location (Ekstrom & Lenke, 1995; Geisinger, 1994; *Standards*, 1985).

Intellectual Disabilities

Assessing the abilities of individuals with intellectual deficiencies may be particularly difficult given the challenges of maintaining the interest and concentration of the test taker. In testing individuals with intellectual deficiencies, an examiner may reasonably expect to contend with self-stimulating behavior, self-injury, destructive behavior, a brief attention span, and noncompliance with requests, which will likely interfere with the ability to administer assessment devices in a standard fashion. Individuals who are severely deficient in motivation or attention may prove to be untestable. Therefore, before attempting a testing session, it is helpful to obtain information, either through observation or from caretakers, about the likelihood that individuals with disabilities will be able or willing to complete the tasks required by particular assessment devices (Sattler, 1988). Frequent breaks and the use of reinforcers are useful accommodations with this population.

Individuals with severe intellectual deficiencies may also suffer from physical handicaps that will make it difficult to assess them accurately. Thus, many will require the kinds of modifications in test content, format, and administration procedures described in the chapters of this book dealing with sensory handicaps and handicaps in speech and language. In administering any assessment device to individuals with intellectual impairments, it is important to be cognizant of their attention, motivation, endurance, and salient reinforcers (Sattler, 1988). Another potential problem with assessing the skills of people with intellectual impairments is the relative insensitivity of some standard measures, particularly traditional intelligence tests, to low levels of ability. The use of an adaptive behavior scale such as the Vineland Adaptive Behavior Scales (Sparrow, Balla, & Cicchetti, 1984), which measure the extent to which individuals demonstrate skills required for daily living (e.g., going to the store), may be more practical and informative in providing information about the functioning and abilities of such individuals (Cohen et al., 1988; Kamphaus, 1993). Because they are completed by caregivers, adaptive behavior scales also circumvent the many difficulties encountered in testing individuals who have severe intellectual deficiencies.

Emotional Disturbances

As with testing individuals with intellectual deficiencies, examiners performing assessments of individuals with severe emotional disturbances will likely struggle to maintain the attention and concentration of test takers. In the case of individuals with severe mental illness who may be experiencing active hallucinations, the timing of testing during non-psychotic periods is particularly important (Kamphaus, 1993). Examiners faced with intense emotional reactions should temporarily suspend testing activities and provide additional rest periods (Sattler, 1988). Required reading levels for many self-administered assessment devices may also necessitate modifications in standard procedures for clinical populations. For example, examiners may need to orally administer paper-and-pencil measures, alter the wording of questions, or clarify the meaning of test items (Griffin & Kogut, 1988).

Autism

Because individuals with autism often have impaired communication skills, an examiner may have to adopt any number of the modifications for people with speech impairments (discussed earlier in this book). Examiners also will likely encounter difficulty in establishing social contact and therefore maintaining the interest and attention of test takers with autism (Kamphaus, 1993; Sattler, 1988). Examiners should alert test takers when important instructions or information are about to be communicated by saying the individual's name. Using short, concrete sentences may also facilitate comprehension and cooperation, although some autistic individuals will require physical gestures or sign language to communicate. Direct physical guidance or teaching an autistic individual to imitate a particular behavior to complete a task may also be required (Kamphaus, 1993; Sattler, 1988). Excellent assessment devices are available that circumvent the difficulties involved in testing in the traditional manner by asking for a caregiver's input. As noted earlier, the Vineland Adaptive Behavior Scales (Sparrow et al., 1984) can be used to assess the ability of children (suffering from autism or not) to care for themselves in an age-appropriate manner. Other measures, such as the Childhood Autism Rating Scale (Schopler, Reichler, & Renner, 1988), deal more specifically with the special problems of children with autism.

Brain Injury

Individuals with brain injuries may suffer a variety of limitations, particularly in terms of cognitive functioning, that necessitate alterations in standard testing procedures. There are several ways that examiners can minimize irrelevant effects of these limitations on the assessment of abilities. Examiners should begin the testing with relatively easy tasks so that test takers will experience initial success, administer difficult tests in the middle of the testing session, and conclude with relatively easy tasks again at the end of the session, when fatigue is likely to affect performance. Relaxing time limits is particularly crucial for individuals with brain injuries, who may require inordinately long periods of time to organize responses. It is particularly important for examiners to face test takers when communicating instructions or important information. It may also be important to repeat instructions and to include more pauses in instructions and administration of test items to allow time for comprehension (Sattler, 1988).

Metabolic Disorders

Diagnostic metabolic disorders such as diabetes often require accommodations (Willis, Culbertson, & Mertens, 1984). Individuals with diabetes must eat small meals frequently. Moreover, individuals with diabetes experience more fatigue than the average examinee. It is therefore important to allow examinees with diabetes to take more frequent breaks. Other metabolic conditions, if not perfectly controlled, require similar accommodations. Examples of such disorders include Wilson's disease, pernicious anemia, and acute porphyria (Strider & Strider, 1985).

Endocrine Disorders

As with metabolic disorders, several endocrine disorders, if not managed well, may necessitate testing accommodations (Strider & Strider, 1985). Hyperparathyroidism may lead to hyperactivity that requires individual, rather than group, testing for example (Martin, 1979). Hypoglycemia induces fatigue that may necessitate frequent rest periods (Ouslander, 1983). Other such disorders include Addison's disease and Cushing's disease (Lishman, 1978).

Motor Handicaps

Individuals with motor handicaps often require testing accommodations. The severity of the motor handicap will obviously determine the degree to which the method of administration and responding will need to be modified. Individuals with minor limitations in upper-body functioning, such as might be caused by rheumatoid arthritis, may require only the relaxation of time limits to compensate for difficulty in manually recording responses, turning pages, performing computation, and drawing diagrams (Eyde et al., 1994; Munger & Loyd, 1991; Sattler, 1988). Individuals with severe motor handicaps who are unable to write or even turn pages may require either audiotape administration and the recording of responses or assistance from a nondisabled individual assigned to fill in answer sheets or turn pages of the test materials (Eyde et al., 1993; Geisinger, 1994). Allowing the assistance of nondisabled individuals risks providing cues to test takers, which, of course, must be avoided (Sattler, 1988).

Because individuals with physical handicaps may tire easily, examiners should consider scheduling several short testing sessions (Anastasi, 1988; Sattler, 1988). People who are confined to wheelchairs or who use corrective braces to compensate for disorders such as scoliosis may also require frequent changes in positions to stay comfortable. Individuals suffering from diseases such as cerebral palsy that affect functioning in more than one area may require significant modifications to standard procedures to accommodate their disabilities (Sattler, 1988). For example, individuals with deficits in motor functioning as well as speech may be able to respond only with head nodding or pointing (Anatasi, 1988). Consultation with a physical therapist or an occupational therapist is often helpful in deciding how best to test individuals with motor handicaps (Willis et al., 1984).

Disadvantages of Special Accommodations

Although special accommodations facilitate the assessment of individuals with disabilities by reducing or eliminating the detrimental effects of the disability, some modifications of standard procedures may actually increase the difficulty of particular tasks and therefore confound test results. For example, relaxing or eliminating time limits may increase fatigue and thus adversely affect performance (Geisinger, 1994; *Standards*, 1985). Printing questions in large type may facilitate reading but may also slow examinees down and potentially interfere with processing ability because the individual test items will be extended over several pages (Geisinger, 1994; Rock, Bennett, & Jirele, 1988). Translating certain test questions such as those including graphs or tables to audio form may be so complicated that the difficulty associated with such items is significantly changed (Geisinger, 1994).

It may prove impossible to modify all test items to a form that is compatible with every disability. When test items cannot be administered, examiners may either estimate the abilities that could not be tested, by using statistical techniques such as multiple regression, or attempt to obtain a more complete picture of overall functioning and capabilities by testing compensatory skills (Geisinger, 1994). For example, individuals who cannot use their hands may have compensated by developing exceptional dexterity in their feet. Testing the extent of motor coordination with their feet may therefore be important in an assessment of educational placement or employment options.

Empirical Investigations

Potential disadvantages to test modifications highlight the need to pretest nonstandard administration and to revalidate modified forms of standardized assessment devices (Geisinger, 1994). To date, there have been few empirical investigations on testing individuals with disabling conditions and even fewer examinations of the effects of modifications in test procedures on test results and their reliability and validity (Kaplan & Saccuzzo, 1989; Rock, Bennett, & Kaplan, 1987; *Standards*, 1985). The 1985 *Standards* require a test user who substantially changes the format, mode of administration, or content of a test to revalidate the modified version (Standard 6.2). Despite the admonition contained in the *Standards* (1985) that test users should assess the validity and reliability of modified versions of tests or risk "not having usable information regarding the meanings of scores for handicapped people" (Standard 14.6, 80), test users routinely interpret scores obtained from nonstandard administrations in the absence of hard evidence about the reliability and validity of the scores.

One reason for the lack of research in this area is the relative infrequency with which test users administer standardized tests to individuals with handicapping conditions. Even more infrequent are requests by people with disabilities for modifications to testing procedures (Geisinger, 1994). For example, Willingham (1988) reported that from 1981 to 1986, only 2.21% of SAT takers and 1.70% of Graduate Record Examinations (GRE) takers required nonstandardized test administration. The 1985 *Standards* recommended pilot testing modifications of tests to evaluate the appropriateness and feasibility of alterations; however, empirical investigations that have been conducted, or at least those that have been published, have relied on data from modifications that have been used in actual testing situations (Bennett et al., 1987; Rock et al., 1988, 1987).

Another issue that limits the ability to conduct empirical investigations of the effects of modifications of standard test administration is the infinite variation in the nature of individual disabilities, which may require an infinite number of different accommodations depending on the particular handicapping condition or set of handicapping conditions. Research on the effects of each combination of accommodations or modifications requires that many people have taken a test under the same conditions (Geisinger, 1994).

An important consideration in testing individuals with disabilities in both standardized and nonstandardized administrations is whether the test measures the same constructs that are measured when nondisabled individuals take the test under standard administration procedures (Rock et al., 1988; *Standards,* 1985). Rock et al. (1988) addressed this issue in a comparison of the factor structure of the GRE in standardized administration to people with and without disabilities. They found that the three-factor model comprising Verbal, Analytical, and Quantitative factors did not fit well for the group with disabilities because the logical reasoning and the analytical reasoning items did not function effectively as a single factor. On the basis of these findings, Rock et al. suggested that interpretations that are based on composite scores combining scores from the Verbal, Analytical, and Quantitative sections should be avoided.

It is particularly important for test users to ensure that tests that have been modified to accommodate individuals with disabilities are measuring the same underlying abilities, even if the method for doing this has been altered. In other words, test users must be reasonably certain that the modified version of a test serves as an adequate substitute for the original standardized test on which it is based. Several studies have provided evidence of the validity of nonstandard administration of standardized tests (Bennett et al., 1987; Dillon & Ward, 1989; Griffin & Kogut, 1988; Rock et al., 1987). For example, in an investigation of SAT scores from nonstandard administrations, Rock et al. (1987) found that the two-factor structure of the SAT functioned in essentially the same way. Using the same data, Bennett et al. (1987) analyzed the performance of respondents with and without disabilities on each item of the SAT. Although they found substantial effects on individual items (e.g., algebra comparisons were significantly easier for the group that was learning disabled and given audio cassettes), they detected no broad classes of differently operating items.

A study of the implications of oral as opposed to written administration of the Beck Depression Inventory and a slightly modified version of the Zung Rating Scale for Depression indicated that, although only the oral administration of the Zung scale, not the Beck Depression Inventory, differentiated at a significant level between depressed and non-depressed patients, both measures correlated significantly with criteria for depression from the third edition of the *Diagnostic and Statistical Manual of Mental Disorders* (Griffin & Kogut, 1988). Finally, a study of the use of the Improved Readability Form of the Minnesota Multiphasic Personality Inventory with illiterate patients found that although judgments of grandiosity from Scale 2, hostility from Scale 7, and suspiciousness from Scale 2 were not in conformity with usual clinical interpretations, the Improved Reliability Form served as a reasonable substitute for the Minnesota Multiphasic Personality Inventory.

It is particularly important to determine whether modifications of standard procedures lead to more accurate measurements of the abilities of individuals with disabilities. If it is determined that a particular modification is not operating in this manner, it should not be used. A study of the effect of speededness on test performance, for example, showed that eliminating time limits had minimal and almost identical effects on the scores of students with and without disabilities who took parallel forms of the Iowa Tests of Basic Skills under both timed and untimed conditions (Munger & Loyd, 1991). Test results in terms of the number of items attempted by both groups of students showed no difference in the speededness of the test. Despite their finding that the students with disabilities were not disadvantaged by the time limits, Munger and Loyd acknowledged that other studies of speededness have produced contradictory results. For example, Pasker (1987, as cited in Munger & Loyd, 1991) and Centra (1986, as cited in Munger & Loyd, 1991) concluded that increased SAT Mathematics scores obtained by individuals with disabilities who were allowed extended testing time were evidence that time increases may be important in reducing the effects of disability on performance.

Test Interpretation

Whether a test has been modified to accommodate individuals with disabilities, the interpretation of test results must include careful consideration of the effects on performance of limitations imposed by disabilities. The Code of Professional Responsibilities in Educational Assessment (NCME, 1995) requires testers to ensure that the scoring of assessments is not affected by factors that are irrelevant to the purpose of the assessment (Section 5.3). The APA ethics code requires psychologists to consider all test factors and characteristics of the test taker that might affect interpretation of assessment results (Section 2.05). The Rights and Responsibilities of Test Takers (JCTP, 1996) advise of the examinee's right to be told whether scores will be treated specially and, if so, in what way (Section 5d). Finally, the *Standards* (1985) require that interpretation of test scores include consideration of the effects on test scores of modifications made for people with handicapping conditions (Standard 14.6).

Norms

A score obtained on any test has little meaning unless it is placed in a context by comparing it with a reference group of scores (*Standards,* 1985). The Code of Professional Responsibilities in Educational Assessment (NCME, 1995) requires testers to objectively evaluate the appropriateness of norms used in the interpretation of test results (Section 6.5). The Rights and Responsibilities of Test Takers (JCTP, 1996) inform examinees of their right to information about the characteristics of any comparison group used in the interpretation of their test scores (Section 7c). Finally, the Code of Fair Testing Practices in Education (JCTP, 1988) recommends that test users inform themselves about the characteristics of any comparison groups and consider major differences between test takers and the comparison groups as well as differences between test takers and the comparison group in interpreting test scores (Sections B9 and B10).

Standardization of an assessment device should include systematic stratification on a number of variables that may affect test scores, including age, gender, level of education, geographic region, and disability. Norms derived from standardization represent the average scores of the standardization sample (Cicchetti, 1994). Ideally, characteristics of the reference group to whom an individual's scores are compared will be similar in terms of important variables that may affect performance on a test, including the presence or absence of a handicapping condition. From a practical standpoint, it is nearly impossible to include a broad enough range of individuals in a standardization sample to render obtained norms universally applicable (Anastasi, 1988). Unfortunately, virtually all standardized tests are not normed on populations that include significant numbers of individuals with handicapping conditions. Most standardized samples include primarily nondisabled individuals, largely because this is the population to whom the test developer expects tests users will administer the test most frequently.

Standardized Administration of Assessment

The choice of norms against which to compare the test scores of people with disabilities should perhaps depend on the purpose of the testing (*Standards*, 1985). Because nondisabled people set the standards in most societies, it is often important to assess the ability of people with disabilities to function in a context in which their performance will be compared with that of nondisabled individuals (Cohen et al., 1988). In this case, individuals with disabilities should be tested under standard administration conditions and the use of standardized norms is most appropriate. On the other hand, if one wishes to determine how well individuals with disabilities will function in a setting in which their performance will be compared with other people with disabilities, then the use of norms for nondisabled people may not be informative and norms on people with disabilities should be used if available (Cohen et al., 1988; *Standards*, 1985). Unfortunately, the problem with this decision rule is that norms appropriate for individuals with particular disabilities often do not exist (Cohen et al., 1988). Faced with this situation, testers should exercise great caution in interpreting scores that are based on standardized norms, taking into account the limitations of people with disabilities who may have had difficulty performing the tasks required by a standardized test (Sattler, 1988). In most situations, it is as important to know *how* an individual earned a test score as it is to know the test score itself. The implications of a low score on a test requiring the copying of designs with blocks are much different if that low score is caused by the slow performance of an examinee with poor motor skills than if that same score is earned by someone with good motor skills.

Nonstandardized Administration of Assessments

The purpose of standardized testing is to provide all examinees with an equal opportunity to demonstrate the abilities assessed by a measure. Standardization of administration and scoring also increases the objectivity of the testing process (Munger & Loyd, 1991). Despite the fact that test procedures are modified for individuals with disabilities in an attempt to ascertain performance on standardized measures assuming that the disability does not exist (Geisinger, 1994), it may be inappropriate to compare scores obtained from modified procedures with norms that are based on standardized administration procedures. The APA ethics code requires that psychologists attempt to identify situations in which standardized norms may be inapplicable because of factors such as a disability (Section 2.04 [c]). The Code of Fair Testing Practices in Education (JCTP, 1988) advises test users to consider differences in test administration in the interpretation of test results (Section B.10). Some would argue that standardization in and of itself precludes deviation in any and all aspects of the testing, including the exact materials used, time limits, and methods of responding to the questions (Anastasi, 1988). By extension, a nonstandardized administration of an assessment device would prevent the use of norms that are based on standardized administration (Sattler, 1988).

Departures from standard testing procedures undoubtedly produce less reliable test results. Because little research has been conducted on modifications of standard procedures, the effects of such modifications on test results remain uncertain (Sattler, 1988). For example, certain modifications may make test items or entire assessment devices differentially easy or difficult for individuals with disabilities or modifications may alter the construct that the test intended to measure. Situations such as this seem to preclude the use of standardized norms.

The extent and degree of the departure from standard testing procedures may determine the ability to compare scores obtained from nonstandardized administration with standardized norms. All assessment devices include a standard error reflecting differences in scores that may be attributed to factors such as examiner characteristics, the conditions of the examination, and timing of assessment, among others (Anastasi, 1988; Cicchetti, 1994; Sattler, 1988). The impact of minimal departures from standard testing procedures such as alterations in the wording of questions or the relaxation of time limits may arguably be no greater than the effects of the unique circumstances of any given assessment that are assumed as part of the standard error. Nevertheless, scores obtained from nonstandard test administration are less likely to be predictive of future levels of ability and functioning and should always be interpreted with caution (Sattler, 1988).

Flagging Scores

The issue of "flagging" scores by reporting any and all aspects of the test administration or interpretation that deviate from standardized procedures is one that often pits tests developers against people with disabilities (Ekstrom & Lenke, 1995). Constantly striving for the opportunity to compete on an even plane with nondisabled people, individuals with handicapping conditions argue that calling attention to modifications that are merely intended to eliminate any bias that would be created by their disabilities represents unfair, differential treatment. Test developers, on the other hand, find that failure to report nonstandard procedures violates the integrity of standardized tests. They also contend that it potentially harms individuals with disabilities, whose scores obtained from a nonstandardized administration may not accurately reflect their abilities to perform tasks required by standardized procedures (*Standards*, 1985). Therefore, many test developers and test users believe that any and all modifications of standard procedures should be noted in the record of the testing (Cohen et al., 1988). The Code of Professional Responsibilities in Educational Measurement (JCTP, 1996) requires that test administrators "administer standardized assessments according to prescribed procedures and conditions and notify appropriate persons if any nonstandard or delimiting conditions occur" (Section 4.5). Some even have argued that test scores generated from a nonstandard administration of an assessment device should be reported as "estimates" (Sattler, 1988).

Conclusion

Testing individuals with disabilities requires consideration of several important issues. Testers are required by law and have a professional responsibility to administer, score, and interpret tests in such a way that test takers will not be disadvantaged by limitations imposed by the disabilities that are irrelevant to the characteristics a test is intended to measure. If an individual cannot demonstrate the skills or knowledge assessed by test items, the individual's performance has not been fairly evaluated. Providing individuals with an equal opportunity to display their level of skill or ability may involve modifying the test administration procedures, altering the method of responding to test items, or offering special accommodations, such as extended testing time or the assistance of a reader or scribe (Cohen et al., 1988).

To adequately address the issue of fairness in testing individuals with handicapping conditions, testers should carefully consider the unique characteristics of the test taker, so they can select tests that commensurate with both the abilities and the limitations of the individual. The ability to administer, score, and interpret a test in much the same way for individuals with and without disabilities greatly increases the robustness of a test (Geisinger, 1994). Some tests may be easily administered to individuals with disabilities. However, many tests require skills or abilities that individuals with disabilities do not have. If testers need to modify testing procedures, these nonstandard administrations should be pretested to ensure the validity of the testing process (Geisinger, 1994; *Standards*, 1985). The ultimate goal in testing individuals with disabilities should be to provide an equal opportunity to demonstrate skills and abilities by eliminating the potential detrimental effects of the limitations imposed by the disabilities. This may be accomplished by granting, when necessary, reasonable and fair accommodations to testing conditions and procedures.

References

American Psychological Association. (1954). Technical recommendations of psychological tests and diagnostic techniques. *Psychological Bulletin, 51,* 201–238.

American Psychological Association. (1992). Ethical principles of psychologists and code of conduct. *American Psychologist, 47,* 1597–1611.

Ammons, R. B., & Ammons, H. S. (1948). *Full-Range Picture Vocabulary Test manual.* Missoula, MT: Psychological Test Specialists.

Ammons, R. B., & Ammons, C. H. (1962). *Quick Test manual.* Missoula, MT: Psychological Tests Specialists.

Anastasi, A. (1988). *Psychological testing.* New York: Macmillan.

Bawden, H. N., & Byrne, J. M. (1991). Use of the Hobby WISC-R Short Form with patients referred for neuropsychological assessment. *Psychological Assessment, 3,* 660–666.

Bennett, R. E., Rock, D. A., & Kaplan, B. A. (1987). SAT differential item performance for nine handicapped groups. *Journal of Educational Measurement, 24,* 41–55.

Burgemeister, B. B., Blum, L. H., & Lorge, I. (1972). *Columbia Mental Maturity Scale, Third Edition.* New York: Harcourt Brace Jovanovich.

Cargnello, J. C., & Gurekas, R. (1987). The clinical use of a modified WAIS procedure in a geriatric population. *Journal of Clinical Psychology, 43,* 286–290.

Cicchetti, D. V. (1994). Guidelines, criteria, and rules of thumb for evaluating normed and standardized assessment instruments in psychology. *Psychological Assessment, 6,* 284–290.

Cohen, R. J., Montague, P., Nathanson, L. S., & Swerdlik, M. E. (1988). *Psychological testing: An introduction to test and measurement.* Mountain View, CA: Mayfield.

Colarusso, R. P., & Hammill, D. D. (1972). *MVPT Motor Free Visual Perception Test manual.* Novato, CA: Academic Therapy.

Dillon, E. A., & Ward, L. C. (1989). Validation of an MMPI Short Form with literate and illiterate patients. *Psychological Reports, 64,* 327–336.

Dunn, L. M., & Dunn, L. M. (1981). *The Peabody Picture Vocabulary Test–Revised.* Circle Pines, MN: American Guidance Service.

Ekstrom, R. B., & Lenke, J. (1995). *Assessment of individuals with disabilities.* Unpublished manuscript.

Eyde, L. D., Nester, M. A., Heaton, S. M., & Nelson, A. V. (1994). *Guide for administering written employment examinations to persons with disabilities.* Washington, DC: U.S. Office of Personnel Management, Personnel Research and Development Center.

Eyde, L. D., Robertson, G. J., King, S. E., Moreland, K. L., Robertson, A. G., Shewan, C. M., Harrison, P. L., Porch, B. E., Hammer, A. L., & Primoff, E. S. (1993). *Responsible test use: Case studies for assessing human behavior.* Washington, DC: American Psychological Association.

Fremer, J., Diamond, E. E., & Camara, W. J. (1989). Development a code of fair testing practices in education. *American Psychologist, 44,* 1062–1067.

French, J. L. (1964). *Pictorial Test of Intelligence Test manual.* Chicago: Houghton Mifflin.

Gardner, M. F. (1979). *Expressive One-Word Picture Vocabulary Test manual.* Novato, CA: Academic Therapy.

Geisinger, K. F. (1994). Psychometric issues in testing students with disabilities. *Applied Measurement in Education, 7,* 121–140.

Griffin, P. T., & Kogut, D. (1988). Validity of orally administered Beck and Zung depression scales in a state hospital setting. *Journal of Clinical Psychology, 44,* 756–759.

Joint Committee on Testing Practices. (1988). *Code of fair testing practices in education.* Washington, DC: American Psychological Association.

Joint Committee on Testing Practices. (1996). *The rights and responsibilities of test takers.* Washington, DC: American Psychological Association.

Kamphaus, R. W. (1993). *Clinical assessment of children's intelligence.* Needham Heights, MA: Allyn & Bacon.

Kaplan, R. M., & Saccuzzo, D. P. (1989). *Psychological testing: Principles, applications and issues.* Pacific Grove, CA: Brooks/Cole.

Lishman, W. A. (1978). *Organic psychiatry: The psychological consequences of cerebral disorder.* Oxford, England: Blackwell Scientific.

Martin, M. I. (1979). Physical disease manifesting as psychiatric disorders. In G. Usdin & J. M. Lewis (Eds.), *Psychiatry in general medical practice* (pp. 337–351). New York: McGraw-Hill.

Munger, G. F., & Loyd, B. H. (1991). Effect of speededness on test performance of handicapped and nonhandicapped examinees. *Journal of Educational Research, 85,* 53–57.

National Council on Measurement in Education. (1995). *Code of professional responsibilities in educational assessment.* Washington, DC: American Psychological Association.

Ouslander, J. G. (1983). Psychiatric manifestations of physical illness in the elderly. *Psychiatric Medicine, 1,* 363–368.

Raven, J. C. (1947a). *Standard Progressive Matrices.* London: Lewis.

Raven, J. C. (1947b). *Coloured Progressive Matrices.* London: Lewis.

Rock, D. A., Bennett, R. E., & Jirele, T. (1988). Factor structure of the Graduate Record Examinations General Test in handicapped and nonhandicapped groups. *Journal of Applied Psychology, 73,* 383–392.

Rock, D. A., Bennett, R. E., & Kaplan, B. A. (1987). Internal construct validity of a college admissions test across handicapped and nonhandicapped groups. *Educational and Psychological Measurement, 47,* 193–205.

Sattler, J. M. (1988). *Assessment of children* (3rd ed.). San Diego, CA: Author.

Schopler, E., Reichler, R. J., & Renner, B. R. (1988). *CARS manual.* Los Angeles, CA: Western Psychological Services.

Sparrow, S. S., Balla, D. A., & Cicchetti, D. V. (1984). *Vineland Adaptive Behavioral Scales.* Circle Pines, MN: American Guidance Service.

Spirrison, C. L. (1992). Form E of the 16PF and adults with mental retardation: Internal consistency and validity. *Journal of Personality Assessment, 58,* 525–536.

Standards for educational and psychological testing. (1974). Washington, DC: American Psychological Association.

Standards for educational and psychological testing. (1985). Washington, DC: American Psychological Association.

Strider, M. A., & Strider, F. D. (1985). Differentiation of hysterical conversion/psychosomatic disorder and physical disease. In D. P. Swiercinsky (Ed.), *Testing adults: A reference guide for special psychodiagnostic assessments* (pp. 49–63). Kansas City, MO: Test Corporation of America.

Vincent, K. R. (1979). The modified WAIS: An alternative to short forms. *Journal of Clinical Psychology, 35,* 624–625.

Willingham, W. W. (1988). *Testing handicapped people.* Boston: Allyn & Bacon.

Willis, D. J., Culbertson, J. L., & Mertens, R. A. (1984). Considerations in physical and health-related disorders. In S. J. Weaver (Ed.), *Testing children: A reference guide for effective clinical and psychoeducational assessments* (pp. 185–496). Kansas City, MO: Test Corporation of America.

Part IV

Looking to the Future

Training Psychologists to Assess Members of a Diverse Society

Kurt F. Geisinger and Janet F. Carlson

This book has provided information about the use of tests and interpretation of test results with members of various diverse groups. Moreover, it has provided advice and recommendations for practitioners on the proper use of tests with members of such diverse groups. A more forward-looking strategy, however, is not only to enhance test use and interpretation by practitioners but also to make improvements in the skills and abilities of those entering the profession. Entry-level professionals not only need to be able to assess individuals from diverse backgrounds, but they also need to adapt to the changing nature of American society and to apply general principles of proper test use to the changing demographics that characterize society today and in the future.

A reasonable starting place for such a review would be a brief description of current training practices in graduate and professional programs in psychology. A survey of this type was performed within the past decade, and its findings argue for the need to change doctoral-level instruction. Aiken et al. (1990) gathered data from 84% of the psychology doctoral training departments in the United States and Canada—what would appear to be a large and representative sample of respondents from among all of the departments on the continent. The researchers requested information on the courses the departments offered, the components of their curriculum, and the skills demonstrated by their students and graduates. With specific regard to the training of psychology doctoral students in measurement, Aiken et al. (1990) reported that "measurement courses, however, are offered by fewer than half of the departments'' (p. 723) and that "over one third of the programs currently offer absolutely no training in measurement" (p. 724). With regard to the skills present in their students and graduates of doctoral programs in psychology, the researchers described the situation as "bleak."

> Only about one fourth of the departments judged that most of their students are competent at methods of reliability and validity assessment; over one third indicated that few or none of their students are. Even smaller percentages of their students are judged to be competent in classical test theory or item analysis. A glance at the remainder of the table indicates that more advanced and newer techniques of measurement and test development are lost on current graduates of psychology programs. (Aiken et al., 1990, p. 725)

Although it is not clear that to assess members of diverse groups and individuals with diverse backgrounds one needs to understand modern test theory (e.g., item response theory), it is apparent that one must understand *psychometric* concepts such as test bias and test fairness if one is to select instruments, administer them, and interpret the results of such assessments, especially when encountering individuals who differ from those with whom the former student was trained. The results of the Aiken et al. (1990) study are especially disturbing if one considers both that the responding departments probably tried to "put their best foot forward" in responding to the survey and that the doctoral programs that responded may provide a more enriched curriculum than the PsyD master's degree, and more practitioner-oriented programs that train so many service providers.

Department faculty need to rethink the place of measurement in their curricula. Additionally, those who teach courses on testing need to reevaluate the way that some of their courses are taught. For example, among the conclusions of Aiken et al. (1990) was a call that graduate students receive more applied training in consort with their psychometrics training. Faculty who teach psychometrically oriented courses need to consider the diverse situations in which practitioners find themselves and not only to present psychometric concepts such as reliability, validity, test standardization, and test bias, but also to provide real-life examples and perhaps pertinent case studies that represent instances in which the proper application of good testing practice helps to solve a thorny situation and in which improper practice causes misinterpretations and inappropriate decisions.

An additional caution, made throughout this book relates to the notion that those using assessment devices must be as concerned about the experiential background of the test taker as they are with the assessment instrument itself. Indeed, one must take characteristics such as language background and disability into account in making proper test selections, administrations, interpretations, and recommendations.

A Proposed Model of Instruction

Classroom Instruction in Testing Concepts

All psychology students who will be using tests should be exposed to the concepts of reliability, validity, test bias, test standardization, norms, and test interpretation. Although they may not need to grasp the mathematical basis of these concepts (e.g., item response theory or generalizability theory), they should have a thorough verbal and abstract understanding of these concepts, at least commensurate with a first-level undergraduate or graduate text such as those of Anatasi and Urbina (1997) and Cronbach (1990). Instruction in these concepts needs to be academically rigorous as well as grounded in the applications in which the majority of test use and test misuse occur. Once the concepts have been presented to students and the students understand them intellectually, the instructor should probably lead a discussion on the ways in which each of these concepts is involved in proper test use. It may also be helpful for the instructor to present situations in which improper understanding of the concepts can lead to test misuse. Class discussions and other active learning techniques are to be encouraged for the effective learning of the concepts. This approach to instruction, that of presenting the material, followed by the presentation of examples and discussion, is likely to prepare students best intellectually to apply testing concepts appropriately.

Students learning to use tests within their psychological work need to learn to read test manuals carefully, giving attention to whether and how the test may be properly used with differing members of society. Students must learn to attend to the information in manuals that will help them make the aforementioned determinations. Such skills are critical if test use is to be fair, appropriate, and useful and if it is to be perceived as being fair, appropriate, and useful. Additionally, a later component of the model of instruction presented in this chapter emphasizes the need to teach those learning to use psychological assessment as a constituent part of their professional work as psychologists to seek consultation with others. One type of consultation is that with test publishers. One will read a test manual and often not be certain about how the test can validly be administered to specific segments of the population. In such instances, the prospective professionals should be encouraged to contact the appropriate experts, including the test publisher, for additional information. Although the responsibility for the assessment always remains with the test users, the test publisher can provide much useful information so that the user can make the most informed decisions.

Classroom Instruction in Individuality

One course that had historical importance in the graduate psychology curriculum and that has been deleted at many schools because of pressure to include other information is the psychology of human differences, sometimes known as "differential psychology." The concept of individuality is critical to the proper interpretation of test results for all individuals, including those with diverse backgrounds. Some schools may wish to adopt such courses once again; others may identify other ways in which the breadth of individual differences may be learned and appreciated. Only when individual differences in behavior is understood can individual differences in test behavior and test results be similarly comprehended. As with instruction in testing concepts, instruction should begin with the conceptual aspects of differential psychology and then graduate to examples (e.g., of gender group or cultural group differences). Differential psychology has sometimes focused primarily on the extent of group differences. To aid students in applying their knowledge to their work, understanding of qualitative differences relating to the processing of information, for example, is more likely to prove useful than a presentation of the extent of intergroup differences.

In light of the influence of individual experiential backgrounds on test behaviors, trainers are obligated to teach students to assess individuals using a person-in-a-context orientation, similar to what Figueroa (1990) suggested and Frisby reiterated earlier in this book (see chapter 4). When interpreting test responses and test behavior, psychologists frequently make some common assumptions about the test taker's life circumstances or, broadly speaking, the context in which the test taker ordinarily exists. For example, in administering a large-print, written cognitive ability test to an individual with a visual disability, the individual will need more time to take the test because reading larger print takes more time than normal print. Yet, if one has made the assumption that all test takers should need an equal amount of time and has adjusted one's perception of the results of the assessment due to the fact that the test taker with the visual disability took more time, this assumption would be mistaken. Similarly, an individual with a physical disability that precludes driving a car may have to spend considerably more time and money simply to arrive at the testing center than an individual without such a disability. However, test administrators often assume that only the disability needs accommodation in the test administration and may overlook secondary effects that could well affect test performance and subsequent interpretations. Another assumption that is potentially mistaken is that rapport between a test administrator and a test taker is equally likely to develop regardless of the match between the two on dimensions such as gender, cultural background, and so on.

The manner in which a test taker experiences an assessment likely will vary on the basis of his or her historical background, a point related to those made previously in this book by Sandoval (see chapter 1) and Frisby (see chapter 4). Many individuals in the so-called mainstream of American culture think little of sitting for a large-scale, group-administered, timed, proctored examination using "bubble" sheets and identification numbers. Test takers who are less accustomed to such circumstances may not fare as well, although the assumption is that all test takers are being treated equally, ergo all individuals had comparable experiences during the assessment process and therefore differences in scores reflect true difference in abilities for the most part. Ultimately, students in training should become aware that many well-informed individuals believe that the assessment instruments currently in use are value laden, with the majority group's values often interwoven into the very fabric of the tests. For example, many tests of achievement or cognitive abilities emphasize individual competition and success under timed circumstances rather than cooperative or steady progress toward achieving competency. Particularly when it comes to interpreting test results and formulating interventions or rendering decisions, it is essential to bear in mind the contextual elements of an individual's life.

Sandoval (see chapter 3 in this book), Figueroa (1990), and Kamphaus (1993) suggested an assessment model in which hypothesis generation and confirmation using additional sources of information is a good—perhaps essential—practice. It behooves faculty to adopt a similar strategy in teaching students. Those who work with graduate students need to teach more about the proper "attitude" to adopt concerning test interpretation, so that students can recognize the value of evaluating a host of hypotheses about test data by systematically amassing additional information to confirm or disconfirm some of them. Training exercises that are integrated into various assessment courses should assist in the development of hypothesis generation skills as well as hypothesis evaluation skills.

A good deal of research has accumulated on group differences in performance on various types of tests. Interpretations of the research on group differences, especially with regard to intelligence, have moved into the popular press as well, so that today's students are confronted not only with the empirical findings but also with the layperson's preconceptions and inquisitiveness as well. Although it is important for students to be aware of research findings in this area, some caveats are in order. It is critical for graduate students to recognize that no pattern of research findings concerning the performance of particular groups of individuals on a particular instrument will reveal anything about the performance of the individual currently being assessed. In other words, faculty must communicate to their students not only what has been shown in research but also the dangers of premature (or downright prejudicial) judgments. As Sandoval noted in chapter 3, it is the nature of test givers to seek to confirm a suspicion quickly, especially one to which they recently have been exposed. Faculty therefore must establish in their students the mindset of continual and skeptical self-examination and must help them to feel justified in reserving judgment at least until all the data are in.

Case Studies

The publication of *Responsible Test Use: Case Studies for Assessing Human Behavior* (Eyde et al., 1993) marks an important early effort in the systematic collection and publication of case studies involving "critical incidents" of test misuse for instructional purposes. Eyde et al. represent a number of professional associations, all with a vested interest in promoting sound testing practices.[1] The authors present examples of test use and test misuse with discussion questions after each case study. Cases

---

[1] These associations are the members of the Joint Committee on Testing Practices and include the American Counseling Association, the American Psychological Association, the American Speech-Language-Hearing Association, the National Association of School Psychologists, and the National Council on Measurement in Education.

are included from schools, counseling centers, workplaces, mental health agencies, and other applied settings and involve linguistic group differences, foreign national groups, cultural background, and individuals with various disabilities.

Cases are organized into seven groups: general and training, training and professional responsibility, test selection, test administration, test scoring and norms, test interpretation, and reporting to clients. The cases emerged from extensive research by the authors on the common types of test misuse and a listing of the 86 elements or competencies of effective test use (as identified by Moreland, Eyde, Robertson, Primoff, & Most, 1995), which are contained in an appendix of the test use volume.

Case studies are perhaps the most effective manner in which students can be introduced to the application of testing before their initial field placements. Students can work on cases individually and discuss them in groups. They can learn from their initial mistakes (e.g., misinterpretations). They can be given many more opportunities to apply principles in solving cases than they would have been able to see in an actual field setting. In addition, the successful application of case studies may provide them with confidence as well as the cognitive skills and strategies to be successful in their field placements.

Field Placements With Field and Academic Supervision

It is incumbent on training programs to ensure that their students are adequately prepared in both content areas and practice arenas. Thus, it is essential for programs to identify field placements and supervisory personnel that provide trainees with opportunities to engage in assessment activities with members of diverse groups as clients, coworkers, and supervisors to the maximum extent possible. Training sites that provide experience assessing members of diverse groups should be eagerly sought by programs concerned with the breadth of their students' abilities. If a particular training program does not have associations with such sites, it should take steps to enter into relationships with such institutions. It may not be easy to establish a working relationship, but these should be pursued nevertheless to make students' training appropriately comprehensive.

Training programs located in remote, isolated, or rural regions may likely need to make special efforts to diversify trainees' experience. Actions taken could include instituting speaker series devoted to such

issues, aggressively seeking faculty members who are able to help ameliorate such curricular deficiencies, arranging for the use of more distant placement sites, establishing exchange programs with training programs that have greater access to training sites serving greater numbers
of diverse groups, integrating relevant case studies into course training
materials, sponsoring students (and faculty perhaps) to travel to appropriate workshops, and so on. Also, trainers at such locations should not
overlook the various dimensions of diversity that may exist within their
own region, as even remote or rural sites have gender and class issues
with which to contend, and frequently there are small pockets of diversity with respect to religion or other cultural factors. Rather than assuming or behaving as if there is no discernible level of diversity within the
surrounding population, training programs in remote locations should
capitalize on whatever dimensions of diversity are available in an effort
to prepare students who appreciate the nuances of these different
groups. In doing so, students will be better prepared for future transitions to other, more obviously diverse settings or times.

Supervision of students while in field settings is a matter of considerable importance and one that has received ample attention elsewhere.
For this discussion, it is probably sufficient to state that optimal supervision will include oversight and tutelage that is based both on the
teaching faculty and on the field site in question. Such field supervisors
can add substantially to the diversity of perspectives to which students
are exposed. The diversity of a teaching faculty is always limited by virtue
of its size and the uneven representations of all components of society.
In the past, graduate programs in psychology habitually sought psychologists as field supervisors who were similar to the teaching faculty
in orientation. In fact, they frequently chose their own graduates. Wise
is the educational program that seizes the opportunity to use field supervisors who can add perspectives, values, and backgrounds that are
not present on the university faculty.

Just as a diverse and representative faculty is imperative for an educational program, student diversity, too, is essential for a program striving to present diverse perspectives on psychological matters of consequence. We have frequently heard students who differ from many of
their student cohort make points in class discussions that simply would
not be made if they were not present. In effect, students who differ by
age, gender, social status, cultural and linguistic group status, disability
status, geographical background, or other such dimensions improve the
instruction of all students. Their ability to impart differing perspectives

to their student compatriots enriches the educational experience for all students. Such an opportunity for an educational program can sometimes prove to be a burden for the students in question, so it is also essential for the educational program to provide positive support structures and institutionally sanctioned mechanisms for such underrepresented students to resolve issues that may occur for such students.

Teaching the Need for Consultation

Professional work in a diverse and changing society necessitates professional development and consultation that were rare in previous decades. A psychologist may be asked to assess an individual who is a member of a group (e.g., a person with a specific disability) or who has an experiential background with which that psychologist has limited or no experience. Although the professional can and should keep current with his or her discipline, no professional is able to anticipate all future assessment needs or requests. In such instances, the professional psychologist should seek information. Such information will frequently come in the form of consultation from other professionals. With regard to assessment issues related to the diversity of American society, it is likely that such consultation could come from another, more specialized psychologist, but it also may come from health care professionals, anthropologists, demographers, test publishers, special education teachers, and so on. To ascertain how best to make an assessment, interpret test findings, or render decisions about a client with a particular experiential background, psychologists may need to talk with other professionals to a greater extent than was necessary in the past.

Consultation should be encouraged among students to a greater extent than it has been traditionally. Some applied graduate programs offer courses in consultation either as elective or required courses, but virtually without exception these offerings are aimed at instructing students in how to be a consultant or how to understand various models of consultation (such as when psychologists provide guidance for teachers, other professionals, or parents) rather than how and when to make good use of consultation themselves. Thus, the traditional model of graduate education in psychology has not fostered among students the need to or benefits of partaking in consultation either during their graduate school years or thereafter as former students become professionals. Independent practice in a variety of contexts has been the order of the day, for the most part, and seeking advice from anyone other than one's primary professor or classroom instructor or direct supervisor is rare. Yet, the need to communicate with other professionals, both within psychology and in other areas or disciplines, appears to be expanding as applied psychologists attempt to better understand diverse individuals. Educational programs need to provide students with instruction and experiences so that they will come to know the circumstances under which consultation is appropriate and to provide ideas in terms of how and with whom such consultation may effectively be secured.

Today's technology (e.g., electronic mail, telephones, "picture-tel" technology) provides unique opportunities to confer with other professionals as never before. A psychologist working alone at a particular site can have "virtual" access to numerous fellow professionals. One must be somewhat cautious in using this technology, however, insofar as ethical practice is concerned (e.g., retention of confidentiality). Nevertheless, relatively recent technological advances and accessibility, such as E-mail and fax transmission, have noteworthy benefits as long as training also includes attention to the special ethical practices brought on by these recent advances.

Self-Study and External Program Review

Self-appraisal is an important component of most high-quality programs and should be undertaken by training programs on a regular basis to address issues as they surface. Training programs are urged to conduct self-studies generally and to consider specifically how well positioned they are to train tomorrow's applied psychologists and assessment professionals. Of note, faculty should assess the degree to which their program adequately trains students in the principles of measurement, the variety and influence of experiential backgrounds, the application of assessment skills generally, the application of assessment skills to members of diverse groups, and the use of peer consultation. To ensure continuing improvement of the program, pragmatic concerns also should be addressed. For example, faculty should work to ensure that library resources are sufficient in the areas of assessment, diversity, and assessment applications. On a related note, faculty should be certain that the holdings in their testing laboratory are current, especially regarding instruments that are specifically meant to aid in the assessment of members of diverse groups. Test publishers might be approached about offering discounted rates for trainers to purchase these materials.

Internal institutional sources of funding also should be explored as a possible means of increasing the training program's holdings in the area of assessing diverse individuals. The American Psychological Association and the National Association of School Psychologists sponsor accreditation processes in which graduate programs may be reviewed by external site visit teams after a thorough internal self-study has been performed. Diversity in curricula, students, faculty, and field placements represent criteria that are included in such reviews. Even departments that do not participate in these accreditation processes may find it formative to conclude a period of self-study with a visit from well-informed, impartial external reviewers of the program.

Conclusion

Training applied psychologists to administer tests and interpret test results to people with diverse experiential backgrounds is an important and forward-looking activity. The instruction provided by professors may focus less on answers to the real assessment problems that the profession faces and more on approaches and processes. Some of the processes that should be emphasized are psychometric and others relate to knowledge about individual differences. Others should emphasize the need for research to improve assessment practices. The accurate assessment of all individuals continues to be imperative; faculty need to communicate such attitudes to students as well as the above-mentioned competencies (e.g., knowledge of different psychology). As applied psychologists continue to seek ways in which to accurately represent an individual's abilities, needs, and so on, they will continue to rely on systematic observations of behavior. The meaning of the data collected and the decisions emanating from those interpretations are influenced by a confluence of factors, including culture, disabling conditions, language, economic conditions, and so forth. Faculty who train future professionals likely will continue to address concerns in this domain, as they are charged with the task of training futuristic problem solvers who are competent to seek, recognize, and rectify both known and as-yet unknown challenges.

References

Aiken, L. S., West, S. G., Sechrest, L., Reno, R. R., Roediger, H. L., III, Scarr, S., Kazdin, A. E., & Sherman, S. J. (1990). Graduate training in statistics, methodology, and measurement in psychology: A survey of PhD programs in North America. *American Psychologist, 45,* 721–734.

Anastasi, A., & Urbina, S. (1997). *Psychological testing* (7th ed.). Upper Saddle River, NJ: Prentice Hall.

Cronbach, L. J. (1990). Essentials of psychological testing (5th ed.). New York: HarperCollins.

Eyde, L. D., Robertson, G. J., Krug, S. E., Moreland, K. L., Robertson, A. G., Shewan, C. M., Harrison, P. L., Porch, B. E., Hammer, A. L., & Primoff, E. S. (1993). *Responsible test use: Cast studies for assessing human behavior.* Washington, DC: American Psychological Association.

Figueroa, R. A. (1990). Best practices in the assessment of bilingual children. In A. Thomas & J. Grimes (Eds.), *Best practices in school psychology—II* (pp. 93–106). Washington, DC: National Association of School Psychologists.

Kamphaus, R. (1993). *Clinical assessment of children's intelligence.* Needham Heights, MA: Allyn & Bacon.

Moreland, K. L., Eyde, L. D., Robertson, G. J., Primoff, E. S., & Most, R. B. (1995). Assessment of test user qualifications: A research-based measurement procedure. *American Psychologist, 50,* 14–23.

Test Interpretation in a Diverse Future

Jonathan Sandoval

I n this final chapter I discuss the future prospects for test usage and interpretation for diverse individuals. It is daunting and perhaps foolish to attempt to predict too far into the 21st century, given the rapidity of both technological and social change. No doubt there are developments that no one can anticipate that will also have a major impact on both assessment and the practice of psychology. Fifty years ago, computers were largely unknown. Today, the modern world and the process of assessment owe much to electronic technology.

Nevertheless, there are trends evident now that must be taken into account as psychologists prepare for a diverse future in North America. Changes in the population, in culture, and testing technology will present new challenges and opportunities for psychologists. In addition, new dimensions of diversity and approaches to assessment may emerge as progress is made in the neurosciences. At the same time, legal challenges and attempts by governmental agencies to regulate testing will continue. In spite of the rapid changes on the horizon, it seems unlikely that the assessment of individuals or the need to draw inferences from tests and other measures will disappear from psychological practice.

Future Demographic Changes

Changes in Cultural Background and Ethnicity

Over the next 30 years, the U.S. population is expected to increase by 72 million to 335 million in 2025. Forty-four million of that increase

(61% of the population growth) will come from Hispanic and Asian groups, who together will increase from 14% to 24% of the national population. Other non-White groups, Native Americans, and Blacks will increase their sizes proportionately, whereas the percentage, if not the numbers, of European Americans will decline. Most of the growth will be in the South and the West, with 45% of the growth in the three states of California, Texas, and Florida. Sometime after 2050, there will be no majority ethnic group in the United States (U.S. Bureau of the Census, 1996).

With increased ethnic diversity, it is reasonable to expect more intermarriage and blending of cultures. One might anticipate increasing numbers of individuals declaring themselves "other" on standard demographic questionnaires. With mixed heritage, what frame of reference does one use to evaluate individuals? Consider Tiger Woods, the most successful amateur golfer in the sport's history and as a professional the youngest winner of the U.S. Masters tournament. He is one-eighth Native American, one-eighth Black, one-quarter White, one-quarter Chinese, and one-quarter Thai, according to *Newsweek* (McCormick & Begley, 1996). He grew up in a middle-class home and went to a prestigious university. How might an assessment of a psychological construct be interpreted in his case?

Also, as time passes, some groups will be absorbed into the mainstream culture. Former groups of immigrants, Irish, Italians, and Jews, for example, over succeeding generations have become part of the majority population, at least for many test interpretation purposes. Second- and third-generation individuals from Latino and Asian backgrounds may come to be considered part of the majority culture in the United States.

It is clear, then, that with increased racial, ethnic, and cultural diversity, psychologists will be working with a different mix of clients in the future than they do now. To the extent that tests will continue to play an important role in psychological practice, an issue to be explored later in this chapter, the issues of test interpretation explored in this book will have increased relevance over the next three decades.

Changes in the Disabled Population

Although the number of members of different ethnic or language groups may increase, the number of people with disabilities may decline. With medical progress moving to a point where genetic engineering becomes more applied, various conditions may become prevented or ameliorated. Genetic diseases such as cystic fibrosis and muscular dystrophy may disappear as innovations in gene therapy become more common. Genetic screening may also help to identify individuals for early intervention that will prevent disabling conditions. Advances in prosthetic devices may someday enable blind people to see, deaf people to hear, and people who are paralyzed or who have lost limbs to retain normal motor control. Nerve regeneration and nerve splicing may help to repair spinal cord injury. The disabled population is likely to decline or change in composition in the future.

A countertrend, increasing the number of individuals with disabilities, is the increased ability of medical personnel to save the lives of severely injured people and prematurely born infants. Those whose lives are saved as a result of heroic interventions may become disabled as a result of surviving, whereas in the past they would have died. Conditions such as cerebral palsy, for example, may increase in prevalence. These trends may balance one another out, with the result that the number or percentage of the population with a disability will remain constant but the types of disabilities and the needs for accommodation will change radically.

Changes in the Age of the Population

In addition to other changes in demographics, Americans will age, with a larger proportion above age 65 than at present (U.S. Bureau of the Census, 1996). Medical advances will permit individuals to live longer, and the birth rate is declining among the developed nations.

As the number of older people increases, there will be an increased need for services yet unanticipated. Assessments appropriate to the problems and the status of older adults will need to be developed.

The Interaction of Population Changes

Previous chapters in this book have focused on single dimensions of diversity that may have importance in interpreting a test. With an increase in diversity, psychologists will also see a combination of factors that might impinge on testing and test interpretation. For example, if a child is born deaf to hearing Latino parents, which is more important to test interpretation, and how does the test interpreter weigh each contribution in gaining an understanding of an individual?

Another example of interaction is between age and ethnicity. As the U.S. population ages, there will be an increasing number of older clients coming from diverse backgrounds. Hays (1996) discussed culturally responsive assessment issues with this population. She argued that the use of standardized tests with older people from diverse groups requires extra sensitivity. She pointed out that the tests are intimidating, do not take into account that older clients tire more easily, and may not have age-appropriate norms (Hays, 1996):

> Even standard mental-status questions may be threatening because they are obviously intended to test an elder's intellect. Furthermore, the questions themselves may assume a particular education and cultural upbringing. For example, although most normally functioning Euro-American elders can be expected to know their birthdates, an older Khmer (Cambodian) woman might not know hers, particularly in relation to the Euro-American calendar. (p. 192)

These interactions of dimensions of diversity will force even more fine-grained considerations in test interpretation as psychologists come to work with clients who vary on many dimensions of diversity.

Future Cultural Changes

As the world becomes more democratic and as transportation becomes less expensive and more accessible, it is easy to anticipate the global economy. One effect of globalization and the increase in the ease of communications is that individuals who do immigrate are much more connected to their country of birth than was true in the past. They may phone or electronic mail relatives, watch a cable or satellite TV channel or rent videotapes featuring entertainment from their country of origin, or travel home for vacations. Today's immigrants have much more contact with their culture of origin while living in the United States than has previously been the case (Cornelius, 1995). It is also a trend for many groups to cluster together in communities and schools, reinforcing cultural contact. Orfield and Eaton (1996) documented how desegregation is reversing in U.S. schools. As a result, one might speculate that new immigrants will acculturate more slowly than previous generations who were more cut off from their homelands. For example, recent data on Mexican immigrants in California suggested that a surprising number return home periodically and plan to retire in Mexico after several years of working in the United States.

This slower rate of acculturation may not be true of all immigrant groups, however. Those fleeing violence, religious persecution, or extreme economic conditions (e.g., Haitians) may have little interest in returning to their birthplace and will want to assimilate quickly.

A countertrend working against the maintenance of culture has also been fostered by the development of global communications. Computers, through devices such as E-mail and the World Wide Web, have increased communication globally. With increases in communication, a greater exposure to different cultures becomes possible, with increased cultural understanding as a potential outcome. Travelers abroad will also note, for better or worse, the development of a world culture in which U.S. movies and fast food franchises, European cuisine, and Japanese electronics and automobiles can be found almost everywhere. The shared experience of younger people today is greater than ever before. Foods are shared, democratic values are commonly articulated, and scientific and technical knowledge is held in common. This phenomenon of a world culture may lead to more universal experiences in society and, hence, in test takers than was previously the case. A universal set of background knowledge and assumptions makes it possible to base assessment on information that is widely shared and thereby make assessments more fair across groups.

Another aspect of globalization will be the continued export of American and European testing technology to the rest of the world. Psychologists can also anticipate that tests that are developed and normed in other cultures may prove useful for clients in the United States. Consultation with foreign psychologists using improved communications will also become possible.

Future Testing Technology

The present time has been described as the information age. There is no doubt that the increase in the power of the computer has revolutionized every aspect of life, from work to leisure time. In addition to increases in the power of computers has come a decrease in their size and weight. As a result, book-sized and smaller PCs have become practical and relatively inexpensive. Assuming this trend continues, computerized tests become much more practical. Paper-and-pencil tests may even eventually disappear. Computers will likely be involved in the testing and interpretation process to a greater extent than they are now.

Computer-adaptive testing has already begun. Currently, the Graduate Record Examinations may be taken in a computer-adaptive format, and the Graduate Management Admission Test can be taken only in this format. These tests have been programmed to present the test taker with new questions depending on how the examinee previously responded. The computer keeps track of responses and draws from a bank of items the next question that will add information to a test score. For example, if a student has already correctly answered questions dealing with two-digit addition, there is little use in asking questions assessing one-digit addition. If the student fails on a two-digit item, the test can then present an item assessing simple one-digit addition facts. When enough information is available to estimate an individual's functioning on a construct, the test can move on to the assessment of another construct. This process is most easily done when there is a clear hierarchy of skills or an underlying ability, but applications of adaptive testing can be made in other areas of testing such as personality or employment testing. One outcome of such adaptive testing is shorter tests and more accurate estimates of true score because more items can be presented at an appropriate difficulty level. Another outcome is that two test takers will likely not be taking identical tests. Perhaps most useful, however, is the capacity of the computer to give immediate feedback on performance so that testing may facilitate learning more easily.

The availability of multimedia, artificial intelligence, and virtual reality on computers also presents some new possibilities for assessment. Having pictures and words and animation available in items makes for intriguing possibilities. A wider range of items will be available, and it may be easier to assess constructs such as artistic ability and musical ability as well as to collect information about reaction time. Testers will be able to move away from multiple-choice formats in testing and still have objective scoring. One current example is the use of a computerized editing simulation to measure writing skills (Davey, Godwin, & Mittelholtz, 1997). Computerized scoring as well as computerized administration are being developed with performance assessments. Multimedia virtual reality assessment is still in its infancy, although it is currently used with aircraft pilots. Exciting new formats for assessment will soon be available.

One question that will have to be answered soon is whether computer-literate people will have an advantage by a shift to computer-based testing. Will there be groups who will be penalized by the presentation of testing materials by computer? There is reason to be optimistic:

> Overall, examinee acceptance of computer-based testing has been very good. Despite concerns about the effects of computer delivery on the performance of people who are not computer literate or who have limited previous experience with the computer, lack of experience does not appear to affect scores, especially if tutorial on using the computer or other practice materials are provided. Many examinees report a preference for computer-administered tests over paper-and-pencil tests. (Scheuneman, 1997, p. 20)

This concern may not be a relevant consideration for long because computers may soon be invisible. Voice recognition and production, handwriting recognition, and other technologies will advance to the point where interacting with a computer will be indistinguishable from interacting with another human being. Tests and questionnaires can already be automatically given over the telephone by computer, wherein the examinee either gives voice responses or enters digits on a touch-tone phone.

Computer technology has permitted the creation, for better or worse, of large data banks on individuals. Data collected throughout an individual's lifetime could be lined together by a network of computers. Concerns about privacy have presumably kept large databases from being constructed, but it is clear that the potential exists. Keeping longitudinal data would certainly aid in the assessment process. One of the features of baseball is the fact that complete data have been stored about every game that is played. This permits the creation of numerous statistics that enable cognoscenti to make sophisticated predictions about players' abilities and even the outcomes of the next pitch by a pitcher in a game. If the same scrutiny were given to a child learning to read or an adult performing a work task, psychologists may be able to make predictions without the use of discrete events called *tests*. It remains to be seen whether routine data come to be collected about people that will be used by assessors. Portfolio assessment has become popular in education, in which children's work is kept and reviewed. Computers might allow for portfolios to be easily maintained and analyzed. Portfolios in work settings or in the home might become possible with new devices for recording behavior. For example, what would an analysis of the videos an individual had checked out from the neighborhood store reveal about his or her interests or aesthetics? Although this kind of data collection would be an invasion of privacy, there may be ways of obtaining similar naturalistic information in an ethically responsible manner. It has already been demonstrated that assessments can be imbedded unobtrusively in instructional programs related to alcohol (Meier & Wick, 1991).

Computer-based scoring and interpretation are a reality. No doubt they will become even more commonplace in the next century. Guidelines have already been prepared on computer-based test interpretation (American Psychological Association, 1986) as well as computer-adaptive tests (American Council on Education, 1995). As psychologists come to rely on these tools more and more, the danger is that clients who have not been considered by the research that has gone into the test interpretation program will be overlooked. The use of test interpretation programs will have to be validated for the populations for which they are used. The validation of test interpretation programs is more important than the validation of the tests themselves. Safeguards could be built into the program data that would signal a user that an interpretation is not appropriate or available. For example, entering information about how English-reading proficiency might trigger a measure to ignore the results. The ease of computer interpretation will need to be guarded against because it is already possible to get an inappropriate comparison with the click of a mouse.

Future Measurement Developments

Psychometric Theory

Classical test theory is being eclipsed by newer models made possible by the application of computers and acceptance of assumptions about test behavior. These assumptions have not all been fully subjected to empirical analysis and verification, but progress is being made. So far, item response theory has written some new rules of measurement (Embretson, 1996). Table 16.1 contains some of the new rules for measurement as outlined by Embretson (p. 342). Consider the cumulative implications in Rules 2, 3, and 4 that shorter tests can be reliable, that comparing scores from multiple forms is optimal when test difficulty levels vary across individuals, and that unbiased estimates of item properties may be obtained from unrepresentative samples. These rules suggest that it may be easier in the future to produce parallel forms of tests across different groups. The fact still remains, however, that item response theory requires a large sample to estimate parameters. Nevertheless, it may become more possible to equate translations to norms

Rule no.	Old rule	New rule
1.	The standard error of measurement applies to all scores in a particular population.	The standard error of measurement differs across scores, but generalizes across populations.
2.	Longer tests are more reliable than shorter tests.	Shorter tests can be more reliable than longer tests.
3.	Comparing test scores across multiple forms depends on test parallelism or adequate equating.	Comparing scores from multiple forms is optimal when test difficulty levels vary across persons.
4.	Unbiased assessment of item properties depends on representative samples from the population.	Unbiased estimates of item properties may be obtained from unrepresentative samples.
5.	Meaningful scale scores are obtained by comparisons of position in a score distribution.	Meaningful scale scores are obtained by comparisons of distances from various items.
6.	Interval scale properties are achieved by selecting items that yield normal raw score distributions.	Interval scale properties are achieved by justifiable measurement models, not score distributions.

Table 16.1

Embretson's Old and New Rules of Measurement

Note. From "The New Rules of Measurement" by S. E. Embretson, 1996, *Psychological Assessment, 8,* p. 342. Copyright 1996 by the American Psychological Association. Reprinted with permission.

for a general population and to verify that a test is functioning similarly or differently across populations. The future may (or may not) bring tests that can be made fair to different groups by providing them with economical parallel forms suited to the group's linguistic and cultural situation. New developments in psychometric theory could make the job of test interpretation for diverse groups easier.

Problem of Measurement Literacy

At the same time that changes are taking place in the field of measurement, psychologists are not being prepared in measurement theory (Lambert, 1991). Measurement literacy, according to Lambert (1991), consists of knowledge in four areas:

1. Knowledge of basic assumptions that underlie rendering or quantification of observations, assigning objects or events to classes, ordering of units of observations from greatest to smallest, or transforming of the number of right and wrong test answers on a formal or informal test.

2. Familiarity with the general rules by which observations, rank orders, item scores, and individual difference data are translated into measurement units, such as frequency counts, probability estimates, measures of central tendency, and measures of variability.

3. Implied familiarity with concepts of validity and reliability and the ability to utilize these concepts in selecting, using or interpreting numbers that are derived from the several approaches to educational and psychological measurement.

4. Knowledge of sources of error and the ability to apply appropriate standard errors of measurement in making psychological or educational diagnoses, classifications, inferences, or predictions. (p. 24)

The requirements for measurement literacy have increased recently with the development of item response theory. Psychologists formerly literate in measurement may not be current, as implied in Table 16.1. Remaining literate is a challenge to practicing professionals. Illiterate professionals will unquestionably be at the mercy of test publishers and salespeople because they will not know how to approach the development of alternate techniques when faced with client diversity. One might speculate that current bad assessment practices with minorities and other clients spring from measurement illiteracy. Bad practices with tests are generally likely to result in even worse practices for members of minorities and people with disabilities.

However, new professionals may not even have the skills of their predecessors. A recent survey of all PhD programs in psychology in the United States and Canada concluded that

> measurement has declined substantially in the curriculum. Measurement-related issues continue to permeate the discipline from psychopathology through psychophysics. Yet, students are often unacquainted with even the classic concepts that underlie basic psychological measurement. This deficiency opens the door to a proliferation of poorly constructed ad hoc measures, potentially impeding future progress in all areas of the field. (Lambert, 1991, p. 730)

Not only are new professional psychologists not being prepared in measurement, but fewer PhDs are being granted in the field of measurement, and fewer of those with PhDs are choosing to begin a career in an academic setting (Lambert, 1991). Thus, psychometric knowledge may become the province of a measurement elite, working for testing companies rather than preparing psychologists to use and understand tests. In addition, psychometricians are often untrained in score interpretation. This development does not bode well for test interpretation in the future.

Future Developments in the Neurosciences

The neurosciences have made remarkable progress in understanding brain functioning. As a result, several new drugs have appeared to address problems ranging from spinal cord injury to depression, panic attacks, and obsessive–compulsive disorder. Using imaging techniques such as magnetic resonance imaging, positron emission tomography, and single-photon emission computed tomography, it has become possible to pinpoint pathways and areas of brain functioning associated with brain functions such as learning and memory. Biochemical studies also reveal different chemical balances, particularly in neurotransmitters, between well-functioning and disordered brains, resulting in new options for pharmacological interventions. Suggestions for non-chemically-based intervention have also come from this research. For example, learning disabilities may be studied with computer-based training in auditory discrimination (Merzenich, Schreiner, Jenkins, & Wang, 1993).

Matarazzo (1992) speculated that

> I predict that we should expect in the decades ahead additional technological advances in both how and what EEG [electroencephalography] and other biological parameters of individual differences are recordable in the measurable aspects of intelligence. It is reasonable to expect that the technology for measuring these neurophysiological parameters of simple and more complex information-processing activities, as well as their executed end-stage target behaviors, also will be improved considerably in the not-too-distant future. For example, . . . I anticipate such improvements will come from the development of new generations of neurophysiological, neurochemical, and neuromolecular measures of information processing and related aspects of cortical functioning, as well as from insights yielded by new generations of advanced systems of brain-imaging techniques such as the successors of today's positron emission tomography (PET). (p. 1011)

What remains to be seen is whether these new techniques show any evidence of cultural differences. An important line of research will be the influence of culture and experience on the formation of brain structure and neurochemistry. There are some suggestions that neurology is shaped by experience. Regardless of the outcome of this research, the inferences from these biologically based measures will be more about current capability than about potential or what might have been under optimal developmental conditions. Whether inferences from biological data will be less invidious than inferences that are based on tests will remain to be seen, however. Genetic screening by insurance companies to avoid indemnifying individuals at risk of disorders such as Alzheimer's disease, Parkinson's disease, and so on has raised some important ethical questions. One possible change is that assessment will shift from the diagnosis of inadequacies to the identification of functions still intact and the rehabilitation of damaged capacities. The implications are that some conditions that formerly had been assessed by psychometric methods may now be made by biochemical, genetic, or noninvasive imaging techniques. The use of the magnetic resonance imaging has already displaced neuropsychological tests in the detection of tumors. Whether these methodologies are less affected by cultural considerations than the current instruments remains to be seen.

The Social, Political, and Legal Future

Assessment practices have been as influenced by political forces, including court cases, as much or more than they have by psychological theory (Sandoval & Irvin, 1990). Legislation and the courts have led to the increased use of tests overall (e.g., the Education for All Handicapped Children Act of 1975) but to the decreased use of tests with particular groups (e.g., *Larry P. v. Riles*, 1979; *Griggs v. Duke Power Co.*, 1971). No doubt forces favorable to testing will continue to contend with those that are unfavorable and will use the legal and legislative area as a battleground. Recently, for instance, a group of blind students sued the Law Schools Admissions Council because they were not permitted to use their own readers or note-taking equipment such as a braille typewriter to take the Law School Admissions Test. Although blind students may take the test in braille, use assigned readers, hear it on audiotape, and have extra time to complete the examination, they are not allowed to have their own readers, with whom they have rapport, who are used to working with blind people and are familiar with legal terminology ("Blind students sue," 1997). The courts have generally been used to secure the use of interpreters and study materials in braille. Another issue that has been hotly debated is the use of separate norms for different groups.

Race Norming

One policy issue of relevance is the issue of constructing separate norms for different racial or ethnic groups (Gottfredson, 1994). Having separate norms for groups who differ on a trait permits different cutoff scores to be applied in decision making and thereby reduces the disparate impact on certain groups. This issue has been pursued most actively in the context of employment testing, in which the General Aptitude Test Battery has been normed by the Department of Labor for different minority groups, a policy supported by a committee of the National Academy of Sciences. Most advocates for minorities perceive tests to be formidable barriers to upward mobility, and, by having separate norms, the best scoring candidates from a group can succeed and be eligible for benefits. Others, concerned about preserving a meritocracy (particularly one in which they are succeeding), argue that tests promote individual fairness and promote standards. This latter point of view has prevailed, and the practice of race norming was banned by the Civil Rights Acts of 1991. The issue will unquestionably arise again, particularly if it becomes easier technologically to create such norms for diverse groups.

On the other hand, the need for separate norms may lessen if the gap in performance between groups on tests disappears. There was much optimism that this might occur when there was a narrowing of the gap between Whites and minority groups on the National Assessment of Educational Progress measures of school achievement during the 1980s. Currently, there is concern that the gap is no longer closing, however (U.S. Department of Education, National Center for Education Statistics, 1996).

Regulation of Testing

Testing and assessment practices have frequently found their way into court cases and legislation. One attack on tests has been to decry their secrecy. Disclosure laws requiring the public release of information about tests have contributed to increases in the cost of testing. Advocates of full disclosure argue that making available the questions and answers to tests provides a means of making testing companies accountable. On the other hand, those arguing against test disclosure are concerned with the cost of disclosure because test security demands that disclosed items be retired and new items be constructed. Test disclosure becomes more difficult when computer-adaptive tests are used. However, individualized test disclosure might also be possible given the computerized nature of testing, in that the individual may receive individualized feedback on-line in a secure context. Calls for increased openness in testing will continue to be heard.

Other sectors in society are calling for the increased use of testing. School reform advocates often place tests at the center of new proposals. Advocates argue that national standards and assessments in English, mathematics, science, history, and geography will permit both excellence and accountability, not to mention comparisons with other industrialized countries, most of which have national standards in place. At the same time there is a push for national standards, there is a call for improved modes of testing aimed at higher order cognitive skills. The types of tests suggested are often performance tests, in which tasks are taken from life or from curriculum-based problem solving. There is clearly a need to consider issues of diversity in the construction of new assessments and to plan for the appropriate interpretation of test results that may result from this and other future test development efforts (Padilla, 1992).

Another arena in which tests are proliferating is in licensure and certification. This is a rapidly growing field with certification offered in an incredibly wide range of fields, from professional erosion and sediment control specialist to cosmology to pest control. Certification takes place at both the national and state levels, and most procedures involve written examinations. What impact the increasing use of written examinations for certification and licensing will have on the ability of minorities or individuals with an assortment of disabilities to gain access to various professions is still largely unknown. Lawyers generally advise the certifying agencies against collecting ethnic or gender information, thereby precluding any analysis of performance. An exception was the well-known "golden rule" case. In this suit, the Multistate Insurance Licensing Examination was accused of being biased against minority test takers. The settlement called for the disclosure of test results, the calculation of item statistics separately for minority test takers, and the use of these item statistics to construct new tests (cited in Denton, 1987).

Limits to Resources

A societal concern that may continue into the next century is the realization that there are limits to resources, particularly human resources (Sarason, 1996). This concept of limits has come to the public's attention most vividly in the current debate about health care. The costs of providing complete medical care to everyone in society has exceeded the amount of funds available in the economy. Expensive procedures involving transplants and genetic implants and even cloning are now possible but are exceedingly expensive. What is possible to provide by way of medical intervention cannot be made available to everyone.

At some point, the costs of what will be possible to do in assessment will strain the resources of those providing the services. This has already happened, to some extent, in special education. Educators question whether the required assessment under the Individuals With Disabilities Education Act diverts too many funds away from the treatment of children with disabilities. It becomes incumbent on psychologists to demonstrate that assessment is cost effective and will contribute to the delivery of better services to clients. If psychologists are not able to do that, there will be no future to testing the diverse population.

Conclusion

The resource issue aside, it is a good bet that assessment will continue into the next century and that the client base will become more diverse. New tests and techniques will replace existing procedures. The need for critical thinking, which includes the cultural context of assessment, will surely continue. All the authors in this book have presented the current research and theory needed to respond to this need for careful reflection as part of the test interpretation process. Diversity will increase along with psychologists' capacity to recognize it. Psychologists can look forward to new and, as yet unanticipated, research and theory that will continue to shape future assessment practice. Psychologists can only hope for increased wisdom to make assessment fair and beneficial to their clients.

References

American Council on Education. (1995). *Guidelines for computer-adaptive test development and use in education.* Washington, DC: Author.

American Psychological Association. (1986). *Guidelines for computer-based tests and interpretations.* Washington, DC: Author.

Blind students sue over test. (1997, April 9). *The San Francisco Chronicle,* p. A14.

Cornelius, W. A. (1995). Educating California's immigrant children: Introduction and overview. In R. G. Rumbaut & W. A. Cornelius (Eds.), *California's immigrant children: Theory, research, and implications for educational policy* (pp. 1–12). San Diego: CA: University of California, Center for U.S.–Mexican Studies.

Davey, T., Godwin, J. & Mittelholtz, D. (1997). Developing and scoring an innovative computerized writing assessment. *Journal of Educational Measurement, 34,* 21–41.

Denton, L. (1987, September). Testing panel weighs science, social factors. *The APA Monitor,* p. 39.

Embretson, S. E. (1996). The new rules of measurement. *Psychological Assessment, 8,* 341–349.

Gottfredson, L. S. (1994). The science and politics of race-norming. *American Psychologist, 49,* 955–963.

Griggs v. Duke Power Co., 401 U.S. 424 (1971).

Hays, P. A. (1996). Culturally responsive assessment with diverse older clients. *Professional Psychology: Research and Practice, 27,* 188–193.

Lambert, N. M. (1991). The crisis in measurement literacy in psychology and education. *Educational Psychologist, 26,* 23–35.

Larry P. v. Riles, 495 F. Supp. 926 (N.D. Cal. 1979).

Matarazzo, J. D. (1992). Psychological testing and assessment in the 21st century. *American Psychologist, 47,* 1007–1018.

McCormick, J., & Begley, S. (1996, December 9). How to raise a tiger. *Newsweek, 128,* 52–56.

Meier, S. T., & Wick, M. T. (1991). Computer-based unobtrusive measurement: Potential supplements to reactive self-reports. *Professional Psychology: Research and Practice, 22,* 410–412.

Merzenich, M. M., Schreiner, C., Jenkins, W., & Wang, X. (1993). Neural mechanisms underlying temporal integration, segmentation, and input sequence representation: Some implications for the origin of learning disabilities. *Annals of the New York Academy of Sciences, 682,* 1–22.

Orfield, G., & Eaton, S. E. (1996). *Dismantling desegregation: The quiet reversal of Brown v. Board of Education.* New York: New Press.

Padilla, A. M. (1992). Reflections on testing: Emerging trends and new possibilities. In K. F. Geisinger (Ed.), *Psychological testing of Hispanics* (pp. 273–283). Washington, DC: American Psychological Association.

Sandoval, J., & Irvin, M. G. (1990). Legal and ethical issues in the assessment of children. In C. R. Reynolds & R. W. Kamphaus (Eds.), *Handbook of psychological and educational assessment of children: Intelligence and achievement* (pp. 86–104). New York: Guilford Press.

Sarason, S. (1996). *Revisiting "The culture of the school and the problem of change."* New York: Teachers College Press.

Scheuneman, J. D. (1997). Testing and measurement issues: Potholes on the road to computer-based testing. *CLEAR Exam Review, 8*(1), 19–24.

U.S. Department of Education, National Center for Education Statistics. (1996). *The condition of education 1996* (NCES 96-304). Washington, DC: U.S. Government Printing Office.

U.S. Bureau of the Census. (1996). *Warmer, older, more diverse: State-by-state population changes to 2025* (PPL-47). Washington, DC: U.S. Department of Commerce.

Author Index

Numbers in italics refer to listings in the reference sections.

Subject Index

About the Editors

Jonathan Sandoval is a professor at, and the interim director of, the Division of Education at the University of California, Davis. He earned his PhD in school psychology at the University of California, Berkeley. He has published three books on mental health crisis prevention in the schools and his research interests include the prevention of school failure, the promotion of metal health in schools, the preparation of educational and psychological professionals, and child assessment.

Craig L. Frisby is an associate professor in school psychology at the University of Missouri—Columbia. He earned his PhD in school psychology at the University of California, Berkeley. He is currently an associate editor of *School Psychology Review,* which is the official journal of the National Association of School Psychologists. His research interests are in assessment, school psychology issues, and multidimensional scaling applications.

Kurt F. Geisinger has been the academic vice president and professor of psychology at LeMoyne College in Syracuse, New York, since 1997. Before LeMoyne, he was the dean of arts and sciences and professor of psychology at the State University of New York at Oswego for 5 years and chaired the department of psychology at Fordham University, where he directed the doctoral program in psychometrics and served on the faculty for 15 years. He is the author of numerous scholarly articles, monographs, papers, and books, including *Psychological Testing of Hispanics* (an APA publication). His areas of research include test validation, translation, and construction and the testing of special populations.

Janice Dowd Scheuneman is the owner of Quality Assessment Services, a consulting company for testing agencies and other providers of testing. She earned her PhD in educational research from Indiana University and spent several years working for large testing companies: the Psychological Corporation, Educational Testing Services, and the National Board of Medical Examiners. She has published numerous journal articles and book chapters. Her areas of specialization include test and item bias and differences in test performance between population subgroups.

Julia Ramos Grenier is the president of Grenier Consulting Associates, Inc., which provides clinical, forensic, and neuropsychological assessment/intervention services as well as training services. She earned her PhD in clinical psychology at the University of Massachusetts at Amherst and has coedited a book on prevention and coauthored several book chapters concerning ethnic minority issues and testing. She is on the affiliate faculty of the University of Hartford's Graduate Institute of Professional Psychology, where she teaches courses in forensic psychology, neuropsychological assessment, ethics in psychology, and human diversity. She is a past chair of the American Psychological Association's Ethics Committee and is currently a member of the Ethics Code Revision Task Force of the APA.